D0175028

THE HISTORY OF
CHRISTIAN
THOUGHT

THE FASCINATING STORY OF THE GREAT

CHRISTIAN THINKERS AND HOW THEY HELPED

SHAPE THE WORLD AS WE KNOW IT TODAY

JONATHAN HILL

InterVarsity Press
Downers Grove, Illinois

InterVarsity Press
P.O. Box 1400, Downers Grove, IL 60515-1426
World Wide Web: www.ivpress.com
E-mail: mail@ivpress.com

©2003 by Jonathan Hill

InterVarsity Press® is the book-publishing division of InterVarsity Christian Fellowship/USA®, a student movement active on campus at hundreds of universities, colleges and schools of nursing in the United States of America, and a member movement of the International Fellowship of Evangelical Students. For information about local and regional activities, write Public Relations Dept., InterVarsity Christian Fellowship/USA, 6400 Schroeder Rd., P.O. Box 7895, Madison, WI 53707-7895, or visit the IVCF website at <www.ivcf.org>.

Cover design: Cindy Kiple

Cover image: Scala/Art Resource NY

ISBN 0-8308-2776-5

Printed in the United States of America ∞

Library of Congress Cataloging-in-Publication Data

Hill, Jonathan, 1976-
 The history of Christian thought/Jonathan Hill.
  p. cm.
Includes bibliographical references and index.
 ISBN 0-8308-2776-5 (cloth: alk. paper)
 1. Theology, Doctrinal—History. I. Title.
 BT21.3.H55 2004
 230'.09—dc22

                               2003020592

P	18	17	16	15	14	13	12	11	10	9	8	7	6	5	4	3	2	1
Y	18	17	16	15	14	13	12	11	10	09	08	07	06	05	04			

CONTENTS

INTRODUCTION

Many readers will perhaps be puzzled by the appearance of a book with this title. What exactly is Christian thought? And why should we be bothered about its history? We might think, after all, that most Christian doctrine is to be found in the Bible, especially the New Testament, and that all Christian writers have ever done is explain it to their contemporaries. Why study the ways in which they explained it in the past?

In fact, the study of the history of Christian thought is both important and fascinating in its own right. If you are a Christian yourself, then you should certainly be interested in why Christianity teaches the things that it does. It may be true that the essentials of Christianity are taught in the New Testament, but the way we read the New Testament today is the product of centuries of speculation and development. And the thought of those who have reflected on Christian faith in the past remains a treasury of inspiration to those doing the same thing now.

Even if you are not religious, the history of Christian thought is well worth knowing about, just like any other important historical subject. People like Augustine, Aquinas and Luther have shaped the very fabric of modern society. Even if many people no longer believe what they did, we are still, most of us, the heirs of the church fathers and the medievals; and because Christianity has spread across the globe, from South America to Japan, from Siberia to New Zealand, that is not just true of Europeans and North Americans. And this is quite apart from the inherent interest of the subject—many Christian writers lived through some of the most turbulent and exciting periods in history, even playing a leading role in those periods, and some of the things they said are worth hearing whatever your own religious beliefs are.

This book offers an introduction to the history of Christian thought for the completely uninitiated. I have assumed no knowledge in the reader of the people involved or the subjects about which they wrote, and I have aimed to avoid all the unpleasant technical jargon with which this subject, like every subject, tends to surround itself. There is also a glossary.

The study of Christian thought—its nature, its development and its content—is the study of theology; and the study of theology inevitably involves dealing, in one way or another, with theologians. If someone is called a "theologian," that means one of two things: either they study theology, just as a historian studies history; or they actually contribute to it, reflecting on what the Christian faith means to them and writing down their thoughts in a more or less systematic way.

This book is largely the story of theologians in the second sense: the people who have made the history of Christian thought what it is. It focuses on their lives as well as their works. On the one hand, of course, we cannot really understand what they said if we do not know the context in which they said it; but on the other, their lives have often been as colorful and as inspiring as their writings. My aim has been to bring their personalities to life in a way that will help show why they said the things they said and why we should still care about them today.

In order to do this, I have looked at the issues that confronted the great theologians of the past and the ways in which they dealt with them. Of course, many of the issues that they faced were each other, and so I have aimed to provide a sense of narrative and progression and to show that many theologians were tackling problems, or developing ideas, first raised by their predecessors. The constraints of space and need for clarity have meant that I generally focus on just the most important or relevant areas of people's thought, rather than attempting to give a comprehensive account of everything that they said.

My goal throughout the book has been twofold. First, it has been to help the reader understand and sympathize with the characters in the book, even when disagreeing vehemently with what they said. If we can hope to understand properly what someone said and why they said it, then it is no great impoliteness if we choose to disagree with them.

Second, I have encouraged the reader to go beyond the claims of the great theologians. Throughout the book I present constructive criticism of the theologians under discussion, partly to explain their thought in a little more detail and partly as a springboard into more general considerations of the issues at hand. The reflections I offer are intended to help readers to think about those issues for themselves; I have sought to present them in as unbiased and objective a way as possible.

The main narrative of the book describes the theologians—their lives and their thought—and major movements in Christian thought in approximately chronological order. The text boxes that accompany the main text provide additional information on events, places and movements that do not quite fit into the main narrative but are relevant to it.

The book is divided into six parts, each dealing with one of the great ages of

Christianity. In a work of this scope, it has not been possible to include every Christian theologian or movement of the past two thousand years, although I have tried to be as evenhanded as possible. As a general rule, I have included those figures whose contribution to Christian thought was especially original or especially influential.

In particular, I begin not with Jesus himself or the New Testament but with the developments that arose immediately afterward. The origins of Christianity is a fascinating subject but one that is far too large and complex to address in this book. I have assumed that most readers will be roughly familiar with who Jesus was and what the New Testament says about him; for those who are not, there is a bit of catching up to do, and there are many books available to help!

The attentive will notice that I have taken the 20th century separately from the modern era. That is not to say that I necessarily think we are living in a "postmodern" age but simply that the issues theologians faced in the 20th century and the answers they gave to them were indeed quite different from those of the two centuries that came before.

I

THE CHURCH FATHERS

𝔇

Our story begins at the height of the Roman empire. By the middle of the 2nd century A.D., the mighty empire stretched from Britain to Palestine, from Germany to North Africa. Millions bowed to the seemingly eternal power of Rome. Yet the empire was more fragile than it seemed. After the 2nd century, its borders were no longer expanding. They were contracting, pushed back by wave after wave of invaders from the north and east: the barbarians. Racked by internal division, feuding emperors and a general sense of malaise, the Roman empire was about to enter a long and terminal decline.

Yet for the church, this was a time of incredible growth. Jesus himself had lived at the time of the great Caesar Augustus, the man who, more than any other, established the might of the Roman empire. By the end of the 1st century A.D., most of the New Testament had been written, and the basic beliefs of Christians had been more or less established: they believed in God, followed Jesus and looked forward to some kind of resurrection. But beyond that there was an awful lot of room for disagreement, and there was still a huge amount to be done before everyone could agree on exactly what Christians did believe and why. This is why the age of the church fathers—the earliest theologians, who tried to establish the basic doctrines of Christianity—is so exciting. It was a time of intellectual and spiritual discovery, when the lines were yet to be drawn, the precedents yet to be established. The great figures of this time may sometimes have lacked the sophistication and powers of sober reflection of their spiritual descendants, but they certainly had vitality.

Greek Philosophy

Christianity first appeared as a development within Judaism. The first issues the early Christians had to deal with concerned the new faith's relations to its parent religion, the most famous example being the circumcision controversy described in Paul's letter to the Galatians. As Christianity grew, however, it had to come to terms with religious and intellectual movements in the wider world—something it has been doing ever since. During those first centuries, theologians had to evaluate these rival movements and try to establish the place of their own faith in relation to them. Should they bitterly oppose anything non-Christian, or should they try to take over the best ideas of their rivals?

The philosophers

The movements that had the most influence on early Christianity were the schools of Greek philosophy. Today philosophy is an academic discipline understood only by specialists. In ancient times, however, it was much broader. Philosophy dealt with issues we would normally associate with science: the nature of the world, what it is made of, where it came from. It also dealt with what we would consider religious issues: the existence and nature of God, the nature of the soul, life after death, suffering and salvation. *Philosophy* had the sense we still use today when we talk about someone's personal philosophy, meaning their moral and spiritual outlook on life as a whole. It was not just intellectual exercises. It was a way of life.

In fact, the life of philosophy was thought—by philosophers, at any rate—to be the most worthy life one could lead; it was a life of enlightenment and contemplation, of virtue and striving after the divine—much like the life of a monk would be in later ages. It is little wonder that Christians came to regard their faith as a rival philosophical school and took on the philosophers at their own game.

So what were these movements?

Platonism. Perhaps the most significant to Christianity was Platonism. Platonism was a development from the thought of Plato, the great philosopher who lived in the 4th century B.C. Plato believed that the physical world, which is always changing and perishable, cannot be the true, perfect reality. It is instead a reflection of a higher realm, a nonphysical, ideal world. Physical objects are pale, fleeting shadows of their eternal, unchanging counterparts—the Forms—in the higher world. The purpose of philosophy, for Plato, is to learn to look away from the material world and come to contemplate the eternal, spiritual beauty of the ideal world.

Plato's works, which are highly readable and enjoyable literary classics quite apart from their philosophical importance, are all dialogues in which different characters discuss various issues and try to reach a conclusion. Although it is often clear which character in the dialogue Plato himself agrees with, sometimes it is hard to tell; and often no clear conclusion is reached. It is the questioning that is important, not the final answer. After Plato's death, however, his followers ignored this questioning approach and created a more dogmatic system around the often fragmentary ideas in Plato's dialogues. In particular, they developed the idea, found in some dialogues, of a World Soul that exists in the ideal world together with the Forms and that shapes and sustains the physical realm. The World Soul, then, was a sort of god; but the Platonists also believed in a higher God, existing above the world of Forms and the World Soul. This higher God was the ultimate cause of the universe. This idea of the two gods, one higher and one lower, would prove very influential on Christianity.

Stoicism. A more widespread school of philosophy was Stoicism. This was founded by Zeno, who lived shortly after Plato and taught at the Stoa, a large portico in the center of Athens. His followers were known for their extremely rigorous and well-developed ethical system. They believed that the only true happiness comes through virtue, and the virtuous person can never be made unhappy by external circumstances, because things like money, health and physical pleasure are not really important. This is why *stoic* is still used to describe someone who can put up with hardship, and why we still describe someone who is not unduly upset by the loss of material things as "philosophical." The truly happy, virtuous life is one ruled by reason, not by emotion or passion; and the Stoics sought to achieve a passionless state of mind.

In contrast to the Platonists, the Stoics denied that anything existed that was not material. However, they did believe in something like the Platonic World Soul, which they called the Logos—a word meaning "reason," "word" or "principle." The Logos is material, consisting of a fiery substance spread throughout the universe, but it sustains and animates the world just as the World Soul does.

Philosophy and early Christianity

This idea of the Logos, or World Soul, influenced Jewish descriptions of God's Wisdom. In later parts of the Old Testament and in the literature written between the two Testaments, the divine Wisdom was thought of as a semi-independent entity, responsible for creating and sustaining the world, just as the Platonic World Soul was a separate being from the High God although connected to it. Some early Christians used this idea, together with those of the World Soul and the Logos, to describe the relation of Jesus to God. The famous opening of John's Gospel, where Jesus is described as the Logos who was with God in the beginning and through whom all things were made, is the earliest example. And it was in the 2nd century that Christian theologians first appeared who were willing to discuss these ideas with pagan philosophers on their own terms, thus pioneering the concept of Christianity itself as a rival school of philosophy. Their leader, and the first real theologian to appear after the writing of the New Testament, was Justin Martyr.

Justin Martyr

The life and work of Justin Martyr, the first true church father, heralds a new and immensely fruitful departure for Christian thought. Virtually singlehandedly he kick-started the Christian dialogue with rival philosophies and set the church on the road to an intellectually coherent account of its faith.

Life

Justin was born a pagan, probably around the year A.D. 100, in Palestine. He must have been well educated, since as a young man he decided on a life of philosophy—although it took him awhile to work out which philosophy he was interested in. In the second chapter of his *Dialogue with Trypho*, he describes his search for the right kind of philosophy and his unfortunate experiences with several philosophers. First he studied under a Stoic teacher but abandoned him when he found that the Stoics couldn't teach him anything about God. He then tried a follower of Aristotle, but when his teacher demanded early payment, Justin concluded that he was "no philosopher at all" and quickly left. He had even less luck with a Pythagorean philosopher, who expected him to study music, geometry and astronomy, about which Justin knew nothing and was not prepared to spend time studying. Almost despairing of finding a suitable philosophy, he turned to a famous Platonist and finally found a philosophy he liked. In fact, he believed that Platonism had shown him the way to God:

> The vision of immaterial things quite overpowered me, and the contemplation of the Forms gave wings to my mind, so that after a short time I thought that I had become wise; and I was so stupid that I expected to be able to see God quite soon, for this is the goal of Plato's philosophy.
> *Dialogue with Trypho* 2

But Justin's search for truth was not yet at an end. One day, walking by the sea and contemplating the eternal Forms, he happened to meet a mysterious old man. After a discussion about God and philosophy, the old man told him that modern philosophers knew less of God than certain ancient prophets, whose works could still be studied. Intrigued, Justin went away and read them:

> Immediately a flame was lit in my soul; and I was seized by a love of the prophets, and those men who are friends of Christ. And whilst turning over his words in my mind, I found this philosophy alone to be safe and worthwhile. So that is why I am a philosopher.
> *Dialogue with Trypho* 4

Justin's tale of the mysterious old man sounds a little improbable; it may be that he hoped to show his readers that he was converted to Christianity through sound, logical reasoning rather than some crazy whim. What is important is the fact that he regarded Christianity as a kind of philosophy, just like Stoicism, Platonism and the rest; and that he became a Christian because he was convinced it was the best of these competing options. Almost as important is the fact that, of the other options available to him, Justin thought Platonism the best. As we shall see, his account of Christianity draws heavily on his Platonic past.

As a Christian, Justin still wore the distinctive cloak common to all philosophers, and he became a teacher in his own right, expounding Christian philosophy to those who would listen. More important, he set out his beliefs in writing. He sought to defend Christianity from its many and varied opponents.

Christians, at this time, were greatly discriminated against. Intellectuals regarded this "barbarian philosophy" with contempt; in particular, Platonists found it laughable that Christians appeared to worship a mere human being instead of an immaterial God. They considered the Christian doctrine of the end times, when all believers would be physically resurrected, to be a garbled and ridiculous travesty of their own doctrine of the immortality of the soul. Worse, the religion was not recognized by the state, and some emperors sought to stamp it out by persecuting its followers. Christians were notorious for refusing to honor the traditional gods of Rome, to which even philosophers paid lip service, and they were called atheists. Dark rumors about what Christians were about were widespread; it was popularly believed that they indulged in incestuous orgies and child sacrifice. To many, including many in positions of authority, simply to call oneself a Christian was to admit to such practices.

Justin therefore set out to defend Christianity against these charges, both moral and intellectual. In about A.D. 155 he addressed a book to Emperor Antoninus, called *The First Apology* (*apology* here means defense). In it Justin complains bitterly about the injustices meted out to Christians simply because of their name and argues—not unreasonably—that a person should be judged on how they have behaved, not on what they call themselves. He vigorously rebuts the charges of atheism and immorality, arguing that in fact Christians are more virtuous than pagans. More significantly, he defends—as a philosopher speaking to philosophers—the intellectual coherence of Christianity.

A *Second Apology*, continuing the themes of the first, soon followed, together with a variety of other works. Unfortunately the only other one that survives is the *Dialogue with Trypho*, a work of great length and extraordinary tedium. It does, however, provide a fascinating counterpart to the *Apologies*. The work is a dialogue, modeled on Plato, between Justin himself and Trypho, a Jewish philosopher. By writing a book in the style of Plato featuring a calm, rational discussion between two seekers after truth, Justin hoped to present Christianity as a philosophy that was as rational and intellectually coherent as any other.

The whole work is remarkable for the friendly way the speakers address each other and the respect each shows for the other's views. Trypho is not a straw man for Justin to ridicule but a sensible person with powerful arguments of his own—arguments that Justin must have heard in real-life conversations with Jews and that he took seriously. In fact, Justin wholly lacks the vitriol and contempt for opponents, particularly Jews, that would mark other Christian writers. At one point he remarks that it would be wrong to shun Christians who continue to follow the Jew-

ROME

Rome was the greatest city of the Roman empire, its ancient capital, its seat of government. Even in later years when the government moved elsewhere and other cities came to eclipse it, Rome remained the symbolic center of civilization. Christianity, the empire's most enduring creation, has also always had a special place in its heart for the Eternal City.

Rome is supposed to have been founded in 753 B.C. by a suspicious character named Romulus, who together with his brother Remus had been abandoned as a baby and raised by a wolf. Romulus killed his brother, thereby saving the new city from being called Reme, but also establishing a precedent for its violent future.

It was in the 3rd century B.C. that Rome, now a republic, began the systematic conquest of its neighbors, including Carthage, Macedonia and Syria, and established itself as the dominant power in the Mediterranean world. In 27 B.C., following his conquest of Cleopatra's Egypt, Caesar Augustus had himself proclaimed emperor, coruler with the Senate. The Roman empire was born, and its power stretched from Britain in the west to Palestine in the east. The metropolis at its center was the greatest city in the West, with up to a million inhabitants and eighty-five kilometers of narrow, mazelike streets. In A.D. 64, much of the city burned down in a fire supposedly started by Emperor Nero, who is said to have been so unconcerned by the disaster that he practiced the violin while the city burned. However, the fire cleared the way for urban regeneration on a massive scale, and the city was exten-

ish law, even though he thinks them mistaken in doing so. This tolerant attitude toward those with differing theologies sharply contrasts with the attitude toward heretics displayed by most Christians in the early centuries of the church.

Still wearing his philosopher's cloak and living in Rome, Justin engaged in real-life philosophical arguments with a variety of opponents, including a well-known pagan philosopher called Crescens. It has been said that Crescens, having lost the debate, complained to the authorities. Whatever the truth, in the year A.D. 165 Justin was arrested for teaching a forbidden religion and brought before Rusticus, the Roman prefect.

According to a contemporary, and probably fairly accurate, account of what happened next, the trial was brief. Justin, still arguing that "to obey the com-

---

sively replanned and rebuilt. Unlike Athens, its equivalent in Greece, Rome was not noted for intellectual or cultural achievements. And unlike Alexandria, it did not produce any great theologians. But it was a central location for the development of Christianity from the earliest times. Paul's letter to the Romans, unlike his other surviving letters, adopts an almost deferential attitude to its recipients. Ignatius of Antioch, a famous bishop who was taken to Rome to be executed in 107—a fate he looked forward to eagerly—praised the church there in fulsome language.

Rome was the only city in the western half of the Roman empire that could claim that its church had been founded by an apostle—and no less an apostle than Peter. This was one of the reasons that as the centuries passed the bishop of Rome became increasingly powerful in the West; as we shall see, early theologians placed great importance on the apostolic foundation of churches as a guarantee of their doctrinal correctness. The East, by contrast, had several bishops who traced their predecessors back to the apostles, and so they did not develop such a centralized organizational structure.

Nevertheless, Rome's status in the early church was more symbolic than real. Major theologians, including Justin Martyr and Tertullian, lived there, but they were imports. Even in the Middle Ages, when Rome would be the undisputed center of European Christendom, it would never be a center for theological activity. Rome was always a seat of power, never of research.

mandments of our Savior Jesus Christ is worthy neither of blame nor of condemnation," refused to make a sacrifice to the gods. Together with six companions who were equally steadfast in their faith, he was taken away, scourged and beheaded. In honor of his death, the church came to call him Martyr almost as an honorary surname.

Thought

Because only three of his works survive, Justin's thought remains somewhat fragmentary. His most important ideas appear in only a few brief passages. Moreover, these surviving works are apologetics, seeking to defend Christianity to its opponents; they are not a calm, reflective discussion of the meaning of Christian doctrines. Perhaps Justin provided such discussion in his lost works meant for Christian readers, but there is no way to tell.

God and Christ. Justin's most significant ideas concern the way God relates to the world and to Christ, and they are a good example of how Christians used concepts of contemporary thought to frame their faith.

Like many Platonists at the time, Justin stresses the greatness of God and his distance from the world. And like the Platonists, he argues that because of the great distance between God and the world, there must be a sort of intermediary entity between them, by which God can act on the world. This intermediary is the Platonic World Soul, the Stoic Logos.

As we have seen, the Greek word *logos* can mean not only "thought," or the mental faculty of thinking, but also "speech" or "word." Justin talks of the Logos as existing within God, as his divine Reason; and indeed he suggests that there was a time when God was alone apart from this reason, or thought, within himself. There came a time, however, when God spoke his thought, and the Logos came to exist outside God, as his speech or word.

Justin is emphatic that this process did not involve God's being diminished in any way—after all, when *we* speak, we do not lose the thoughts that we express. Justin uses the analogy of fire: just as one fire can ignite another without becoming diminished, so God begets the Logos without losing any part of himself.

So are there two Gods? Justin is concerned to avoid saying this. The Logos is not an independent power: it is the means by which God acts on the world, just like a person using a tool. But the relationship is closer than that:

> We call him the Logos, because he carries tidings from the Father to men:
> but maintain that this power is indivisible and inseparable from the Father.
> It is just as we say that the light of the sun on earth is indivisible and insep-

arable from the sun in the heavens. When it sinks, the light sinks along with it. In the same way, we say, the Father, when he chooses, causes his power to spring forth, and when he chooses, he makes it return to himself.
Dialogue with Trypho 128

It should be stressed that by this account of God and the Logos Justin is concerned to explain how God acts on the world. It is not a description of what God is like in himself. So the original begetting, or speaking, of the Logos was done for the purpose of creating the world—and the Logos continues to exist as an intermediary between God and the world. Every appearance of God in the Old Testament was in fact the Logos, God's emissary on earth, and it was the Logos who inspired the prophets.

All of this is essentially a reworking of the standard Platonist position regarding the high God and the lower World Soul. Where Justin's account diverges is in the identification of the Logos with a historical person: Jesus Christ. Christ is the Logos by whom the world was made and who governs the world today; it was he who appeared to Moses and spoke by the prophets. And that, of course, is something that no orthodox Platonist could accept.

Christians and non-Christians. Justin is well aware that much of what he says is repeated by other philosophers. Indeed, this is part of his defense of the reasonableness of Christianity. But how can the similarities be explained if Christians are to avoid accusations of simply dumbing down Plato?

Justin has two answers to this. The first is that the Christians have not taken ideas from philosophers; on the contrary, philosophers got their best ideas from the Bible. He argues—rather improbably—that Plato had read the Old Testament but not fully understood it, which is why Platonism has much in common with Christianity. In Justin's day, any belief system was regarded with more respect if it could be shown to be particularly ancient. Justin's claim that the books of Moses were older than those of Plato was therefore an important apologetic argument, and one that was repeated by Christians for centuries.

The second explanation is more interesting and involves the role of the Logos. The Logos, as we have seen, is God's reason. Every person, of course, has a "logos" of their own—their own rationality. Justin suggests that human logos comes from the divine Logos. That is, everyone who is rational is so only through sharing in the Logos. This idea is largely taken from the Stoics, who believed much the same thing. As a result, Justin can show how it is possible for those who live according to reason to share in the Logos and glimpse something of the truth. This is why philosophy, even pagan philosophy, is worthwhile:

I confess that I both boast and with all my strength strive to be found a Christian; not because the teachings of Plato are different from those of Christ, but because they are not in all respects similar. And neither are those of the others, Stoics, and poets, and historians. For each man spoke well in proportion to the share he had of the seed of the Logos, seeing what was related to it.
Second Apology 13

However, Justin stresses the imperfect nature of this understanding. The philosophers had only the "seed of the Logos," whereas Christians have the whole Logos himself. The philosophers saw reality only darkly, whereas Christians have a firm grasp of the truth.

Justin goes further, however. If anyone can follow the Logos by living a rational life, then that means it is possible to follow Christ even if one has never heard the Christian message. So Justin claims that the prophets and philosophers who lived before Christ were Christians, even though they didn't know it:

We have been taught that Christ is the firstborn of God, and we have declared above that he is the Logos of whom every race of men were partakers. And those who lived according to reason (logos) are Christians, even though they have been thought atheists; as among the Greeks, Socrates and Heraclitus, and men like them; and among the barbarians, Abraham, and Ananias, and Azarias, and Misael, and Elias, and many others whose actions and names we now decline to recount, because we know it would be tedious.
First Apology 46

The notion is an intriguing one and reflects Justin's benevolent attitude to those of other faiths. It was revived in the twentieth century by the theologian Karl Rahner.

Reflections

In Justin Martyr we see Christianity beginning to invade the territory occupied by contemporary philosophy, using common concepts and terminology as vehicles for its own teachings. Like anyone opening up new avenues for thought, however, Justin left as many problems for his successors as he solved.

Perhaps the most obvious is the Holy Spirit. Justin's Christianity seems to feature a duality rather than a trinity: he says much about the Logos but little about the Spirit. Indeed, if the Logos is God's intermediary in all of his dealings with the world, including inspiring the prophets, then there seems little for the Spirit to do. At the same time, Justin often refers to the Holy Spirit in connection with Scripture. In general, he seems quite confused on this whole issue. This is shown by one particularly jumbled remark that mixes angels into the equation:

> Both the Father, and the Son (who came forth from him and taught us these
> things), and the host of the other good angels who follow and are made like
> him, and the prophetic Spirit, we worship and adore.
>
> *First Apology* 6

Perhaps it is unfair to criticize Justin for this, since it is to judge him by the standards of later orthodoxy. But more serious is his handling of the Logos itself. Is the Logos really God? Or is it simply the first and greatest of God's creations? If part of what it is to be God is to be immeasurably distant from the world, then the Logos cannot be God. On the other hand, Justin speaks of worshiping the Logos and even talks about "two Gods." Yet it seems clear that the Logos is worshiped only in the second place, after the Father. The account may have been adequate for Justin's purposes, which was to defend the Christian adoration of Jesus to a skeptical, philosophical audience. But the lack of clear definitions was to cause huge problems for the future, as Christians became divided between those who thought the Logos was indeed God and those who regarded him as a creature: a great and powerful one, but not fully divine.

It causes tensions within Justin's thought itself. The Logos is the point of mediation between God and the world. Very well: so what about Jesus? He is the Logos incarnate. But if the Logos is *already* mediating between God and the world, then why does it need to be incarnate? Later theologians, writing after the Council of Nicaea, which defined the Logos as equal to the Father, would tend to think of the incarnation as the point at which God meets the world. The person of Jesus is the point of mediation. But for Justin the preincarnate Logos is already a mediator—and indeed we find that he speaks little of Jesus himself compared with the Logos. His theology is as abstract and timeless as the philosophy of Plato: he shows little interest in the concrete and the historical, in the person of Jesus and what he did and said on earth.

Justin Martyr was not the first Christian to try to defend his faith to its critics or the first to present it as a kind of philosophy. But he was the first to produce a new way of thinking, as a Christian, using the philosophical concepts of his day. If he didn't do a very thorough job, that is hardly to his discredit. When, inevitably, greater minds arose to reflect on Christian doctrine, they did so according to the preliminary lines laid down by Justin.

Irenaeus of Lyons

Irenaeus of Lyons occupies a strange place in the history of Christian thought. He

GNOSTICISM

In its first years Christianity was just one of a large number of religions, of varying novelty and originality, vying for the hearts of Roman citizens. Most died out or had little influence. But apart from Christianity, one other survived and grew popular: Gnosticism.

Gnosticism is hard to define, because it was closely related to Christianity and seems to have existed in a variety of forms. Some of these forms were probably very similar to "normal" Christianity—given that Christianity, too, was varied at this stage and there was no standard of orthodoxy. Other forms were less similar to Christianity and essentially constituted an independent faith.

The origins of the movement are obscure. It probably developed out of a mixture of Platonism and Eastern influences such as Zoroastrianism as well as Judaism and Christianity. It seems to have appeared at around the same time as Christianity; some parts of the New Testament, such as the letters by John and the first letter from Paul to the Corinthians, attack beliefs that we now associate with Gnosticism.

Although Gnosticism varied greatly, it was marked by one basic belief: Matter is evil. The physical world and all its contents are fundamentally flawed and corrupt. Only the spiritual realm, uncontaminated by base matter, is good.

This has several consequences. First, if God is good, he cannot be responsible for the material world. Many Gnostics therefore believed in a lower god, the Demiurge (Creator), who, through a combination of ignorance and wickedness, created the material world and set himself up as its god. This was the God of the Old Testament, a God of justice and violence, who was supplanted by the true High God of the New Testament, a God of love and mercy.

But where did the Demiurge come from? Many Gnostics developed a complex mythology to explain his existence. Instead of one God, they spoke of a whole pantheon or system of divine beings, known as the Divine Fullness. This had the High God at the top and ranged down through various divine beings including the divine Wisdom, the divine Word and so on. One of these beings fell out of the Fullness, and it was from this primordial disaster that the Demiurge and matter came into being.

Another consequence of matter's being evil is ethical. The body, being ma-

terial, is evil. Some Gnostics therefore lived very ascetic lives, trying to avoid bodily pleasures as much as possible. Others concluded that since all matter is evil, it makes no difference what you do to it, and they led extremely loose, immoral lives.

A third consequence was in Christology. If the body is evil, then a divine being could not have one. So many Gnostics believed that Christ did not really have a body: he appeared human, but in fact this was an illusion. He never ate, blinked or left footprints. This belief, known as docetism (from a word meaning "seeming"), is attacked in the New Testament in the first letter of John. Other Gnostics accepted the true humanity of Jesus but thought that he was distinct from the divine being who spoke through him. As the Messiah, Jesus was sent by the Old Testament God, the ignorant Demiurge—but if we read his words carefully and spiritually, we can hear the message of the divine being from the Fullness, sent by the High God.

The Gnostics believed that salvation for human beings consists of the spirit's escaping the prison of flesh in which it is trapped. They thus rejected the Christian doctrine of the bodily resurrection of the dead. Moreover, they thought that salvation could be attained only by knowledge—by learning secret teachings originally given by the divine being of Jesus. The name Gnosticism comes from the word meaning "knowledge." It was thus an intellectual, elitist faith. Many Gnostics considered their faith a special, advanced sort of Christianity, a philosophically acceptable one that put them one notch above ordinary Christians who were unable to understand it. Some, indeed, believed that most people do not even have spirits capable of being saved.

Gnosticism proved a remarkably resilient movement, surviving the attacks of both non-Gnostic Christianity and non-Christian philosophy for hundreds of years. In the 3rd century A.D. a Persian prophet named Mani founded his own religion, known as Manichaeism; essentially a sophisticated version of Gnosticism, it proved very popular throughout the Mediterranean world until the Middle Ages. Zoroastrianism, the ancestor of Gnosticism, still survives in the Middle East and India, as do versions of Gnosticism itself.

appears to have made virtually no impact on his contemporaries and immediate successors. His work is patchy and often tedious or trite. Yet it is punctuated by flashes of brilliance and poetry that together form a Christian vision of remarkable profundity. In modern times, even if not in antiquity, the greatness of Irenaeus has been fully appreciated.

Life

Little is known of Irenaeus's life. In his youth he knew the famous martyr Polycarp, who in *his* youth had sat at the feet of St. John the apostle. So Irenaeus, like Polycarp, was probably from modern Turkey, and he was probably born sometime in the second quarter of the 2nd century A.D. One thing seems clear: Irenaeus was not an adult convert to Christianity. Unlike most of his predecessors, including Justin Martyr, he was brought up within a Christian household. It is likely that his strong sense of orthodoxy owes much to this background.

He later moved to what is now France and joined the church at Lyons. In A.D. 177 this church suffered a severe persecution by the state, and Irenaeus was sent to the bishop of Rome with a letter describing the heroism of those who suffered.

Irenaeus's precise role in the church is uncertain. The letter he took to Rome names him a "presbyter," suggesting a fairly lowly role. But at that time this term might have been used to refer to any church official. So he may never have officially become a bishop, but he seems to have acted as bishop after the persecution, and he is remembered as such.

Nothing else is known about Irenaeus's life. The church remembers him as a martyr, but there is no evidence for the manner of his death. He probably died around the turn of the 3rd century A.D.

While he was bishop, Irenaeus wrote several books. By far the most important—and the only major work to have survived—is *On the Detection and Overthrow of the So-Called Gnosis,* normally referred to as *Against Heresies.* This five-volume work was written in response to the religious movement known as Gnosticism, which Irenaeus was shocked to discover when he moved to Lyons. In his work Irenaeus describes the Gnostic systems in detail and argues against them at great length. In the course of his argument he introduces much positive teaching of his own. It is this positive element that ensures Irenaeus's continuing popularity.

Irenaeus was not a major figure in the early church. He seems not to have been very famous either in his lifetime or after his death, and apparently he had few disciples. Most of the original Greek of *Against Heresies* was lost, and the work survives only in a Latin translation, probably made very soon after Irenaeus wrote the original. Through this translation and other fragments of his works, Irenaeus's thought survived and came to be recognized as a valuable resource long after his death. In modern times some of the most distinctive aspects of his thought, particularly his views of the purpose of evil, have been very influential on theologians and philosophers of religion.

Thought

No one is sure how original a thinker Irenaeus was. Some of the most interesting ideas in *Against Heresies* seem to be his own, since they are developed in response to particular Gnostic beliefs. But it is certain that some ideas are taken from earlier theologians; and since much of *their* work has been lost, it is hard to tell how much Irenaeus depends on them. It should be remembered, too, that Irenaeus, like Justin Martyr, did not write a systematic account of his ideas.

God. Irenaeus has much to say about God, since it was the Gnostics' views of God that distressed him more than anything else. Rejecting both the Gnostics' distinction between the High God and Demiurge and their belief in different entities within the Divine Fullness, he emphasizes God's unity: there is one and only one God, who transcends all ordinary categories. Here Irenaeus seems to anticipate elements of *via negativa* (the "negative way"), the tradition of spirituality that emphasizes the unknowability of God. This was a common idea in Platonic philosophy at the time, and Irenaeus seems here to be influenced by that kind of writing.

Despite God's unknowability, we can know something of him through the goodness of the created world. The world, created by God, is itself a potent argument for God's existence and nature. In fact, God sustains the world from moment to moment. Only God truly exists; created things exist only in a secondary way because God keeps them in existence. This great emphasis on the fundamental difference between God and his creation anticipates a similar emphasis found in the work of post-Nicene writers, especially Gregory of Nyssa, and even Thomas Aquinas.

One idea unique to Irenaeus is that of God's containing the whole universe within himself—there is nothing outside God. This is quite different from Justin Martyr's view that God exists at a great *distance* from the world. Irenaeus often uses the image of God's holding the world in the palm of his hand. So God is fundamentally different from the world; but because he sustains it, holding it in his hand, he is very close to it. The inexpressibly mighty and exalted God is present within us and knows our hearts better than we do ourselves:

> The heavenly treasuries are indeed great: God cannot be measured in the heart, and he is incomprehensible in the mind; he who holds the earth in the

hollow of his hand. Who perceives the measure of his right hand? Who knows his finger? Or who understands his hand—that hand which measures immensity; that hand which, by its own measure, spreads out the measure of the heavens, and which holds in its hollow the earth with the abysses; which contains in itself the breadth, and length, and the deep below, and the height above the whole creation; which is seen, which is heard and understood, and which is invisible? And for this reason God is "above all principality, and power, and dominion, and every name that is named," of all things which have been created and established. He it is who fills the heavens, and views the abysses, who is also present with every one of us.

Against Heresies 4.19.2

Irenaeus does use Justin's terminology of the Father and the Logos, but he prefers to talk of the Father and the Son; and he regards the Son as the invisible Father made visible. As he puts it, "The Father is the invisible of the Son, but the Son is the visible of the Father" (*Against Heresies* 4.6.6).

Irenaeus also describes the Son and Holy Spirit as the "hands of God." This potent image is meant to suggest God's immediate relationship to the world—he needs no tools to work on the world, just his two hands. So the Son and Spirit are very close to the Father but still distinct from him, just like the two hands of a human being.

Humanity. Irenaeus's thoughts on human nature are some of the most original and interesting in his work. He begins with the claim of Genesis 1:26 that God intends to make humankind in his own "image and likeness." For Irenaeus, the whole of the rest of the Bible describes this process of making. Human beings are made in God's image right at the start, but they attain his likeness only gradually, throughout the whole of history. Right from the start, God intended humanity to develop slowly in this way. So Irenaeus makes the startling claim that Adam and Eve were created as children. This may mean physically, but Irenaeus primarily means that they were *morally* immature. When they disobeyed God, it was in a childish way, because they wanted to grow up too soon, before the right time. Irenaeus thinks of this as a childish mistake, not a terrible, catastrophic act of rebellion. It represents humanity's failure to rise to greater things, not a loss of original perfection. It should be clear that this is a quite different view of the Fall from that found in later Western writers such as Augustine. Irenaeus also has no notion of original sin or inherited guilt.

According to Irenaeus, everything that has happened since Adam and Eve's petulant mistake is intended by God to help humanity grow up. God always intended that humanity should mature over a long historical process. The actions of Adam and Eve may have altered the details of his plans, but not the basic process. Even if Adam had not sinned, Christ would still have been sent, although he might not have come as a savior.

So things that seem evil, such as death, are planned by God as part of this maturing process. They help us learn about good and evil by experience and, ultimately, learn to choose freely what is right. If Jonah had not been swallowed by the whale, he would not have repented and turned to God. In the same way, suggests Irenaeus, without death and other evils we would never repent either. This approach to the problem of evil has been very popular in recent theology; it is entirely different from the more common view associated with Augustine, whereby all evil comes from creatures' misusing their free will. For Irenaeus, by contrast, evil comes from God: ultimately it serves a good purpose. Irenaeus does believe in free will, though, and thinks that without it good actions would be worthless because they would be too easy to do. He argues that nothing is really worthwhile unless it is difficult to attain. But he does not use the notion of free will in the context of explaining the existence of evil, as Augustine does.

An important part of the maturing process for humanity is coming to accept that we are God's creation. Just as Adam and Eve wanted to grow up before their time, so we also want to have it all now. We must learn to be patient. Irenaeus uses the image of a clay figure molded by a potter:

> You do not make God, but God makes you. If, then, you are God's workmanship, await the hand of your Maker which creates everything in due time; in due time as far as you are concerned, you whose creation is being carried out. Offer to him your heart in a soft and tractable state, and preserve the form in which the Creator has fashioned you, having moisture in yourself, lest, by becoming hardened, you lose the impressions of his fingers. By preserving this framework you will ascend to that which is perfect, for the moist clay which is in you is hidden by the workmanship of God. His hand fashioned your substance; he will cover you over on the inside and outside with pure gold and silver, and he will adorn you to such a degree that even "the King himself shall have pleasure in your beauty." But if you, being obstinately hardened, reject the operation of his skill, and show yourself ungrateful towards him, because you were created human, then, by becoming ungrateful to God in this way, you have lost his workmanship—and, with it, life.
> *Against Heresies* 4.39.2

Christ and salvation. Christ, for Irenaeus, is central to God's plan for helping humanity become mature. He is the invisible God made visible on earth; but he is also human, made from the same lump of clay as everyone else. This mere fact, that the Creator has become joined to the creation, begins the process of salvation. It is as though creation has been *infected* with God's nature. Divinity begins to spread throughout the created order. Before, humans were mortal and corruptible, but now they can take on the divine qualities of immortality and incorruptibility.

> It was for this purpose that the Logos of God was made man, and he who was the Son of God became the Son of man, that man, having been taken into the Logos, and becoming adopted, might become the Son of God. For in no other way could we have achieved incorruptibility and immortality, unless we had been united to incorruptibility and immortality. But how could we be joined to incorruptibility and immortality, unless, first, incorruptibility and immortality had become what we are, so that the corruptible might be swallowed up by incorruptibility, and the mortal by immortality, so that we might be adopted as sons?
>
> *Against Heresies* 3.19.1

The end of the reign of death and decay marks the beginning of the new era in human nature. It is the start of our becoming whole and mature. Only God could bring this about, but only as man could he do it, which is why the incarnation was necessary (this is an intriguing anticipation of the views of Anselm of Canterbury).

> As I have said, he caused humanity to cleave to and to become one with God. For unless man had overcome the enemy of man, the enemy would not have been legitimately vanquished. And again: unless it had been God who had freely given salvation, we could never have possessed it securely. And unless man had been joined to God, he could never have taken on incorruptibility.
>
> *Against Heresies* 3.18.7

Irenaeus thus regards the incarnation as beginning a process of divinization, of humanity taking on God's qualities. As he puts it, "How shall man pass into God, unless God has passed into man?" (*Against Heresies* 4.33.4).

This is not to say that we are absorbed into God like rivers into the sea. The fundamental distinction between Creator and creation is never abolished, but we can share in the divine qualities and the divine life. This is what it means to become made in God's likeness, and the process never reaches an end. The immensity of God means that there is no end to our pressing forward, becoming more like him every day. Here again Irenaeus anticipates the views of Gregory of Nyssa.

However, what Christ did is just as significant as who he was. Irenaeus describes

Christ's work as "recapitulation" or "summing up." Christ "sums up" human nature by living a human life—he passes through all stages of human life, sanctifying them as he goes, until he passes through death and sanctifies that too:

> He did not despise or avoid any condition of humanity, or break the laws which he had set up for humanity, but sanctified every age by passing through it himself. For he came to save everyone through himself—everyone, I say, who through him is born again to God—infants, and children, and boys, and young people, and old people. He therefore passed through every age, becoming an infant for infants, thus sanctifying infants; a child for children, thus sanctifying those who are of this age, and being at the same time an example of piety, righteousness, and obedience; a young person for young people, becoming an example to them, and thus sanctifying them for the Lord. And in the same way he was an old person for old people, so that he might be a perfect Master for all, not only by showing them the truth, but also by sharing their age, sanctifying at the same time the aged, and becoming an example to them.
>
> *Against Heresies* 2.22.4

In making this claim, Irenaeus has to argue that Christ did not die until he was quite old—a very unusual view! Although Irenaeus does not use this image himself, we can think of the process as rather like a king's reconquering his kingdom, reclaiming it as he passes through it. In the same way, Christ passes through and reclaims human nature. Moreover, Christ's life mirrors Adam's—except that where Adam was disobedient, Christ is obedient. For example, Adam's supreme act of disobedience involved a tree, and Christ's supreme act of obedience also involves a tree (the cross). And where Eve was faithless, Mary was faithful. So Adam's sin is reversed, and humanity can come to wholeness.

Irenaeus's view of the atonement is therefore based on the incarnation. He lays little emphasis on Christ's death, treating it as part of his life, the *whole* of which brings about our salvation. Irenaeus is the first of the church fathers to present an account of the atonement like this, and he sets the tone for all the rest. His basic approach was repeated by Athanasius and remains central to Eastern Orthodoxy.

Reflections

Irenaeus's theology is often profound and quite striking, especially to those more used to a Western kind of Christianity influenced by Augustine and Luther. But there are problems: for example, Irenaeus's most influential doctrine, from a 21st-century point of view, seems especially vulnerable.

The doctrine in question is Irenaeus's explanation for the existence of evil. We are told that the world is frequently an unpleasant place because it is intended to help us grow up. In other words, God deliberately creates evil in order to change us for the better. Does this really make sense? For one thing, it might be said that it is not worth the price. If all the horrific things that have happened throughout history are necessary to help us grow up, then we might be excused if we prefer to stay children. But more fundamentally, why on earth should God *need* to create evil?

The issue revolves around ends and means. For example, if I want a cup of tea, I have to boil water in a kettle, find a tea bag and so on. Having a cup of tea is my end, or goal, and the process of making it is the means I use to achieve that end. But if I were omnipotent, I wouldn't have to bother with the means. I could simply click my fingers and *have* a cup of tea, completely bypassing the process that is normally unavoidable. In other words, part of being omnipotent is the ability to achieve one's ends without having to take intermediate steps to get there.

Irenaeus, however, is telling us that God takes certain actions (creating evil) as a means to an end (helping humanity mature). But if God is omnipotent, this doesn't make sense. The end—mature humanity—should be available to him without needing the means, the creation of evil. To say that the existence of evil is necessary if we want mature human beings is to miss the point: that may well be the case in the normal run of things, but not where God is concerned. Anyone planning to use Irenaeus's theology to explain why God allows evil and suffering to exist needs to be able to show either why God should choose this method of improving humanity despite its intrinsic unpleasantness or why no other method was available to him even though he is omnipotent. Irenaeus, at least, does not even attempt this.

Tertullian

As Irenaeus was forging the distinctive Eastern understanding of Christianity, Tertullian was doing the same thing for the West. The first Latin theologian stamped his unique personality into the character of Western Christianity with a force few have equalled. Tertullian's biting wit, cruel sarcasm and obsessive fanaticism retain their power and vitriol as surely today as when he committed them to paper 1,800 years ago. By turns insulting, courageous, brilliant and pedantic, Tertullian is never dull.

Life

The extraordinary vigor of Tertullian's work may reflect something of the vigor of the African church to which he belonged. The splendidly named Quintus Septimius Florens Tertullianus was born in Carthage, the greatest city of North Africa, sometime in the middle of the 2nd century. Nothing is known of his early life, except that he seems to have indulged happily in worldly pleasures to what he later considered an extravagant degree.

He certainly received a good education. Intriguingly, it seems that there was a prominent lawyer at the time called Tertullian, and the two Tertullians may have been the same person. Certainly his theology uses many legal ideas; and many have detected in his vigorous self-righteousness and general rudeness unmistakable signs of a legal mind!

At some point, however, this well-educated and talented Roman converted to Christianity. Although Tertullian does not tell us how or why this happened, it is often thought that he was impressed by the courage of Christians being thrown to lions or burned in public. Throughout his writings Tertullian dwells on the glories of martyrdom, pointing out to the authorities that their persecution of the church has the opposite effect to that intended: "The more we are mown down by you, the more numerous we grow; the blood of Christians is seed" (*Apology* 50). Or as it is usually misquoted, "The blood of the martyrs is the seed of the church."

It is likely that Tertullian was quite young when he became a Christian, since he had not yet married; he later married a Christian woman. After his conversion he threw himself wholeheartedly into his new faith, immersing himself in its Scriptures to a profound degree. It cannot have been long before he began writing in its defense.

Tertullian's appearance on the literary scene must have caused something of a stir. Christianity was a predominantly Greek-speaking religion, and even Christian writers who lived in Rome, such as Justin Martyr, wrote in Greek. Tertullian was the first important theologian to write in Latin. Equally striking was his style. Instead of the calm reasonableness of Justin's apologies or the roundabout rambling of Irenaeus, Tertullian's works were short, brutally direct and completely uncompromising. His masterful *Apology* makes Justin's look like the work of an amateur; in it he harangues the rulers of the Roman empire like an angry schoolmaster.

In fact, Tertullian was happy attacking practically everyone with whom he disagreed: not simply pagans and persecutors of Christianity but also those within the church whose doctrines he considered erroneous or whose morality left something to be desired. His attacks often seem to go beyond what Christian charity would normally consider appropriate. Virtually all his works contain graphic warnings of fiery judgment. Consider, for example, the following notorious passage, in which he seems to suggest that what he most looks forward to in heaven is a good view of hell:

What a wonderful spectacle then bursts upon the eye! What about it do I admire? What do I laugh at? Which sight gives me joy? Which do I exult at?—as I see so many great kings, whose reception into heaven was publicly announced, groaning now in the lowest darkness with great Jupiter himself, and with those who announced their exultation! And governors of provinces, too, who persecuted the Christian name, in fires more fierce than the ones that they proudly threatened the followers of Christ with! And the world's wise men, those same philosophers, in fact, who taught their followers that God was not concerned about anything below the moon, and would assure them that either they had no souls, or that they would never return to the bodies which they left when they died, now covered with shame before the poor deluded ones, as one fire consumes them! Poets also, trembling not before the judgment-seat of Rhadamanthus or Minos, but of the unexpected Christ! I shall find it much easier then to hear the authors of tragedies, much louder in their own misfortune; of viewing the play-actors, much more dissolute in the dissolving flame; of looking upon the charioteer, all glowing in his chariot of fire; of seeing the wrestlers, not in their gyms, but bobbing in the fiery waves.

On Spectacles 30

In fairness to Tertullian, it should be pointed out that his gleeful vision of an over-populated hell was written at a time when the whole world, from politicians to intellectuals, seemed united against Christians. Tertullian himself could easily have suffered an end as horrific as the tortures he imagines for Caesar and Aristotle.

Tertullian's reputation as a great theologian certainly doesn't rest on his talent as a polemicist. In opposing what he saw as doctrinal error, he pioneered new avenues for Christian thought. His works against his theological opponents laid down the lines along which later thinking on the Trinity and the person of Christ would run.

However, Tertullian's rigorous ethics and inability to compromise eventually led him to join a sect known as the Montanists, a sort of early-3rd-century charismatic movement that spread throughout the church. The Montanists believed that their leaders were receiving new prophecies from the Holy Spirit about church discipline and Christian morality. The movement proved especially popular in the enthusiastic, hot-blooded African church, and Tertullian embraced it eagerly. Perhaps he felt that the new prophecy provided a more secure foundation for his rigorous ethics than mainstream church tradition.

Most Christians, however, rejected Montanism; and so Tertullian finally turned

his pen against the mainstream church he had once defended. His later works cas-
tigate the church for rejecting the new prophecy, and it is for this reason that he
has not been remembered with wholehearted approval. It is not known what happened to Tertullian. It may be that he split away from the Montanists, founding a
splinter group of his own. A schismatic group called the Tertullianists did exist in
Carthage in the 4th century, possibly the successors of Tertullian's followers, although more probably just later admirers. There was a later tradition that Tertullian
lived to extreme old age; however, if he did, then he seems to have stopped writing,
which would seem rather out of character. It is not impossible that he finally gained
the prize of martyrdom that he had praised so highly in his work.

Thought

Tertullian is the first of the church fathers to have left a large body of work, although not all of it survives. Although he wrote only short, occasional polemics
and essays, they reveal a remarkably systematic pattern of thought for someone
who professed to hate philosophy. Here only the most important points can be sur-
veyed. Perhaps more than with any other author in this book, there is no substitute
for reading Tertullian firsthand.

The sources of theology. We saw earlier that Justin Martyr believed that since Christ
is the Logos or divine Reason, those who live according to reason are followers of
Christ and may dimly grasp the truth. The philosophers were therefore forerunners
of Christianity, much like the prophets.

Tertullian is having none of this. He can see no good whatsoever in either philosophy or philosophers themselves:

> Where is there any likeness between the Christian and the philosopher? be-
> tween the disciple of Greece and of heaven? between the man whose goal is
> fame, and whose goal is life? between the talker and the doer? between the
> man who builds up and the man who pulls down? between the friend and the
> foe of error? between one who corrupts the truth, and one who restores and
> teaches it?
> *Apology* 46

Where Justin regarded philosophy as a potential ally of Christianity, because it
dealt with many of the same subjects, Tertullian sees in it a rival, for much the same
reason. He argues that all heresies come from the influence of philosophy, adding,
in a famous aphorism, "What has Athens to do with Jerusalem? What has the
Academy to do with the Church?" (*Prescription Against the Heretics* 7).

Worldly wisdom has no place in the church. The philosophers can tell Christians nothing that they don't already know—and anything truthful that philosophers may say was stolen from the Scriptures anyway.

Human reason, then, is not the source of our knowledge of God. But neither is Scripture alone, since the heretics appeal to Scripture as well. Tertullian argues for a "rule of faith," the public teaching of Christ, given to the apostles and taught in the churches that they founded.

> It is clear that all doctrine which agrees with the apostolic churches—those moulds and original sources of the faith—must be considered true, as undoubtedly containing what those churches received from the Apostles, the Apostles from Christ, Christ from God. And all doctrine must be considered false which contradicts the truth of the churches and Apostles of Christ and God.
>
> *Prescription Against the Heretics* 21

So we know that what the churches preach is true because it was handed down to them by the apostles. The Scriptures are true because they too have been handed down in this way and are the sole property of the apostolic churches; heretics do not even have the right to quote them. In other words, Tertullian seems to suggest that the ultimate authority in matters of doctrine is tradition. This is not to say that he does not regard Scripture as authoritative. The idea that Scripture and tradition could be at variance would never have occurred to any Christian of the time. In practice Tertullian, like most ancient Christian authors, draws most of his arguments from Scripture, falling back on tradition and reason when necessary.

The Trinity. Tertullian's greatest contribution to Christian doctrine is undoubtedly his treatment of the Trinity. He is the first author to devote a whole treatise to the subject, and as might be expected, his approach is bold and clear. There is none of the vagueness that we saw in Justin and Irenaeus.

Tertullian begins with the Logos doctrine of Justin. Like Justin, he speaks of God's Reason existing within him in primordial times and then being "spoken forth" as his Word for the purposes of creation. It is striking that he uses this theology even though, writing in Latin, he cannot rely on the ambiguities of the Greek word *logos* as Justin did. However, he stresses the personality of the Word more than Justin did, arguing that even before it was spoken, God's Reason was like a second person within him.

Where Justin never really defined the Logos or stated whether it was really divine, Tertullian is quite clear. The Word is God. So too is the Spirit. Yet they are not identical with God the Father. In a famous definition, he writes:

All of them are One, by unity of substance; while we still keep the mystery of the distribution which spreads the Unity into a Trinity, placing in their order the three Persons—the Father, the Son, and the Holy Spirit. But they are three, not in state, but in degree; not in substance, but in form; not in power, but in appearance; yet of one substance, and of one state, and of one power, inasmuch as he is one God, from whom these degrees and forms and appearances are understood, under the name of the Father, and of the Son, and of the Holy Spirit.

Against Praxeas 2

This complex statement is a remarkable advance on the theology of Justin and his immediate successors. For one thing, Tertullian clearly teaches a trinity rather than a duality—he includes the Holy Spirit in the Godhead as well as the Son. This is unsurprising given Tertullian's association with the Montanists, whose worship was based on new teachings from the Spirit.

But there are more innovations here. Perhaps most striking is that Tertullian lists some ways in which the three Persons are one and ways in which they are three, recognizing that there is something paradoxical in what he says. The brief discussions of the subject in Justin and Irenaeus lack this sense of the complexity of the issue.

Equally important is the terminology developed here. The very word *trinity*—*trinitas* in Latin—is applied to God for the first time. Tertullian is also the first to describe the three members of the Trinity as "persons" and the first to talk of their unity of "substance." These terms remain the standard way of discussing this subject. What did Tertullian mean by them?

On the one hand, of course, *substance* can mean what something is made of. More technically, it refers to the essential qualities something has—qualities without which it would not be what it is. For example, an iron object would not be iron if it were not hard, though it could be square, round or any other shape without ceasing to be iron. Hardness is therefore part of the substance of iron, but squareness and roundness are not. So to say that the three Persons share one substance is to say that they share the same essential qualities—they are essentially the same kind of thing. They are all God.

But more: they are one and the same God. *Substance* also has a legal meaning, equivalent to "property." And a person is someone who owns a substance. So to say that the three Persons share substance in this sense is to suggest a very close relation between them, just as there is between a married couple who own everything in common.

Tertullian expands on his theme by using traditional imagery. He argues for the unity of the Persons by appealing to the "monarchy" or the unity of their rule: there is only one power in heaven. More strikingly, he uses images drawn from nature to argue that three things can be distinct and yet inseparably joined:

> I should not hesitate to call the tree the son or offspring of the root, and the river the son of the fountain, and the ray the son of the sun; because every original source is a parent, and everything which comes from the origin is an offspring. And this is even more true of the Word of God, who is actually called Son as his own name. But still the tree is not severed from the root, nor the river from the fountain, nor the ray from the sun; nor, indeed, is the Word separated from God. . . . Now the Spirit is third from God and the Son; just as the fruit of the tree is third from the root, or as the stream out of the river is third from the fountain, or as the apex of the ray is third from the sun. But nothing is different in character from its original source. In the same way, the Trinity, flowing down from the Father through intertwined and connected steps, does not at all disturb the Monarchy.
>
> *Against Praxeas* 8

Despite the originality and boldness of his ideas and language, this passage shows that Tertullian still lives in the thought world of Justin and his followers. He thinks of the Father as the origin of the Trinity, just as the sun is the origin of the ray of light that comes from it. In other words, the Son and the Spirit are divine because they come from God the Father. The Father is identical with the divine substance of the Trinity: he is the reference point of divinity.

This is known as "subordinationism," since although it recognizes the divinity and unity of all three Persons it regards the Father as the source of the Trinity and therefore as greater than the other two members. It would not be until the 4th and 5th centuries, with the work of Augustine, that this legacy of Logos theology would finally be laid to rest. Yet this later development beyond Tertullian's thought would always use the terminology and basic ideas that he developed.

Christ. In another pioneering move, Tertullian applies the same terminology he uses for the Trinity to Christ. He writes:

> The truth is, we find that he is clearly set forth as both God and man . . . certainly in all respects as the Son of God and the Son of man, being God and man, differing no doubt according to each substance in its own qualities, inasmuch as the Word is nothing else but God, and the flesh nothing else but man.
>
> *Against Praxeas* 27

In other words, where the Trinity is three Persons with one substance, Christ is one Person with two substances. He is wholly God and also wholly human. These two substances remain distinct from each other and are not mixed, since otherwise Christ would be neither properly divine nor properly human but a sort of half-and-half mixture of both. He is, however, one person, not two; and moreover, that one person is identical with the divine Word who existed with the Father before the incarnation. Yet we must stress his humanity and his divinity equally. As Tertullian demands of those who forget this, "Why do you halve Christ with a lie?" (*On the Flesh of Christ* 5).

As with the Trinity, Tertullian is aware that what he says seems paradoxical. In one famous passage he delights in his own apparent intellectual perversity:

> I am safe, if I am not ashamed of my Lord. . . . The Son of God was crucified; I am not ashamed because others are ashamed of it. And the Son of God died; it is definitely to be believed, because it is absurd. And the one who was buried rose again; it is certain, because it is impossible.
> *On the Flesh of Christ* 5

His point, of course, is not that Christianity is stupid or contrary to reason: it is that it is so extraordinary that no one could have made it up.

Tertullian's christological teaching is not only clearer than that of his predecessors but basically identical to what would become Christian orthodoxy at the epochal Council of Chalcedon two and a half centuries later. That council would set forth its teaching in language originally developed by Tertullian and also by his younger contemporary Origen Adamantius, the "Iron Man."

Origen

Origen is, together with Augustine and Luther, one of the most important figures in this book. Almost single-handedly the "Iron Man," as he was known, dragged Christianity into intellectual respectability. One of the greatest minds of his age, he debated with pagan philosophers as their superior. And as the first truly professional theologian, he also created the first true Christian philosophy, much of which would remain in place throughout Christendom for centuries. Yet this very originality was regarded by many as heresy. The systematic destruction of most of his writings after his death—by churchmen unworthy to inherit them—robbed the church of one of its greatest treasures. This tragic loss, together with the aura of suspicion that still surrounds the name of Origen, has meant that that name has not received the praise due to it by the church at large.

Life

Origen was born in about A.D. 185 in Alexandria. His father, a Christian named Leonides, not only ensured that he received the best education available but had

ALEXANDRIA

Alexandria was founded in 332 B.C. by Alexander the Great during a brief stopover on his way to conquer the rest of the known world. By the time of the church fathers it was one of the greatest cities in the world.

The city was perfectly sited on the Egyptian coast. It had two harbors opening onto the Mediterranean, dominated by the great Pharos Lighthouse, one of the Seven Wonders of the World, which stood on an island a mile offshore. To the south was a third harbor, on Lake Mareotis, which was even busier than the other two put together. The lake was connected by canals to the River Nile and the Red Sea. All trade between the Mediterranean and Asia therefore passed through Alexandria, and the city prospered beyond the dreams of avarice. It was blessed with the enormously fertile Nile Delta close to hand, and after its incorporation into the Roman empire in 30 B.C. it played a central role in the empire's food supply. Every year an enormous shipment of grain was dispatched to Rome and, later, to Constantinople.

Alexandria was carefully planned on a grid layout, and its wide paved streets, which were illuminated at night, were a definite advance on the tiny, narrow alleyways found in most Egyptian towns of the time. At the center of the city was a magnificent mausoleum that housed the body of Alexander the Great himself; but Alexandria's greatest treasure was its fabled library. The library was said to possess over 700,000 books and was by far the most important resource for knowledge and learning anywhere in the world.

It is no surprise, therefore, that Alexandria was the foremost center of philosophy, science and scholarship in late antiquity. Galen the great medical writer and Ptolemy the astronomer and geographer worked here, as did the mathematicians Archimedes and Euclid. One Alexandrian scientist, Hero, even invented the steam engine. The 600,000 inhabitants were justifiably proud of their city and felt rather aloof from the surrounding countryside; sometimes, in defiance of normal geographical laws, it was known as Alexandria "next to" Egypt.

him learn and recite the Scriptures every day. That Origen was no ordinary child is indicated by the fact that he apparently enjoyed this. Like all fathers, Leonides soon found himself unable to answer his son's questions about what he was learning, but

Alexandria was a center for religious thought too. The city had a large Jewish population, many of whom were extremely well educated. This community's most distinguished product was Philo, an extraordinary thinker who lived at around the same time as Jesus. Philo sought to combine Platonic philosophy with the Jewish faith and developed new methods of expressing traditional Jewish ideas in the technical vocabulary of Platonism. He also pioneered the allegorical method of interpreting Scripture, using the text as a window into deep philosophical mysteries. Philo's work appears to have been completely ignored by the philosophical community in general—but it was of supreme importance for Christian thinkers who came after him with very similar projects.

Christianity seems to have become an important force in Alexandria sometime in the 2nd century, although it must have arrived earlier than that. Tradition claimed that it was brought by St. Mark the evangelist and that he was the first bishop of Alexandria. Whatever the truth of the matter, by the late 2nd century the Christian community was as prominent and vigorous as the Jewish one, and it was producing thinkers of major significance. Theologians like Clement of Alexandria and Origen, and their successors, drew on the unparalleled resources and traditions available to them to forge a new Christian philosophy that would eclipse that of their predecessors and blaze new trails for posterity to follow.

Their time was brief. The rise of Constantinople in the 4th century meant that Alexandria was no longer the premier city of the East, to its inhabitants' enormous irritation. A major blow to the city's standing came in 391, when the great temple of the pagan god Serapis was destroyed by a raging mob led by Theophilus, the unscrupulous bishop of Alexandria. The temple happened to contain most of the collection of the Great Library, so that was the end of that. The city's intellectual decline was swift, and its capture by Muslim forces in the 7th century marked the end of its ancient importance.

was secretly delighted that he had produced such a brilliant child. We are told that he would often stand by his son's bed at night and kiss the chest that he believed must house a divine spirit.

Still, the young Origen seems more self-righteous than admirable. When Origen was 17, his father was arrested for his faith. Origen, who, like most Christians of the time—especially in Africa—idolized martyrs, wrote him a letter urging him not to forsake his faith for fear of leaving his family fatherless. Leonides took his son's advice and was duly executed. Origen was keen to follow him into martyrdom, but his mother, evidently deciding that it was bad enough to lose her husband without losing her son as well, hid his clothes. Teenage modesty prevailed over religious enthusiasm, and Origen remained safely at home.

With Leonides' execution, the state confiscated his property, leaving the family destitute. Origen had to provide for the rest. Luckily he had continued to excel at all his studies, and he had mastered the standard literary curriculum sufficiently to scrape out a living as a teacher. On this he managed to support his mother and many siblings.

At the same time his own studies were becoming more and more advanced. Two teachers in particular seem to have held his attention at this time. The first—although we are not certain he taught Origen—was Ammonius Saccas, a famous pagan philosopher. This teacher was later to become the mentor of Plotinus, the celebrated founder of Neoplatonism. Virtually nothing is known of Ammonius, who left no writings; but if he inspired Origen and Plotinus, the two greatest minds of the 3rd century, then he must have been a remarkable man.

The second great teacher is not mentioned anywhere in Origen's surviving works but cannot have failed to influence him. Clement of Alexandria was head of the catechetical school that instructed those preparing for baptism. An extraordinarily erudite and capable theologian, Clement strove to prove to the world that Christians were not uneducated barbarians. His works, which burst with quotations from poets and philosophers alike, speak of an advanced Christian philosophy known and practiced by the spiritually and intellectually adept but unknown even to the common run of Christians. In this respect Clement's thinking is reminiscent of Gnosticism, and he did indeed describe the Christian sage as a "gnostic" or "knower." But where the Gnostics claimed to possess a secret teaching handed down from the apostles, Clement believed that the advanced Christian philosophy was publicly available in the Bible. But he argued that only those with great spiritual insight were capable of looking beyond the plain meaning of the words and understanding the deeper meaning of Scripture.

These ideas were undoubtedly hugely influential on Origen, who was starting to gain a reputation as a good teacher not only of secular arts but of Christian doctrine too. Indeed such was his reputation that when a fresh wave of persecution left the catechetical school with no teacher, Bishop Demetrius of Alexandria asked the 18-year-old Origen to take on the job.

As a Christian instructor, Origen now felt qualms about the degree to which he had immersed himself in non-Christian learning. Despite his great philosophical ability and the remarkably successful way he created a synthesis of Christian faith and Greek philosophy, Origen, at least consciously, could never think of them as really compatible. His general outlook had more in common with that of Tertullian than that of Clement or Justin. It was an "us and them" outlook, the outlook of a man who had seen his own father arrested and killed by a hostile, pagan society.

Origen therefore sold his books, lived on the paltry sum that he received for them and devoted himself only to the Scriptures. His lifestyle can hardly have been extravagant to start with, but now he took it to new extremes of hardship in an effort to train his body and soul for a life pleasing to God. Fasting regularly and sleeping erratically on the floor, he went about barefoot, trying to follow the strict ethic of the Sermon on the Mount (Mt 5—7).

Origen was later to write that the Sermon on the Mount represents an impossible ideal, one that no human being can hope to follow. Perhaps that reflects his experience as a young man leading an ascetic life of self-denial that ultimately achieved nothing but the near ruin of his health. Perhaps, too, his later insistence that not all of the Bible is to be taken literally had some of its roots in his failed attempt to follow Jesus' hardest commands.

And his youthful fervor seems to have had some highly regrettable consequences. We are told that, misled by an overly literal reading of Matthew 19:12 and worried that teaching female catechumens might lead him into sin, Origen "made himself a eunuch for the kingdom of heaven's sake." It is not certain that he actually took this drastic step, since the evidence varies; according to some hostile accounts, Origen's sexual self-control was brought about by the use of drugs or a minor operation of some kind. However, although illegal except under special circumstances and frowned upon by the church, self-emasculation was certainly not unknown in Christian circles of the more enthusiastically ascetic variety. If Origen was indeed one of those who did this, then he came to regret it. Toward the end of his life, he wrote a commentary on Matthew's Gospel in which he vigorously rejects any literal interpretation of the fateful verse.

Instructing those who wished to be baptized was not the placid, otherworldly occupation we might imagine today. The persecution was still going on in Alexandria, and many of Origen's pupils were arrested and executed for their faith. Bravely,

Origen accompanied and supported them as they were led away; and he quickly became known as one of the most prominent Christian leaders in the city. Attacked by angry mobs and hunted by groups of soldiers, he had to be bundled from house to house simply to survive. Luckily, he seems to have realized that he could do the church most service by continuing to teach, and he no longer tried to become a martyr himself.

It was, perhaps, partly as a result of Origen's bravery and seeming invulnerability to the hostile authorities that he acquired a nickname: Adamantius, meaning "Unbreakable," or we might say "Iron Man." His fame as an inspirational teacher was beginning to spread throughout the world: in A.D. 222 he was invited to Arabia to meet the Roman governor.

When he wasn't teaching new Christians, dodging the city guards or rubbing shoulders with the famous and powerful, Origen was still learning. He continued to immerse himself in the Scriptures but found his progress hampered by textual problems. He realized that before he could hope to understand the text, he had to establish exactly what the text was. To this end he undertook one of the most impressive feats of scholarship of ancient times: the *Hexapla.* This work was a critical collection and comparison of all the versions of the Old Testament on which Origen could lay his hands. It was divided into several columns, with the Hebrew original on the left and six different translations into Greek on the right. In order to accomplish this, Origen had to learn Hebrew. He never became proficient in the language, but still it was an almost unheard-of thing for a Christian to do. He also consulted learned Jewish rabbis—an equally astonishing act. At this time Jews and Christians spent much of their time fighting tooth and nail over the correct way to interpret the Old Testament. Origen's recognition that Jews might have something worthwhile to say on the matter was therefore extremely unusual.

The *Hexapla*—named for the six Greek translations it contained—was an ongoing project for much of Origen's life. By the time he had finished, some sections had even more translations—up to nine in the case of the Psalms. One of the translations he used had only recently been discovered in a clay pot near Jericho, rather like the Dead Sea Scrolls in modern times. In those days of papyrus scrolls, the *Hexapla* must have been physically huge, occupying a whole room by itself, like a computer from the 1950s.

Origen was not to be allowed to devote all his spare time to this mammoth labor of love. At some point in this period, he met a wealthy Alexandrian called Ambrose, who was a Gnostic. Origen befriended him and before long had him converted to mainstream Christianity. He soon found, however, that this was something of a mixed blessing. Ambrose was greatly impressed by his new mentor and decided to commission some books from him. He even provided Origen with state-of-the-art writing equipment: a team of over 20 shorthand writers, copyists and calligraphers. Origen merely had to dictate, and his staff would take down every word, turning it into publishable prose.

Origen seems to have been a reluctant author. He complained in one letter that Ambrose never left him in peace:

> I am in danger of refusing his demands; for when we are collating the texts we cannot eat, go for a walk, or rest. Even at the times set apart for these activities, we have to engage in learned discourse and correct the manuscripts. And we cannot sleep at night to rest our bodies, since our learned discourse goes on long into the evening.
> Quoted in Joseph Trigg, *Origen: The Bible and Philosophy in the Third-Century Church*, p. 147

Not only did Ambrose have to force Origen to write anything, he was lucky if he got a finished book out of him. Origen's works were so ambitious in scope and minute in detail that he often seems to have got tired of them and abandoned them for new, more interesting projects. Despite these failings, Ambrose's apparently limitless financial resources and enthusiasm for Origen's work eventually allowed the haphazard genius to become quite possibly the most prolific author of all time. Approximately 800 titles of his books are known, and ancient sources estimate the total number as to 6,000 items, ranging from short letters and pamphlets to weighty commentaries on the Bible and philosophical tomes.

Many of these works were published, but some seem to have been written for the sole edification of Ambrose and his friends. Origen was reluctant to commit his more advanced speculations to paper, believing, exactly like Clement of Alexandria, that most Christians would be unable to understand such difficult teachings. He therefore confined such ideas, on the whole, to works not intended for publication. One of these, *On First Principles*, was the first work of systematic Christian theology ever written; in it Origen set forth his fundamental ideas about God, Christ, the world and humanity. Unfortunately, pirate editions of this and other books, originally written as advanced, private research material, were soon circulating among the Christian community at large—something that would cause their author serious problems later.

Sometime shortly after he began writing, Origen gave over leadership of the catechetical school to his assistant Heraclas and left Alexandria to settle in Caesarea, on the coast of Judea. Perhaps he hoped to establish close links with the sizable community of Jewish scholars there and enlist their help with the *Hexapla* and the biblical commentaries he was then working on.

Theoctistus, the bishop of Caesarea, was delighted to welcome the famous teacher to his church and, together with Alexander, bishop of Jerusalem, asked Origen to preach at services. The invitation had unforeseen consequences. Origen's own bishop, Demetrius of Alexandria, interpreted it as a direct assault on his authority and wrote angrily to the Judean bishops, who responded in kind. Eventually Demetrius sent a delegation to Origen to persuade him to return, which he did.

Church leaders were not the only people jostling for Origen's attention. In A.D. 231 Julia Mammea, the powerful mother of the teenage emperor Alexander Severus, sent a military escort to Origen and had him conveyed to Antioch to talk with her son. On his return, Origen again visited his friends at Caesarea, where he was ordained as a presbyter by Theoctistus.

As Theoctistus and Origen must both have anticipated, this infuriated Demetrius, who believed that rival bishops had no business ordaining members of his own church. Where Demetrius had once admired Origen and entrusted him with important responsibilities, he now began to work against him as an enemy. He raised the support of his fellow Egyptian bishops and wrote to Pontian, the bishop of Rome, to persuade him to join him in condemning Origen. His case was threefold: first, Origen could not be ordained by a foreign bishop; second, as a eunuch he was technically ineligible for ordination anyway; and third, he was teaching heretical doctrines.

As Origen had feared, the common run of Christians could not appreciate the bolder and more advanced elements of his teaching. Some of the books he had written for private circulation had been leaked and were misunderstood by lesser minds. The doctrine that Demetrius objected to in particular was Origen's supposed claim that the devil would be saved. On the basis of this, the church in Egypt condemned Origen's teachings and excommunicated him.

Since Origen was in Caesarea, this condemnation meant little as long as Alexander of Jerusalem supported him. Indeed the rather otherworldly Origen seems to have been most annoyed not by the slur to his reputation but by the interruption to his work. His ever-present team of secretaries had abandoned him, leaving him unable to write. Fortunately, Origen managed to produce, without their help, an eloquent refutation of Demetrius's charges, maintaining that he had claimed only that the devil *could* be saved if he repented, not that he certainly *would* be. Alexander pledged his support to Origen and wrote to Pontian of Rome defending him.

At the same time, Origen's life was made easier by the fortuitous death of Demetrius. He was succeeded as bishop of Alexandria by Heraclas, Origen's erstwhile assistant at the catechetical school. Unfortunately, Heraclas harbored no nostalgic feelings toward his old master, whom he regarded not only as an excommunicated heretic but as a personal rival. Origen therefore remained in Caesarea, where he could pursue his studies in peace with the aid of his newly returned secretarial staff.

Away from his enemies and enjoying again the full support of local bishops, Origen resumed his work as a teacher. Instead of the introductory lessons he had given those preparing for baptism at Alexandria, he now offered an advanced course in Christian philosophy, covering all the secular literature and science taught in normal higher education but with a Christian focus. One fascinating testament to this time survives, a speech delivered by one of Origen's pupils, traditionally identified with a famous missionary and teacher called Gregory the Wonderworker. This speech extravagantly praises Origen as a perfect teacher and example of Christian living. The speaker stresses the great man's immense learning and the remarkable way he expounded all the works of pagan philosophers and poets, showing how there was useful material in them all. Unlike most teachers of philosophy, who taught only the ideas of their own tradition—Platonism, Stoicism and so on—Origen had mastered it all. And the speaker wonders at Origen's supernatural understanding of the Bible. The only possible conclusion is that Christ himself "has honoured this man as he would a friend" (*Panegyric to Origen* 15).

Now in his late 40s and 50s, Origen was becoming something of a sage to the worldwide church. His sermons and homilies were recorded for general circulation, something he had never allowed before. He was also called upon to help with doctrinal disputes. Origen's formidable debating powers, combined with his zeal for orthodoxy and fair-handedness in dealing with those who disagreed with him, made him a valuable presence at a number of synods. By remarkable good fortune, the transcript of one of these occasions survives, recording a synod that met to investigate the christological views of a bishop named Heraclides. In it Origen quickly but fairly refutes Heraclides' mistakes and converts him to orthodoxy, before discussing at length several related issues raised by members of the assembly. That an august gathering of venerable bishops should have taken part in what was essentially a seminar taught by a mere presbyter is an eloquent testimony to Origen's charisma and spiritual power.

However, controversy was never far away. In about A.D. 246 documents came into the hands of Heraclas, bishop of Alexandria, which accused Origen of teaching that the devil ought to be saved. Origen must have been horrified that this old scandal, which he had believed had been laid to rest 15 years earlier, had flared up again. Heraclas, Origen's former pupil, still regarded his old master as a personal rival, and like Demetrius before him, he condemned Origen before passing the offending material to Fabian, the bishop of Rome.

Strangely, the affair ended in the same way as the earlier one: Heraclas died, and the matter was dropped. Heraclas's successor as bishop of Alexandria was Dionysius, yet another of Origen's former pupils. Luckily, Dionysius held his old teacher in high esteem, and in later years he proved to be an able theologian himself and staunch defender of the Origenist tradition.

Origen once again picked up his studies and continued pouring forth commentaries, treatises and other works. But he was not to be left in peace for long. In A.D. 249 Emperor Philip was replaced by Decius, who did not share his predecessor's sympathetic attitude toward Christians. A wave of persecution—the first major attack in 50 years—was unleashed. This time, instead of killing large numbers of Christians and creating martyrs, the authorities focused their efforts on Christian leaders. They aimed for the most part not to kill them but to use torture to force them into recanting their faith. In this way they hoped to crush the spirit of the church.

Fabian of Rome and Alexander of Jerusalem both died in prison. Origen's pupil Dionysius of Alexandria survived only because the guards, searching for him for several days, did not think of going to his house, where he was patiently awaiting their arrival.

Origen's name must have been at the top of the list. The old man was arrested, incarcerated and cruelly tortured in an effort to force a recantation. But a lifetime of ascetic training supported his faith, and neither stretching on the rack nor threats of fire could induce the Iron Man to renounce it.

Origen was released after a few days, his faith intact, but physically a broken man. Virtually nothing is known of the last years of his life; his literary and ecclesiastical activities were no more. He is thought to have ended his days in obscurity at Tyre in about A.D. 254.

Condemnation

Even in his own lifetime, Origen was a controversial figure. After his death, although he was remembered as a great teacher and model Christian, the controversies continued. His ideas were cherished and developed by some skilled theologians, including Dionysius of Alexandria, and an enduring Origenist tradition developed among the monks of the Egyptian desert. However, as the years passed Origen's name became increasingly associated with unorthodox ideas.

Emperor Justinian, who took a keen interest in theological matters, called the Second Council of Constantinople in A.D. 553 to condemn Origenists who had developed his doctrines beyond what Origen himself had taught. A series of statements attributed to Origen was condemned. Although it is probable that Origen himself was not formally branded a heretic, the order was given for his works to be destroyed.

It is quite likely that by this stage much of Origen's vast output had been lost anyway. At a time when every copy of a book had to be made by hand, it was simply too great an effort to preserve so much. All the same, there must still have been a huge amount of material circulating in A.D. 553. The work of destruction therefore commenced in earnest and was remarkably successful. The greatest storehouse of Christian learning ever laid down by a single individual was reduced to a few miserable shreds.

Thought

Today only a tiny fraction remains of Origen's original writings. Only one major treatise, *Against Celsus*, survives in the original Greek, together with a few lesser works. Fragments of his commentaries remain. Luckily, many more works survive in Latin translation, although these translations are often inexact and untrustworthy. Other works can be reconstructed by a painstakingly putting together of fragments quoted in various later authors. In particular, *On First Principles*, in many ways the most interesting and important of Origen's works, exists only as an unhappy patchwork of unreliable Latin translation, occasional Greek fragments and inferences from later reports.

One way or another, however, enough Greek fragments and Latin translations exist to piece together a sizable body of work from which we can reconstruct most of Origen's thought. But because we must often rely on inexact translations or on reports by later, hostile writers, there is a great deal of uncertainty over much of Origen's teaching—particularly over the most original and interesting facets of his thought, which later generations considered heretical.

Scripture. Origen's thought revolves around the Bible. He devoted much of his life to establishing the definitive text of the Old Testament and to commentating or preaching on Scripture; his other works too are drenched in scriptural quotes and imagery. Every word Origen wrote was based on his conviction that the whole Bible was God's revelation to humanity.

Yet Origen was highly aware of the problems posed by the Bible. He knew that much of the Old Testament, for example, either seems dull and irrelevant or contains bloodthirsty tales of a highly unedifying nature. His answer is that these passages—and indeed the entire Bible—have a deeper meaning.

Most texts, taken literally, are true and useful. But some are not. Origen cites the Genesis account of creation and the impossible laws of Moses. Even Jesus' refer-

NEOPLATONISM

The 3rd century was one of the worst times in history to be living in Europe. Wave after wave of barbarians threatened to overwhelm the borders of the Roman empire. Terrible plagues reduced mighty cities to charnel houses. And the political system was in free fall. Emperors were murdered within months of seizing power, puppet rulers were installed by military juntas, and any talented politicians who were left spent most of their time simply trying to stay alive.

Yet in the middle of this appalling turmoil appeared some of the most profound, calm and otherworldly thought ever produced. The work of Origen was part of this extraordinary awakening. The rise of Neoplatonism was another.

Neoplatonism was founded by Plotinus, the last great pagan philosopher of antiquity. It derives its name from the fact that it was both a revival of Platonic philosophy and a major advance on it. Plotinus—who according to his biographer Porphyry was sweaty but good-looking—spent many years in Alexandria studying under Ammonius Saccas, the teacher of Origen. After traveling in Asia he eventually wound up in Rome, where he opened a school and started teaching.

Plotinus was an incredibly inspirational teacher, attracting a wide circle of listeners. They urged him to write his ideas down. It must have taken some persuasion, because Plotinus was not a gifted writer. His handwriting was so bad and his eyesight so weak that he was unable to read over what he had written; he also cared nothing for trifles such as spelling and grammar. The result was a series of tortuous works, rambling unpredictably as their author struggled to find words to convey the extraordinary visions he had experienced.

Like all Platonists, Plotinus believed in a higher reality than the world we see around us, but the higher reality he described was rather complex. The physical world is ordered and managed by Soul, by which is meant both the individual souls of creatures and the World Soul itself, a sort of benign Mother Earth. Soul is subject to an even higher reality, the Divine Intelligence, which contains the Forms, the eternal pattern on which the physical world is modeled. Yet even Divine Intelligence is not the highest reality; above it dwells the One, mysterious and unknowable, transcending all qualities, completely incomprehensible to the human mind.

So the One is the highest pinnacle of reality, the undivided Unity from which everything else, in all its diversity, cascades. Just as a blob of paint when smeared out with a brush becomes gradually fainter, so too reality becomes less "real" and less good the further down from the One it goes. Thus for Plotinus evil has no existence in itself but is simply an absence of good, in the same way that darkness is an absence of light. The physical world, being furthest from the One, is the least real and good part of existence. So we must turn our back to it and direct our mind to the higher planes of reality until we can hope to become united with the One itself.

This gradual spreading of reality from the highest divinity down to the physical realm is a central tenet of Neoplatonism. It contrasts strongly with the post-Nicene Christian insistence on a radical difference between God and the world. After Plotinus's death, later Neoplatonists would develop intricately detailed accounts of all the different levels of reality, elaborating greatly on Plotinus's relatively simple trinity of One, Intelligence and Soul.

Another central tenet of Neoplatonism is the incomprehensibility of the One. The One transcends not only our understanding but even reality itself, for the eternal Forms of reality exist at the level of Divine Intelligence, below the One. This extremely negative conception of the One was a development of ideas already current in Platonic thought. Christianity, which was also absorbing these Platonic ideas, would prove highly receptive to this aspect of Neoplatonism.

While Plotinus was teaching his followers about the beauty of contemplating the eternal divine realities, the plague was sweeping through Rome. Plotinus contracted the disease, which may have been some kind of leprosy. Disfigured, deserted by his followers, the philosopher was left alone on his estate in Sicily. One disciple alone returned to him. He arrived just in time to hear Plotinus announce from his deathbed, "It is time to return the divine element in me to the divine element in the universe." The great man died, but he left an intellectual and spiritual legacy that would change the world.

ence to being struck on the right cheek cannot be taken literally—Origen points out that one always strikes people on the *left* cheek with one's *right* hand! He suggests that "impossible" passages like these have been deliberately put into Scripture by the Holy Spirit, so that the intelligent reader will realize that there must be a deeper meaning to them. In fact every passage, even literally true ones, has a deeper meaning.

This deeper meaning can be discovered by the use of allegory. This essentially means treating the text as a cryptic crossword clue to some deep truth. Thus Origen finds mystical secrets about Christ and human destiny in even the most forbidding passages of the Old Testament law.

The technique often seems fantastical, and Origen has received much criticism for reading his own ideas into the text. But three points should be made in his defense. First, the use of allegory was widespread in late antiquity, when Homer and other classic authors were regarded almost as Christians regarded the Bible. Only through extensive allegorizing could Homer, with his bloodthirsty battles and conniving gods, be considered edifying material. Origen was simply treating the Bible in the same way.

Second, the method is part and parcel of Origen's Platonism. We have seen that a distinction between the visible, material world and a higher, invisible, intellectual or spiritual world is at the very heart of Platonic philosophy. It was at the very heart of Origen's philosophy too. His distinction between the two senses of Scripture was simply an application of that basic belief to the Bible.

Third, Origen's allegorizing is not quite as arbitrary as it at first appears—at least in theory. He was convinced that the key to unlocking the hidden meaning of any text was in that text itself. Each word had to be analyzed and checked against every other passage where it occurs. Thus each passage is interpreted by reference to the whole of the rest of the Bible. This is one reason Origen's biblical commentaries are so incredibly long!

So Origen, like Clement before him, believed that a body of higher, deeper doctrine existed beyond what ordinary Christians knew about. Contrary to the Gnostics' claims about a secret tradition handed on behind closed doors, Origen believed that this higher truth was publicly available in the Bible but concealed from those who lacked the intellectual and spiritual abilities to see and understand it. So what was this teaching?

God. The Bible speaks of a God with emotions, who is angry and jealous, who changes his mind, who moves from place to place and even has hands, a face and eyes. For Origen, it would be the height of stupidity to take this sort of thing literally. He insists repeatedly that God is incorporeal, which means he not only lacks a body but exists everywhere. He is a perfect mind:

> God must not be thought to be any kind of body, nor to exist in a body, but
> to be a simple intellectual existence, without any addition whatsoever, so that
> he cannot be believed to have in himself a more or a less, but is Unity, or if
> I may so say, Oneness throughout, and the mind and fount from which orig-
> inates all intellectual existence.
> *On First Principles* I.1.6

This very abstract God is the God of Platonic philosophy. Origen's doctrine, which
closely parallels that of contemporary pagan theologians, is a development of the
philosophical theology of Justin Martyr and Irenaeus and an important step on the
road to the "classical" doctrine of God of Thomas Aquinas centuries later. We
should take note in particular of the claim that God is a mind. It follows that it is
by using our mind—through intellectual activity—that we can become most like
God. Origen's spirituality, as we shall see, is therefore extremely intellectualist.

The fact that Origen is still thinking within the bounds of Platonic philosophy
is shown by his striking claim that God is not infinite:

> We must maintain that even the power of God is finite, and we must not, un-
> der pretext of praising him, lose sight of his limitations. For if the divine
> power were infinite, of necessity it could not even understand itself, since the
> infinite is by its nature incomprehensible.
> *On First Principles* 2.9.1

Today we are so used to thinking of God as infinite that we forget that this is not
explicitly stated in the Bible. To the ancient mind, to be infinite would actually be
an imperfection, because it was thought that to be infinite would involve being in-
definite, vague, incomprehensible—all marks of an imperfect being. So Origen's
claim here is intended to support the divine perfection. It would not be until Gregory of Nyssa, 150 years later, that the notion of God's infinity would be introduced
into Christian thought.

The Trinity. Origen occupies a pivotal place in the history of trinitarian thought,
poised between the Logos theology of the past and true trinitarianism of the future. His ideas are very similar to those of Tertullian, his older contemporary, but
with some important changes.

Like Tertullian, Origen firmly upholds a divine Trinity. Each of the three Persons is God. But he is quite clear: they are not equal. He stresses this point more
strongly than Tertullian:

> The God and Father, who holds the universe together, is superior to every
> being that exists. . . . The Son, being less than the Father, is superior to ra-
> tional creatures alone (for he is second to the Father); the Holy Spirit is still
> less, and dwells within the saints alone.
> *On First Principles* I.3.5

Origen even goes so far as to say that the Son is not good in his own nature; he is
good only inasmuch as he reflects the Father's goodness. For this reason, he holds
that it is wrong to pray to Christ: "If we understand what prayer is, perhaps we
ought not to pray to anyone born, not even to Christ himself, but only to the God
and Father of all, to whom also our Saviour prayed" (*On Prayer* 15.1). The notion
of praying to the Holy Spirit does not seem to have even occurred to him.

All of these ideas would be rejected by later orthodoxy. But Origen did introduce one idea that was to become central: eternal generation. Tertullian, like Justin
Martyr, had believed that there was a time when the Father was alone and that at
some point he had begotten the Son and emanated the Spirit in a sort of divine big
bang. Origen points out that if this is true, then we can reasonably ask why God
generated the Trinity at this point rather than, say, five minutes earlier or later. In
fact, the Son and Spirit always existed. They are generated from the Father eternally. The Son is always being begotten, and the Spirit eternally emanates. This
idea, in the hands of Athanasius, would be central to the fight against Arianism in
the 4th century and would become a central plank of the doctrine of the Trinity.

The cycles of the universe. The reader may have noticed a flaw in Origen's argument
for eternal generation. If it would be arbitrary to identify one point in time when
the Son came into being, does this not also apply to the creation of the world? Origen bites the bullet. It would indeed be arbitrary. Just as the Son and Spirit are eternally generated from the Father, so too the universe is eternally created. There was
no time when the world did not exist. For God is Creator and he cannot change,
so there cannot have been a time when he was not Creator.

Yet the Bible quite clearly speaks of a time when the world was created—and of
a time when it will come to an end. Origen resists the temptation to allegorize these
away but points out that this present world is just one of many. There was a universe
before this one was created, and after the present order of things is wrapped up a
new one will be created—and so on and on, through countless eons.

To modern ears it sounds like science fiction. But it was more reasonable in Origen's day. The Stoics believed that when the world comes to an end, another world
will replace it—exactly the same in every respect—and so on forever. Origen rejects
this rather depressing doctrine: it is central to his system, as we shall see, that each

world is different from its predecessor.

The Fall and human nature. We have seen that Origen thinks of God as a mind. More controversially, he applies the same idea to human beings. Origen rejects the idea that humans are intrinsically embodied, physical beings and accepts instead Plato's belief that the body is simply a temporary container for an eternal, immaterial soul. When the body dies, the soul survives. But it goes the other way too: the soul existed before the body. This life is not the first we have lived.

Origen believes that there was a time when we had no body at all. We existed as a pure mind, united to God. But this state of primordial bliss didn't last. All of the souls for some reason abandoned the beatific vision and fell away from God. As they fell, their pure intellectual nature became sullied; the result is the tumultuous human soul that we know today, where the intellect is frequently overwhelmed by passion.

In response to this disaster, God created the physical world to act as a sort of safety net. The newly passionate souls were placed in bodies and put into this world. This explains our current situation, enmeshed in a physical world, enslaved by sin, but with longings to return to our original, pure state.

Why did the souls fall? It was caused by free will, a central doctrine for Origen. They freely chose to abandon God for something worse. And they chose this to differing degrees, which meant that some fell farther than others. This explains the diversity in the world. The souls who fell only a little way were given ethereal bodies and became angels. Those who fell the farthest became demons. And those in the middle became human beings of varying degrees of depravity.

These ideas are very similar to those of Gnosticism, especially the notion that the physical world came about as a result of a fall and that we are trapped in it, yearning to return to a higher realm. But Origen opposes the notion that the physical world is intrinsically evil. It was created by God and serves a good purpose.

Christ and salvation. Not all of the souls fell. One alone chose to remain faithful and united to God. From this union it began to take on God's qualities itself:

> Suppose a lump of iron is placed for a time in the fire. It takes on the fire through all of its pores and veins, and becomes completely changed into fire, as long as the fire is never removed from it and it is never removed from the fire. . . . In this way, then, that soul which, like a piece of iron in the fire, was forever placed in the Word, forever in the Wisdom, forever in God, *is* God in all its acts and feelings and thoughts.
> *On First Principles* 2.6.6

This soul is of course the human soul of Christ. Origen is unique among the early fathers in his emphasis on Christ's human soul; at this period it was usual to think of Christ as a human body animated directly by the Logos. But for Origen the soul is an essential component of Christ, because it mediates between God and Christ's body. In later centuries to deny Christ's soul would be regarded as heretical, since without it Christ would not have been truly human.

Although Origen refers to Christ as Savior, he seems to lack a clear doctrine of Christ's role in salvation. In fact, he thinks of the whole of creation as playing a role in our salvation. Christ is simply part of the divine plan, not the whole of it.

Just like Irenaeus, Origen believes that the universe was created as a place in which we could better ourselves. He stresses that God cannot simply restore us to our original perfection by divine decree: that would override free will. We must get there ourselves, by the exercise of the free will that caused us to fall in the first place. The world is an arena for us to do that, to choose what is right, to make mistakes, to fall and slip, to pick ourselves up again and to continue progressing toward God.

The process is clearly a very long one. Origen is not particularly optimistic about the human ability to progress and seems to think in terms of a succession of success and failure, with only a very gradual progression up to God. This is because we are always free to choose which way we want to go: "It lies with us and with our own actions whether we are to be blessed and holy, or whether through sloth and negligence we are to turn away from blessedness into wickedness and loss" (*On First Principles* I.5.5).

In fact, the process lasts far longer than any one lifetime. This is why there is a long succession of universes. After our life in one world, we progress to the next, in a new body and new position in life, reflecting how we did in the previous world. As we progress from life to life, we gradually improve ourselves and edge closer to the final consummation, when, in the very distant future, the succession of physical worlds will finally come to an end.

Lest this sounds too idealistic, Origen stresses that it is a long and painful process:

> For the sake of bodily health we occasionally find it necessary to take some very unpleasant and bitter medicine as a cure for the ills we have brought on through eating and drinking, and sometimes, if the nature of the illness demands it, we need the severe treatment of the knife and a painful operation, yes, and if the disease has progressed beyond even these remedies, in the last resort it is burnt out with fire. So how much more should we realise that God our doctor, in his desire to wash away the diseases of our souls, which they have brought on themselves through a variety of sins and crimes, uses penal

remedies of a similar sort, even punishing with fire those who have lost their soul's health.

On First Principles 2.10.6

For those lost in sin, life is literally hell on earth—and there is a hell after earth waiting for them too. But the punishment they receive there is not retribution for their crimes; it is a remedy for their sickness. However unpleasant it is, divine punishment is intended for their own good. Eventually the soul will be cleansed and the punishment will end. What this means is that hell is not eternal. And that means that all creatures will in the end be restored:

> There is a resurrection of the dead, and there is punishment, but not ever-lasting. For when the body is punished the soul is gradually purified, and so is restored to its ancient rank. For all wicked men, and for demons, too, punishment has an end, and both wicked men and demons shall be restored to their former rank.
>
> *On First Principles* 2.10.3

It was this doctrine, the salvation of the devil, that got Origen into trouble in his lifetime. It is not clear exactly how explicitly he held it; when challenged, he denied that the devil would certainly be saved, and argued that it was merely possible. On the other hand, the doctrine of universal salvation does follow inexorably from the claim that God punishes his creatures only in order to improve them. It also follows from another of Origen's oft-expressed principles, that the end must be like the beginning. If after all the succession of universes and near-infinite trials of life, not all souls have returned to their original perfection and union with God, what would that say about God's power and wisdom? As St. Paul put it in I Corinthians 15:28, after the last enemy, death, has been conquered, "God will be all in all."

It is a striking fact that, the devil aside, Origen's belief in universal salvation appears to have excited very little controversy in his lifetime or shortly thereafter. Only a few other ancient theologians appear to share it, but hardly anyone seems to have written against it. Gregory of Nyssa, probably the greatest Greek-speaking theologian after Origen, and a central pillar of the Orthodox faith, repeatedly states in his works that all creatures will be saved, and does so far more explicitly than Origen himself. It is only in modern times that less generously minded critics have picked up on this optimistic doctrine as Origen's central error.

The resurrection. In the beginning, we were pure minds without bodies. So if the end is really like the beginning, it would seem that after the final consummation we will again be bodiless. Yet Origen's teaching here is among the most obscure in all his work. On the one hand, he certainly denies the crudely literal doctrines of some Christians that at the end of time all people will be resurrected in the same physical body they now possess, complete with arms and legs, hair and nails. He seems instead to have built on the claim of Paul in I Corinthians 15 that what is "sown" as a physical body will be raised as a spiritual body: that is, the same body rises as the one that dies, but it is transformed. It may be that the resurrection body is like the bodies of angels, thin and ethereal, although not immaterial. It will certainly not need to move from place to place, to eat or to reproduce, and will therefore lack the parts of the body associated with those activities.

Whatever his exact doctrine, Origen was later bitterly attacked for teaching it. He was accused of denying the resurrection of the dead altogether or, bizarrely, of teaching that the resurrection body will be perfectly spherical. It was on this basis, together with his insistence on the preexistence of the soul and reincarnation from life to life in different bodies, that he was condemned in the 6th century.

The spiritual life. How, in practice, do we purify ourselves and come closer to reattaining our original state? Origen's answer is that we must do our best to overcome the bodily passions, lead a life as free from sin as possible and, above all, immerse ourselves in Scripture. In other words, we ought to try to live much like Origen himself.

The study of Scripture is central to the spiritual life. For Origen it is a purely intellectual activity, the goal of which is to understand as fully as possible every word of the inspired books. This is not to deny that it is an emotional, spiritual experience. For Origen, the intellectual and the spiritual are the same thing. Just as God is a mind, so are we, and salvation involves abandoning the lower parts of the soul and becoming pure intellect once again:

> We see that human beings have a kind of blood-relationship with God; and since God knows all things . . . it is possible that a rational mind also, by advancing from a knowledge of small to a knowledge of greater things and from things visible to things invisible, may achieve an increasingly perfect understanding.
>
> *On First Principles* 4.4.6

As we read the Bible, progressing in knowledge of spiritual reality and becoming more like God, we come to know God more closely. Just as Moses encountered God in the burning bush, God comes to us in a blaze of light, illuminating our intellects. But it is a long process. Origen bases his account of spiritual progression on the three books of Scripture he believed to have been written by Solomon. First, in the book of Proverbs we learn how to live correctly. This purification process is the essential prerequisite to drawing close to God. Next we learn about the world around us, both the physical and spiritual realms. This process is described in the book of Ecclesiastes. Finally we come close to God himself and are united with him. This is described in highly allegorical language in the Song of Songs, which Origen interprets as a love song between God and the soul of the mystic.

It is not a smooth process. In one famous passage Origen touchingly describes his own experiences at the hands of the heavenly Bridegroom:

> Often—God is my witness—I have felt the Bridegroom come close to me, so that he was almost with me, and then he suddenly went away, and I could not find what I was looking for. Again I find myself desiring his coming, and sometimes he returns; and when he appears before me, and I reach my hands out towards him, he escapes me again and disappears, and I must start searching again. He does this again and again, until I hold on to him firmly and ascend, leaning on my beloved.
> *Homilies on Song of Songs* 1.7

This personal experience and utter devotion to "my Christ," as he calls him, lies at the basis of every word Origen wrote. He was the first great Christian mystic, and his account of the mystical progression toward union with God is arguably the most influential part of his whole system. It would form the basis for the work of Gregory of Nyssa and Pseudo-Dionysius, and through them most of the medieval and early modern mystics.

Influence

The jailers who tortured Origen in the imperial dungeons did him more harm than they ever realized. By keeping him alive and denying him the martyr's death that would have ensured he was honored as a saint by later generations, they allowed those later generations to tarnish the name of the church's greatest teacher. Yet despite his unorthodoxy in many areas and the destruction of his works, the teaching of Origen has continued to exercise enormous influence down to the modern day.

The thought of the Cappadocian fathers and of Augustine would have been impossible without Origen's trailblazing combination of Christian faith and Platonic philosophy. Even where they disagreed vehemently with Origen, they were still following his lead. The spiritual teaching of Pseudo-Dionysius and Boethius in the Dark Ages continued the same tradition. Even as the medieval Scholastics argued over whether Origen's soul could have been saved, they still believed in the abstract God he had introduced to Christianity; and in the monasteries the mystics were

THE CONVERSION OF CONSTANTINE

Few realized it at the time, but A.D. 312 was one of the most momentous dates in history.

Emperor Constantine was marching to battle against Maxentius, his bitter rival for the imperial throne. Suddenly, we are told, he and his troops were dazzled by a shining cross in the sky. A voice from heaven boomed, "By this sign you will conquer." Constantine duly won a spectacular victory at the Battle of the Milvian Bridge, and, attributing it to the power of the cross, surrendered to the Lord. The Roman emperor had become a Christian.

Constantine was one of the most remarkable and powerful figures ever to rule Rome. The collapse of the empire, apparently inevitable in the 3rd century, had been staved off by the reforms and firm rule of his predecessor Diocletian, and Constantine continued in his footsteps. He built spectacular monuments in Rome, including the great Arch of Constantine, which still stands. His victory over the Eastern emperor, Licinius, in 324 made him the sole master of the empire. He quickly consolidated his power by founding a new city in the East, which came to be named after himself: Constantinople.

still allegorizing the Bible and following the threefold path of enlightenment he had pioneered.

Today few could accept Origen's allegorical treatment of Scripture, his fantastic account of a primordial fall and successive universes, or his careful analysis of the bodies of the angels. But his belief in a world designed by a caring God to bring willful creatures back to him is still enormously powerful. His ultimate optimism, that all creatures would be saved and that God would never abandon anything he had created, continues to inspire. And his spiritual writings remain among the most powerful ever committed to paper. Wherever Christians try to work out the meaning of their faith with intellectual, spiritual and scientific integrity, the influence of Origen may still be detected.

Arianism

In A.D. 323 a synod met in Egypt to condemn the doctrines of Arius, a presbyter in the church at Alexandria. The bishops who took part could have had little ink-

The city was to be the new Rome, the new capital of the mighty empire. By the end of the century it had eclipsed old Rome and rivaled Alexandria as the greatest city in the East, even the world.

Almost overnight Christianity had been transformed from an illegal religion to the faith of the emperor himself—not merely tolerated but actually promoted.

It was to prove a mixed blessing. Christians no longer had to fear execution, but they did have to come to terms with the fact that the emperor, the sole ruler of Rome and Constantinople, now considered himself to have jurisdiction over the church as well. In the last years of his life, Constantine began to stamp his powerful personality on the Arian controversy, which was beginning to engulf the church. His dominance set a worrying precedent that would be extended by later 4th-century emperors and eventually develop into the Byzantine institution of "Caesaropapism," the total union of church and state with a single, all-powerful monarch ruling both.

ling of the cataclysm they were unleashing on the church.

Arius had denied that the Son, the second Person of the Trinity, was fully divine. He was the greatest of God's creatures, a mighty archangel, but not God. This was no innovation. We saw that Justin Martyr left the matter vague; and where Tertullian and Origen took the route of affirming the Son's divinity, Arius took the equally open one of denying it.

A remarkably charismatic man, Arius wrote popular songs about his beliefs; people actually went around Alexandria singing about how the Son was inferior to the Father. Refusing to submit to those who condemned him, he toured the Roman empire, drumming up support. Another, much larger council met at Nicaea in A.D. 325 to condemn him.

The matter seemed closed. But many people sympathized with Arius's views. And some of them persuaded the emperor that peace might best be restored by reversing the decisions of Nicaea. In A.D. 336 Constantine duly ordered the church to receive Arius back into the fold. This was foiled only by the timely and rather gruesome death of Arius, who suffered a horrific hemorrhage in a public toilet at Constantinople and, as his opponent Athanasius put it, burst asunder like Judas.

The church split between Arians and those who upheld the faith of Nicaea. Constantine's death in A.D. 337 only worsened matters, as his successors, first Constans and then Constantius, were full-blown Arians (as well as having unoriginal names). Council after council was called to settle the escalating civil war, and anathemas were hurled back and forth like missiles. It was said that the imperial postal service actually suffered as the roads were clogged with bishops dashing

THE FIRST COUNCIL OF NICAEA

It was one of the most important meetings ever held. Over three hundred bishops, in the presence of the emperor himself, solemnly laid down the definitive statement of the Christian faith. It would become the primary standard of Christian orthodoxy for the rest of time.

Arius had been causing a problem for some years. Although condemned by a council at Alexandria in 320, he had continued to travel around the empire raising support for his theological cause. Emperor Constantine, newly converted to Christianity and desperate to secure peace and unity within the empire, decided to settle the matter once and for all. He called all bishops throughout the empire to a great council.

The council met in 325 at the town of Nicaea, in modern-day Turkey, chosen for its easy accessibility. Tradition records that 318 bishops were present, but there may have been even more. Most were Greek.

The bickering had already begun when Constantine himself entered, dressed in gold from head to foot, adorned with flashing gems of every kind. Taking his seat on a magnificent golden throne, the emperor declared the Ecumenical Council in session.

The council quickly condemned Arius and his heresy and put together a statement of faith that everybody could sign. The statement became known as the Symbol of Nicaea, and it would become the basis of Christian orthodoxy for all time. It read:

> *We believe in God the Father almighty,*
> *maker of all things, visible and invisible.*
> *And in one Lord Jesus Christ,*

from one council to another. And now that the empire was Christian, the emperors felt that they had authority over the church. At a synod in Milan in A.D. 355, the meeting degenerated into a brawl as the bishops, unable to agree, knocked the pen out of each other's hands. When Emperor Constantius burst in with a sword to force them to reach the decision he required, some of them protested: "This is against the rule of faith!" "I am the rule of faith!" roared the emperor, before forcing all present to sign the disputed documents.

Bishops who dared defy Constantius were exiled and replaced with Arians. New

the only-begotten of the Father,
God from God, light from light, true God from true God,
begotten not made,
of the same substance as the Father,
through whom all things were made, in heaven and earth;
who for us humans and our salvation came down, took flesh, and
  was made human,
suffered and rose again on the third day,
ascended into heaven,
and will come to judge the living and the dead.
And in the Holy Spirit.

All but two bishops agreed to sign this. These two were exiled and the writings of Arius symbolically thrown onto the fire. The voice of the Ecumenical Church had spoken.

As it happened, the Arian controversy raged for another fifty years, during which time the Symbol of Nicaea was just one of many conflicting "definite answers" to the problem. Constantine himself would come to order the reinstatement of Arius, and successive emperors would openly overrule Nicaea and support the Arians. But eventually, at the Council of Constantinople in 381, the Symbol of Nicaea would be restated as the official creed of the church. Every council that came after, however great, would claim only to be explaining the Symbol of Nicaea, not adding to it. Today a version of the Symbol is still recited in churches across the world as the definitive statement of the Christian faith.

Arian theologians arose with powerful arguments for their position. As Athanasius, their most vehement critic, put it, "The world awoke and discovered itself Arian."

To Christians ever since, the Arian conflict of the 4th century was possibly the biggest theological crisis of the church's history. Only the Reformation, over 1,000 years later, saw so much new theologizing being done with such urgency. Yet the scale of the dispute, its political ramifications and its overwhelming importance to those who lived through it meant that the conflict had positive effects. A new trinitarianism was forged by the opponents of Arianism, based on the doctrine of Nicaea. Creative theologians like Hilary of Poitiers, Athanasius and the Cappadocians were forced to find new ways to express their faith.

The struggle ended only in A.D. 379, when Theodosius became emperor and for the first time made Christianity the official religion of the empire, something that Constantine had never actually done. A staunch Nicaean, he swept aside the Arian orthodoxy his predecessors had tried to establish and called the Council of Constantinople, which became known as the Second Ecumenical Council after Nicaea. The Nicaean faith, and with it the doctrine of the Trinity, were permanently safeguarded.

Athanasius

Athanasius stands out as the preeminent defender of the Trinity in the Arian conflict. An extraordinarily forceful personality and bold theologian, he never lived to see his ideas ratified as Christian orthodoxy.

Life

Born in about A.D. 295, Athanasius quickly rose through the ranks of the Alexandrian church. Becoming personal assistant to the bishop, Alexander, he was present at the epochal Council of Nicaea in 325. When Alexander died in 328, Athanasius succeeded him as bishop of Alexandria. There must have been times in the years that followed when he wished that he had not.

He inherited a whole host of problems. A schismatic sect known as the Melitians existed in Alexandria, and they bitterly opposed Athanasius. They brought a variety of complaints against him, in the light of which he was summoned to the imperial court in A.D. 330 to explain himself to Constantine. His defense must have been satisfactory, since the matter was dropped, but in 334 a council was called in Caesarea to investigate charges of misconduct against Athanasius. He was accused of a strange variety of crimes, ranging from imposing illegal taxes to murder and witchcraft. The charges were dropped when the man Athanasius was supposed to have killed was found alive and well, which must have given his prosecutors a bit of a legal headache. All the same, a subsequent council at Tyre in 335 found him guilty of misconduct and removed him from his see, despite his personal popularity among the people of Alexandria.

Athanasius took advantage of the death of Constantine in A.D. 337 to return home. But his opponents protested, and in 339 he was forced to flee to Rome, where Bishop Julius supported him and pronounced him the rightful bishop of Alexandria. There he remained until 346, when his replacement in Alexandria died. Making his peace with the new emperor, Constantius, Athanasius returned home once more. The whole city celebrated the return of their beloved bishop, and there was something of a religious revival.

But the church was now in the grip of the Arian crisis. Constantius was a staunch Arian; and Athanasius, who was becoming known as a leading proponent of the rival Nicene faith, could no longer count on his protection. In A.D. 356 a new military commander named Syrianus was posted to Alexandria. Athanasius's pleas that he was the rightful bishop fell on deaf ears. On the night of February 8, as Athanasius presided over a packed church, Syrianus and his troops entered the building to arrest him. Undeterred, the bishop remained seated on his throne and announced the psalm. But as the soldiers advanced up the aisles the congregation panicked. In the resulting chaos, Athanasius's friends bundled him out of the church.

He spent the next six years in hiding. On the run from the guards, he moved from house to house in the city, spending most of his time in the isolated cells of loyal monks in the desert. Here he continued to administer his see via intermediaries and letters, despite the fact that he had officially been replaced by an Arian called George of Cappadocia. However, contrary to later legends, it is unlikely that he fled to Spain and worked as a cook!

Help came from an unlikely quarter. In A.D. 361 Constantius died and was succeeded by Julian "the Apostate," a pagan who hated the newfangled Christian religion. In order to cause the church as much confusion as possible, the new emperor ordered all bishops exiled by his predecessor to return home. Athanasius accordingly reappeared in public in 362. His people showed their appreciation by tying the unhappy George to a camel and burning them both to death—which sounds like an especially undignified way to die.

This time Athanasius remained in Alexandria until his death in A.D. 373. He had been bishop for 46 years but had spent only 29 of them in the city. He had maintained his position through extraordinary charisma, total dedication and an enormously ruthless strength of character.

Thought

Athanasius had little leisure for advanced theological reflection. But somehow, while dodging the guards in the monasteries of the Egyptian desert, he found the time to compose the forceful demolition of Arianism that would pave the way for the establishment of the faith of Nicaea as official orthodoxy.

The Arians argued that God is by nature essentially uncreated and owes his existence to nothing else. That being so, the Son cannot be God, because he owes his existence to something else—the Father. And if the Son was begotten by the Father, then there was a time when he did not exist, which is hardly compatible with being God. Moreover, how can there be two Gods?

The Arians had a powerful case, and the fact that Athanasius spent so much energy rebutting it shows that he recognized its strength. His position, however, was quite simple.

Athanasius answered the Arians' taunts of polytheism the same way Justin had

CONSTANTINOPLE

With the conversion of Emperor Constantine to Christianity and his subsequent securing of power over the whole empire, a new age seemed to be dawning. The most spectacular symbol of this new age was the founding of a new imperial capital: the city of Constantinople.

The emperor founded his new city in 330 on the site of an ancient town called Byzantium, located on the west coast of the Bosporus, the channel linking the Black Sea to the Mediterranean. It was to be the administrative and military capital of the East just as Rome was of the West, and it was to be known as the Second Rome. Like Old Rome, it was built on seven hills, and with its mighty walls and splendid palaces it would be a beacon of civilization.

But where Old Rome was a pagan city, full of temples to the traditional deities, New Rome was to be a Christian capital. In addition to a senate house, baths and all the other amenities of civilization, Constantine provided the city with an array of splendid churches. He decreed that no pagan rites would ever be performed in the new capital. Nothing could have symbolized better the new foundations of the Roman empire.

The city was an enormous success, acquiring a substantial population and vigorous culture in a matter of a few years. It was quickly established as a center of theological thought, becoming associated in particular with the traditions that had arisen in the nearby older city of Antioch. These repre-

replied to his pagan opponents. The Son is not an independent God, any more than a ray of light is independent of the sun. In fact the Son's divinity and all that he is derive from the Father. Even though there are two of them, there is only one power in heaven.

The argument is clearly based on old-fashioned Logos theology. But Athanasius supports it with more subtle points. He developed an idea suggested by Origen, of the Son as the image of the Father. Origen took the term from Colossians 1:15 but interpreted it as stressing the similarity between Father and Son, not their difference. Origen suggests that the Son is the Father's image in the same way that a human son is the image of his father. In other words, they appear similar because they *are* similar: they have the same nature. Athanasius says the same thing: if Christ is the image of the Father, then he has the same nature as the Father. And further-

---

sented something of a rival Christian tradition to that of Alexandria, and it was not long before the two great centers of Eastern Christianity came to clash: first in the rivalry between Theophilus of Alexandria and John Chrysostom of Constantinople, and later in that between Cyril of Alexandria and Nestorius of Constantinople. Both of these bishops of Constantinople originally came from Antioch, and the tremendous prestige they enjoyed as bishop of the imperial city was enormously resented by their Alexandrian counterparts. The proud Alexandrians regarded the new city as an arrogant upstart, especially when Alexandria had to start sending grain supplies to keep New Rome fed.

Theological discussion in Constantinople was not confined to the churches. In fact, even professional theologians could get tired of the endless interest that the city's inhabitants had in such matters. Shortly before the Council of Constantinople in 381, Gregory of Nyssa described the mood of the city to a friend:

> Garment sellers, money changers, food vendors—they are all at it. If you ask for change, they philosophize about the Begotten and the Unbegotten. If you inquire about the price of bread, the answer is that the Father is greater and the Son inferior. If you say to the attendant, "Is my bath ready?" he tells you that the Son was made out of nothing.

more, he is not just the same *sort* of thing as the Father—as Son he is distinct from the Father, but as God they are identical.

The central point of Athanasius's theology is thus twofold: first, the Father and the Son are essentially the same, and second, this similarity is intrinsic to the nature of God. This is not quite as confusing as it may sound. The Arians argued that the Son could not be God because his existence depended on the primordial decision of the Father to beget him, and nothing divine could depend for its existence on a decision of the will. Athanasius replies that the divine will has nothing to do with it. It is in the nature of the Father to beget the Son, just as it is in the nature of the Son to be begotten. And that means it is essential to the divine nature itself that it exists in this way—on the one hand begetting, and on the other begotten. Imagine a plate: a plate can be fashioned from clay or molded from plastic or carved from wood or stone. There are many different ways a plate can come into being, but they are all equally plates. But God is different: we could not imagine a God who did not exist as begetting and begotten. It is part of being God to exist in this way, in a way that it is not part of being a plate to exist in one way rather than another.

We should therefore not think of one God choosing to beget another. Rather, there is one God who exists as Father and Son, the one eternally begetting, the other eternally begotten. Athanasius therefore upholds Origen's doctrine of the eternal generation of the Son, and it is indeed central to his doctrine. Contrary to Origen, of course, he does not think that the world is eternally created. This is because "begetting" and "creating" are totally different, something the Arians failed to realize. In Athanasius's book, the Arians are right to say that God cannot be created, but they are wrong to think that he cannot be *begotten.* The Son is not created, he is begotten—and that is quite compatible with being divine.

In any case, the Son *must* be God. If he were not, he could not save us. Athanasius, like Irenaeus before him, believes that we are saved by the union of divine and human in Christ, which raises all of humanity up to the level of divinity. In his eyes, to deny Christ's divinity is to deny the whole basis of salvation.

Athanasius's theology represents a halfway house between the old and the new. Like Justin and his followers, he thinks of the Son as mediating in some way between the ineffable Father and the world. Moreover, he describes the Son as divine only inasmuch as he comes from the Father. These ideas are, in general intent, essentially subordinationist. Yet at the same time, Athanasius stresses above all else the doctrine of Nicaea that the Son is wholly divine, totally different from creation and essentially the same as the Father. He vigorously defends Origen's doctrine of the Son's eternal generation while rejecting his outspoken subordinationism. These ideas look forward to the even subtler doctrines of the Cappadocian fathers and

Augustine. For them, as for succeeding generations, Athanasius was a theological hero, a bold defender of orthodoxy in the face of the Arian menace.

The Cappadocian Fathers

Cappadocia is an extraordinary region in central Turkey: a land of striking mountains, almost like an alien planet, where people still live in well-appointed caves carved from rock. In the 4th century this beautiful landscape was home to three equally striking theologians. Together, Basil of Caesarea, his friend Gregory of Nazianzus and his brother Gregory of Nyssa transformed Christian thinking on God. They occupy a place in the evolution of Eastern theology much like that of Augustine in the West, a man who took many of his best ideas from them.

Lives

The natural leader of the three Cappadocians was Basil the Great, who was one of the most forceful personalities of the 4th century. He was born in A.D. 330 to an aristocratic family, who ensured that he had an excellent education, first under the famous secular teacher Libanius of Antioch and then at Athens. He spent five years there, together with his closest friend, Gregory, who came from Nazianzus, also in Cappadocia.

Gregory had just undergone a terrifying experience: on the way to Athens, his ship had been caught in a violent storm, and Gregory, believing that all was lost, had promised God that if he was spared he would be baptized as soon as they reached land. At this time it was usual to delay baptism until late in life or even until the point of death, but Gregory was as good as his word.

The two Cappadocians were both very devout. Gregory would later recall that they had only known two roads from the lodgings they shared—one to the church and the other to the library. Perhaps all the parties happened at their house. But it was here that they hit upon the plan of forming a tiny community in some beautiful location, a pastoral retreat where they could follow the example of famous hermits and escape the world.

After completing their studies, Basil and Gregory collaborated on a compilation of the writings of Origen, known as the *Philokalia (The Love of Beauty)*—one of the most important sources for the original Greek of many of Origen's writings. Like Origen, they both felt that Christianity could profitably be combined with the best of classical culture. And Basil set up the retreat they had planned at a place called Pontus, a beautiful spot by a river, surrounded on all sides by thickly forested mountains.

Gregory, however, was unable to join him there for very long. His aging father, who was confusingly also called Gregory, was bishop of Nazianzus, and the younger Gregory felt honor-bound to stay there and help him in his duties. He would speak to Basil about how much he longed to come to Pontus; and when his father had him ordained as a priest he even ran away to the retreat rather than take on the responsibility. But somehow he always found an excuse not to leave his duties. It was as if, despite his protests, he rather liked a public role in the church and could not decide between that and the life of private seclusion he had planned with Basil.

Basil, meanwhile, was rapidly making a name for himself. In A.D. 360 he appeared at a council that condemned the Arian theologian Eunomius, and shortly afterward he published a work against him that marked a major advance in Nicene anti-Arian thinking. In 370 he was consecrated as bishop of Caesarea, the most important city in Cappadocia, and was soon known as one of the most prominent

THE FIRST COUNCIL
OF CONSTANTINOPLE

It must have seemed as if the glory days of the empire had returned. Theodosius the Great, a powerful general, had been made emperor of the East and had successfully beaten back the barbarians who were threatening the empire. He was also taking a firm role in the West, and indeed in a few years' time he would invade and conquer the West, ending the squabbles between various claimants to both halves of the empire and reuniting it. In fact, Theodosius would rule an undivided empire for less than a year, and he would be the last man to do so. But he had ended the theological civil war that had been raging for half a century. Not only did Theodosius finally make Christianity the official religion of the empire, but he was an avowed supporter of the Nicene party.

The Council of Constantinople was convened in 381 to put an end to Arianism once and for all. One hundred fifty bishops from the East gathered at the imperial city under the leadership of Meletius of Antioch. Meletius died during the proceedings and was replaced by Gregory of Nazianzus, the most prominent theologian in the East and a leading defender of Nicaea. His friend Gregory of Nyssa also played a pivotal role in the proceedings.

The council upheld the teaching of the Council of Nicaea over fifty years earlier and overruled all the councils that had taken place in the meantime,

supporters of the Nicene doctrine, a successor to Athanasius. But as we shall see, his theology had moved beyond that of the great bishop of Alexandria and was not only more sophisticated but designed to be more easily accepted by a broader range of parties within the church.

As bishop of Caesarea, Basil introduced major reforms: in particular, he established large hospitals for the poor and wrote an enormously influential set of monastic rules. At the same time he was a major player in ecclesiastical politics. Emperor Valens, who was an Arian, sought to limit his power by dividing up Cappadocia and putting some of its bishops under a different authority. Basil responded by creating a large number of new dioceses within his own part of Cappadocia and appointing his friends to them. In 372 he made his old university friend Gregory bishop of Sasima, something Gregory found very hard to forgive.

which had been Arian to varying degrees. The council was therefore essentially a confirmation of Nicaea rather than a supplement to it, and it seems that no new creed was introduced. One important new point, however, was the divinity of the Holy Spirit, something that Nicaea had skimmed over quickly. The council was quite clear that the Spirit, as well as the Son, is fully divine.

One other major innovation was made: the council decreed that henceforth the bishop of Constantinople would be superior to all other bishops in the East and second only to the bishop of Rome. There was some understandable annoyance at this, particularly in Alexandria, and also in the West, which had no representatives at the council.

In fact, the lack of Western representation, among other factors, meant that the Second Ecumenical Council was not quite the epochal, universally binding event it was meant to be. Many people did not accept it, and even Gregory of Nazianzus, who had been booted out before the end, criticized its decisions. But just like Nicaea before it, the council would come to be taken as a definitive expression of the faith of the church when it was ratified seventy years later at the great Council of Chalcedon.

He thought he had already made it quite clear that he did not want the responsibility of leadership, and he hated the tiny village of Sasima. In fact he never lived there but remained at Nazianzus. Gregory's rather otherworldly character made him a hopeless administrator, at least in Basil's eyes; and he often had to be bailed out by his famous friend.

At the same time, as part of his plan to bolster his own power in the church, Basil made some of his own brothers bishops. The most significant of these was yet another Gregory, who was assigned the new see of Nyssa, which, like Sasima, was the absolute back of beyond. Unlike Gregory of Nazianzus, Gregory of Nyssa made little protest at this unexpected change in his fortunes. A year or two younger than Basil, he had not studied at Antioch or Athens and had not gone into the church, he had instead become a secular teacher of rhetoric and (very probably) married. He was enormously in awe of his brother, whom he always called "the Master," and he claimed that Basil had taught him everything he knew. Basil, for his part, seems to have had a relatively low opinion of his brother, who was a rather innocent character. On one occasion Basil had fallen out with his uncle, and Gregory, eager for peace, forged a letter from the uncle patching things up with Basil. Basil soon realized it was a forgery, so Gregory did exactly the same thing again—to Basil's enormous exasperation.

Mention must also be made of another of Basil's siblings, Macrina. Gregory of Nyssa was greatly in awe of her as well and referred to her as "the Teacher," claiming she had filled the few gaps in his knowledge that Basil had overlooked. She was certainly a striking and forceful woman, and an extremely devout one; she lived in a retreat next door to Basil's at Pontus. But Gregory is the only person to mention her; judging by Basil's writings alone, we would never know that he had a sister. This probably tells us a lot more about Basil than it does about Macrina.

In A.D. 379 Basil died, exhausted by church politics and an ascetic lifestyle. Now, freed of his rather overbearing personality, his friend and brother stepped into the limelight. In the year of Basil's death, Gregory of Nazianzus preached five "theological orations" at Constantinople in which he defended the Nicene doctrine of the Trinity with unprecedented skill. It is in honor of these orations that Gregory is remembered by the Orthodox Church as "Gregory the Theologian." In 380, in recognition of his standing as a major theologian, he was made bishop of Constantinople, the most important ecclesiastical post in the Eastern empire. Needless to say, he protested against such a responsibility, but he still took it on. He played a leading role in the great Council of Constantinople that took place the following year, and he even chaired it for a while—until his opponents pointed out that it was contrary to church law for a bishop to move from one diocese to another. Gregory, of course, was still supposedly bishop of Sasima. So he was deposed, and he retreated to Nazianzus, where he spent the remaining years of his life writing extremely melancholy poetry about what a rotten life he had led.

Gregory of Nyssa was also extremely prominent at the council, having written a massive refutation of the Arian Eunomius which continued the argument where Basil had left off. He was a favorite with Emperor Theodosius and preached at the funerals of both his wife and his daughter. He was also becoming known as a major spiritual master and wrote extensively on mysticism as well as dogmatic theology. Gregory of Nyssa probably died sometime toward the end of the 390s.

Thought

The theologies of Basil of Caesarea, Gregory of Nazianzus and Gregory of Nyssa are extremely closely linked. The three of them were in constant communication, and all contributed ideas to each other. But they were still quite distinct. Basil was essentially an administrator and a theological pioneer. Gregory of Nazianzus was really a poet and rhetorician, capable of stating complex ideas in a clear and beautiful way.

They were both overshadowed by Gregory of Nyssa. Despite Basil's low view of his brother's abilities—a view endorsed by Gregory himself—he was a far greater theologian and more profound mystic than Basil ever was. In fact, the works of Gregory of Nyssa form what is arguably the most complete system of genuine Christian philosophy to appear before Aquinas. Even more than Origen, Gregory of Nyssa remains something of a well-kept secret among academics and Orthodox priests; his popular profile is nowhere near as high as it deserves to be. Gregory was perhaps less original and wide-ranging than Origen, who was a huge influence on him, or Augustine, who was hugely influenced *by* him; but he achieved a much greater synthesis of Christianity and classical culture than they ever did. He was a true Christian philosopher, with equal emphasis on both words; for Gregory, there could never be any conflict between them.

The Cappadocians were wide-ranging theologians, but they made two supremely important contributions to Christian thought. In both of these, especially the second, Gregory of Nyssa dominates.

The Trinity. Funnily enough, given that the Cappadocians emerged as the greatest defenders of Nicaea after Athanasius, their thoughts on the Trinity developed from a doctrine known as Semi-Arianism, a movement Basil was associated with in his youth. The Semi-Arian theologians sought to steer a moderate path between the true Arians, who argued that the Son is inferior to the Father, and the Nicenes, who identified the two Persons, at least at some level. The Semi-Arians suggested that the Father and Son are similar but not identical.

This forms the basis for Basil's distinction between the general and the particular, which in turn is at the heart of the Cappadocian doctrine of the Trinity. Basil invites us to consider the difference between, on the one hand, the word *human* and, on the other, the names Peter, Paul and Timothy. *Human* is a general term; it refers to a class of beings; the names pick out particular members of that class. In the same way, when we talk about "God," or the divine substance, we are using a general term. The three Persons are three separate manifestations of that substance, just as Peter, Paul and Timothy are three separate manifestations of human nature.

This seems pretty strange. If the three Persons of the Trinity are three in the same way that three people are three, then there are three Gods! It looks as if we have drifted away from monotheism altogether. But the situation is more complex than this. Gregory of Nyssa helps to explain it. He points out that when we have several different members of one class, there are usually certain ways to tell them apart: they may be different sizes, shapes or colors; and most fundamentally they must all be in different locations in space. But none of these things apply to the divine nature. God is incorporeal, a fact that Gregory, like Origen, is quite insistent on. So although the three Persons are different members of the one class, they cannot be distinguished from each other in the normal way.

In fact, there is only one difference between them: their mutual relations. This central idea was first articulated by Gregory of Nazianzus, in his famous *Theological Orations*. The Father has no characteristic that the Son lacks, and vice versa—because otherwise they would not be equally God. The only thing that is true of the Father but not the Son is that he *is the Father of* the Son; and similarly the Son *is the Son of* the Father. And the Spirit is the only one that *proceeds from* the Father. In every other respect except their mutual relations, the three are identical.

Gregory of Nyssa repeats the same idea and also points out that it is impossible to think of any one Person without also thinking of the others. To talk of the Spirit is to think of the Son who sends him, and to talk of the Son is to think of the Father who begets him. Gregory likens the process to a chain: pull one end and the rest follows.

This notion that the three Persons of the Trinity are differentiated only by their mutual relations represented a major advance on earlier trinitarianism, such as that of Origen or Athanasius, and it has proved the most durable of the Cappadocians' achievements. It was to be central to Augustine's doctrine of the Trinity and to that of Aquinas after him. In the 20th century the idea was rehabilitated in the form of "social trinitarianism." If the divine Persons are known through their relationships, then perhaps the same is true of human persons too. We should think of people not as autonomous individuals but as inextricably bound up in a social web of relationships with others.

The unknown God. This highly sophisticated doctrine of the Trinity was not the Cappadocians' only weapon against the Arians. Eunomius, the foremost Arian theologian of the time, argued that the divine nature is intrinsically unbegotten. If the Son is begotten, he cannot be God. We have seen that the Cappadocians' answer to this is that "begottenness" and "unbegottenness" are not characteristics as such at all: they express the *relation* between the Persons. But they also deplore Eunomius's rationalism. Basil argues that we just cannot make such bold sweeping statements about the nature of divinity. In fact, God is essentially unknowable. The logic-chopping of Eunomius has no place in this field.

Basil was accused of agnosticism on this account, and it was left to Gregory of Nyssa to explain that there is a difference between God's essence and his activity. The essence, or true being, of God is unknown and unknowable. All that we can know is God's activity, his actions among us, which includes those times that he seems to appear to people like Moses. In fact the name God, and all other descriptions of God, actually apply to these activities, not to God himself.

Gregory of Nyssa develops this anti-Arian argument into a profound mystical theology. We have seen how Origen described the mystical life as one of increasing illumination, as the mystic's mind becomes attuned to the mind of God and gradually learns more about him. Gregory keeps the idea of a progression in stages, but for him it is a progressive *darkening.*

How can this be? The point is that God is not simply unknown as a matter of fact: he is *unknowable.* And this is because he is unlimited. We saw that for Origen, as for most Greeks, God is limited, because only limited things can be known; to be unlimited is to be imperfectly formed. But Gregory introduces the notion of God's infinity, a notion so commonplace today that it is hard for us to imagine that someone was once the first to defend it. Gregory argues at length that if God were limited then he would be inferior to whatever limits him—so if God is perfect then he must be infinite. And this means that he is intrinsically unknowable.

The mystic's journey is therefore a gradual realization of this fact. Gregory uses the life of Moses as an image of the mystical path—like Origen, he always interprets Scripture in a highly allegorical fashion. Moses' journey begins with a moment of illumination, as he meets God in the burning bush and turns from the path of darkness to light. But he soon realizes that although he has left forever the darkness of God's absence, he is plunging toward a deeper darkness still—the darkness of God's presence. On the holy mountain, as Moses climbs to receive the law, he passes into the cloud, which signifies that God cannot be perceived with the physical senses. But moving still higher, he plunges into the darkness where God is, and finds that God cannot be perceived with the mind either. Gregory comments:

> Leaving behind everything that can be perceived—not just what the senses see but also what intelligence thinks it sees—the mind keeps on penetrating deeper, until by the intelligence's yearning for understanding it reaches what is invisible and incomprehensible, and there it sees God. This is the true knowledge of what is looked for. This is the seeing that consists of *not* seeing. The thing that is looked for transcends all knowledge, and is surrounded by incomprehensibility like a kind of darkness. This is why John the sublime, who penetrated into the luminous darkness, says, "No one has ever seen God"—meaning that knowledge of the divine essence is unattainable by human beings, and by all rational creatures.
> *The Life of Moses* 2.163

And there is more. We saw how Origen's understanding of history, although based on the idea of immense cosmic cycles, was ultimately static: the end of the whole process is the same as the beginning, with all intelligent beings reunited to God, knowing him perfectly. But in Gregory's system, the infinity of God means that we never reach this end—the more we journey into him, the more we see that there is still to go. The mystical journey is therefore a never-ending one. If this sounds like eternal unfulfillment, Gregory thinks quite the opposite: it is eternal fulfillment, forever moving from horizon to horizon. We do not progress *toward* perfection; progress is itself perfection, at least for limited creatures like us:

> This is truly the vision of God: never to be satisfied in our desire to see him. But by looking at what we do see, we must always rekindle our desire to see more. So there can be no limit interrupting our growth in ascending to God, because there is no limit to the Good, and our desire for the Good is not ended by being satisfied.
> *The Life of Moses* 2.239

Gregory of Nyssa is the first great Christian representative of "apophatic" mysticism, also known as *via negativa* (the negative way), a spirituality that stresses the unknowability of God and the breaking down of intelligence in the face of the divine. It had already been pioneered by some pagan Middle Platonists and above all by Plotinus, who was a major influence on Gregory. But Gregory was the first to incorporate it into a Christian philosophy, and it would prove enormously influential. The most famous exponent of this kind of spirituality would be Pseudo-

Dionysius the Areopagite, and he would base his thought very closely on that of Gregory of Nyssa. Through him it would become central to both Eastern and Western thinking on God and would be enshrined in the theologies of Thomas Aquinas and Gregory Palamas alike.

The Desert Fathers

Sometime in the A.D. 280s, an extraordinary figure appeared in the trackless wastes of the Egyptian deserts. His name was Antony, and he was pioneering a new way of life.

Antony was a solitary ascetic, one of a number of holy men who lived on the outskirts of towns and villages, trying to dedicate their lives to God. But Antony felt that even such a life was too close to the world. By going to the desert he hoped to escape the world and its entire works and be close to God alone. The desert was beyond the boundaries of the inhabited world. Going there was like leaving the planet altogether.

His solitude did not last. By the time Antony died in A.D. 356—at the age, supposedly, of 105—his reputation had attracted a huge number of disciples, all living in huts and cells in the desert. Communities sprang up throughout the wilderness. Some monks lived by themselves, as Antony had, and met only occasionally. Others shared their meal and worship times, living in loose-knit communities. Still others lived together, developing rules to govern their way of life.

The movement spread. In an age of political and social uncertainty, when it seemed to many that the end of the world must be coming, huge numbers of people from all walks of life abandoned the world for the security of a lonely cell and a closer walk with God. Some monks became celebrities for their holy way of living and were forced to spend most of their time trying to avoid visitors.

Farther east, in Syria, people believed that the power of God could be directly witnessed in the lives of these men. This could sometimes be quite spectacular. Symeon Stylites spent decades perched on top of a pillar, arms outstretched, ignoring the crowds that jostled for a better view 60 feet below. Imitators appeared, and in some places there were veritable forests of pillars, each topped by an ascetic trying to outdo his rivals in holy self-denial. It is said that when Symeon died, no one realized for several days—they just thought he was adopting a particularly holy position.

These practices may seem ridiculous to us, but they testify to the awesome sense of the presence of God that these people had. To a man like Antony, God was more real than the shimmering desert around him. The hermits in the wilderness, together with the spiritual theology being developed by Origen, Augustine and others, were part of a great mystical movement that would later blossom in the medieval monasteries to produce some of the most profound writing of all time.

Pelagianism

At the end of the 4th century A.D., a remarkable character called Pelagius arrived in Rome. He was a huge man, broad and powerful, but slow moving and gentle. Pelagius looked like a wrestler but rapidly gained a reputation as a very holy man. Although not technically a monk, he worked as a spiritual adviser to a wide cross-section of Roman society.

Now that Christianity was the official state religion and rather fashionable, standards of behavior had fallen in the church. When Pelagius arrived in Rome from his native Britain, he was shocked at what he saw. He was even more shocked when he found that some people justified their sinful life theologically. They told him that they had no power to overcome original sin. It was impossible to do anything good unless God directly brought it about by an act of grace. So if we are predestined to sin or grace, why make any effort?

Matters came to a head one day when Pelagius was attending a reading of Augustine's *Confessions.* The reader came to the line where Augustine implores God: "Command what you will, and give what you command." Pelagius was outraged at the implication that God should control his creatures like puppets, and he angrily shouted down the hapless reader.

Pelagius felt that Christians should, above all, try to live right. So he stressed the fact that human beings have free will and it is up to them to use it properly. He rejected the notion, which was being developed by Ambrose, Augustine and others, of original sin as a kind of implacable force that makes people sin even after they have been baptized. He also rejected the idea that anyone other than Adam is guilty for Adam's sin. Adam's sin was a disaster because it set a precedent and showed later generations how to disobey God. It wasn't passed on to them like a genetic defect.

In fact, Pelagius argued that it is possible to live without sin if you really put your mind to it. He pointed out that it would be unjust if God were to command us to do what is beyond us and then punish us when we fail. But the Bible tells us to live perfectly, so it must be possible to do that.

So Christianity is about leading a perfect life. When we are baptized as Christians, the guilt of our past life is washed away through the cross of Christ. After that it is up to us to keep from sinning. We must look to Christ's death as an example of perfect obedience, but it is up to us to follow it.

Pelagius quickly got into serious trouble. Jerome, the famous author of the Vulgate translation of the Bible and a fanatical anti-Origenist, saw the influence of Origen in Pelagius's doctrine of free will and possible perfection. More seriously, Augustine felt that Pelagius's emphasis on free will and human merit denied divine grace and the power of the cross of Christ. In fact Pelagius did believe in grace, but he thought that it consisted of the gift of human reason and the provision of the law. He did not accept that God's grace can work directly within the human heart, turning it toward what is right. That would be a denial of the human power to choose right or wrong freely.

Pelagius and his followers were condemned in 415, and Pelagius was soon sent into exile, a fate he meekly accepted. The movement, however, continued under the leadership of his friends and followers. It proved particularly persistent in Gaul and Britain, and a number of talented theologians arose to defend versions of it—some less extreme than Pelagius himself, some more so.

The term *Pelagianism* actually represents a caricature of the views of Pelagius: the heretical notion that human beings can save themselves without needing God's grace. In medieval times, Peter Abelard was accused of it; in the Reformation, the Reformers accused the Catholics of it.

Today Pelagius is often regarded as a sympathetic figure—especially by British theologians, who obviously want to defend their earliest-known colleague. He is sometimes thought of as a sort of early liberal whose optimistic belief in humanity led him to oppose Augustine's depressing notion of original sin. In fact, Pelagius's theology was far more negative than that of Augustine. His emphasis was not so much on the human ability to live perfectly as on our *responsibility* to do so. His teaching could be called a kind of "ethical cleansing," a highly rigorist rejection of any kind of imperfection in the church. If Pelagius had had his way, the church would have been a very small society, composed entirely of monks. He would certainly have consigned even more souls to hellfire than Augustine did. Despite his obsession with sin and universal guilt, Augustine's faith in the saving power of divine grace makes him, ultimately, a far more sympathetic thinker.

Augustine of Hippo

Augustine of Hippo is unquestionably one of the greatest theologians of all time. His influence over Western thought—religious and otherwise—is total; he remains inescapable even over 15 centuries after his death. He has been hailed as the first medieval, or even the first modern man; and his greatest works rank with the timeless literature of the ages. Yet he has also been derided and despised as a perverter of Christianity and the chief architect of the great schism between the Eastern and Western churches.

Life

The man who would stamp his character and mind indelibly across Western thought was born in Tagaste, a small town in North Africa, in 354. Although his father was a pagan, his mother, Monica, was a devout Christian and had her son educated in Christianity from the cradle on. Augustine accepted the faith unquestioningly.

He excelled at school in every subject except Greek, a language he hated and was unable to master. This fact would have major theological ramifications later. Despite this failing, Augustine's parents decided to send their precocious son to the great city of Carthage to complete his education. Since they were not well off, they had to save up for this, and Augustine found himself hanging around with little to do while he waited for the money to be found.

Augustine was now 16, with all the psychological and physical pressures of a typical adolescent. As he later put it, "The thorns of lust rose over my head, and there was no one to root them out" (*Confessions* 2.2.6). He and his friends spent their time comparing their sexual excesses, and Augustine—again like most teenagers—soon found himself having to invent experiences just to keep up with the others.

One particular incident stuck in his mind from this period: he and his friends robbed a pear orchard just for the fun of it, throwing most of the pears to pigs as they ran off. It was this careless attitude that would later cause terrible feelings of guilt:

> I became evil for no reason. The only motive I had for this wickedness was the wickedness itself. It was disgusting, but I loved it. I loved the fact that I was ruining myself. I loved falling—not the thing that I had fallen for, but simply falling itself. My depraved soul plummeted from God's firmament into ruin.
> *Confessions* 2.4.9

If he could get this worked up over the theft of a few pears, far worse was to come when he finally arrived at Carthage, the city he later described as "a hissing caldron of illicit love" (*Confessions* 3.1.1). Carthage, the premier city of Africa, offered unparalleled resources to a lustful teenager, and Augustine made full use of them:

> I found it sweet to love and be loved in return—especially if I could also enjoy the body of the person I loved. So I polluted the fresh water of friendship with the filth of lewdness, and muddied its clear stream with the hell of lust. But even though I was so disgustingly sinful, I was also so incredibly vain that

I would act as though I was an elegant man about town.
Confessions 3.1.1

Augustine actually led a relatively stable life during this period. He soon settled down with just one woman and continued to excel in his studies. A respectable and lucrative career as a teacher of rhetoric beckoned. When he was 19, however, Augustine discovered a book by Cicero, the great Latin rhetorician and philosopher. Seduced by Cicero's legendary style and elegance of thought, Augustine became determined to learn philosophy.

Cicero also led him to reject the faith he had been taught by his mother. The Bible now seemed to him poorly written and barbarous, compared with the beauty of Cicero's style. Religious truth had to be found elsewhere.

He found it in the teaching of the Manichees. About a century earlier, a flamboyant Persian painter named Mani, who habitually wore red and blue trousers with a green tunic, had decided to found his own religion. Manichaeism, a form of Gnosticism, taught that good and evil are both powerful forces locked in an eternal struggle. Augustine, with his strong sense of sin as a power within himself that he could not resist, found this teaching very appealing and became a member of the Manichaean church.

Augustine spent the next decade as a professional teacher of rhetoric and earnest Manichee. When he returned to Tagaste to teach, his mother was horrified by his new faith and prayed for him constantly. The prayers must have had some effect, because as Augustine became more adept at pagan philosophy and science, he gradually found that the Manichees could not answer all of his questions and doubts. They seemed to be plain wrong on many scientific issues.

Matters came to a head with the arrival of a famous Manichee bishop named Faustus. Augustine's friends had assured him that this man would be able to answer all of his questions easily. As it turned out, Faustus knew far less about science and philosophy than Augustine did, and could not help him at all. Completely disillusioned, Augustine gave up trying to advance any further in Manichaeism. He was 29.

Augustine now decided to leave for Rome, where he hoped the students would be better behaved than those in Africa. His mother begged him not to go; Augustine, exasperated, told her he had to meet a friend urgently at the docks, and he escaped.

The Roman pupils turned out to be as bad as the African ones, so Augustine quickly moved to a better teaching position in Milan. By this time Milan was actually a more important city than Rome. Although it lacked the historical and cultural importance of the older city, it was now the usual residence of the emperor of the Western empire. Its bishop, Ambrose, was a highly influential figure, a champion of the Nicene faith against the Arians and a mentor to both Eastern and Western emperors. He was also famous as a great speaker. Augustine therefore went to listen to his sermons, hoping to learn some tricks of public speaking. In fact, he found himself learning about the Christian faith.

For the next three years, Augustine remained in a state of intellectual and spiritual uncertainty. The pressure on him increased when his mother arrived in Milan, still hoping to persuade him to accept orthodox Christianity. Augustine began to read the Scriptures again but found more solace in the works of Plotinus and the Neoplatonists.

But he was increasingly unhappy. Now that he had become a successful man of culture, it was decided that he should marry. His mother arranged a marriage with a suitable woman, and Augustine's girlfriend from Carthage was forced to return to Africa, leaving behind their son. Unfortunately, the marriage to the new girl was postponed for two years. Unable to contain himself, Augustine soon found a third woman with whom to console himself in the meantime. Strangely, he seems to have suffered less guilt over this shabby behavior than he did over the trivial pear episode from his youth.

Augustine's emotional and spiritual turmoil eventually brought him to a crisis point. As he put it, "I was twisting and turning in my chain until it would break completely" (*Confessions* 7.9.25). The crisis came in 386, as he was sitting in his garden torturing himself with guilt and longing, tearing his hair and weeping bitterly. Suddenly he heard a child's voice from the next garden, saying over and over again, "Take up and read, take up and read." It was part of some kind of game—Milanese children clearly had particularly cultured games in those days—but in his overwrought emotional state, Augustine took it as a divine command:

> I hurried back to where my friend Alypius was sitting, where I had put down the book of the Apostle. I seized it, opened it, and silently read the first passage I saw: "Not in riots and drunken parties, not in eroticism and indecencies, not in strife and rivalry, but put on the Lord Jesus Christ and make no provision for the flesh in its lusts." I neither wished nor needed to read any more. At once, as I read the last words of the passage, it was as if a light of relief from all anxiety flooded into my heart. All the shadows of doubt were dispelled.
> *Confessions* 8.12.29

The passage from Romans 13 had done what the combined efforts of his mother and Ambrose could not. Augustine broke down and committed himself to Christ. His first act as a new Christian was to go and tell his mother.

Augustine now abandoned his career and his marriage and retired to a small monastic retreat with his mother and a few friends. Here he contemplated philosophy and faith, which for him had now become indistinguishable—for he did not cease to be a Neoplatonist when he became a Christian; on the contrary, he thought at this stage that most of the Christian faith could be found in Plotinus.

He was able to take great comfort in his faith when his beloved mother died shortly afterward. After this, Augustine decided to return to Africa and lead a life of quiet contemplation there. His wishes were not to be granted. In 391, praying in a church in the town of Hippo, he was suddenly surrounded by an enthusiastic crowd who begged the bishop to ordain Augustine as a priest. Reluctantly, tears streaming down his cheeks, Augustine submitted to the will of the people.

As a priest he proved remarkably popular and successful, founding a monastery and debating with his former allies the Manichees. He also became popular as an author. He had written some literary and philosophical works before his conversion and immediately after it, but these were of doubtful quality. Now he threw himself into the battle for orthodoxy, writing powerfully against Manichaeism, forging a new vision of free will, grace and the nature of evil.

In 396, at the age of 42, Augustine was made bishop of Hippo. A devoted pastor of his flock, he now lived a life that revolved around the daily services over which he presided. The vast numbers of sermons that survive testify to what a compelling preacher this former professor of rhetoric must have been.

At the same time he stepped up his literary activities. One of his first works after becoming bishop was the famous *Confessions*, one of the most popular and profound works of literature of all time. The bulk of the book tells the story of his life up until the death of his mother, all in the form of a prayer to God, interspersed with spiritual and doctrinal musings and teachings. The book was one of the first autobiographies ever written. Its emphasis on the self—the author's own individual self and soul in relation to the world and to God—was something new as well. Earlier Christian mystics, such as Origen and Gregory of Nyssa, had of course spoken of the mystic's soul becoming united to God, and they had spoken of their personal experience of God. But this was confined to their "mystical" work, and passages describing their personal experiences are very rare. On the whole, Christians had focused on God's relationship to humanity in general, not to individual human beings. Most people did not have a very strong sense of personal individuality. To ancient Christians, it is humanity as a whole—or the church—that is saved; the individual believer is saved by being a member of that group, not through any personal merits or qualities.

Augustine changed all that. The emphasis on the individual's emotional and spiritual voyage and relationship to God and others, as found in the *Confessions,* would become so central to Western thought that it is hard to imagine a world without it. In the West, in the hands of the medievals and the Reformers, Christianity would become a religion of the individual. Even modern Western philosophy and science rest ultimately on this strong distinction between the subjective self and the objective world that the self experiences and observes.

Brilliance aside, it was a brave act to publish the *Confessions,* a work that dwells at enormous length on its author's sinfulness. It might equally be called a self-indulgent act. It encapsulates Augustine's peculiar genius: extraordinary honesty combined with a remarkably morbid outlook on life.

During this period Augustine became embroiled in another controversy, this time with the Donatists, an enthusiastic schismatic sect in North Africa. They were rather like the Montanists, whom Tertullian had joined two centuries earlier, in that they had an extremely rigorist ethic and considered the Catholic Church to have abandoned any pretense to morality. Augustine's arguments against them laid the foundations for the Catholic understanding of the church and the sacraments until modern times.

As the years went by, commentaries, homilies and treatises on a vast variety of subjects, religious and secular, flowed from Augustine's pen. A new Christian philosophy was forming, the greatest since Origen. Yet it found no definitive written form until 410. In that year Alaric the Visigoth and his hordes swept across Italy, destroying everything in their path, and finally captured and ransacked Rome itself. The shockwaves were felt in the farthest corners of the empire: its ancient capital had fallen to a horde of screaming barbarians from the outer wilderness.

Some people pointed out that this disaster had come only a few years after the empire officially adopted Christianity, and they argued that Rome's traditional gods were wreaking a petulant revenge. Augustine responded with a new work, *The City of God,* vigorously refuting the accusation. As he warmed to his theme, the book grew and grew. Years in the writing, it was eventually published in 22 massive volumes, an all-encompassing account of the "city of God"—God's kingdom in the world—and the "city of the earth," its ancient foe. Augustine had written the definitive treatment of the nature of Christianity in relation to the old pagan order of things. It was his masterpiece, one of the most influential works on theology and politics ever written.

At the same time, Augustine was working on a project that was in many ways even greater: the monumental *On the Trinity,* which revolutionized Western thinking on the subject. This is his most erudite, philosophically advanced and intensely spiritual and personal work; even Origen had never approached its brilliance.

Augustine was becoming the most famous theologian in the world, possibly the greatest ever. Yet controversy was never far away. Hardly had he finished his struggle with the Donatists than a new one began, with Pelagius. Pelagius himself was soon condemned and exiled, but he had struck a chord with a great many people who felt uneasy about the theological route the bishop of Hippo and his followers were taking. Augustine therefore spent the last decades of his life engaged in a long-running war of words with the Pelagians, especially a young and brilliant theologian named Julian of Eclanum. At the start Augustine and Pelagius had addressed each other with great respect. Julian, by contrast, had no love for Augustine and filled his works with bitter personal attacks, sinking so low as to attack the bishop's beloved mother. The aging Augustine, for his part, endured his opponent's relentless sarcasm with infinite patience and set forth his own views in volume after volume.

While the empire's greatest minds were tearing each other to shreds over these matters, the empire itself was falling apart. The ransacking of Rome had been merely the start. In 430 Genseric the Vandal and his warrior horde rampaged across North Africa and laid siege to Hippo. As his city lay beleaguered by the barbarians' blockade, Augustine died. With him died antiquity itself. The Western empire was crumbling, and the Dark Ages were beginning.

Thought

The church and the Bible. As an intellectual North African, Augustine was heir to the Origenist tradition of veneration for the Bible. He commented that "the scripture, which is called canonical, has supreme authority, and we ought to agree with it in all matters" (*City of God* 11.3). At the same time he was, like Origen, aware that much of the Bible is obscure, and he even devoted a whole four-volume treatise, *On Christian Doctrine*, to explaining how to understand it. Although in that book he uses Origen's method of allegory, he does so in a limited way: "Whatever we think is the meaning of some obscure passage should be either backed up by what is obviously the case, or it should be stated in other, clearer texts" (*City of God* 11.19). This reflects Augustine's down-to-earth, practical nature, compared with Origen's more mystical and intellectualist approach.

In practice, Augustine's work is drenched in biblical quotation and imagery. This is combined with a very strong sense of the authority of tradition and the church. His views on these matters were developed during his controversy with the Donatists. The Donatists believed that the church, and especially its priests, should be morally blameless. Since this was not the case with the Catholic Church—some members of which had been known to reject Christ rather than suffer death for his sake—they separated from it, forming their own church. Throughout much of North Africa, the Donatist Church was actually more popular than the Catholic one: Augustine could even hear the hymns of a Donatist church as he preached in his own! The Donatists argued that Catholic sacraments, including baptism and ordination, were powerless because they were performed by morally lax priests. This rigorist position was very popular in Africa, and the Donatists could appeal to the works of the revered bishop-martyr Cyprian of Carthage, a contemporary of Origen who, although a Catholic, had believed many of the same things as the Donatists.

This was clearly a pressing issue for a Catholic bishop in Africa, and it forced Augustine to lay the concept of the church and the sacraments on a wholly new foundation. He argued that the worth of a sacrament has nothing to do with the morality of the priest who administers it. This is because the sacrament is actually performed by Christ; the priest is simply his instrument. As Augustine put it, "When Peter baptizes, it is Christ who baptizes. When Paul baptizes, it is Christ who baptizes. When Judas baptizes, it is Christ who baptizes."

So anybody, no matter how steeped in evil, can administer valid sacraments, because they are performed not by that person but by the power of God. This applies to schismatics and heretics, and Augustine believed that the sacraments of the Donatists themselves were valid even though the Donatists were in error. He even worried about whether children pretending to be priests, or actors playing priests, might accidentally consecrate bread and wine for real!

Although in theory anyone *can* perform the sacraments, in practice not everyone *should* do so. Augustine stresses that only the Catholic Church has the authority to ordain priests and perform the Eucharist. The Donatists' sacraments are real and valid, but they have no right to perform them, and by doing so outside the authority of the one true church they blaspheme and condemn themselves. The notion that the one body of Christ might be represented on earth by a variety of different denominations was totally alien to Augustine, as it was to all the church fathers. Anyone who split off from the one true church was a schismatic, no different from a heretic who denied some essential point of doctrine. In fact, to deny that the church was the one true body of Christ *was* heresy.

The Trinity. Augustine's work on the Trinity is among his most brilliant and important. He represents the final stage in the evolution of the doctrine in the early church, from the vague Logos doctrine of Justin Martyr to a clearly defined, rigorously presented dogma that would form the basis of medieval theology.

Augustine begins with the Cappadocians' claim that the three Persons of the

Trinity are distinguished from each other only by their mutual relations. So they are not three different substances (which would be tritheism, the belief in three Gods), and they are not just different qualities of one substance (which would be modalism, the denial of any real distinction between the Persons). So far, Augustine agrees with Gregory of Nyssa.

But he differs greatly from the Cappadocians in his analysis of what the relations between the Persons actually are. The Cappadocians had thought that the Son is the Son of the Father, and the Spirit proceeds from the Father. So the Father is the one who is basically God, while the other two are God because they come from the Father. They are God just as much as the Father is, but only because they come from him and take their divinity from him. Like all theologians before them, including Tertullian, Origen and Athanasius, the Cappadocians therefore thought of the source of divinity in the Godhead as being the Father. The Father is divinity itself.

Augustine's conception is totally different. For one thing, while he agrees that the Son is the Son of the Father alone, he says that the Spirit proceeds from the Father *and the Son*, not just from the Father. This may seem a trivial difference, but it is in fact enormously significant. It means that the Father is not the sole source of both of the other Persons, because the Spirit is derived from the Son as well.

In fact Augustine does not think of the Father as the source of divinity in the Godhead. No one Person is to be identified with divinity itself. Augustine thinks of divinity as something distinct from each of the Persons, in the same way that human nature, for example, is not identical with any particular human being. To be human is to share in human nature, which is something logically distinct from ourselves; in the same way, each of the divine Persons shares in the divine nature, which is something distinct. This means that no one Person is greater than the others— in fact, because they are all God and of infinite greatness, no two taken together are greater than the other one. The Son is still generated from the Father, and the Spirit proceeds from the other two, but this is a relation merely of logical priority. The generation and procession happen eternally—as with Origen and Athanasius— and do not mean that the Son and Spirit gain their divinity from the Father or are inferior to him in any way.

Augustine has thus purged the doctrine of every trace of subordinationism, the belief that the Father is greater than the other two Persons because their existence and divinity depend on him. The Persons are all equal and take their divinity from the same source—the Godhead itself, which is not identical with any one of them.

Such a sophisticated doctrine could easily become abstract and irrelevant. Yet in Augustine's hands it becomes a spiritual meditation on the nature of God and his relation to humanity. Reflecting on the fact that humankind is made in the image of God, Augustine suggests that we can see a dim image of the Trinity in human love: "Whenever I myself, the person investigating these things, love anything, three things are involved. These are myself, the thing I love, and love itself" (*On the Trinity* 9.2). The point is that you can't have love without someone doing the loving and someone else being loved. They are three different things, but they always come packaged together, as it were. And the three Persons of the Trinity are rather like this.

But Augustine is not content with his analogy and suggests a couple of others to modify the image. The final one revolves around human memory, intelligence and will. These three mental faculties are obviously not different people and indeed cannot exist without each other—but neither are they the same as each other.

Augustine's pioneering use of psychological analogies to the Trinity illustrates again his deep interest in the subjective life of the self and its relation to God. It also illustrates what many have seen as a flaw in his doctrine of the Trinity. Memory, intelligence and will may be different faculties, but they are possessed by a single person. Their unity is more fundamental than their diversity. Similarly, Augustine seems to emphasize the unity of God more than he does the diversity of the Trinity.

For this reason he is disliked by the Eastern Church, which, like the Cappadocian fathers, has always tended to emphasize the diversity over the unity. But far worse in Eastern eyes is the denial that the Father is the sole source of divinity in the Trinity. Some critics argue that to talk of divinity apart from the Father is to introduce "divinity" as a fourth member in the Trinity! Augustine's claim that the Spirit proceeds from the Son as well as from the Father is simply a symptom of this, and the Orthodox Church has always vigorously rejected the doctrine.

Augustine himself was under the impression that everyone, Greek and Latin, believed that the Spirit comes from the Son as well as from the Father. This was because his Greek was too bad for him to realize that although hints of the doctrine could be found in some Greek writers, it was not really there. It is sobering to think that the history of ever-deteriorating relations between Eastern and Western Christianity might have been eased if only Augustine had tried harder in school.

Sin. Without question, Augustine's doctrine of human nature, its fall and its redemption, is the most famous—or notorious—part of his thought. It is also among the most personal, springing, like his *Confessions,* from a profound sense of his own guilt.

When he was a Manichee, Augustine believed that evil was a powerful force, a substance in its own right opposing the power of good. When he became a Christian he rejected this belief, arguing instead that evil actually does not exist. What we call evil is really just an absence of good, in the same way that cold is an absence of heat. This idea, which would be very popular in later centuries, is taken from Neoplatonism and is also found in Origen.

Yet Augustine combines this denial of the reality of evil at the metaphysical level with a great emphasis on its reality at the *existential* level. Nobody can escape sin. It is an unstoppable force within us, the direct result of Adam's original sin:

> Because of Adam's sin, the whole race which descended from him became corrupted in him, and punishable by death. So everyone who is descended from him . . . is tainted with the first sin. Because of it they are drawn through all kinds of errors and suffering until they reach the last, never-ending punishment that they suffer together with the fallen angels, who corrupted and control them and share their doom.
> *Enchiridion 26*

This cheerful doctrine was an advance on anything that had been said before. Earlier theologians, especially Augustine's mentor Ambrose, had indeed talked of "original sin" as a power, caused by the fall of Adam, which influences us to do evil. Augustine expanded on this theme, dwelling at length on the ineluctable power of sin within us. One of the most pernicious manifestations of this, in his view, is sexual desire. Augustine's views on the terrible potential for sin that sexual desire creates have cast a heavy shadow over the church's attitude toward sex for centuries. But Augustine went still further. The notion that all of Adam's descendants actually share his *guilt* for that first sin was new. It is not to be found in Romans 5, the source passage for the doctrine.

How could Augustine have believed such a thing? It was partly due to his Platonism. Platonists, as we have seen, believed that all physical objects are simply copies of eternal, immaterial templates or Forms. This means that two objects of the same kind have a sort of connection because they both depend on the same Form. So the terrible taint of Adam can spread to those who share his Form, the Form of humanity.

The doctrine also had something to do with ancient theories of genetics. It was believed that everything a child inherited from its parents came from the father alone. The mother contributed nothing material to the development of the baby within her; she was just a convenient incubator. So it was also believed that before being implanted into the mother's womb, a baby exists in its entirety in its father, in seed form. The father once existed in seed form in his father too, and so on all the way back. So Augustine could plausibly believe that the entire human race really did exist "in Adam" at the time of his sin, like a set of Russian dolls. And since we were there, we share the guilt for what happened.

Thus, as Augustine memorably puts it, the human race is a "mass of damnation." All people are guilty and are justly condemned to eternal punishment. Augustine has no time for Origen's faith in the ultimate salvation of all and is quite clear that hell is going to be decidedly overstocked. But what of free will? Augustine suggests that before the Fall, Adam was free to sin or not to sin. After the Fall, the irresistible power of sin means that we no longer have the choice. We can only sin— although this is not to say that everything we do is sinful or that some sins are not worse than others. These latter doctrines would be introduced at the Reformation as extreme extensions of Augustine's ideas.

It seems that Augustine hung on to some of his Manichaean beliefs longer than he realized. This strong, even cruel doctrine of original sin and universal guilt and the inescapable power of the sinful impulse is highly reminiscent of the Manichaean belief in the substantial power of evil. Yet it is just part of the story. Augustine's great sense of sin is equaled by his great sense of grace.

Grace. It seems that humanity is in a bad way. Augustine stresses that it is impossible for human beings to help themselves in any way. We cannot even choose what is right, far less save ourselves by doing it. So we must be helped by an external power, divine grace:

> This grace, which perfects strength in weakness, brings everyone who is predestined and called by God to supreme perfection and glory. This grace not only shows us what we ought to do, it makes us do it. It not only makes us believe what we ought to love, it makes us love it.
>
> *On the Grace of Christ* 13

So then, just as the power of original sin forces us to do what is wrong, the power of grace forces us to do what is right. Augustine teaches an "internal" doctrine of grace: grace is the action of God within the human will itself, turning that will toward what is right. This contrasts with the "external" grace taught by Pelagius, whereby God provides us with the means to do what is right but leaves the final decision up to us.

Augustine therefore denies free will, if by "free will" we mean the belief that people are free to choose right or wrong. According to him, everyone is predestined—either by sin, to do wrong, or by grace, to do right. But to put it like this is to miss Augustine's point. The point of grace is not that it forces us to do what is right; rather, it makes us *want* to do what is right and enables us to do it. Through grace, God transforms the human will. It is almost as if the will cooperates with

God in the performing of good actions.

This, for Augustine, is true freedom—the freeing of the will from the shackles of sin, freeing it to be able to do good. He believes that this process will be perfected in heaven, when humans will no longer even be able to sin. And this is the most perfect freedom of all.

So we are saved by grace, not by ourselves. This grace is channeled through the death and resurrection of Christ, and Augustine draws his theology of salvation from Romans 6, where Paul speaks of dying with Christ and being raised with him. If we have faith in Christ, Augustine assures us, the divine grace will put our sinful self to death with him and raise us again.

All of this reflects Augustine's interest in the individual self and its relation to God, and we can see why the Reformers and their evangelical successors approved. But Augustine is no Pietist. The personal transformation in the heart of the individual brought about by grace has meaning only within the context of the church. The Catholic Church is the city of God, and those who are not members of it dwell in the city of the earth. Augustine takes very seriously Paul's claim in Romans 6 that we are saved by being baptized into Christ's death. He concludes that baptism, the sacrament by which we enter the church, is an essential precondition for salvation. Anyone who does not participate in the life and sacraments of the church— by which, of course, he means the Catholic Church, not any schismatic sect like the Donatists—is playing with fire, however devout they may appear to be otherwise. Even babies, if they die before they are baptized, cannot be saved, and God justly condemns them to eternal punishment on account of the guilt they bear for Adam's sin. Augustine tempers this notorious doctrine with the suggestion that there are degrees of punishment in hell and unbaptized infants suffer only the lightest variety. But this is as much as he will allow.

Influence

It is little exaggeration to say that the whole history of the Western Church for the last 1,500 years is the story of Augustine's influence. His doctrines of the Fall, sin and grace would become unquestionable orthodoxy, and the man himself would be honored with the title "the Doctor of Grace"—reflecting the essentially grace-centered, optimistic interpretation of Augustine common to medieval theologians. His doctrine of the Trinity would become the only acceptable one. The greatest theologians of the Middle Ages, including Thomas Aquinas, regarded themselves merely as his disciples; and spiritual writers from Bernard of Clairvaux to Julian of Norwich were immersed in his thought. Later, in the Reformation, Catholics appealed to his views on the church and the impossibility that grace could exist outside it. Protestants responded by appealing to his emphasis on grace and the impossibility of saving oneself. The great work of Calvin himself was essentially a revision and expansion of the parts of Augustine's thought with which he agreed.

At the same time Augustine came under heavy fire from the Orthodox Church, which disagreed with most of his most characteristic doctrines, above all his doctrine of the Trinity. To this day the Western belief that the Spirit proceeds from the Son as well as from the Father is a major barrier to ecumenical dialogue between East and West. Moreover, many Protestant theologians themselves deplore the hold that Augustine has exercised over their history, lambasting him for his pernicious views on sin, damnation and sex.

Augustine remains a highly controversial figure, perhaps the most debated and high-profile theologian ever, with the exception of Paul himself. As long as issues like the nature of God and humanity, life, death and salvation are discussed, Augustine will continue to be alternately revered and deplored.

Cyril of Alexandria

He hardly seemed a likely candidate for sainthood. Vitriolic, tactless and despotic, Cyril, bishop of Alexandria, wielded as much power in Egypt as the pharaohs

THE COUNCIL OF EPHESUS

The Third Ecumenical Church Council was a complete shambles from start to finish. It was Nestorius's idea to hold it, rather than meekly submit to Pope Celestine's demand that he recant his doctrines, and it was arranged by the Eastern emperor Theodosius II. The emperor wrote to Augustine, hoping that he would play a central role, but unfortunately the famous bishop of Hippo had died the previous year, and no one knew because his city was still besieged by barbarians.

Cyril and Nestorius both arrived in Ephesus on the same day, each accompanied by a large cohort of bishops who all refused to attend church with bishops of the other party. The proceedings were delayed by the late arrival of Nestorius's ally John, bishop of Antioch, where Nestorius had been trained. Tempers were short as everyone sat about in the oppressive heat, and a couple of bishops even died. Nestorius refused to appear before the council without John. Cyril eventually lost patience, called the council to order and had Nestorius solidly condemned. A letter announcing this was pinned to

themselves. He would stop at nothing to retain that power, even rousing mobs to loot and murder his enemies. Yet this man is remembered as one of the greatest teachers of the church. After his death, his writings became canonized as the ultimate authority on the doctrine of Christ.

Life

As a nephew of the all-powerful Theophilus, bishop of Alexandria, Cyril was assured of a good career in the church.

The previous century and a half had seen successive bishops of Alexandria, from Demetrius to Athanasius, become more and more powerful. Theophilus had completed the process, becoming one of the most ruthless church politicians in history. He had destroyed the celebrated Great Library of Alexandria, persecuted Origenists, sent armies of storm troopers into monasteries to root out his enemies, and engineered the exile of his chief rival in the Eastern empire, Bishop John Chrysostom of Constantinople. In Egypt his power was total.

Within three days of Theophilus's death in 412, Cyril had himself installed in his place, amidst riots between his supporters and opponents. It was an inauspicious beginning to an episcopate that would be almost as ruthless as that of his uncle.

Nestorius's front door, since he refused to receive it in person.

Several days later John of Antioch finally arrived, declaring that everything that had happened so far was invalid and accusing Cyril of heresy. A fortnight after this the pope's envoys, who had also been delayed, turned up and supported Cyril. Eventually, after many sessions, accusations and counteraccusations, it was decided that the original session of the council and its decisions were in fact valid. In securing his victory Cyril was greatly helped by Memnon, bishop of Ephesus, who like Cyril was bishop of a waning city and greatly resented the growing power of the bishop of Constantinople.

The net result of all this was the deposition of Nestorius and the condemnation of his heresy. However, it would not be until the more orderly Council of Chalcedon, twenty years later, that the christological disputes between Alexandria on the one hand and Constantinople and Antioch on the other would be laid to rest.

Cyril must have wanted to establish his authority as bishop quickly after the riots. His first act was to close down the churches of a schismatic sect known as the Novatians. This was something that only the civil authorities could normally do. So it seemed that the bishop of Alexandria was now a secular ruler as well as a spiritual one.

This was something of a mixed blessing. The city of Alexandria, once the serene intellectual capital of the world, had become a seething hotbed of fanaticism and hatred. The population, divided between pagans, Christians and Jews, lived in an uneasy state of truce that could erupt at any time into rioting and lynch mobs. Sadly, Cyril lacked the diplomatic skills necessary to handle the delicate situation.

Trouble began when one of Cyril's henchmen was discovered attending a meeting where Orestes, the civil governor, was announcing some of his policies. Orestes, who although a Christian was unhappy about Cyril's growing power, had the man removed and publicly tortured. Enraged, Cyril met with the leaders of the Jewish

THE COUNCIL OF CHALCEDON

If Ephesus had been a victory of Alexandria over Constantinople, Chalcedon was Constantinople's revenge. The council met in 451 to decide the fate of Eutyches, an elderly and rather woolly-thinking abbot in Alexandria. He had taken Cyril's teaching to extremes, claiming that when Christ became human his humanity was swallowed up by his divinity, so that he had only one nature. The teaching was endorsed by Dioscorus, who had succeeded Cyril as bishop of Alexandria—in fact, in 449 Dioscorus had attempted to emulate Cyril by presiding over a rather violent synod at Ephesus, at which he allowed only his friends to speak and deposed the bishop of Constantinople for disagreeing with him.

The bishops at Chalcedon, however, lost no time in condemning this "Robber Council" and both Dioscorus and Eutyches with it. Not content with this, they set about defining exactly what the orthodox doctrine of Christ was to be. First they endorsed the Symbol of Nicaea, in a slightly longer version than the original, with an extra paragraph about the Holy Spirit. They attributed this version to the Council of Constantinople, and it is this creed that is recited today in many churches throughout the world as the "Nicene Creed."

The council added to this a statement of its own. The Council of Ephesus had decreed that no creed should ever be used as definitive apart from the Symbol

community, who for some reason he thought were responsible, and ordered them to stop harassing Christians. This undiplomatic move caused such anger among the Jews that a group of them organized and executed a brutal massacre of Christians.

Cyril thereupon stirred up his followers to march on the synagogues, which they destroyed and plundered. Any Jews who survived were driven from the city, many never to return.

The situation now became more complicated with the arrival of several hundred monks from the Egyptian desert. These monks were fanatically loyal to the bishop of Alexandria and feared for his safety. The governor, Orestes, rode out to talk with them, but the situation turned nasty and one of the monks threw a stone at him, inflicting a serious head wound. At this, a mob rushed out of the city to their governor's defense. The monk who had thrown the stone was arrested and executed. Astonishingly, Cyril's reaction was to venerate the monk as a saint who had given his life in the cause of Christ. This, unsurprisingly, did not help his rapidly deteri-

of Nicaea, so the council was careful to assert that this new statement was simply an unpacking of the teaching of Nicaea, not an additional creed. It ran:

> Following the holy fathers, all of us agree in teaching people to believe in one and the same Son, our Lord Jesus Christ, at once complete in his divinity and complete in his humanity, true God and true man (with both a rational soul and a body); of one substance with the Father as far as his divinity goes, and at the same time of one substance with us as far as his humanity goes; like us in every way apart from sin; as far as his divinity goes, begotten of the Father before the ages, but as far as his humanity goes begotten for us and our salvation of the Virgin Mary, the Mother of God; one and the same Christ, Son, Lord, Only-Begotten, recognized in two natures—not confused, not changing, not divided, not separated—the distinction of the natures being in no way compromised by the fact that they are united, but the qualities of each nature being kept and united to form one person, not divided or separated into two persons, but one and the same Son and Only-Begotten God, the Logos, Lord Jesus Christ; just as the prophets spoke of him from the earliest times, and the Lord Jesus Christ himself taught us, and the creed of the Fathers handed down.

orating relations with Orestes.

The crowning disaster was the death of Hypatia. This woman was a pagan Neo-platonist philosopher, a prominent public figure in the city and a good friend of Orestes. Convinced that she had been bad-mouthing Cyril to the governor, a Christian mob waylaid her and dragged her into a church, where she was stripped, torn to pieces and finally burned. While Cyril was probably not involved in this personally, he had certainly done nothing to overcome the atmosphere of hatred in which such a crime could be committed.

Eventually Cyril managed to get matters in his own city under control. But events were unfolding overseas that would lead to even greater disturbance. In 428 a monk named Nestorius became bishop of Constantinople. He immediately proved to be almost as heavyhanded as Cyril, burning an Arian church, deposing bishops and generally alienating everybody with whom he dealt. This sort of thing seems to have been fairly common practice for archbishops of this time. But Nestorius was not content with attacking "old" heretics like the Arians; he was convinced that a new heresy was afoot concerning the person of Christ. He denounced those

Simple! In fact, the care with which every word was chosen makes the statement quite straightforward. The council is insistent that Christ was one person, not two—and furthermore that this one person was identical with the Second Person of the Trinity. In this it is in full agreement with the heart of Cyril's doctrine—and the description of Mary as the Mother of God is a swipe at Nestorius, who had claimed that she was mother of only the human part of Christ, not the divine part. But Cyril had never said that Christ had two natures; in affirming this, the council was taking account of the genuine concern Nestorius and his allies had had for acknowledging Christ's humanity. The doctrine of Eutyches, that Christ's divinity swamps and overrides his humanity, is firmly prohibited. In fact Nestorius, who was still living in exile, declared that the council's decision was a vindication of his own doctrine—although he decided not to say so publicly. He did not want the true doctrine to become suspect by being associated with the despised name Nestorius.

Some staunch Cyril fanatics refused to accept the teaching that Christ had two natures. They rejected the Council of Chalcedon and with it the Orthodox Church. From then on there were two churches in Egypt: the Orthodox Church and the Monophysite (meaning "one nature") Church. In Syria, meanwhile, there was also a church that had refused to accept the Council

who called the Virgin Mary "the Mother of God." This, he claimed, was heresy, for God could not be born of woman; Mary was the mother of the human part of Christ but not the divine part.

Nestorius had gone too far. Cyril, horrified that a fellow archbishop should teach such a thing, wrote to him saying as much. He also wrote to other bishops to enlist their support and to the emperor. Nestorius, naturally, didn't budge, even when Cyril sent him a harshly worded ultimatum in the form of 12 "heretical" propositions drawn from Nestorius's own works, which he demanded Nestorius condemn. A council met at Ephesus in 431 to settle the matter, and Nestorius was condemned and deposed.

The whole affair was an unhappy confusion of theology and politics. Twenty-five years earlier Cyril's uncle Theophilus had hounded John Chrysostom, bishop of Constantinople, out of jealousy of his rival's influence over the emperor and the Eastern Church in general. And now here was Cyril, Theophilus's nephew, persecuting another bishop of Constantinople and securing his exile. No wonder tongues wagged. But there were real theological issues involved too. Cyril was gen-

of Ephesus—the Nestorian Church. These two communions would survive for centuries, although the Monophysites were eventually overwhelmed by Islam. The Nestorian Church in particular was vigorous and produced good theologians and spiritual masters: indeed, China first came to learn of Christianity through the efforts of Nestorian missionaries, and the church remains active in India. But these two churches, known collectively as the Coptic Churches, would pass almost entirely out of the consciousness of the West. This was the first great split of Christendom, a rift that has never been healed, and an anticipation of the still greater divisions between Catholics and Orthodox and, later, Catholics and Protestants.

In a way, the Fourth Ecumenical Council was the most important church council ever held. Its teaching remains the definitive statement of the classical doctrine of Christ. And it was the last of the great councils that are accepted as authoritative by all churches throughout the world, including Orthodox, Catholic and Anglican. Three more would be held, making seven in all; but the later ones are accepted only by the Orthodox Church. The Council of Chalcedon was therefore the last truly ecumenical council. Its date, 451, is generally taken as marking the end of the Patristic period, the age of the church fathers, the most creative and important centuries of the church's history.

uinely alarmed at Nestorius's ideas and spent much time and effort trying to correct them.

Two years of controversy followed, as Nestorius's followers refused to accept the decision. In 433 Cyril made his peace with them, Nestorius himself having given up the fight and resigned. The theological warfare continued as Cyril attacked the works of earlier theologians whom the Nestorians cited in support of their views. But his heart seems not to have been in these more abstract battles, and he retired from them shortly before his death in 444.

Thought

Cyril made a lasting contribution to only one area of Christian thought, but what he said on that matter was of immense importance. His teaching on the person of Christ developed as a direct response to Nestorianism.

Nestorius was bishop of Constantinople, but he originally came from Antioch, where there was a strong tradition of placing great importance on the humanity of Christ. Like his compatriots, Nestorius distinguished carefully between the human "part" of Christ and the divine "part." He believed that the human part was formed in the normal fashion in the womb of the Virgin, whereupon the divine part—the second Person of the Trinity—entered her womb. The two parts were then joined together, forming Christ. So Mary was the mother of the human part of Christ, not the divine part. Think of a hat, which is made of two parts, the crown and the brim. In exactly the same way Christ is "made" of a human part and a divine part, without being identical with either one of them by itself.

This was nonsense as far as Cyril was concerned. To him it sounded as if Nestorius was talking about two separate persons, a divine person and a human one, operating as a sort of committee. Quite apart from the implausibility of such a picture, it meant that Christ, the human being who lived on earth, was not identical with the Son, the second Person of the Trinity, for the Son only made up half of him.

This, then, is the heart of Cyril's thought. Just as the Nicene Creed stated, it was the Son himself who was incarnate, suffered and died. Jesus Christ *is* the second Person of the Trinity—the two are the same person. We are dealing with only one person, not two glued together.

Instead of thinking of a divine Person coming down from heaven and becoming united to a human person, we must think of a divine Person descending and becoming human himself. An analogy might be a lollipop being dipped in chocolate: the Son was plunged into human nature, taking it upon himself. That does not mean simply that he animated a human body, taking the place of a normal human soul, which some of Cyril's predecessors at Alexandria had believed. On the contrary, it meant becoming fully human, and Christ had a human soul as well as a human body. He did not put on human nature like a coat, with the possibility of taking it off again and remaining unaffected in his real being. He became really human, just as he was already really divine.

So Christ was one person, both divine and human—not two persons, one divine and one human. The Virgin Mary was therefore the Mother of God, because the whole of her son was God as well as man.

These ideas would form the basis of the Creed of Chalcedon, the definitive expression of the church's doctrine of Christ; and the council would even canonize two of Cyril's letters as fully authoritative on the matter. There were actually subtle differences between Cyril's doctrine and that of Chalcedon, to the extent that Nestorius—still living in exile—could claim that Chalcedon was a vindication of his own theology. But the differences were really minor. In effect, Cyril was the author of the orthodox doctrine of Christ. That this doctrine owes so much to a man of such unscrupulous ambition and irascible character is an abiding paradox in the history of Christian thought.

2

THE BYZANTINE EMPIRE

As Rome fell to the barbarian hordes, the western half of the empire withered away. But Constantinople, the New Rome, held firm. The Christian city of Constantine, also known by its ancient name of Byzantium, was now the sole capital of the eastern half of the Roman empire—what became known as the Byzantine empire.

For 1,000 years the Byzantine empire stood fast. Here scholars and theologians continued to write and argue, sifting through the Scriptures and the writings of the church fathers and producing ever more sophisticated reflections upon them. The Orthodox Church, more than any other Christian denomination, has always set great store by tradition. This means that the Byzantine theologians tended to be less original than the Fathers they studied and less daring than their Western medieval contemporaries. They are certainly not so well known in the West. But for beauty of writing and profundity of spirituality, few could match them.

Byzantium

In Byzantium, at last, Constantine's dream of a perfect union of church and state was realized. The inhabitants of the city believed that they were living in a foretaste of the heavenly Jerusalem, so pervasive was Christianity in all spheres of life. The magnificence of the city set the seal on its status as an icon of heaven itself. It had a distinctive architectural style, shown to great effect in buildings like the immense cathedral of Hagia Sophia, built by Emperor Justinian in the early 6th century, which required 625 priests simply to keep it operational. Throughout the Middle Ages Constantinople was the largest and most glorious city in Europe.

The splendor of the city was matched by the sophistication of its scholarship, which kept alive the flame of antiquity. The refined elegance of its inhabitants was surpassed only by the complexity of their political system, which revolved around the imperial court. *Byzantine* has meant "incomprehensibly complicated" ever since.

All of this was in stark contrast to the empire's status in the world at large. Its dominions were limited to the Balkans and modern-day Turkey; after the 6th century it had no power in the West, a fact that was forcibly brought home by Charlemagne's coronation as Holy Roman emperor in A.D. 800. The rise of Islam in the 7th century quickly meant that Byzantium was no longer the major power in the East either, and in addition it had to contend with the Slavs and Avars to the north.

The emperor was the supreme ruler of Byzantium and its dominions; he was also the supreme figurehead of the church. His immense, magnificent palace and his splendid vestments proclaimed him the true regent of God himself. Although he had no priestly office and was matched in his spiritual authority by the patriarch of Constantinople, the emperor filled a symbolic role similar to the one that was increasingly occupied in the West by the pope.

This tendency is known as Caesaropapism—treating the emperor like the pope—and the Orthodox Church, which lacks a strong ecclesiastical leader, has often been prone to it. After the collapse of Byzantium in 1453, the Russian czar would claim a similar authority and prestige.

Pseudo-Dionysius

The mysterious person who wrote under the name Dionysius the Areopagite is one of the most intriguing figures in Christian history. His works are among the most impenetrable and perplexing possessed by the church, but there have always been a few kindred spirits in every age who have been transfixed by his ethereal teachings of the darkness and the eroticism of God.

Life

The writings in question consist of four short treatises and a few letters, which the author passes off as the work of Dionysius the Areopagite, an individual mentioned in Acts 17:34 as one of Paul's few converts in Athens. Nothing else at all is known of the actual Dionysius, although later legends had him becoming the first bishop of Athens. One thing, however, is certain: he did not write the works that have survived under his name. These appeared suspiciously suddenly in the 6th century but were generally accepted as genuine 1st-century works quite quickly. The real identity of the author is unknown. It is thought that he was a monk living in Syria sometime at the start of the 6th century, which would make him a member not of the Orthodox Church but, probably, the Monophysite or maybe the Nestorian Church. Beyond that he is shrouded in mystery.

It was quite common in the ancient world to write under the name of some famous person. There are books by "Plato," "Aristotle," "Seneca" and other worthies, supplementing the genuine books by these authors, and all quite spurious.

And Christians did the same thing. Among such works are those by "Pseudo-Justin," "Pseudo-Tertullian," "Pseudo-Augustine" and so on. Today we would regard this as dishonest forgery, but in ancient times it was more acceptable, since the author was supposedly only writing what the famous person would have said if they had got around to writing on that topic. It was also a good way of ensuring that your work got noticed. People were sometimes suspicious when a "newly discovered" work of some ancient worthy suddenly appeared, but most books of this kind were generally accepted as genuine, copied and preserved. An author who was willing to sacrifice personal fame in return for a better chance of his work's actually being read could do a lot worse than choose a famous pseudonym.

Pseudo-Dionysius's ghostwriting was clever and fooled the church for centuries, but he is betrayed by his use of ideas and language that never existed when the real

THE SECOND COUNCIL OF CONSTANTINOPLE

Of the seven great ecumenical councils, the fifth is surely the least interesting. It was held in 553 at the prompting of Byzantine emperor Justinian. Justinian was a great leader who had succeeded (temporarily) in recapturing much of the western half of the old empire, including Rome. He was also an amateur theologian who was keen to reconcile the Monophysite Church to the Orthodox faith.

He had a document known as the Three Chapters drawn up, a compilation of quotations from several writers. These included Theodore of Mopsuestia, a famous 4th-century theologian from Antioch, and Theodoret of Cyrus, a 5th-century supporter of Nestorius. Although both figures were remembered fondly, their thought had been quite similar to that of the heretic Nestorius, and the Three Chapters was an anthology of their most objectionable comments. Justinian hoped to have the document condemned, thereby reassuring the Monophysites that the Orthodox Church was not Nestorian after all.

Most bishops were reluctant to cast aspersions on long-dead writers, but the council was duly called and the Three Chapters condemned—although the council was careful not to condemn the revered authors themselves. Hardly any Westerners were there. Pope Vigilius was present, although Justinian

Dionysius lived. Pseudo-Dionysius is a Neoplatonist philosopher who also happens to be a Christian. Like the Cappadocians and Augustine, his aim was to create a true "Christian philosophy." In his case this meant using the concepts and categories of contemporary Neoplatonism to express his Christian faith. Perhaps this is why he chose to write under the name of the legendary first bishop of Athens, the home of Greek philosophy.

Thought

Pseudo-Dionysius made two major contributions to Christian thought. The first was his concept of "hierarchy," a word he invented.

Hierarchy. By Pseudo-Dionysius's day, Neoplatonists had developed sophisticated theologies of the various levels of reality that existed above the visible world.

had to exile him for a while before securing his agreement to the council's decisions.

Most bishops were reluctant to cast aspersions on long-dead writers, but the council was duly called and the Three Chapters condemned—although the council was careful not to condemn the revered authors themselves. Hardly any Westerners were there. Pope Vigilius was present, although Justinian had to exile him for a while before securing his agreement to the council's decisions.

The more lasting consequence of the council was tacked on almost as an afterthought. Justinian had been involved in a struggle against fanatical Origenists who had taken the ideas of the 3rd-century theologian to strange and extreme lengths. In fact it seems that the Three Chapters affair had been partly their leaders' idea, in the hope of diverting the emperor's attention away from themselves. The plan failed, however, and the council condemned twelve propositions supposedly drawn from Origen's work. It is not clear whether Origen himself was condemned; if he was, it was while the pope was not there, and so Origen's defenders still argue that the great theologian has never been formally branded a heretic. Nevertheless, the damage was done, and his voluminous writings were systematically destroyed.

These were far more complex than the relatively simple scheme sketched out by Plotinus and generally revolved around groups of three. Pseudo-Dionysius christianizes this worldview. He provides an elaborate description of the inhabitants of the higher realms—angels, cherubim, seraphim, archangels and so on. There are nine classes of angels, arranged into three groups of three. The same is true of the church, where there are three classes of priests, three classes of ordinary believers and three sacraments. Capping both sets of hierarchies is the Trinity, itself a triple "Thearchy" of Father, Son and Spirit.

Pseudo-Dionysius does not think that one ought to try to climb these hierarchies like a ladder, starting as an ordinary believer and ending up as an archangel. On the contrary, everybody has their own fixed place on the hierarchy. Because the hierarchies are images of the divine Trinity, it is possible to know God and become more like God by keeping to one's place in the hierarchy and performing the duties of that position properly. The idea is not that knowledge of God trickles down the hierarchy like a waterfall, benefiting the lowest members only indirectly. That would be a more common Neoplatonic way of thinking. Instead any member of the hierarchy can gain immediate knowledge of God through their place on the hierarchy.

Because both God and the world are hierarchies, there is an intrinsic similarity between them. This is why the whole of creation yearns to be united to God. This idea is again taken from Neoplatonism, but Pseudo-Dionysius turns it on its head to say that God too yearns to be united to the world—something that could never be said of Plotinus's ineffable One. Pseudo-Dionysius, like Origen before him, uses the language of romantic love, particularly the word *eros*, meaning yearning desire. He thinks that the world is essentially erotic and reflects God, who is also erotic: each is desperate for the other. This notion of the intrinsically erotic nature of both God and world is one of the most intriguing and unusual aspects of Pseudo-Dionysius's thought.

Yet this rather strange similarity of God and the world is transcended by a more profound dissimilarity. This is Pseudo-Dionysius's second great contribution to Christian thought.

Via negativa (the negative way). Pseudo-Dionysius is a profound mystic in the tradition of Gregory of Nyssa. Like Gregory, he declares that God transcends all normal categories, so we cannot really say or think anything about him at all.

> Indeed the incomprehensible One cannot be reached by any use of reason. Nor can any words match the unspeakable Good, this One, this source of all unity, this Being beyond existence. Mind beyond mind, word beyond speech,

it is encompassed by no speech, by no intuition, by no name.
The Divine Names I.1

Even more than Gregory, Pseudo-Dionysius is heavily influenced by the language of Neoplatonism here. Indeed his language sometimes seems quite unorthodox. He points out that while it is more wrong to say that God is evil than that he is good, nevertheless we must ultimately reject both these terms as inadequate to describe God. Nothing can really be said of God at all. God is not mind or soul; he is not life or love; he is not power or light; he is not unity or trinity. Nothing can truly be said of him, and nothing can truly be denied of him. He simply transcends the ways in which we normally think of objects.

This being so, we cannot hope to know God in an intellectual way. Again like Gregory of Nyssa, Pseudo-Dionysius uses the imagery of Moses' ascending the holy mountain and meeting God in the cloud and the darkness:

> He breaks free of them, away from what sees and is seen, and he plunges into the truly mysterious darkness of unknowing. Here, renouncing all that the mind may conceive, wrapped entirely in the intangible and the invisible, he belongs completely to him who is beyond everything. Here, being neither oneself nor someone else, one is supremely united by a completely unknowing inactivity of all knowledge, and knows beyond the mind by knowing nothing.
> *The Mystical Theology* I.I

This intensely poetic language is intended to convey the paradoxical way one can know God only by consciously "unknowing" him. "Unknowing" does not mean simple ignorance; it is the conscious recognition that God transcends knowledge, and the active grasping after God in that recognition.

Influence

The influence of the self-styled Areopagite was immense, undoubtedly due in part to the belief that his works really were written by a disciple of Paul. It also helped that Dionysius the Areopagite was often confused with another Dionysius or Denis, the patron saint of Paris, and so Parisian scholars were particularly interested in him. In fact, Pseudo-Dionysius was the last major theologian to be an important influence on both Western and Eastern Christianity. In the West, his theology of hierarchies resounded through the Middle Ages. It provided a theology to support the social system of feudalism and the correspondingly hierarchical structure of the Catholic Church.

THE THIRD COUNCIL
OF CONSTANTINOPLE

The monothelite controversy had been raging for decades. It had driven a wedge between the great sees of Rome, where monothelitism, the belief that Christ had only one will, was rejected, and Constantinople, where it was affirmed, pushing the two wings of the church even further apart. It was time to do something about it.

The sixth great council of the church accordingly met at Constantinople in 680. Emperor Constantine Pogonatus was in the chair. His predecessor, Constans II, had been murdered in his bath twelve years earlier. Constans had supported monothelitism but tried to restore order with his Typus, an imperial ban on discussing the matter at all. That had totally failed.

The death of Constans had removed one good reason for upholding mono-

Yet despite the huge importance of this theology, it is dwarfed by Pseudo-Dionysius's place in the roll of mystics. It was through him that the mysticism of negation, pioneered by Gregory of Nyssa, was transmitted to the future. It was a central influence in the doctrine of God of the medieval theologians, particularly Thomas Aquinas. It was also the basic foundation on which the medieval mystics and the early modern Spanish mystics built. His influence in the East was even greater; for centuries the works of the Areopagite remained the standard by which all spiritual theology was judged.

Maximus the Confessor

Maximus is one of the most cherished heroes of the Orthodox Church. He is remembered as a great theologian and profound spiritual writer who stood virtually alone against the doctrinal errors of a generation. He is also honored for the terrible sufferings he endured for his faith, for which he is given the title Confessor, one rank below a martyr.

Life

Maximus was an aristocrat, born in Constantinople in about 580. He enjoyed an excellent education before rising to become personal secretary to the emperor. However, he soon found even the Christian majesty of the imperial court unsatis-

thelitism. Another good reason had been removed by the Muslim empire, which had swept across the Middle East and North Africa with dizzying speed, overwhelming the Monophysite and Nestorian churches that lay in its path. With the Monophysites a dwindling force, there was less and less reason for the Orthodox to try to win them back by holding on to monothelitism, a doctrine that was similar to what Monophysites believed and that appealed to them.

The council therefore condemned the monothelite doctrine, laying down as unassailable orthodoxy the doctrine of Maximus the Confessor that Christ had a human will as well as a divine one. As the Sixth Ecumenical Council, its teachings would become the standard of truth in the Eastern Church.

fying and retreated to the Chrysopolis Monastery. He later became the abbot of the community.

At Chrysopolis, Maximus quickly became known as a powerful and profound theologian. Unfortunately he was also a rebel. He saw no need to keep quiet when he disagreed with others, even the emperor himself. The result was a series of ignominious exiles and even beatings at the hands of his enemies. Little wonder that he commented morosely, "Friends are everywhere—that is, when you are doing well. In times of trial you can hardly find one" (*Four Hundred Chapters on Love* 4.94).

Maximus was fighting a doctrine that had become prevalent in the Orthodox Church, the doctrine that Christ had only one will. *Will* here means the decision-making part of the mind; it is our ability to decide things for ourselves. It was thought that the divine will within Christ overruled his human will so completely as to swallow it up. This notion became known as monothelitism, meaning "one will."

Monothelitism had become accepted by almost everyone in the East, since the alternative—two wills in Christ—seemed to make him into two people, the old Nestorian heresy. That seemed to open up the possibility that the human part of Christ might want one thing and the divine part another, clearly a ridiculous idea. Acceptance of the monothelite doctrine also had the happy consequence of calming the anxieties of the Monophysite Church in Egypt, which had split off from Orthodoxy after the Council of Chalcedon in the 5th century. Persuaded that the

Byzantines perhaps weren't quite as Nestorian as they had feared, some Monophysites joined the Orthodox Church again. Even the emperor, the all-powerful head of the church, believed in monothelitism. Only Maximus and a few others stood out against it, but they proved a persistent thorn in the flesh of the authorities.

In an effort to calm the situation, Heraclius, bishop of Constantinople, issued a statement in 638 suggesting that Christ had one will but two "energies." Nobody understood what this meant, and nobody agreed with it. The row intensified. Ten years later Emperor Constans II issued a decree called the Typus in which he simply forbade any argument over the matter and outlawed discussion of either "will" or "energy" in Christ. That didn't have much effect either.

The Roman Church disagreed with the monothelites, and Maximus found sanctuary in the West, rebuffing a series of Eastern envoys who tried to get him to submit to the Typus. Maximus said that to forbid the use of an expression was to deny its truth, and he would not give up the doctrine of two wills in Christ. He also rejected the suggestion that Christ had one will according to his unity but two wills according to his natures—a pretty desperate formula designed to please everybody that made no sense whatsoever.

Eventually, in 662, Maximus was brought to Constantinople and tried for heresy. His right hand was cut off and his tongue ripped out to prevent him from spreading his errors, and he was dragged around the city so that everyone could see his mutilated condition. He died later that year in exile.

But Maximus's arguments did not die with him. Within 20 years monothelitism had been condemned by the Third Council of Constantinople, and Maximus was revered as the champion of orthodoxy.

Thought

Maximus spent his life battling the doctrine—or heresy, as he saw it—that Christ had only one will. He pointed out that the will is a faculty that derives from nature. That is, part of what it is to possess human nature, to be a human person, is to have a will of your own. If you are inherently unable to make decisions for yourself, you are lacking something that is essential to human nature. So to deny that Christ possessed two wills, a human one and a divine one, is to deny that he has two natures. To deny that he had a fully human will is to deny that he is fully human. It is to deny the orthodox faith as laid down at Chalcedon and to slip into Monophysitism, the heretical notion that Christ had only one nature. At the same time, Maximus did deny that Christ's two wills could have disagreed. Christ the man was totally obedient to God and perfectly united to him; his two wills were therefore in perfect harmony and always willed the same thing.

Why was Maximus so obstinate? The issue of how many wills Christ had hardly seems important enough to risk the imperial wrath over—in fact we might think it a fairly petty and unimportant matter. But Maximus was not just a dogmatic theologian, rigidly refusing to abandon what he saw as the logical consequence of Chalcedon. He was also a mystic, a spiritual writer in the tradition of Origen and Pseudo-Dionysius. The heart of his spirituality was the union of humanity with Christ and the union of Christ with God. Through Christ, humanity can become united to God. This very Christ-centered mysticism depends on the true union of Christ with both humanity and God and demands that he be fully God and fully human. So the heart of Maximus's faith rested on the doctrine of Chalcedon, and he was prepared to risk anything to defend that doctrine. Just like Athanasius and Cyril before him, he recognized that what might seem like pedantic bickering over irrelevant matters actually cut right to the heart of Christianity itself.

Symeon the New Theologian

"The Theologian" may not sound like a particularly exciting title, but the Orthodox Church has seen fit to bestow it on only three people: John the Evangelist, Gregory of Nazianzus and Symeon. These three alone are considered to have been wholly suffused with longing for and intimacy with the divine to the extent that they could truly talk about God.

Life

Like Maximus the Confessor, Symeon was the son of a Byzantine nobleman. Born in 949, he received an excellent education and was sent to work in the imperial court, where he became a diplomat and senator. While a teenager, he met the venerable Symeon of Studia, a famous monk, and decided he wanted to follow in his footsteps. The older man told him he was too young, however, and forced him to continue his worldly career until the age of 27. Young Symeon did his best, spending his evenings in quiet contemplation and prayer; even in Byzantium this must have been fairly unusual behavior for an imperial senator.

When he was finally allowed to enter the monastery, Symeon's great zeal for the holy life annoyed even the other monks, who thought him a bit extreme. He was forced to move to a smaller monastery, where his exemplary life brought him to the post of abbot within three years. As abbot he sought to enforce a rigorous rule of life on the monks, true to the teachings of Christ and the Fathers. Unfortunately some of the more worldly monks were not happy about this and rebelled. A riot during a church service ended with Symeon's opponents being repelled and sent into exile, but his reputation had been damaged.

THE SECOND COUNCIL OF NICAEA

The Seventh Ecumenical Council was called to deal with the last great theological dispute of the Orthodox Church—the iconoclasm controversy.

Icons were an integral part of Orthodox worship. An icon is a picture of Christ or a saint, painted in a heavily stylized manner. It is intended not only as a work of art of great beauty but as an aid to devotion, both in private and in church. But many people in the Byzantine empire disapproved of this tradition. They were possibly influenced by Islam, which forbade all images, as well as by lingering Gnosticism, which distrusted all material things. Like some of the extreme Protestant Puritans in the West in later centuries, they felt that the use of such things in worship was basically idolatry. They were known as the iconoclasts, or "icon-smashers."

Controversy erupted in 726, when the Byzantine emperor Leo III took up the iconoclast cause enthusiastically, smashing icons everywhere and persecuting those who stood up for them. Monasteries were destroyed, monks were killed, and relics as well as pictures of saints were burned. When Germanus, bishop of Constantinople, protested at the destruction of a famous picture of Christ over the palace gateway, he was swiftly deposed and replaced. Leo was resisted by the most outstanding theologian of the day, John of Damascus, who, ironically, was safe to say what he liked because he lived in Muslim territory.

The iconoclasts argued that the use of icons was idolatry and contravened the First Commandment. John replied:

> *In the old days, the incorporeal and shapeless God was never depicted. Now, however, when God is seen clothed in flesh, and conversing with humanity, I make an image of the God whom I see. I do not worship matter, I worship the God of matter, who became matter for my sake, and was prepared to inhabit matter, who worked out my salvation through matter. I will not cease from honoring that matter which works my salvation. I venerate it, though not as God.*

On Holy Images

For John and his supporters, the veneration of icons represented a profound faith in the incarnation. God appeared as a human being: that means not only that material things are intrinsically good but that God can be represented. And he can be validly known and experienced through images of Christ and of his saints. Those images are not worshiped in themselves, but those who look on them with eyes of faith can look through them to the invisible mysteries beyond, just as those who saw Jesus could, if they chose, look through him to the Father. In a roundabout sort of way, the iconoclast dispute was the last of the great christological debates of the early church. For a man like John, just like Maximus the Confessor before him, and Cyril of Alexandria before him, and Athanasius before him, the issue had to do with the deepest truth of Orthodox Christianity—the union of God with humanity.

As with so many disputes before, this one continued for as long as the emperors provoked it. Leo's son, Constantine V, was even harsher than his father. But eventually the less puritanical, more profound spirituality of John and his followers won out. In 787 Empress Irene called the Second Council of Nicaea, at which over three hundred bishops condemned iconoclasm. Iconoclast has since taken on the general meaning of a cultural maverick who goes against what most people believe; and today Orthodox churches are still full of icons of every description.

It was quite fitting that this council should have taken place at Nicaea (it would have been at Constantinople, but there were too many iconoclastic soldiers there), for it was the last of the great ecumenical councils of the Orthodox Church. There is no reason, in theory, why there should not be an eighth, but there never has been yet. Since 787 the Orthodox Church has been the Church of the Seven Councils.

The foremost theologian at the imperial court, Stephen, called Symeon's orthodoxy into question and challenged him to a public debate on the Trinity. Symeon's simple devotional theology was no match for Stephen's hard-line logic-chopping, and the abbot was forced into exile. In 1009 he founded a new, small monastery in a ruined chapel in a remote village. Here, together with a few followers, he devoted himself to writing and prayer. His orthodoxy was eventually vindicated, and Sergios, bishop of Constantinople, even offered to make him a bishop; but Symeon would have none of it. He remained at his retreat until his death in 1022.

Thought

Symeon was a master of spiritual theology rather than dogmatic theology, as his duel with Stephen showed only too well. He was first and foremost a monk concerned with living a holy life, and he had little time for those who complained that a holy life was impossible because of human imperfection or original sin. Like Pe-

THE RISE OF ISLAM

In the 630s a new barbarian horde appeared from the East. It was not just another raiding party from the Arabian peninsula. A new world power had arisen.

Islam had been founded by Muhammad, a prophet and military commander from Mecca, who had received a series of divine revelations that would later be written down in the Qur'an. Under his leadership the first Muslims had fought battle after battle to win the political and spiritual allegiance of the Arab world. Now, after his death in 632, his followers were organizing themselves into a mighty military force that would win half the world for Allah and his Prophet.

The word Islam means "submission," and a Muslim is one who submits to God; the first Muslims did not take lightly their duty to spread this submission by any means possible. Within five years of Muhammad's death the Persian capital, Ctesiphon, was under Muslim rule. By 638 the Muslims had defeated Byzantine forces and occupied Jerusalem. Throughout the 640s and 650s they swept through North Africa.

By the 8th century, Spain had been conquered. Most of the old Roman empire bowed to the Caliph, and still the expansion continued into Asia and Sicily. In Syria and Egypt, the Nestorian and Monophysite churches found them-

lagius centuries before, he declared that no one other than Adam is guilty for Adam's sin, and he emphasized human freedom to choose right or wrong.

But he was no Pelagian in the sense of denying an integral divine role in salvation. Like the Fathers before him, Symeon thinks of salvation as consisting of union with the divine, brought about by the incarnation of God as man, but he put a very personal and individual spin on this idea. It is not simply that Christ unites the whole human race to God, as in the theology of Irenaeus. Rather, personal union with Christ, and through him with God, is the goal of every individual life. We must spend our whole life striving toward this.

Yet it is not simply a goal that we hope for at the end of our life. Union with Christ and the presence of God in our heart can be grasped even now, transforming our life in love. There is a "now but not yet" element to Symeon's theology, which remains very true to the spirit of the New Testament.

Symeon emphasizes the reality of God to the believer and the possibility of

selves being slowly swamped and strangled by the Muslim flood. They began to dwindle in both numbers and theological activity. Meanwhile the once-mighty Byzantine empire, having lost most of its territory, retreated into Constantinople, which for centuries even the power of Islam seemed unable to topple.

From the Muslims' point of view, the loss of Spain between the 13th and 15th centuries was more than compensated for by the final conquest of Byzantium in 1453. The Byzantine empire was crushed. Its capital, now known as Istanbul, became the capital of the Islamic world.

The incredible rise of Islam as a military and spiritual power had an immense influence on Christianity. Superficially, it provided medieval Christendom with a rival power, an "infidel" in a cold war that simmered for centuries before finally erupting into the Crusades. But there was a more positive influence too. Islam developed a rich spiritual tradition known as Sufism and a flourishing revival of mathematics, science and philosophy. The works of Muslim philosophers and theologians such as Avicenna and Averröes influenced Christian thinkers such as Thomas Aquinas. Even more important, the Muslim philosophers rediscovered the ancient works of Aristotle, and it was through the Muslims that the medieval West came to learn of them.

drawing near to him. He is a theologian of light, using this imagery to stress both
the glory and the positive self-revelation of God to the mystic. At the same time he
is careful to stress the incomprehensibility of God. In this way he develops the illumination spirituality of Origen but tempers it with an element of the darkness
spirituality of Gregory of Nyssa.

> Whenever someone sees God revealed, he sees light. He is amazed at what
> he sees—but at the same time he does not know straight away who has ap-
> peared. He does not even dare ask. How could he? He cannot even lift up his
> eyes and gaze upon that majesty. Instead, overcome by fear and trembling, he
> looks down at his own feet.
> *On the Mystical Life*

Origen had described the process of divine illumination as an intellectual progression—the purifying of the mind and learning of divine doctrines. For Symeon, by
contrast, it is a deeply emotional process, experienced fully by the whole person. In
one striking passage he describes how, as a novice, he experienced it for the first
time:

> Father, that light appeared to me. The walls of my cell melted away and the
> whole world vanished. I think it was fleeing before his face. I alone remained,
> in the presence of the light. And father, I do not know if I was still in my
> body or carried outside it. I completely forgot that I even have a body. I felt
> such great joy within me—and it is still in me now—great love and also great
> longing—and I wept streams of tears, just as you see me doing now.
> *On the Mystical Life*

Symeon's works are full of passages like this, brimming over with wonder and
love at his rapturous experiences of God. The extraordinarily personal and in-
timate character of his writing, combined with his strong emphasis on the individual's experience of God, gives Symeon a claim to be considered the Augustine of the Orthodox Church. Yet he lacks the morbid obsession with guilt that
pervades Augustine's works. This makes Symeon one of the most engaging and
attractive mystics in Christian history. The renewed interest in him today
among writers on Orthodox spirituality is well deserved.

The Great Schism

In 1054 a group of ambassadors from Rome stormed into the great cathedral of
St. Sophia in Constantinople. They marched up to the magnificent altar and placed

upon it a papal bull of excommunication. As they left, the cathedral's priests chased after them, trying to give the bull back. There was a scuffle, and the solemn document ended up in the road.

The pope had excommunicated the entire Eastern Church. How could such a thing have happened?

The Eastern and Western wings of the church had been drifting further and further apart for centuries. In the West, the collapse of the empire had led the church to become more centrally organized under the pope. In the East, the supreme figurehead of the church was the Byzantine emperor. Ultimate authority in the West lay with the pope; in the East it lay with the seven great councils, and although the bishop of Constantinople was regarded as the most important ecclesiastical figure, he was the first among equals. The Western Church was a monarchy, while the Eastern one was a republic.

The Westerners were increasingly irritated at the Easterners' refusal to accept the total authority of the pope. The Easterners, for their part, were incensed by the West's stubborn insistence that the Spirit proceeds from the Son as well as the Father, an innovation that went back to Augustine. Not only did the Catholics hold this erroneous teaching, they had the audacity to insert it into the Nicene Creed, supposedly the very bulwark of the faith. The inferior scholarship of the West meant that the Latins, for their part, genuinely believed that the doctrine was in the Nicene Creed and that the Greeks had erased it.

Given these differences, there was little prospect of reconciliation between the Latin-speaking West and the Greek-speaking East. The condemnation of 1054, which was followed by a series of counter-condemnations, was simply the most dramatic moment in a long and painful divorce. In later years the squabble was to become even more bitter, culminating in the ransacking of Constantinople by Catholic Crusaders in 1204. The Roman Catholic and Eastern Orthodox churches have remained at odds ever since, each convinced that it alone holds the true teaching and tradition of the Fathers. Only in recent decades, following the Second Vatican Council in the 1960s, has a new spirit of mutual respect and cooperation appeared.

Gregory Palamas

Gregory Palamas is the last of the great Byzantine theologians. Like Aquinas in the West, he summed up and reformulated the traditions of his predecessors, creating a touchstone of orthodoxy for the future. He accomplished this at a time of enormous uncertainty, as the empire spiraled toward oblivion and as he was taking a leading political role in the attempt to bring about peace and stability.

Life

Like most other great Byzantine theologians, Palamas did not exactly work his way up from a humble background. His father was a senator, close friend of the emperor and tutor to the emperor's son and heir. Born in 1296, Gregory was the same age as the young prince—and when his father died, the 7-year-old Gregory was taken in by the emperor.

Palamas received the best possible education, excelling at the Imperial University, which at that time was in the charge of the famed Theodore Metochites, known (with typical Byzantine panache) as the Great Logothete. When he was 17, Palamas gave such a good interpretation of Aristotle before an assembly that included the emperor that the Great Logothete declared that if Aristotle himself had been present he would have bowed to the young philosopher.

However, Palamas was not very interested in secular learning, which he regarded as a good thing but incompatible with a truly spiritual life. It was the latter that really attracted him, even as a teenager; at the age of 20 he finally rejected the glittering career that lay ahead and headed for Mount Athos, the holy mountain that was the heart of Byzantine spirituality.

Palamas stayed for eight years, until Muslim attacks in 1325 forced many monks to leave. He then made his way to Thessalonica, where he was ordained priest, before retiring again to a hermitage on a mountain near Berea. Here he continued his forays into the spiritual world, spending weekends attending services with other hermits and the rest of the week in total isolation. He was becoming a master at the hesychastic tradition of spirituality, a technique that stressed the position of the body and the mantralike repetition of short prayers to bring about a state of complete calm and awareness in which the mystic could hope to meet God.

Then it was Serb attacks that put Palamas's life in danger, and after five years at Berea he returned to Mount Athos. There his profound spirituality began to make him well known, and he started to write.

Although he was venerated by many, some people considered hesychastic spirituality heretical, and the rising star of the movement inevitably encountered controversy. In about 1330 a man named Barlaam appeared in Constantinople. Although an easterner, Barlaam had been educated in the West, and he quickly established a reputation as a leading philosopher and man of science. It seems that no one believed in this reputation more than Barlaam himself. Ambitious and arrogant, he had little time for anyone he considered his intellectual inferior, which included virtually everyone he met. In character he seems to have been a lot like the Western theologian Peter Abelard—but unlike Abelard, the reality did not really live up to the hype.

Barlaam particularly didn't get on with Palamas. They first fell out over the doctrine of the Trinity. Hoping to reunite the Catholic and Orthodox churches, Barlaam had argued that differences between the two churches' doctrines of the Trinity were irrelevant since no one can have certain knowledge about God anyway. Palamas vigorously objected to this relativist outlook and to the worldly Aristotelian logic that underlay it. Barlaam responded with an attack on the spiritual methods used by Palamas and the other hesychasts. He laughed at their breathing techniques, use of verbal repetition and belief that the body can be used in prayer; and he mockingly dubbed them the "belly-soul people."

In 1338 Barlaam appealed to the bishop of Constantinople to have the hesychasts condemned. The bishop ruled in favor of the monks and ordered Barlaam to leave the matter alone. Barlaam ignored this, and the affair began to spiral out of control. Barlaam and Palamas exchanged increasingly hostile pamphlets, and Barlaam stepped up his calls to have Palamas condemned. The bishop of Constantinople, John Calecas, was an ambitious politician and reluctant to be drawn into an unsavory doctrinal dispute; but he finally agreed to call a council in 1341 to try to settle the matter.

Both Barlaam and Palamas attended with large numbers of supporters, but Palamas had the advantage since Emperor Andronicus III, who presided, had been his childhood friend. Barlaam was accordingly ordered to confess his errors. Even the death of the emperor five days later did not reverse the general anti-Barlaam feeling of most of Constantinople, and after some further sniping Barlaam eventually got fed up and returned to the Western Church, where he was really happier.

Unfortunately, matters now became complicated by the outbreak of civil war. The dead emperor's son was only nine years old, and there were two claimants to the regency: John Calecas, bishop of Constantinople, and John Cantacuzene, the Great Domestic, another splendid Byzantine title meaning a powerful minister or chancellor. Cantacuzene was called away on military business, so Calecas promptly seized the throne.

Palamas supported Cantacuzene and deplored Calecas's ambition, which he feared threatened the safety of the empire. But he submitted to Calecas and pressed for peace between the two sides. Calecas, desperate to rid himself of someone he regarded as a dangerous subversive, tried to have Palamas's theology condemned and eventually arrested him and had him imprisoned in a monastery. This cannot have been much of a punishment from Palamas's point of view, but it was reinforced in 1344, when Calecas secured his excommunication. However, in 1346 Cantacuzene returned. Calecas's support melted away, Cantacuzene was crowned emperor (his supposed status as mere regent being forgotten), and Palamas was raised to the post of bishop of Thessalonica in reward for his loyalty.

But there was to be no durable peace in the closing century of the Byzantine

MOUNT ATHOS

The holy mountain of Athos is one of the most awe-inspiring Christian sites in the world. A rocky peninsula jutting out from the Greek mainland, its sandy coves and thickly forested flanks sweep majestically up to the two-thousand-meter-high peak of the holy mountain itself. Twenty monasteries and innumerable smaller communities jostle for space in this remarkable setting, some perched high on the crags, floating ethereally over the Aegean Sea.

According to legend, the Virgin Mary saw Mount Athos while making a sea journey with John the Evangelist. Struck by its beauty, she persuaded God to give it to her as a garden of refuge to those seeking salvation.

It was a while before the promise was fulfilled, since monks arrived only gradually during the Dark Ages. But the rugged beauty and seclusion of the peninsula was a powerful magnet for those who disliked the harsh and increasingly overcrowded Egyptian and Syrian deserts, and by the middle of the 11th century there were seven thousand monks there, in several monasteries. Various special privileges were granted to the communities by the emperor at this time, including a law, which remains in effect, forbidding all females of any species to set foot on the mountain.

empire. Continuing anti-Cantacuzene protests prevented the new bishop from entering Thessalonica until 1350. Even worse, the young John, son of the old emperor, grew up and launched a fresh civil war against the self-proclaimed emperor and former Great Domestic Cantacuzene. John was based in Thessalonica and in close contact with Palamas. The peace of Mount Athos seemed further away than ever.

One of the most extraordinary events in Palamas's life occurred in 1354. Emperor John sent the bishop as a special envoy to discuss peace terms with Cantacuzene, something the peace-loving Palamas was more than happy to do. Unfortunately his ship was blown off course to Gallipoli, where he and his companions were captured by Muslims who had just occupied the town. The Muslims treated their illustrious prisoner very well, allowing him to visit various towns throughout Turkey and finally taking him to the court of the great emir Orkhan.

The emir was very keen to learn about Christianity and arranged a meeting between Palamas and his Muslim theologians. The amicable discussion that resulted was disrupted by a third group that was present, some former Christians who had

Cats were the only exception allowed.

Deprived of female interference, the holy mountain became the beating heart of Byzantine spirituality. As Byzantine politics degenerated into petty intrigues, civil wars and political back-stabbing, Mount Athos became a refuge to those tired of it all.

The inevitable collapse of the empire hit the monasteries hard, particularly after 1424, when the Turks captured the peninsula and imposed crippling taxes on the monks; but the church provided the wherewithal to allow them to remain.

Today, despite centuries of decline, the monasteries remain on Mount Athos and operate as a semi-autonomous state within Greece. There chants are still sung and icons still painted as they have been for over a millennium, with only the cries of seagulls to punctuate the numinous silence. Yet the mountain is no museum. The revival enjoyed by Orthodox spirituality in recent decades has caused the twenty monasteries to thrive in a way unknown for centuries. The holy mountain remains the center of Orthodox spirituality and seems likely to do so for the next thousand years.

converted to Judaism as a sort of middle road between Christianity and Islam. This group came off worst in the argument, and one of them punched Palamas before being dragged off to face the wrath of the emir.

In general, apart from this bust-up, Palamas seems to have had a thoroughly pleasant, if unexpected, holiday in Turkey and was so pleased to have the opportunity to experience Islam and discuss Christianity from a new point of view that he stayed for over a year. On his return home he found that John had defeated Cantacuzene, although the latter remained an important political figure.

Palamas was becoming increasingly unwell, despite his continued activities both in his see and at court. He died in 1359 and was almost immediately venerated as a saint throughout the empire. He was officially canonized in 1368.

Thought

Gregory Palamas is often thought of as the Orthodox Church's answer to Thomas Aquinas. Like Aquinas, Palamas was not a hugely creative theologian; he sought to restate the classical Christian doctrines in a newly integrated and relevant way and as a result created something like the final word in classical Orthodox theology. His work is a distillation of the 13 centuries of Orthodox theology that preceded it, enriched by a lifetime of meditation on the New Testament and the church fathers. There is little in it that cannot be found at least in some form in the Fathers; from the point of view of the Orthodox Church and of Palamas himself, of course, this is its greatest strength.

Palamas's most interesting contributions to the history of Christian thought are his doctrine of God and his defense of hesychastic mysticism.

God. Like that of all Byzantine theologians, Palamas's thinking concerning God ran along the lines laid down by Pseudo-Dionysius centuries before. He emphasizes the fact that God transcends all earthly ways of thinking and cannot really be known:

> It is not just a "God" who transcends beings, but something more than God; the greatness of the one who transcends everything is not only higher than all positive descriptions, but also higher than all negative ones; it transcends all greatness that you could think of.
> *Triads* 2.3.8

But he is not content to leave it like this. Simply saying that God is unknowable leads ultimately to the relativism of Barlaam, which Palamas strenuously opposed. Instead Palamas wants to stress the fact that through Christ we do in fact know this unknowable God.

How can this be, if God is intrinsically unknowable? Palamas answers with what at first seems a rather strange distinction: the difference between God's essence and his "energies." God's essence is eternally unknowable. When we experience God, or when God acts on us, we are dealing with his energy, which is something different.

It might seem that Palamas is reverting to the old Logos theology of Justin Martyr and inventing a "half-God" to hover between the unknowable God and the world—and indeed his opponents accused him of ditheism, or belief in two Gods. Palamas is certainly motivated by similar concerns to Justin's: a desire to reconcile God's greatness with the fact that he can be experienced by imperfect creatures. But the divine energy is not a separate entity from God. It is God himself, acting. That is, to say that we experience God's energies rather than his essence is to say that we know God through his actions. We know him only when he acts on us.

Palamas's understanding of God is therefore a dynamic one, a significant advance on the static Neoplatonism of Pseudo-Dionysius. It owes much to the similar theology of Gregory of Nyssa.

The distinction between God's essence and his energies also allows Palamas to reconcile different views of God, because he can accept that certain claims are true of the energies that are not true of the essence. For example, he strongly upholds the Orthodox belief that the Spirit proceeds from the Father alone but accepts that while this is true for God's essence, the Spirit may proceed from both Father and Son at the level of the energies. Put another way, we may *experience* the Spirit as given by both Father and Son, although in the heart of the Godhead he proceeds from the Father alone. So without compromising Orthodox tradition, Palamas is able to open up an avenue of dialogue with the West.

Palamas's doctrine of the energies is rooted in the Christian conviction that we know God fully, but not through our own efforts, only through his action on us. It is based in part on Palamas's own experience as a hesychastic mystic.

Hesychasm and human nature. The word *hesychasm* means "silence" or "tranquillity." In the 4th century it came to mean the peaceful state achieved by mystics who have successfully risen above the clamor of the body's passions and who are close to seeing God.

By Palamas's time, hesychasm was a special form of spirituality that emphasized the role of the body. Influenced by mystics like Symeon the New Theologian, hesychast monks used breathing exercises to achieve mental calm, repeated short prayers over and over again, and adopted particular bodily positions. The practices were quite similar to Eastern meditation or yoga and resulted in a self-hypnotic state of heightened awareness in which the mystic could hope to see God.

Opponents of the practice, such as Barlaam, argued that only the mind can come to see God. They appealed to the tradition, going back to Origen, that the mind is the true part of human nature, the part that is like God, and to see God we must rise above bodily things. Prayer should be a purely mental affair with no contribution from the body at all.

Palamas, who quickly became a master of the hesychastic technique, argued vigorously against these ideas. In doing so he elaborated an alternative, more sophisticated theology of human nature.

For Palamas, the body is not a discardable appendage to the mind, like a coat that can be removed at death. On the contrary, it is an essential part of human nature. In fact, he even argues that human beings are superior to angels because they have bodies. It is through the body that humans have dominion over the earth, and it was the body as well as the soul that Christ elevated to the heights of divinity when he became incarnate. In fact it is through the body of Christ that we are united to God. The incarnation is a guarantee of the goodness of the body.

Palamas therefore distances himself from the Origenist, and Neoplatonic, idea that the body is somehow the cause of sin. He is much closer to the Syrian, and biblical, tradition of viewing human nature in an integrated way, without drawing a clear line of separation between body and soul.

So it is entirely appropriate that the body should have a part to play in prayer, and Palamas points out that Orthodox tradition regards bodily posture during prayer as an important matter. It reflects the presence of Christ in the person who prays, not just in their mind but throughout their whole person.

Hesychasm, then, is central to Palamas's conception not only of human nature but of salvation itself. He defends the practice so vigorously because he considers its opponents to be attacking the doctrine of the incarnation, a doctrine that for Palamas revolves around the body of Christ.

The Third Rome

The fall of Constantinople to the Muslims in 1453 must have seemed like the end of the world to Eastern Christians. The Orthodox Church had been shattered.

Yet the fall of Byzantium coincided with the rise of a new power to defend the church. Russia had been converted to Orthodoxy in the late 10th century and had become an important Christian power until 1237, when it was invaded by the Mongolian armies of Genghis Khan, also known as the Tartars. Kiev, the political and spiritual center of Russia, was sacked.

The church, however, remained and became a focus for Russian nationalism. The monasteries prospered and spread north and east into the great northern forests, just as their spiritual ancestors had once done in the deserts of Egypt. Like their equivalents in the West, the monasteries were major centers of learning and of art, and the great traditions of Byzantine iconography were successfully transplanted to Russia.

The power of the Tartars was waning by the end of the 14th century, and by the time of the fall of Constantinople, Russia was, for all intents and purposes, a free nation again. Its new capital was Moscow, a city whose importance was based on its location on a major trade route and which had led the fight against the Tartars. Many Russians felt that it had been raised up providentially just as the Byzantine empire fell. In 1510 a monk named Philotheus of Pskov wrote in a famous letter:

> The Apostolic Church stands no longer in Rome or Constantinople, but in the blessed city of Moscow. She alone shines in the whole world brighter than the sun. . . . All Christian empires are fallen and in their stead stands alone the Empire of our ruler in accordance with the Prophetical books. Two Romes have fallen, but the third stands and a fourth there will not be.

Rome had fallen and had been replaced by Constantinople, the Second Rome; now that too had been found unworthy. Just as Charlemagne in the West had once styled himself "the New Roman emperor," so now the rulers of Russia claimed to inherit the temporal and spiritual power of the Byzantine emperor. In 1472 the Russian king Ivan the Great legitimized this claim by marrying the niece of the last Byzantine emperor; and in 1547 his successor, Ivan IV, became the first to call himself Czar—a corruption of "Caesar." The double-headed eagle, which had once been the symbol of Rome, was now the symbol of Russia. Moscow began to reinvent itself, embarking on a major rebuilding program. New cathedrals were erected, together with a new palace, the Kremlin, all in the style of Byzantine architecture. For four and a half centuries after the fall of the Second Rome, the Third Rome would stand unassailable as the bastion of Eastern Christianity.

3
THE MIDDLE AGES

The Middle Ages saw a new Europe arise from the ruins of the empire, a continent of nations with a strong sense of their identity. United by the Catholic Church and the power of the papacy, the Middle Ages was the age of "Christendom," an age that reached its peak in the 13th century. Great cathedrals and monasteries were built throughout Europe, and a new breed of theologian arose. Where once Europe's greatest minds had devoted themselves to philosophy and science, they now turned to careful systematizing of Christianity. Faith and religion, reason and science and philosophy were all united into a seamless body of learning.

To modern minds the works of the medieval theologians can seem strange, incomprehensible or just plain dull. They certainly don't seem to have much to do with Christianity as most people know it today. But beneath the arid appearance of these writers lies a profound spiritual vision, a depth of emotion and poetry that has rarely been equaled. That, together with the unsurpassed intellectual sophistication of their thinking, makes their theology timelessly valuable.

The Dark Ages

The barbarians were on the move. Throughout the 3rd and 4th centuries, wandering tribes were migrating across Russia and Europe—the Goths, Visigoths, Vandals and countless others. These new peoples swept across the borders of the old empire in wave upon endless wave.

The strengthening of the government and reunification of the battered empire in the 4th century by Diocletian and Constantine saved the system from collapse for 100 years, but the end was inevitable. In 410 Rome itself was ransacked by the Visigoths. In 476 the ancient capital was actually captured by a barbarian king, Odoacer, who installed himself as ruler.

The Eastern part of the empire survived for nearly 1,000 years more, in the form of the Byzantine empire, ruled from the mighty city of Constantinople. Here learning and scholarship flourished, although it was a sterile blooming, endlessly dwelling on the intellectual glories of the past and lacking in innovation or originality.

In the West the empire was gone, replaced by various small tribes and kingdoms. The imperial army was no more, and the imperial postal service, the symbol of central government and political integrity, had ceased to run.

As political unity collapsed, the unity of the church grew. Most of the barbarians were Christians, although they tended to be Arians, and people found a sense of unity in the church that was no longer provided by the state. Where a single ruler had once governed the whole empire, so now the power of the church began to be collected into the hands of a single figure, the bishop of Rome. The title Pope, meaning "father," had originally been applied to any great and powerful bishop— so there had been a pope in Carthage and another in Alexandria—but now there was only one pope, and he was in Rome.

One of the most important popes of the period was Gregory the Great, who ascended to the post in 590. Unwilling to accept the responsibility of the job, he had himself smuggled out of Rome in a huge wicker basket and fled, but he was soon caught and installed. As pope, Gregory, a man of great humility, called himself "the servant of the servants of God." Yet he also acted, in the absence of anyone better, as civil and even military governor of the city of Rome, which Gregory had seen reduced to a pathetic remnant of its former greatness as it was conquered and reconquered by Byzantine and European forces. Sweeping reforms were introduced into the church, including important monastic and liturgical shakeups; Gregory's revision of church music gave rise to the tradition of Gregorian chant.

Gregory was the most powerful pope yet, setting a highly significant precedent for the future. The Catholic Church was taking the place of the Roman empire as the greatest force for unity in a fragmented and uncertain world. The West, under the pope, and the East, under the Byzantine emperor, were drifting apart. They would never be reconciled.

The Holy Roman Empire

On Christmas Day the Frankish King Charles was praying in the great cathedral of St. Peter's in Rome. Suddenly Pope Leo entered. Striding to the king, he produced a crown and set it on his head. Kneeling before him—the only pope ever to make such obeisance to a mere king—he proclaimed Charles the new Roman emperor. The year was A.D. 800.

Charles the Great, or Charlemagne, was the most powerful ruler in Europe. By 800 he had conquered not only all of modern France but also parts of Spain, most of Italy, Hungary and Austria, and a significant part of Germany. The coronation at Rome—a strangely stage-managed piece of early medieval spin doctoring—was a formal recognition that Charlemagne, and not the Byzantine emperor in the distant and mysterious East, was the true successor to the Roman emperors, the founder of a new empire.

This empire was to be ruled not by Romans but by North Europeans. Tall and powerful, Charlemagne was a prototype for the medieval kings who followed him. He was also a fiercely patriotic Frenchman who refused to wear anything other than his national dress. The world had moved on since the collapse of Rome. The future belonged to northern nationalistic monarchs like Charlemagne.

The new empire saw a revival in learning. Although he himself could hardly read, Charlemagne was determined to promote scholarship and attracted to his court the greatest intellects of his day. A new beacon of enlightenment was being raised to rival Byzantium in the East and Ireland in the West.

AUGUSTINE OF CANTERBURY

Gregory the Great, soon to become one of the most dynamic and influential popes of all time, was walking through the marketplace of Rome when he saw some tall, golden-haired boys for sale as slaves. "Who are they?" he asked. On being told that they were Angles—from Anglo-Saxon England— he replied, "Not Angles, but angels. What a shame that God's grace does not dwell within these beautiful brows!"

Gregory bought the slaves and had them raised in his monastery. He never forgot his wish for the rest of the Angles to be converted, however, and in 596, now pope, he sent a monk called Augustine from his monastery, together with a team of missionaries and translators, to distant Britain.

Britain was a strange and wild place. It had once been one of the most civilized parts of the Roman empire, but the withdrawal of imperial forces in 407 had left the island open to attack from foreign invaders. Angles, Saxons and Jutes had streamed across the North Sea and settled in the eastern and southern regions of the island, driving the Roman–British population west and north. The Roman Britons were Christian, and the kingdoms they established in Wales and Ireland would become beacons of enlightenment and learning as the Dark Ages settled over Europe. Meanwhile, back in what would become England, the Anglo-Saxon invaders had established

Despite this promise, the new Roman empire did not last. Charlemagne's death in 814 left his empire without a strong ruler. It continued to exist, technically, for just over 1,000 years, but by the end of the Middle Ages it had shrunk to become just one of the emerging nation-states of Europe. By the 10th century it had split into two, rather like the Roman empire it had supposedly replaced: the western half became France, while the eastern half became Germany and Austria. In 962 Pope John XII gave the rule of the empire to King Otto the Great of Germany, as a reward for chasing away the king of Italy, who had occupied the papal territories. John was a notoriously immoral and incompetent pope who was said to run the Vatican like a brothel and who subsequently fell out with Otto shortly before being mysteriously murdered. But he had made his mark on European history, because from then on the empire was ruled by Germanic rulers.

By the 12th and 13th centuries it had become known as the *Holy* Roman empire, and it is usually known by that name, even back to the time of Charlemagne, to

several powerful kingdoms—Kent, Wessex, Northumbria and others. These pagan kingdoms were engaged in a constant and bloody struggle for supremacy over each other.

Augustine—an Italian monk, not to be confused with the great theologian Augustine of Hippo—arrived in Kent, at that time the most powerful kingdom in England and the closest one to continental Europe. King Ethelbert of Kent was intrigued by the exotic visitors and allowed them to stay at his capital, Canterbury. Here they preached and won converts, including, in 597, Ethelbert himself. Augustine was duly consecrated as the first archbishop of Canterbury later that year.

The Christianization of the Anglo-Saxons had begun. Churches were built and more missionaries sent. A strong church structure was established, but the rowdy Anglo-Saxons took a long time to settle into line. Real order and structure did not come to the English Church until nearly a century after Augustine's landing, under Theodore of Canterbury. Theodore was a rather strange choice for English archbishop, being an aged Greek monk, but he surprised everybody by being remarkably good at his job and completely reshaping his church. The foundations of the future Church of England had been laid.

distinguish it from the "real" Roman empire. The empire finally came to an official end in 1806, when, under pressure from Napoleon, Francis II relinquished the title Holy Roman Emperor to become plain old emperor of Austria. Times had certainly changed in the many centuries since the glory days of Charlemagne—but the empire he had ruled was a political forerunner of the uniform religious Christendom, which, under the Catholic Church, would settle like a blanket over Western Europe throughout the Middle Ages.

Erigena

John the Scot, "Erigena," is one of the most fascinating and mysterious characters in European history. His influence has been detected behind everything from medieval Thomism to modern rationalism and even the Freemasons and the hippy movement. In the Dark Ages, popularly thought of as a period of unrelenting misery and barbarous ignorance, Erigena stands as a beacon of free thought.

Life

"Scot" means "Irishman" (the northern part of the British mainland was settled by the Irish, which is why it came to be called Scotland), and John was born in Ireland sometime after 800. Both intellectually and spiritually, Ireland was leagues

THE MONASTERIES

The Dark Ages had been a time of intellectual stifling. The Christian empire of Byzantium in the East and the growing centralization of the Catholic Church in the West permitted no independent philosophical or scientific thought outside the church. The old philosophical schools lay empty.

Yet learning was kept alive in the monasteries. The ideal of the desert fathers, hermits who took seriously the gospel command to forsake the world, had developed into tight-knit communities of monks all over the world. After the 4th and 5th centuries the monasteries were increasingly tightly organized as the monks took binding vows and followed rigid "rules" drawn up by a great monastic founder like Basil of Caesarea or Benedict of Nursia. Here the Scriptures and the Fathers were copied and read. The genius of antiquity had burned itself out, but its remains were preserved for the future.

Monasticism became very popular throughout the devout Byzantine empire. All monks obeyed the Rule of Basil just as they sought the Divine Darkness

ahead of most of the rest of Europe. The country had escaped the foreign invasions suffered everywhere else in the 5th and 6th centuries and rather like Byzantium in the East, it remained as an island of classical enlightenment. When Christian Britain had been overrun by pagan Anglo-Saxons, the Celtic Church had flourished in Ireland, and before the arrival of Augustine of Canterbury it had already begun sending missionaries to England and Scotland.

As an Irishman, then, John the Scot had access to unparalleled scholarly resources. These were becoming valuable commodities in his lifetime: the Holy Roman empire had been founded by Charlemagne shortly before John's birth, and classical learning and spirituality were flourishing in continental Europe. An Irish scholar could do a lot worse than head for France and offer his services to the court, and that is just what John did in about 845.

He quickly made a name for himself as one of the foremost scholars of the time and was invited by King Charles the Bald, Charlemagne's grandson, to become head of the Palatine Academy. Unlike most Western Europeans, John could read Greek, and he has become known by the Greek version of his name, Erigena, which simply means "Irish." In an age when Catholics were almost completely ignorant of the Eastern Orthodox tradition, Erigena devoted his time to studying mysterious authors like Gregory of Nyssa, Pseudo-Dionysius and Maximus the Confessor.

taught by his brother, Gregory of Nyssa. As the centuries passed, the desire to escape the world became even stronger, and monasteries were founded in increasingly inaccessible places. First there were the Meteora, monasteries built on spectacular mountain peaks in Turkey, safe from barbarian hordes. And then there were the famous monasteries of Mount Athos.

In the West, monasteries were places of learning as well as devotion. Unlike their Eastern counterparts, they changed greatly over the years. The Rule of Benedict was followed throughout western Europe for centuries, but the end of the Dark Ages saw the rise of new forms of monasticism to rival it. The great monastery of Cluny began founding daughter monasteries, all of which owed allegiance to the powerful abbot of Cluny. In this way the learning and spiritual teaching of Cluny spread throughout the world. The Cistercians, by contrast, established large numbers of independent monasteries all following the same Rule.

His most important endeavor was begun in about 858, when at the request of the Byzantine emperor he translated the works of Pseudo-Dionysius into Latin. So it was through Erigena that these immensely influential writings would become widely known in the West and central to the thought of Thomas Aquinas.

If the mystical writings of Pseudo-Dionysius seemed exotic to the scholars of the imperial court, they were nothing compared to Erigena's own works. These were the product of a mind completely rational, entirely individual and apparently wholly unconcerned by the need to conform to traditional dogma. Erigena had little time for those he considered heretics, but judging by his own books he must have had a fairly fluid notion, to say the least, of what counted as orthodox.

Trouble was inevitable. It began in 855, when Erigena's work on predestination, in which he denied that God foreordains some people to sin and damnation, was condemned as "Irish porridge." Tempers flared further when, in 870, he published his masterwork, *On the Division of Nature.*

One tradition concerning Erigena's death survives, which, if it is not true, certainly should be. It is said that he was recalled to Britain by King Alfred the Great and put in charge of the scholars at a monastery in Malmesbury, where his students eventually stabbed him to death with their pens because he made them think too hard.

Thought

Erigena was not a major theologian in the sense of making important new advances in doctrine or being very influential. But he is important as an example of the sort of philosophical theology that was possible even during what we call the Dark Ages and as a forerunner of the great things that were to come in the high Middle Ages.

In *On the Division of Nature* Erigena divided the world into four parts: God the Creator, the Logos and Platonic Forms, the material world, and God the goal of creation. This was a very Neoplatonic way of thinking, and indeed the whole work is permeated with Neoplatonism. Erigena, like Plotinus, thought of the universe as an ordered hierarchy, with reality spreading down by degrees from God at the top to matter at the bottom. Yet the lower parts of the hierarchy are not distinct from the higher ones; they are simply the self-manifestation of God. There is thus a strong streak of pantheism, the belief that God and the world are the same thing, in Erigena's thought. He is also strongly influenced by Origen in his belief that all reality not only spreads down from God but will return to him in a universal restoration.

Erigena lacks the conviction, common to later medieval theologians, that although reason and revelation are both acceptable sources of knowledge, revelation is better. Yet his strange mixture of rationalism and Neoplatonic mysticism would prove very influential in Western theology, at least indirectly. Thomas Aquinas may not have known Erigena's work directly, but he would attempt the same sort of project on a much larger scale. At the same time, those on the shady border of theology and philosophy, tinkerers in magic and alchemy, would be inspired by Erigena and his not exactly orthodox writings. The association of his name with such freethinkers and dabblers in the dark arts was partly responsible for his condemnation in 1225 and the banning of his books by the Catholic Church in 1681.

Anselm

The Dark Ages end here. Anselm was the first of the great philosopher-theologians of the Middle Ages who took Christianity to new heights of sophistication. Yet writing as he did before the medieval intellectual tradition had become rigid and codified, he produced work that remains enormously fresh and appealing. Perhaps this has something to do with the fact that Anselm seems to have been one of the most thoroughly likable people of the Middle Ages.

Life

Anselm was born in 1033 in northern Italy. Precociously, he decided before the age of 15 that he wanted to be a monk. Unfortunately the local abbot refused to take him on. As a result, Anselm began to behave rather more like a normal teenager, forgetting his earlier religious fervor and giving himself up to society and pleasure. The death of his mother, evidently a severe blow to him, accelerated the process.

A terrible falling-out with his father was the result. Life at home became intolerable, and Anselm left for good, taking with him a single servant. Together they set off across the Alps, until the wayward teenager found he could go no further. He collapsed and tried to revive himself by eating snow. Fortunately, a loaf of bread was miraculously discovered in his pack, and the journey was completed safely.

Anselm wanted to study, and he made his way to Bec in Normandy. This monastery was becoming famous as a center of learning under the wise guidance of its celebrated prior, Lanfranc. Anselm became devoted to Lanfranc and soon began to work at Bec as a teacher himself. Here, studying day and night, it occurred to him that his life was no easier than it would have been if he had become a monk after all. He toyed with the idea for a while and finally, in 1059, took Lanfranc's advice and became a monk at Bec.

Anselm was soon making up for lost time. Immersing himself in the Scriptures and the Fathers, he became fascinated by theology and the intellectual problems it raised. At the same time he progressed spiritually, fasting and meditating until his prowess was such that he had to spend all night giving spiritual advice to the other monks.

After three years, Lanfranc left and Anselm was made prior in his stead. While some monks were annoyed that a relative newcomer was so favored, Anselm treated them all with such love and friendliness that everyone was won over. He then proceeded to take such enormous trouble over the well-being of his flock that many monks became his devoted disciples in the hope of winning his special friendship. He took a particular interest in the training of the young, which he thought should be done as far as possible through kindness. When another abbot complained that his young novices remained badly behaved no matter how much he beat them,

FEUDALISM

The spiritual and political power of the Catholic Church was steadily spreading across western Europe. "Christendom"—a continent united by one faith and one pope—was fast becoming a reality. But with the waning of the Holy Roman empire, there was no strong central political institution to correspond to it. Feudalism developed as a response to that problem.

Feudalism arose with the emerging idea of the nation-state and was based on the idea that the king of the nation personally owned all the lands he ruled. But he allowed a class of overlords to occupy and administer the lands on his behalf. They, for their part, might lease out their domains to lesser lords, and so on in a complex hierarchy, until one reaches the peasants who actually worked the lands. These "serfs" were owned by their overlord and provided him with labor and crops in return for land and military protection.

Feudalism was based on the ideal of personal relations. The overlord would forge a close bond with his underling or vassal, which in the early years of feudalism might be sealed with an elaborate ceremony. The overlord allowed the vassal to live on and run his lands, in exchange for which the vassal promised personal devotion to his lord. So it involved a strong social bond rather than simply being a convenient political system.

Much of this developed as a way of allowing monarchs to raise armies quickly, since the underling vowed to fight for his lord if necessary. Thus once the monarch ordered an attack, a large force could quickly be mobilized as members of each tier of the hierarchy called upon their vassals to don armor.

Anselm told him that boys who were treated as beasts would soon act like them.

Anselm seems to have been criticized for being too lax with those under his care and for not leading a sufficiently austere life himself. In fact Anselm was well versed in fasting, austerity and self-denial. But he tried not to be ostentatious and sometimes deliberately lived in a less severe way when he thought others might find it embarrassing or not understand why he did it.

At the same time, he was becoming more interested in philosophy and theology and began writing some short works. In particular, he was fascinated by the problems raised by the nature of God, such as how one can be sure that God not only exists but is good and all-powerful. Anselm became so absorbed in the matter that he forgot to eat, sleep or attend services. Eventually, we are told, the solution sud-

And the overlords were often military leaders, knights who were given their lands in exchange for great military service and who sought to live a life of chivalry and honor.

Why is this relevant to theology? For one thing, it was seen to reflect the spiritual world. Just as there was a complex social hierarchy between the king and the serfs, so too there was an elaborate hierarchy of angels between God and human beings. This was based on the hierarchies sketched by Pseudo-Dionysius, and by the Middle Ages the system had become very detailed.

In fact, God was often thought of as a sort of cosmic feudal monarch, leasing out his lands to his underling, the pope, who in turn administered his rule via the bishops. The Catholic Church was thus seen as an extension of the cosmic hierarchy. Again, much of this derived from Pseudo-Dionysius.

The idea of God as a feudal overlord influenced theology in important ways. Most famously, it formed the basis of the enormously influential theory of the atonement developed by Anselm of Canterbury in the late 11th century. At the same time, the element of personal devotion in feudalism and the personal vows exchanged by overlord and vassal influenced later medieval spirituality. We can see this in the work of Julian of Norwich, for example, who thinks of God as a gracious feudal overlord, brimming over with chivalry and courtesy.

denly came to him in the middle of the night. In the morning Anselm wrote it down on a wax tablet and gave it to a monk for safekeeping—and the man promptly lost it. Anselm wrote it again; this time the tablet was mysteriously destroyed. Since the devil was clearly trying to keep Anselm's discovery under wraps, he now wrote it out properly and had it published. This book, the *Proslogion*, would become the most famous of Anselm's works. It contains his celebrated "ontological argument" for the existence of God.

Before long Anselm was—in the face of his own protests—promoted to abbot of Bec. Meanwhile his old mentor Lanfranc was made archbishop of Canterbury. In 1089 Lanfranc died. Bereft of its archbishop, the English Church was soon being taken advantage of by the new king, William Rufus. Anselm was persuaded by a group of noblemen to come to the country and try to sort things out. Fortunately, the king was delighted to see the famous monk. He did not even seem put out when Anselm admonished him in private for his heavyhanded treatment of the church. In fact he decided that Anselm was the perfect choice for archbishop. Unhappy at this elevation in his fortunes, Anselm had to be carried bodily to the church, where, in 1093, he was consecrated as archbishop of Canterbury. The bishop's staff had to be pressed against his fist, for he refused to take it.

Trouble came almost immediately. The king expected the new archbishop to present him with 1,000 pounds to help finance a military expedition. Anselm, unwilling to take money from the people of his diocese, refused to give more than 500. Relations were further soured when Anselm again complained to the king about his unjust style of governing. This time William Rufus declared that he would do nothing that Anselm told him to. He was clearly beginning to regret his choice of archbishop. Anselm, for his part, was extremely put out at having been wrenched from his peaceful cloister into the world of secular politics. He was happy only when surrounded by his friends in the monastery; controversy made him so miserable that he would become ill.

Some relief from the constant bickering with the king came when Anselm made a pilgrimage to Rome to visit the pope and was welcomed with great honor. There he busied himself with sorting out some knotty problems to do with the Trinity and the incarnation and produced his greatest book, *Why God Became Man*, one of the most important works of theology of the Middle Ages. When he and the pope visited the army, only the rich and important were allowed into the pope's magnificent tent. But everybody was made welcome in Anselm's modest tent, even Muslim mercenaries.

In 1100 William Rufus was killed in a hunting accident. To the surprise of those with him, Anselm burst into tears when he heard the news. The new king, Henry

I, proved just as problematic as his predecessor. Anselm was forced to remain in continental Europe while Henry seized all his possessions because of his loyalty to the pope.

Eventually the two were reconciled, and Anselm returned to Canterbury in 1106. Old and increasingly frail, he was still obsessed with theological problems— now predestination and the soul. But he no longer had the strength to see them through. One evening, one of the monks read to him Luke 22:28-30, in which Jesus promises that his faithful disciples will be with him in the kingdom. As he heard these words, Anselm passed peacefully away.

Thought

Although Anselm was the first great thinker of the Middle Ages, his inquisitive, open-minded approach was not enormously influential on those who came after. However, he did make two hugely important contributions to the development of Christian thought. These were his proof of God's existence and his doctrine of salvation.

The existence of God. Anselm's famous proof of God's existence came to him in the middle of the night. He was not the last person to have his sleep disturbed by it; the proof has probably caused more mind-bending and furrowed brows than any other piece of writing in the history of philosophy. It is known as the "ontological argument," meaning that it aims to prove God's existence from an analysis of his nature rather than from observing the world.

Anselm begins with the claim of Psalm 13:1, "The fool has said in his heart that there is no God." He points out that the fool referred to here, even though he denies God's existence, still understands what "God" means.

Anselm now makes two crucial moves. First, he defines God as "a being such that we cannot think of a greater being." Second, he points out that if there are two identical things, one of which exists but the other doesn't, then the existing one will be greater, since it is greater to exist than not to exist.

The conclusion follows swiftly. The fool agrees that God is "a being such that we cannot think of a greater being" and claims that this being does not exist. But then he must admit that if another being identical to God in every other respect *were* to exist, then it would be greater than the nonexistent God, because it is greater to exist than not to exist. And of course we can imagine such a being. So the fool thinks he can imagine a greater being than "a being such that we cannot think of a greater being." But this is obviously impossible. The fool is wrong. He really is a fool if he does not realize that the greatest imaginable being has to exist, or it would not be the greatest imaginable being. Atheism is not simply wrong; it is incoherent.

CHIVALRY

The mounted knight, putting his sword and lance to the service of honor and justice, is one of the most abiding images of the Middle Ages. In fact chivalry, the code and institution of the knights, was one of the strangest offshoots of Christian theology ever to develop.

In previous centuries the church had usually discouraged its followers from entering a military career. In the tumultuous Dark Ages, however, this became increasingly difficult. Eventually a new ideal emerged: the religious warrior who fought for justice and protected the innocent and weak. The medieval knight was born.

Knights took their vocation seriously. A knight was ordained only after proving his military and spiritual worth. At a special ceremony, robed in white, he would swear a solemn oath before a cleric and be charged to fight for Christian truth.

The knights came into their own in the 11th century with the announcement of the Crusades by Pope Urban II, who hoped not only to capture Jerusalem but also to divert attention away from some domestic problems. His call to arms was enthusiastically taken up by a fanatic called Peter the Hermit, who raised a rabble peasant army. After slaughtering as many Jews as possible, this "People's Crusade" then left for the East, where they were promptly wiped out by Muslim forces.

The real Crusaders arrived soon after, in 1097, and after a series of incredibly bloody battles and sieges, Antioch, Tripoli and Jerusalem were all taken—or what was left of them after appalling massacres of all the Jews and Muslims the Crusaders could find. But the newly established Crusader States based in these cities found themselves at odds not only with the enraged Muslims but with each other. The Outremer, as the states were called, became just another player in the power struggles of the Middle East.

The loss of the Crusader State of Edessa to the Muslims in 1144 prompted a Second Crusade to retake it. This crusade, vigorously supported by the famous spiritual writer Bernard of Clairvaux, was a complete disaster. When, in 1187, Jerusalem was lost, a Third Crusade was mounted by King Richard the Lionheart of England. Much land was regained, but Jerusalem remained in the hands of the "infidel."

Over the next couple of centuries a variety of Crusades were launched against the Muslim world, all to varying degrees of failure—a notable exception being the Reconquista, which retook the whole of Spain from the Muslims in 1492. The worst disaster was the Fourth Crusade, which never even reached the Holy Land; instead the Crusaders attacked the Christian city of Constantinople and massacred its people in 1204. This appalling atrocity destroyed any hope there might have been for reconciliation between the Catholic and Orthodox churches and is still remembered with great bitterness by the Orthodox.

The Crusades represented the epitome of the chivalric ideal, combining Christian devotion with military fervor. They are a graphic example of the way that spiritual warfare, practiced for centuries by monks and ascetics, was becoming identified with real warfare. Yet they had positive effects too. The knights who traveled to the Middle East brought back elements of Islamic culture when they returned, including silk and chess.

The knighthood itself developed significantly in the wake of the Crusades. Chivalric orders sprang up to provide for the defense of the new Crusader States. Orders such as the Knights Templar and the Knights Hospitaller represented the perfect marriage of Christian morality and European warrior codes. They rivaled the monasteries as noble institutions dedicated to carrying out the will of God, and the heroic exploits of their members were soon being celebrated by bards across Europe. These were the glory days of the "knight errant," a holy adventurer who, rather than setting forth to liberate the Levant, roamed Europe righting wrongs.

Gradually the religious element of chivalry became less important. The knights began to undertake their quests not out of obedience to God but to win the hand of a fair lady. Courtly love replaced the love of God as the ideal of the chivalric orders. By the 14th century the military purpose of the knights was also being forgotten. They had become courtiers, favored nobles, rather than crusading warriors.

The appearance of Cervantes's comic novel Don Quixote in 1605 completed the process. Knights errant were figures of fun, outdated relics of an old-fashioned, hopelessly idealistic age. They had no place in the modern world.

At first glance, Anselm's argument looks stupid. It seems to "prove" God's existence by wordplay, without any reference to reality. Yet it is much harder to fault Anselm's logic than it seems. I leave the reader to try to find the chinks in the armor—rest assured that they are there!

Although few accepted the reasoning in the Middle Ages, Anselm's argument is important because it demonstrates the assumption—common to all medieval thinkers—that there is no fundamental difference between God and the world when it comes to reason and science. Most religious people today would be likely to think that while rational arguments of this nature may be able to prove things about the world, you can grasp spiritual truths only through faith. Few people today believe that it is possible to prove God's existence like a mathematical theorem—or disprove it either. Either way, it has to be taken on faith. But this is a very modern view, one that became prevalent only after the revolution in philosophy and theology that Immanuel Kant instigated in the late 18th century. In medieval times science, philosophy and theology were a seamless whole, and there was no idea that different methods were needed to deal with different areas.

As for the ontological argument itself, the reasoning was revived—in a much cruder form—by René Descartes in the 17th century and proved very enduring. Even the devastating criticisms of Kant did not kill it completely, and some forms of the argument are still defended even today.

The atonement. Besides this puzzle for philosophers, Anselm's greatest legacy to posterity was his work on the incarnation and death of Christ.

His ideas are presented in *Why God Became Man,* where he seeks to prove—by reason, rather than from Scripture or tradition—that the incarnation *had* to have happened. The ostensible plan is to prove the doctrine to Jews and Muslims, who would not accept arguments based on Scripture and tradition. The argument is presented in dialogue form, the two speakers being Anselm himself and a disciple with the unfortunate name Boso.

Anselm begins with the problem that the incarnation solves: the problem of sin. He defines sin as disobedience to God. Any failure to submit totally to God's will places us immediately into a state of sin.

Unfortunately, once this has happened, there is nothing we can do to rectify the situation. As Anselm puts it:

> Anyone who does not give this honour to God steals from God what belongs to him, and dishonours God, and this is sin. What is more, as long he does not repay what he stole, he remains guilty. And it is not enough simply to

repay what he stole. Because he insulted God, he must give back something more than what he took.
Why God Became Man I.11

Anselm's ideas are drawn directly from medieval society. People in the feudal system of the Middle Ages owed allegiance to a lord, whom they had to obey. Failure to do this was a gross insult to the lord and was regarded as a kind of theft since it robbed the lord of his honor. If the thief could not make reparation to the lord, together with extra payment in view of the insult he had caused, he would be punished.

In the case of sin, Anselm goes on to point out that we cannot make reparation to God. To do that, we would have to give him something that we would not otherwise owe him. But we owe God everything as it is; we exist only because he created us, and even if we had never sinned we would owe him total allegiance and everything we have. Anselm asks Boso the crucial question:

Anselm: So what will you pay God for your sin?

Boso: If I owe him myself and everything I can do even without sin, then after I have sinned, I have nothing left to repay him.

Anselm: So what will become of you? How can you be saved?

Boso: If I think about what you have said, I cannot see any way.
Why God Became Man 1.20

There is worse to come. To disobey God is the very worst thing that could possibly happen. It is a crime of infinite wickedness. So to repay God his honor, we would have to offer him something that outweighs this infinite crime. And how could we possibly do that?

The problem is that, as the guilty party, humanity must make satisfaction to God. But humanity is incapable of this. In fact, only God himself could. The conclusion is clear:

Anselm: So no one except God can make the satisfaction.

Boso: That follows.

Anselm: But no one except humanity ought to do it—otherwise, humanity has not made satisfaction.

Boso: Nothing could be more just.

Anselm: . . . So if no one except God *can* make it and no one except man *ought* to make it, there must be a God-Man to make it.

Boso: Blessed be God!
Why God Became Man 2.6

For the plan to work, the God-Man must be wholly God and wholly human. He needs to offer a gift of infinite value. Since he is God, his death has infinite value. Therefore the God-Man allows himself to be killed, offering his death to God as reparation for the insult to God's honor caused by humanity. This more than repays the theft, and sinful humanity can be forgiven.

Anselm's doctrine is an "objective" account of salvation. It sees sin as a sort of cosmic overdraft, which God pays back to himself. Sinful humanity is something of a passive observer of this exchange. The doctrine does not speak of a changed relationship with God or the way sinful humanity may be changed to a better life. Of course those things are important to Anselm, but they do not play a part in his theology of salvation, strictly speaking. For Anselm, human beings are like criminals who have escaped their sentence. Any subsequent change of heart and improved living comes as a reaction to being saved: it is not part of being saved itself. This contrasts very strongly with the later doctrine of Abelard, as well as with the earlier emphases of Augustine.

Anselm's legalistic understanding of salvation would be immensely influential. It is at the root of the doctrines of the atonement of Luther and Calvin and through them became the received wisdom of Protestantism at large.

But Anselm's doctrine differs from these later ideas in important ways. He does not think of Christ dying "in our place." Christ makes satisfaction to God *on our behalf*—he does not *take our place*, because God does not inflict on him the punishment due to sinful humanity. The notion of Christ's being punished by God is alien to Anselm. He thinks of Christ's death as a gift that he offers to God to repay what sinful humanity stole from him. It is not a punishment for humanity's crime; it is reparation made so that God does not have to punish anyone.

The later doctrines changed because legal systems changed; the notion of making reparation to avert punishment would have made no sense to Calvin. By basing his doctrine on contemporary practices, Anselm made it relevant and understandable to others; but in so doing he made it liable to become outdated. The same is true of any theologian who seeks to retell the Christian faith in a contemporary way. Much of Anselm's greatness lies in the fact that even though his work is couched in outdated terms and ideas, it is still easily readable today.

Peter Abelard

Peter Abelard is almost certainly the only major theologian to be considered one of the great lovers of history. The story of his doomed affair with Heloise is one of the best-known love stories of the Middle Ages. What's more, the theme of love is at the center of his most lasting contribution to Christian thought, his account of salvation. There is something a little paradoxical about this, since Abelard himself does not seem to have been a very lovable person.

Life

Peter Abelard was born in 1079, the son of Berengar, lord of Pallet, a town near Nantes in modern-day France. Instead of the military career that might have been expected of the son of a nobleman, he decided to devote his life to philosophy and left home at about 15 to study under whoever would be willing to teach him. He must have been a very aggravating student. Not only was he cleverer than most of his teachers, but he was well aware of the fact and saw little point in deferring to their age and authority. At Paris he took part in a public debate with his teacher, the renowned William of Champeaux, archdeacon of Notre Dame, and defeated him, much to William's annoyance. After this, he studied under Anselm of Laon (not to be confused with Anselm of Canterbury), a man of great erudition whose lectures Abelard found too boring to bother attending. To prove his own superiority, Abelard gave a lecture himself on an obscure text of Ezekiel without doing any preparation. The lecture proved far more popular than Anselm's on the same subject, and Abelard's fellow students even begged him to give more lectures on it. Anselm, understandably, quickly put a stop to this, so Abelard returned to Paris and became head of the school there.

As the most forceful debater of his age, Abelard made a great impression on all around him. In fact he became a major celebrity, one of the most famous men alive. Students flocked from all over Europe to hear his lectures, and under his leadership Paris became the greatest center of learning in the world. But he was merciless to his intellectual opponents and lacked humility, since he could never find anyone who could outargue him. In his autobiography, the cheerily titled *History of My Misfortunes*, he admits that "I had by this time come to regard myself as the only philosopher remaining in the whole world."

It was at this point that Fulbert, a canon of the cathedral, asked Abelard to give private tutorials to his young and beautiful niece Heloise. What Fulbert didn't know was that Abelard had fallen in love with the girl.

Whilst pretending to study we spent our hours in the happiness of love, and

PARIS

Paris was originally a small fishing village on the River Seine, but under the Romans it was transformed into a major administrative center. It retained its importance even after the fall of the empire and became the seat of power of the kings of what would one day be France. With the founding of the Holy Roman empire in 800, Charlemagne set out to transform Paris into a city of learning. There Alcuin, Charlemagne's chief scholar, sought to introduce a rigorous secular and religious curriculum that would set new standards for scholarship. Although the hoped-for renaissance never really happened, the measures that were laid down persevered and formed the basis for the great explosion of learning that was to come in the Middle Ages.

It was in the 11th and 12th centuries that Paris really blossomed. It spread over both banks of the Seine as well as the Ile de la Cité in the middle; the roads were paved, and major projects such as the massive Cathedral of Notre Dame were initiated. Even more significant was the development of various colleges and halls that appeared on the left bank of the Seine in the early Middle Ages. Scholars flocked to these colleges and to the great churches of the city. Under the guidance of men like William of Champeaux and Peter Abelard, the schools of Paris became the greatest center for learning in Europe. Finally, in 1231, the pope recognized them collectively as the University of Paris.

The curriculum was still based around the study of literature and theology,

learning gave us the secret opportunities that our passion craved. We talked about love rather than the books which lay open before us; our kisses far outnumbered our reasoned words. Instead of the book, our hands reached out to each other's bosoms—love drew our eyes to each other far more than the lesson drew them to the pages of our text. . . . Our passion left no stage of love untried, and if love itself could imagine any wonder as yet unknown, we discovered it. And our inexperience of such delights made us all the more determined in our pursuit of them, so that our thirst for one another was still unquenched.

The History of My Misfortunes

Heloise clearly learned a lot more with Abelard than Fulbert had intended. The re-

as laid down by Alcuin centuries earlier. Students began their courses at the age of fourteen and studied the trivium or "three ways"—grammar, rhetoric and letters—before moving on to the quadrium—arithmetic, geometry, astronomy and music. This took six years in total, after which students would choose a particular subject to specialize in for the next five or six years. Until the 13th century, however, the only specialized subject on offer was theology.

All studies were in Latin, the language of the church and of scholars, an international language that transcended the various vernacular tongues that were developing in the different nations of Europe. Few people spoke Greek, but there were enough to translate and circulate the works of Aristotle in the 12th and 13th centuries. Paris was at the center of this as well as all other major intellectual movements of the Middle Ages.

The greatest of the colleges was the Sorbonne, founded in 1257 to provide lodgings for students who were not attached to the great monasteries or mendicant orders. Some of these scholars were very poor, even to the extent of having to study in the street; it was therefore in everyone's interest to found colleges and lodginghouses to keep them out of sight. Despite these humble beginnings, the Sorbonne quickly became one of the premier educational establishments in the world, boasting Albertus Magnus and Thomas Aquinas among its alumni.

lationship remained secret for some months, Abelard helped to maintain the illusion that he was teaching Heloise by hitting her, though, he says, not too hard!

The affair became the talk of the whole of Paris. Heloise later wrote that all the women were jealous of her because Abelard was not only young and handsome but wrote outstanding love songs to her which were popular all over the city. Because of this, it wasn't long before Fulbert found out, and he was furious, particularly after Heloise gave birth to a son, to whom they gave the strange name Astrolabe. Abelard decided that they should marry, to appease Fulbert. Heloise did not want to marry, quoting in her defense the letters of Jerome, which are all about the horrors of marriage. However, unlike Jerome, she did not want to lead a life of virtuous chastity—she just did not want to be tied down. She pointed out that it was better to love Abelard because she wanted to rather than because she had to. As usual,

Abelard won the argument, and they were married secretly.

Unfortunately, the couple kept the marriage a secret, enraging Fulbert still more, and Abelard tried to protect Heloise from her uncle by moving her to a nunnery. This was the last straw. Convinced that the philosopher had grown tired of his niece, Fulbert hired some thugs who, with the help of Abelard's own servant, broke into his house in the middle of the night and exacted a very unpleasant revenge. As Abelard put it, "They cut off those parts of my body with which I had done that which was the cause of their sorrow."

Overcome with shame, Abelard felt compelled to flee public life and become a monk. He also persuaded Heloise to become a nun. The letters they wrote to each other in later years discuss love and religion, and it is because of these letters that their love affair is famous.

Abelard now turned his formidable talents to theology, studying Scripture and the Fathers—especially Origen, with whom, understandably, he now felt a special affinity. He wrote several important works on theology. One of these, *Yes and No*, applied his aggressive debating style to religion. It was a collection of quotations from the church fathers, arranged so that they contradicted each other. The aim was not to discredit the Fathers but to force the reader to think. Abelard believed that faith is based on authority, but authority can be ambiguous or contradictory. It is therefore necessary to use reason to draw out the details of the faith. In this he was quite similar to Anselm, although far more provocative.

Abelard's method of doing theology angered many people. Although he distinguished between revealed truth and his own speculations, his self-confidence and popularity as a teacher—even after becoming a monk—made him dangerous in the eyes of more conservative thinkers. One of these, William of St. Thierry, believed that Abelard's reliance on reason was at the expense of authority, and he said as much to the mystical theologian Bernard of Clairvaux. Bernard was appalled not only by the style of Abelard's work but also by its content—particularly, as we shall see, his view of the atonement. He denounced Abelard as an Arian, a Pelagian and, just for good measure, a Nestorian and wrote to Pope Innocent II to have him condemned.

A council met at Sens in 1140 or 1141 to settle the matter. Believing that he would have a chance to debate freely with Bernard, Abelard traveled to the council, only to find that he was in fact on trial for heresy and had to listen silently to his accusers. Abelard was condemned and his books burned. This was not a new experience for him, since some of his views on the Trinity had been condemned at Soissons in 1121, but this time it was a more serious blow to his career. He was sentenced to be confined to the abbey at Cluny, where he remained until his death sometime between 1142 and 1144.

Thought

Abelard made his name as a philosopher, although today most of his philosophical writings are of interest only to specialists. The same is true of most of his theological work, such as his writings on the Trinity. However, Abelard is saved from being consigned to the more boring pages of Christian history by his contribution to the doctrine of the atonement. This strikingly modern area of his thought remains relevant today, having been enthusiastically rehabilitated by several modern theologians.

It is strange that Abelard's doctrine of salvation should be the best-known part of his thought, given that he did not write very much on it. The one aspect that does receive a full treatment is his account of the problem of sin. He wrote a whole book on this, *Ethics* or *Know Yourself*. Abelard's position on sin is both clear and simple. He argues that sin lies not in the act but in the intention. That is, if I kill somebody, the act is not in itself sinful. The original idea to do it is not sinful either, for that is just temptation. What is sinful is my decision to act on that desire. Abelard points out that if, for example, I kill somebody accidentally, I have not sinned, although I may be careless—and, conversely, if I intend to kill someone but fail, I am both sinful and incompetent. As a result, Abelard denies that we can inherit guilt from Adam, since we are guilty only of our own sinful intentions.

The problem of sin, then, is inside us: sin is seen as a *subjective* problem. For God to eliminate sin, he must change us from within. This is quite different from Anselm's view that sin is an objective problem, a record in the cosmic ledger book that God must somehow erase.

How, then, are we to be saved? This is the crucial part, but surprisingly Abelard devotes very little space to it in his writings. In fact, the most famous passage where he describes it is both vague and ambiguous.

Now it seems to us that we have been justified by the blood of Christ and reconciled to God in this way: through this unique act of grace manifested to us—in that his Son has taken upon himself our nature and persevered therein in teaching us by word and example even unto death—he has more fully bound us to himself by love; with the result that our hearts should be enkindled by such a gift of divine grace, and true charity should not now shrink from enduring anything for him.

Commentary on Romans

Abelard describes Christ's incarnation and death as the supreme demonstration of God's love for us. That in itself may not seem very striking—all Christians might agree with it. But Abelard seems to suggest not simply that love is God's motivation for saving us through Christ but it is the means by which he does it. Through the cross God's love flows into us, changing us from within and making us love him and each other. Our intentions are no longer sinful.

This is a subjective account of the atonement. All the action happens inside us, changing us for the future, rather than outside us, canceling out what we have done in the past, as with Anselm.

We can see that Abelard thinks of salvation in primarily ethical terms when he goes on to say:

> Everyone is made more righteous, that is more loving towards God, after the passion of Christ than he had been before, because a realised gift incites greater love than that which is only hoped for. Therefore, our redemption through Christ's suffering is that supreme love in us which not only frees us from slavery to sin, but also acquires for us the true liberty of sons of God.
> *Commentary on Romans*

Everyone who considers Christ's death, then, is inspired by love to be a better person, and that is how we are saved. Salvation is a matter of being really changed from within—it is not just a matter of God's treating us differently, as Anselm thought.

This account is both simple and appealing and has proved very popular in recent years. It takes into account the experience of many Christians of their lives' being changed and makes this central to salvation, rather than just a pleasant side effect. In fact, one of the most striking aspects of this account is its emphasis on the experience of the individual, rather than what happens to the church as a group. Abelard seems very modern in this psychological concern; one could almost call him an existentialist. His account also completely avoids the unattractively legalistic overtones of objective theories of the atonement like Anselm's or Calvin's. But there are a couple of serious flaws.

Bernard of Clairvaux pointed out the first problem. It seemed to him that Abelard was saying that Christ only shows us God's love and salvation; he doesn't actually give them to us. In other words, if we are saved simply by imitating the example of Christ's love, don't we save ourselves? No wonder Bernard called Abelard a follower of Pelagius. In fact, this is one of the most ambiguous aspects of Abelard's account. It may be that he did indeed think of Christ's death simply as an example that we are to follow, in which case Bernard's accusation of Pelagianism was justified. However, his defenders argue that this "exempliarist" interpretation is a caricature. Abelard actually means that through Christ's death God's love flows out into us. The love that transforms us is not our own, responding to God's love, but God's love itself entering us and lifting us up. It is therefore God who saves us, by actively changing us for the better. We do not save ourselves by following Christ's example.

The second problem is more serious. Abelard claims that the cross is the supreme example of God's love for us and that this saves us. But we may ask, why is it the supreme example of God's love? The obvious answer: because it is the means by which God saves us. But then the argument seems circular. If the salvation is on the basis of the love, then that love cannot be on the basis of that salvation. There must be something else.

In that case, we could say that the cross saves in some other way; then our love is a response to that salvation. In fact Abelard himself seems to hint at this. In some passages he talks of Christ's making supplication to the Father on our behalf and imparting his merit to us—which sounds very Anselmian. He even talks of Christ's bearing the penalty of our sins, which seems an anticipation of Calvin's ideas. But this hardly solves the problem, because if we are saved in that way then there seems to be no point in having the original theory at all. This, then, is a serious problem with many subjective accounts of the atonement. Either they seem too weak, failing to explain why Christ's death should change us so much as to save us, or they seem superfluous, riding on the coattails of another theory of the atonement.

Like Pelagius, Abelard is often treated very sympathetically by modern theologians. He is seen as a sort of liberal whose career was cruelly cut short by conservative zealots who could not understand his work. Of course it would be just as anachronistic to think of Abelard like this as it is with Pelagius. But it is nevertheless true that his theological method strikes a chord with many today and his work is used as the basis of a lot of modern thought about salvation. He is still considered the godfather of the subjective understanding of salvation, and for that alone his place in the history of Christian theology is assured.

The Mendicant Orders

The 13th century saw an extraordinary new movement that at once threatened the monastic way of life and breathed new life into it. At first glance the friars were much like the monks, but in fact they were quite different.

Francis of Assisi

The story began with Francis of Assisi, one of the most famous of all Christian saints and one of the most likable and attractive men in history. He was the son of an Italian aristocrat, but he found that wealth and privilege brought him no pleasure. In fact he was happiest giving things away. Eventually, after a day spent trading places with a beggar, he realized that true faith in God—and true happiness—can be found only by radically rejecting all other potential sources of security. So he vowed to give himself to "Lady Poverty"—to live without any money, home or property whatsoever. To the astonishment of their friends and families, he and his first companions found that this lifestyle, which seemed so grueling, in fact made them completely free. They had no worries or responsibilities; they had completely opted out of the system of money, power, avarice and care that made normal society so stressful and selfish. They were so happy and laughed so much that they became known as "God's jesters."

The idyll couldn't last. Before long Francis had hundreds of followers, known as "friars minor" or "lesser brothers." Hundreds became thousands, in every part of Western Europe, including many who had never met Francis himself. It was not possible for such a huge organization to rely on the simple rule of life that Francis and his friends had worked out for themselves, and Francis spent the last years of his life struggling with powerful figures in the movement who wanted to impose order and structure on it. Francis's greatest fear was that he had inadvertently created a new church within a church, a human organization with none of the freedom of those early days. He died, prematurely aged and exhausted, in 1226. He was only 44. And though he had died, at his own request, lying on a scrap of blanket on the ground, his body was interred in a magnificent mausoleum—a stark contrast to the simple life of poverty and humility he had tried to lead.

The friars

That was the tragedy of St. Francis of Assisi; but the movement he founded went from strength to strength. It took a while for the rival trends within the movement—simplicity and poverty on the one hand and structure and order on the other—to calm down; in fact the tension was never really resolved. But the friars were a major new force in the church. Unlike monks, who tried to seal themselves away from the world so they could contemplate God, the friars went out into the world. They too spent many hours of each day contemplating God, but they felt that God was to be found through identifying themselves with the world. The spirituality of Francis himself had revolved around the idea that God is the Creator of all things and that to honor God it is right to honor even the lowliest of his creations—which is why he wrote a canticle praising the sun, spoke to animals, preached to birds and even rescued worms from being trodden on.

Most specifically, however, the friars identified with the poor and downtrodden. In Francis's home town of Assisi "friars minor" was a term applied to the poorest classes in society—so even the name of the movement was a conscious identification with the poor. In a way, this idea that God is to be found through social action, in the world, not apart from it, anticipates the theology of Reinhold Niebuhr and Dietrich Bonhoeffer in the 20th century.

The friars also preached, and this, combined with their holy lives, made them enormously popular—although the fact that they lived by begging and looked ragged and poor meant that they were never really respectable. The Franciscans were joined by the Dominicans, who had been founded by Francis's friend St. Dominic and who specialized in preaching. The two orders were known as the "mendicant orders," meaning that they traveled about begging, unlike the monks; but they also established major centers of learning for those friars who felt more inclined toward a sedentary lifestyle. In fact, between them, these two great orders produced most of the brilliant theologians—Aquinas, Bonaventure, Scotus and others—who made the 13th century one of the most remarkable periods of intellectual creativity in European history.

Thomas Aquinas

The thought of Thomas Aquinas is one of the glories of the Middle Ages. Drawing on centuries of tradition, he created the definitive statement of medieval Christianity, which remains the official teaching of the Catholic Church to this day.

Life

Thomas Aquinas was assured of a good career even before he was born. His parents were Landulph, count of Aquino, and Theodora, countess of Teano, and he was related not only to much of the Italian aristocracy but also to the kings of several countries and even an emperor or two. His birth, which occurred in his father's castle of Roccasecca, near Naples, probably in 1225, was said to have been preceded by portentous prophecies by a local hermit, who foretold that the child would become the greatest teacher in the world.

Thomas was a precocious child. His teachers, the local Benedictine monks, were puzzled by his meditative nature and his often-repeated question "What is God?" Eventually, convinced that the boy was destined for greater things, they persuaded his parents to send him to the University of Naples. There, at the age of 11, he was soon displaying greater mastery of every subject than his teachers.

In his late teens, the rising star of academia suddenly astounded everybody by donning the habit of a Dominican friar. He had decided to renounce the career that seemed to be opening up and devote himself instead to poverty and meditation. His family shared the general distaste for the ragged, begging friars that many aristocrats felt. Horrified, his mother traveled to Naples, but the Dominicans sent their new initiate to Rome so that she could not dissuade him from his chosen course.

On the way to Rome, however, Thomas was captured by two of his brothers, who were soldiers. They took him to the castle of Roccasecca, where they imprisoned him while they tried to find some way to stop his throwing his future away. For nearly two years Thomas remained incarcerated in the fortress, studying hard and memorizing the Scriptures, while his whole family tried every means possible to dissuade him from his chosen life, all without success. They even hired a prostitute to go to Thomas's room and seduce him. Instead of succumbing to her wiles he grabbed a flaming log from the fire and, brandishing it like a sword, drove the naked woman out, before slamming the door, burning a black cross onto it with the flame and returning to his books.

Clearly, the young man was not going to be diverted from his course, and his

THE REDISCOVERY OF ARISTOTLE

Tertullian looked forward to watching him burn on Judgment Day. Gregory of Nyssa called him an evil genius. Yet by a millennium later, Aristotle had been elevated by the church to a position of supreme authority, a pagan saint equal to the Fathers themselves. How did this remarkable change of fortune come about?

The story begins in A.D. 529, when the Byzantine emperor Justinian ordered the closing of the philosophical schools. Philosophers who were unwilling to turn their attentions to Orthodox doctrine fled to the Middle East. There they continued the philosophical practices of late antiquity, which essentially consisted of translating and commenting on the works of great philosophers of the past. These included Aristotle, the pupil of Plato, who had lived in the 4th century B.C. and acted (without much success) as tutor to the famous general Alexander the Great. Aristotle had always had his followers throughout late antiquity, but they were not as prominent as those of Plato or the Stoics—and the Christians had never liked them. Now, in the 6th century, a strong Aristotelian tradition arose.

In the West, meanwhile, Aristotle was almost forgotten. His works on logic survived and were studied, but everything else was lost. He fared better in Byzantium, where he continued to be studied. But Orthodox scholars, coming from the Neoplatonic worldview of Pseudo-Dionysius, had little love for the more arid Aristotle, who lacked the religious sensibility of Plato and his successors.

As the Muslim empire swept across the Middle East, the Aristotelian schools they found there prospered. Islam was developing a lively philosophical tra-

family eventually released him, possibly fearing the political scandal that the affair might cause. Both the pope and the emperor had expressed their displeasure at the situation. Thomas was lowered in a basket from the tower by his sisters and rescued by the Dominicans, who were pleased to find that he had advanced in his studies as much as if he had remained at the friary.

Now confirmed in the order, Aquinas headed for Cologne, where he arrived in about 1245. There he studied under the most famous teacher of the day, Albertus Magnus (Albert the Great), a remarkable philosopher, alchemist and all-round mystic. Albertus's other students found their new colleague hard to understand;

dition around such pivotal figures as Ibn Sina—known to the West as Avicenna—an encyclopedic thinker of the early 11th century who occupied a rather similar place in Muslim thought to that of his contemporary Anselm in Christianity. Muslim philosophers began to incorporate Aristotle's ideas into their theology, creating a powerful Aristotelian Islam, rather like the Platonic Christianity of the church fathers. The most important figure in this development was Ibn Rushd, or Averröes, a Spanish philosopher of the late 12th century. Averröes was a thoroughgoing rationalist who seemed to think philosophy a more certain means than religion of acquiring truth. He even distinguished between religious truth and philosophical truth and did not seem very bothered if they contradicted each other. So something can be religiously true but philosophically false, and vice versa.

Through the work of Averröes and other Spanish Muslims, the Christian West eventually rediscovered Aristotle. In the 12th and 13th centuries Latin translations of his works appeared, made from the Greek and Arabic versions preserved by the Muslims and also from those of Byzantine scholars who visited the West. These works, and the ideas they contained, were something of a shock to medieval Christendom. The notion of scientific inquiry had largely vanished in the West; it was generally accepted that all questions about life and the world could be answered by the church. Philosophy was simply a logical tool for sifting the doctrines laid down by great saints of the past. Aristotle showed that a totally different approach was possible. He speculated about the world and its causes without reference to divine revelation. He went out and actually looked at the world and wrote

they called him "the dumb ox" because he rarely spoke and also because of his decidedly corpulent appearance. His months of incarceration with no physical exercise may have done wonders for his soul, but they clearly had not been so good for his body. Albertus, however, was impressed with his student and commented, "One day this dumb ox will make a bellowing that will be heard throughout the world."

Albertus soon moved to Paris, the greatest center of learning in the world, and then, in 1248, back to Cologne. Aquinas accompanied him both times and in about 1250 was ordained priest. Within a couple of years, at Albertus's recommendation, he was sent back to Paris in a teaching capacity. There he began to make a name for himself. Controversy over the newly discovered writings of Aristotle was raging throughout Western Europe at this time, and Aquinas threw himself into it passionately. Albertus Magnus was an enthusiastic interpreter of Aristotle, and

down what he saw. He was a practical scientist as well as a theoretical thinker, and this must have been enormously exciting to people who until then had spent most of their time poring over volumes of Augustine.

At the same time Aristotle represented a challenge to Christianity, which was still deeply influenced by Platonic ways of thinking. Plato had taught that the visible world is not the real world; it is simply a pale reflection of a higher spiritual reality. He urged his followers to look away from the particular toward the universal, for particular things are just images of eternal, universal forms. Aristotle, by contrast, was interested in the material world. He believed that physical objects are really real, not shadows of something unseen, and he tried to explain them in physical terms—by reference to what they are made of, what shape they are, what caused them to exist and so on. Since everything is caused by something else, Aristotle postulated that there must be a final cause, an "unmoved Mover," responsible for all movement and life in the universe. This is his rather impersonal conception of God. So where Plato thought of the divine in a religious way, as the realm to which the human soul must rise, Aristotle thought of it in a scientific way, as the explanation for the world we see around us.

Theologians disagreed over how to approach the new philosophy. Some condemned Aristotle, since some of his ideas conflicted with Christian doctrine. The prime example was his claim that the world had no beginning, which contradicted the doctrine of creation. In 1215 Aristotle's scientific works were banned at the University of Paris—although his logical works were

Aquinas shared his zeal—but not to the extent of some theologians who sided with the philosopher even when his doctrines contradicted those of the church. Aquinas argued against this approach and also the opposing attitude that regarded Aristotle as a dangerous enemy of the church. Aquinas sought to find a middle way, using Aristotle constructively in the service of Christian theology without succumbing to his errors.

In 1257 Aquinas was granted the degree of doctor of divinity. According to legend, he received his degree on the same day as Bonaventure, and the two of them were so humble that neither wanted to receive his degree first. Aquinas's reputation grew quickly and before long eclipsed that of his famous teacher. He had also begun work on an ambitious project, the *Summa Against the Gentiles*. A *summa* was a complete, systematic exposition. In this book Aquinas hoped to present the doctrines of

compulsory texts. Attempts were made to impose the ban elsewhere too. But other theologians enthusiastically defended Aristotle without reservation, some appealing to Averröes's idea of double truth to claim that it is a religious truth that the world is created and at the same time a philosophical truth that it is not.

Other theologians, unhappy with this kind of doublethink, sought various kinds of middle ways. Bonaventure represents one approach. He was critical of Aristotle but was prepared to use his ideas cautiously where they seemed helpful. But ultimately the most fruitful approach was that pioneered by Albert the Great and perfected by Thomas Aquinas. For these thinkers Aristotle was the supreme secular authority. They refer to him simply as "the Philosopher," as if none other existed. Where he contradicts Christian revelation, they accept that he is wrong, for no secular authority can be infallible. But for the most part, and in all purely philosophical or scientific matters, Aristotle is the authority.

This attitude was highly controversial in Aquinas's lifetime. However, after his death and canonization the rapid acceptance of Aristotle by everyone else was almost inevitable. Ironically, the exaggerated reverence for his ideas meant that there was little creative philosophy of the kind that Aristotle himself had done. It would be two centuries before the Renaissance would pull Aristotle off his medieval pedestal, as thinkers like Thomas Hobbes and René Descartes redirected the course of philosophy and scientists like Galileo demolished his physics.

Christianity in such a way that its opponents, Jews and Muslims, would be rationally convinced of their truth. An even more ambitious aim of the book was to promote Christian unity by focusing on what was believed in both Catholic and Orthodox churches.

Over the next decade Aquinas traveled from university to university, teaching, writing and preaching. His reputation and his waistline increased in roughly equal proportions. Aquinas, who liked wine and good food, was certainly no haggard ascetic. He became so fat that—it was said—he could no longer reach his desk, and a large semicircle had to be cut out of it into which his enormous stomach could fit.

Nevertheless, his true obsession was thinking, not eating. He would pace for hours around the cloisters, lost in a world of his own as he worked out some tortuous problem. On one occasion he was invited to a feast at the court of King Louis of France. He sat silently, ignoring the festivities around him, for a whole hour before suddenly slamming his fist on the table, declaring, "That's the way to refute the Manichaeans!" After a stunned silence, the king simply ordered his secretaries to go and write down whatever it was Aquinas had come up with before he forgot it.

He continued to write prodigiously, turning out book after book on a wide range of subjects. Like Origen before him, Aquinas was helped in this endeavor by a team of secretaries, made necessary by the fact that his own handwriting was atrocious to the point of illegibility. It was said that he could dictate different books to several different secretaries at once and even that he could dictate intelligently in his sleep—something his critics might think would explain a lot. He could also call on the aid of other scholars. Most of Aristotle's works were available only in poor translations of Arabic versions of the Greek originals; Aquinas, who could not read Greek, had new, superior translations made directly from the original texts.

Completing his first *summa*, Aquinas began work on another, even more ambitious one—the *Summa Theologiae*. This massive but never completed work would be his masterpiece, a definitive exposition of Christian doctrine, a distillation of 12 centuries of theology, sorted, categorized and commented on by Aquinas's ever-critical mind.

The *Summa* is no dry, dogmatic exposition but a journey of discovery. It takes the form of a series of questions, arranged thematically. For each question Aquinas considers a possible answer and presents a wide range of arguments in its favor, drawn from reason, Scripture or the Fathers. He then analyzes the arguments, demolishes them, forms an alternative answer to the question and supports it with arguments of his own. The result is almost like a detective thriller as the evidence is sifted and the truth emerges. It gives a fascinating insight into what it must have been like to attend one of Aquinas's teaching sessions, with the students jousting for position in a passionate debate and the genius master dissecting their arguments and pronouncing the victor.

Despite the intellectual scale of the *Summa,* it was based not on dry rationalism but on a warm spirituality grounded very firmly in the life of the church. Aquinas had a strong sense of the role of mystery in religion, even if this does not always come across in his writings. Indeed he found his greatest joy in presiding over Mass; and he would frequently become so enraptured in the proceedings that he would stop talking and remain wrapped in his own thoughts until someone prodded him, at which point he would pick up the liturgy where he had left off.

It was during one of these lapses while saying Mass, in 1273, that Aquinas's career came to an abrupt end. He underwent what he interpreted as a profound spiritual experience and emerged from it something of a broken man. He immediately ceased his writing, explaining that "compared to what I have seen, everything I have written seems like so much straw." It is quite likely, given his physical condition and the emotional intensity he experienced during Mass, that Aquinas had suffered a stroke.

He never wrote another word. In 1274, while traveling to attend a council, Aquinas suddenly fell ill and died at Fossanova, just a few miles from the castle where he was born. He was 49 years old.

Thought

Aquinas is sometimes underrated as a thinker. His reliance on earlier tradition can make him seem unoriginal, and his modern status as *the* Catholic authority can make him seem more dogmatic than he really was. In fact Aquinas's use of the authorities at his disposal is one of the most interesting aspects of his thought.

Aquinas's most important source is Augustine, whom he cites constantly. Despite his avowed love of Aristotle, Aquinas's basic position is closer to Neoplatonism, as mediated by Augustine, and also by Pseudo-Dionysius, another major influence. So Aquinas is basically a Neoplatonist in outline, although the details of his system are filled in using Aristotle. For example, he accepts the basic Aristotelian belief that all knowledge comes ultimately from what we experience with our physical senses, but he adds the Neoplatonic insistence on the importance of using the mind to go beyond this experience and look to God.

The sources of theology. How can we know about God? It is not much of an exaggeration to say that Thomas Aquinas spent his whole life trying to answer this question.

Aquinas recognizes two distinct sources of knowledge: reason and revelation. So there are two ways human beings can come to know things—through their own intellectual and observational powers and by being directly told by God. We might say that for Aquinas Aristotle represents the first way and Paul the second.

However, the two sources of knowledge are not equally important. Reason can teach us a great deal, but not everything we need to know for salvation. Only revelation can supply that. But what reason teaches us is nevertheless true. Reason and revelation do not contradict each other, and both are ultimately gifts of God.

The prime example of knowledge available to reason but perfected by revelation is knowledge of the existence of God. Aquinas did not like Anselm's ontological argument, but like Anselm he thought that it is perfectly possible to prove God's existence. In fact he presented five ways to do this.

1. *Proof from change.* Aquinas points out that when things change, they are invariably changed by something else. Think of a line of carriages: the one at the end is pulled along by the one in front, which in turn is pulled by the one in front of it, and so on. But you cannot have an infinite line of carriages all pulling each other; there must be a locomotive at the front, which pulls everything else. In the same way, there must be some unchanging cause of all the change in the world.

2. *Proof from explanation.* We can ask of any object, "Why is this the way it is?"— and we can always give an answer referring to another object or group of objects. But again, we cannot keep doing this to infinity, like a small child asking, "Why? Why?" ad nauseam. There must be some final thing that is, as it were, the ultimate explanation for everything else, and that needs no further explanation.

3. *Necessity.* No object necessarily exists; it *could* have been the case that it did not exist. So why does any particular thing happen to exist rather than not exist? In fact, why does the universe exist at all, if it might not have? It must have been brought into existence by something that could not fail to have existed. There must be a *necessary* being.

4. *Degrees of goodness in the world.* Some things are better than others. And this suggests the notion of a perfectly good thing.

5. *Argument from design.* If something is perfectly fitted for its task, it must either be intelligent or have been designed by intelligence. But clearly animals and plants are well adapted for life without intelligence; they must therefore have been designed by a greater intelligence.

Clearly Aquinas's arguments are of variable quality. But there are three interesting points to make about them. First, they are basically Aristotelian. They argue for God's existence on the basis of observation of the physical world; and Aquinas rejected Anselm's argument that God's existence could be proved from an analysis of the meaning of the word *God.* He is the classic exponent of the "cosmological" proof of God, the proof based on the existence and nature of the observable universe. Second, the arguments suggest a rather impersonal God. He is the unchanging Changer, the Necessary Being, the Designer. And third, they bring us to a belief in God; they do not bring us to Christian faith and belief in a Trinity. In other words, unaided human reason—what later generations would call "natural theology"—can get us only so far. We cannot do without revelation. To put it another way, knowledge is all very well, but we need to go beyond it in faith.

God. Having proved God's existence, Aquinas informs us that we cannot know what God is, only what he is not. It is perhaps surprising that he then devotes rather a lot of pages to telling us a great deal about God.

In fact, the doctrine of God presented in the opening sections of the *Summa Theologiae* is the most highly developed and sophisticated version ever produced of Pseudo-Dionysius's *via negativa.* The essence of this approach is that God transcends our ordinary ways of thinking to such an extent that no statement we make can do him justice, so we cannot really say anything about him at all. Where Pseudo-Dionysius, not unreasonably, stopped here, Aquinas's genius is shown in the way he makes it his starting point.

If God transcends all earthly categories, argues Aquinas, then he lacks qualities like motion, location, shape, color. In fact, he has no qualities at all. This is the notion of divine *simplicity*, and it is for Aquinas the most fundamental fact about God. Ordinary objects are complex, made of several pieces—a hat, for example, is made of a crown and a brim. This does not apply to God; he is not compounded out of bits but is perfectly simple.

God, then, might seem to be a sort of atom, or quark, or particle that cannot be broken down into smaller particles. But there is more to it than this. Aristotle had argued that there is a difference between substances (ordinary things, like a hat) and qualities (such as the hat's color, its shape, its function and so on). A substance and its qualities are not the same, although you cannot have a substance without any qualities or a quality that does not belong to a substance.

Aquinas accepts this commonsense distinction and adds another: the qualities a substance has are, taken together, its *essence*—its definition, if you like. But in addition to this a substance may have *existence.* If you ask, "What is a hat?" then the answer is the essence of a hat—it is worn on the head, may be made up of a crown and a brim, and so on. But if you ask, "Does a hat exist?" you are not asking about the qualities that the substance possesses; you are asking whether that substance and its qualities can be found at all.

What all this boils down to is that, for Aquinas, even the tiniest particle that cannot be broken down into further particles is, logically speaking, complex. It is a substance with an essence and an existence. But if God is totally simple then this does not apply to him. There is no distinction at all between his substance, his essence and his existence. God is the one thing whose essence *is* his existence. To put it differently, God is not simply something that exists—he is existence itself.

What can this possibly mean? If Aquinas was setting out to prove that God transcends human understanding, it seems that he succeeded. It is a sophisticated attempt to pin down an insight almost as old as Christian thought itself. In the 2nd century Irenaeus had spoken of God as the only truly existing thing, holding the whole universe in the palm of his hand. When Aquinas informs us that God's essence is existence, he is trying to express the same idea—that God is not simply one of a large number of objects that litter the universe. We cannot point to something and say, "That is God," as we can say, "That is a chair," "That is an elephant," and so on. He is not an object like that, not even the greatest one of them all. He is the reality underpinning every object and the universe itself. He is not an existing thing; he is what makes existence possible.

This has profound implications:

> Now, since God's essence is existence, created things are what he causes. . . . Therefore, for as long as a thing exists, God must always be present to it, in whatever way it exists. But existence is within every thing, completely and fundamentally present within them. . . . So God must be completely within all things.
> *Summa Theologiae* Ia.8.1

Paradoxically, Aquinas's emphasis on the transcendence of God has led him to affirm that God is immediately present to every existing thing.

The rest follows swiftly. Since God is the cause of everything else, he must be perfect, because a cause is better than what it causes (this is an essential Neoplatonic belief). Because he is perfectly simple, he has no limits, any more than he has qualities. So he is infinite. He cannot be constrained in any way.

This leads Aquinas to the doctrine of God's timelessness. God is not simply everlasting, in the sense of having no beginning or end, as Aristotle thought about the world. He is outside time altogether. Aquinas uses the image of a man on top of a tall tower, watching a procession passing beneath. The lofty observer can see the whole of the procession and is not part of it. Similarly, God exists outside history and sees the whole of it at once. With God there is no past, present or future. This idea had been stated clearly by Plotinus and less clearly by Origen and Augustine; the 6th-century philosopher Boethius also used it. But Aquinas was the first to work out rigorously what it actually meant. Whether his account is really coherent is, of course, another matter.

How can Aquinas say all of this when God is supposed to be so great that we cannot apply human concepts to him? Aquinas replies that all talk of God is simply analogy. If we say, "Aquinas is a good man," and "This is a good cheesecake," then the word *good* does not mean the same thing in each sentence. The qualities that make a person good and those that make a cheesecake good are obviously not the same. So *good* has a variety of meanings, depending on the context. Similarly, if we say "God is good" then it means something quite different again. There is an analogy between God's goodness and Aquinas's goodness—and the cheesecake's—but it does not follow that God has the good qualities possessed by either Aquinas or the cheesecake. In other words, the terms that we use to describe God do not mean exactly what they mean when we normally use them. They mean something *similar* instead.

Whether this really makes sense is not clear—for one thing, if the word *good* means something different from normal when it appears in the sentence "God is good," then what *does* it mean? If it is not something that we would normally recognize as goodness, then why use the word at all? Duns Scotus would raise serious objections like this to Aquinas's doctrine of analogy, and by extension to Aquinas's whole doctrine of God.

As we found earlier, then, Aquinas presents us with a very impersonal, abstract notion of God. He is existence itself, infinite and perfect, unlimited, beyond time. This is the "classical" Christian doctrine of God, and it might be thought to bear little relation to the dynamic and interesting God of the Old Testament or the loving Father of the New. For this reason, 20th-century theology was marked by a series of vigorous rebellions against the classical doctrine.

Yet this is a little unfair. Aquinas does not deny that we can relate to God personally; on the contrary, God possesses all perfections, including those of personality. It is just that he transcends them. And as we have seen, he is infinitely close to every created thing. But what of prayer? It is true that there seems little point in asking Aquinas's God to do things: since he is outside time, he has either done them or not done them already. And it would be hard to have a two-way conversation with Transcendent Existence. But for Aquinas, prayer is really a matter of mystical contemplation, not conversation. Its purpose is to bring our will into alignment with God, not to try to get God to do what we want. In this respect, we can see that Aquinas's doctrine of God can have valuable spiritual consequences.

Salvation and the church. Like Augustine, Aquinas believes that Adam, before his fall, was essentially perfect, and he therefore rejects Irenaeus's belief that the incarnation would have happened even if Adam had never sinned. He also rejects Anselm's argument that, in the circumstances, the incarnation was necessary; instead he asserts that since God is omnipotent he could have saved us another way, but the way he chose was the most fitting. Aquinas describes the process in terms drawn from Anselm. Like Anselm, his doctrine of Christ is essentially a restatement of Chalcedon: Christ is the second Person of the Trinity, fully God, who has become fully human. One important point connected to Aquinas's understanding of Christ is his defense of the doctrine of the immaculate conception of Mary. This doctrine holds that Jesus' mother was herself born in a special way: although she had a human father in the normal fashion, the stain of original sin was not passed on to her. Unlike all other human beings since Adam, she was therefore born in a sinless state, which was necessary so that she could herself bear Jesus. This was made possible by God's retroactively applying the benefits of Christ's death to Mary—she is not sinless independently of the salvation that Christ wins. The doctrine is intended to honor Christ indirectly, by honoring his mother, just as the affirmation that Mary was *Theotokos*, "God-bearer," had been in the 5th century. However, in the Reformation, Protestants would reject the doctrine as unbiblical and in a sense idolatrous, because it focuses too much attention on Christ's mother instead of on Christ himself.

Again like Anselm, Aquinas believes that the purpose of the incarnation was so that Christ could pay to God what humankind could not. He thinks of this as an excess of merit earned, as it were, by Christ in virtue of his perfect obedience, which is imputed to our account by God. Whereas in the Eastern Church salvation was associated with humanity's becoming deified, or united to God, in Aquinas's thought this is replaced by the ideal of the *vision* of God, and this is at the basis of much medieval and later Catholic spirituality.

The important thing for Aquinas, however, is that salvation, although won by Christ, is mediated via the church. In this respect he is in firm agreement with Augustine. Indeed, he has a higher view of the priesthood than Augustine, arguing that when a priest is ordained, God essentially makes an unbreakable promise to perform the miracle of the sacraments whenever the priest utters the appropriate prayer. The promise holds even if a priest is later disgraced. So a priest can invoke the sacraments almost like magic, infallibly, simply by performing them.

And the sacraments have real power; they are not mere symbols. In the miracle of the Mass, the bread and wine really become Christ's body and blood, and as such they are the means by which salvation is extended to believers. This is not to say, of course, that the sacraments *cause* salvation; we are saved only by Christ's death. God uses the sacraments as a channel whereby grace is given to us, just as a gardener uses a hose to administer water to the garden.

This emphasis on the church's role in mediating salvation may seem to hark back to pre-Augustinian Christianity, when salvation was thought of as a corporate affair, not a matter between God and the individual. Paradoxically, however, there is a strong element of individualism in Aquinas's sacramental theology. Although the church administers the sacraments, they are received by individuals, and it was the highly personal relationship they allow between God and the communicant that was at the basis of Aquinas's own intense devotion to Mass.

Influence

Aquinas was a controversial figure in his own lifetime, mainly because of the way he used Aristotle. Indeed, some of his ideas were condemned after his death by the bishop of Paris in 1277; this provoked a strong reaction from the Dominicans, who supported their late colleague, as well as from the aged Albertus Magnus. It was not until 1323 that Aquinas was completely vindicated, when Pope John XXII had him canonized as a saint. Waving aside objections that Aquinas had performed few of the miracles normally associated with saints, the pope asserted that every page of the *Summa Theologiae* was a miracle.

Before long the *Summa Theologiae* had become the standard textbook for theology students, and the thought of Thomas Aquinas, now known as the "Angelic Doctor," was universally acclaimed as authentic Catholicism. His followers commented on his works and developed his ideas, creating a powerful school of thought known as Thomism. Despite the weakening of Aristotelianism during the Renaissance, Thomism remained strong, and if anything, the Reformation strengthened it as Catholic scholars and theologians pored through the pages of the Angelic Doctor to refute the Protestants.

Nevertheless, Thomism declined in the 18th and 19th centuries even in its strongholds in the Catholic Church. Strikingly, its revival was associated with the appearance of a new enemy, seen by many as equal in danger to Luther: Charles Darwin and the revolution in the life sciences of the 19th century. In 1879, Pope Leo XIII declared Aquinas's teaching to be the official teaching of the Catholic Church. Since then his admirers have sought to find new ways to restate Thomism in terms acceptable to modern thought—just as Thomas himself sought to restate Augustinianism in terms of the then-new Aristotelianism.

Bonaventure

Bonaventure is remembered by the Catholic Church as the "Seraphic Doctor," a man of such intellectual and spiritual powers that he deserves to be mentioned in the same breath as his friend and sparring partner Thomas Aquinas.

Life

Bonaventure's real name was John of Bagnorea, but he took the name by which he is remembered, meaning "good luck," when he became a Franciscan friar. It is said that he was given the name by St. Francis of Assisi himself, when the infant John was taken to him to be cured of an illness in 1221.

Whether or not Bonaventure really had such an early encounter with the famous founder of the Franciscans, he rose through the ranks of the order with astonishing speed. The Franciscans sent him to study at Paris, where he quickly became known as one of the university's most promising scholars; and by 1248 he was lecturing. In 1257 he became minister general of the Franciscans, the leader of the whole order, an extraordinarily important job for someone still so young.

This was the period, 30 years after the death of St. Francis, when the Franciscan order was divided between those who wanted to impose the rules regarding poverty as strictly as possible, and live as Francis had lived; and those who urged a more liberal interpretation in the interest of order and stability. Bonaventure allied himself with neither group but clamped down on extremists from all sides, reforming the order along moderate principles and expelling those who failed to toe the line. The process was finalized when Bonaventure ordered all existing biographies of St. Francis of Assisi to be destroyed, since different factions were appealing to their own interpretations of the founder's life. He then sat down and wrote his own, "definitive" biography to replace all earlier ones, an act that has enraged generations of scholars trying to uncover the real facts of St. Francis's life.

Bonaventure's other writings were also causing a stir. He was involved in the controversy then raging at Paris over Aristotle, whose newly discovered works were being championed by Albertus Magnus and Thomas Aquinas. Bonaventure, who was essentially a theological conservative, railed against what he regarded as unthinking acceptance of unchristian ideas. He was happy to use Aristotle in his own thought, and indeed the works of Bonaventure are just as rationalist as those of Aquinas. But he was far more concerned to stay faithful to tradition, and particularly to Augustine.

Bonaventure's growing prestige in the church was equaled only by his humility. Like many other saints, he was particularly reluctant to accept high office. In 1265 Pope Clement IV appointed him archbishop of York, but Bonaventure refused to take the job. Eight years later Gregory X, a less easily swayed pope, made him cardinal of Albano. The papal envoys who delivered the red hat of office to Bonaventure found the saint outside the monastery washing the dishes; he told them to hang the hat on a convenient tree until he had finished.

Even before he became a cardinal, Bonaventure was at the heart of the Catholic Church's policy-forming unit and played a central role at the Vatican. He called councils and advised his fellow cardinals in papal elections, and he always had the ear of the pope. He was the guiding force behind the 1274 Council of Lyons, during which he suddenly died. It is said that he was poisoned, but who did it and why remains a mystery.

Thought

As far as speculative and creative theology goes, Bonaventure was not in the same league as his friend Thomas Aquinas. But this was more a matter of general outlook than one of ability. Bonaventure's main concern, theologically, was to remain true to the vision of Augustine. This meant, on the whole, retaining a far more Platonic outlook than Aquinas did. It meant thinking of the world primarily not as an ordered system of natural causes but as a reflection of God, a vast and numinous mirror from which the mystic will eventually turn his gaze to see God himself. We can see how this has much in common with Francis of Assisi's own spirituality, which revolved around God's relation to the world as Creator. There is a sense in which Bonaventure's Neoplatonic worldview is far more "religious" than Aquinas's Aristotelian, "scientific" one.

So Bonaventure was, at heart, not a dogmatic theologian like Aquinas but a mystic. His works and life were suffused with the ideal of contemplative prayer. Like other medieval Western theologians, he spoke of the vision of God as the goal of the mystic's life, and he thought of this vision as coming about through personal devotion to the person of Christ. This very Christ-centered mysticism would be common in later medieval devotional writing, such as that of Julian of Norwich. Both Julian and Bonaventure think of the spiritual life as involving devotion and love toward Christ at a very personal level, and therefore they tend to dwell more on the role of emotion than on intellect in the spiritual life. Their devotions also revolve around the passion of Christ and the extraordinary love that it demonstrates.

In fact, their spirituality has many parallels with the much later Protestant movement of Pietism. Aquinas once asked Bonaventure where his great learning came from. Bonaventure pointed to a crucifix, answering, "I study only the Crucified One, Jesus Christ." Any Protestant evangelical would approve!

John Duns Scotus

The original "dunce," Scotus was in fact one of the most brilliant, if hard to understand, thinkers of the Middle Ages. The Catholic Church remembers him as the "Subtle Doctor"; the title is well deserved.

Life

All that is known of John Duns Scotus's life can be stated in a few sentences. He was probably born around 1266, he was a Franciscan friar, and unlike John the Scot ("Erigena," who was Irish), he probably was Scottish. It was in England that he made his name, however, after arriving in Oxford in 1288. By 1302 he was known as one of the university's outstanding scholars and had moved to Paris, where he gained his doctor's degree. Together with 80 other academics, he was expelled from the great university the following year for siding with the pope in a dispute against the king; but he was allowed back in 1304. Three years later he moved to Cologne, where he died in 1308.

Scotus's early death robbed the world of an extraordinary talent. In his short

OXFORD

"Will no one rid me of this turbulent priest?" cried King Henry II of England in an unguarded moment at dinner. Four knights fresh from the Crusades happened to overhear, and correctly taking him to mean Thomas à Becket, the archbishop of Canterbury, with whom he had fallen out, they promptly went off to Canterbury and killed him in the cathedral. The year was 1170.

The assassination, together with the king's subsequent public penance and the swift elevation of Becket to the sainthood, transformed Canterbury into a major pilgrimage destination. The affair also transformed Oxford, an important market town in the center of England, whose wealth had allowed several monastic schools to settle there. Becket, while on the run from Henry II, had sought shelter with the king of France; the furious Henry thereupon ordered all English scholars studying at Paris to return home immediately. They flocked to the schools of Oxford. A new university was born.

The new university was much like its older counterpart in Paris. It consisted of a diverse collection of halls and colleges, and most of the teaching took place in the university church in the center of the city. Gradually more formal courses and faculties evolved, until a standard curriculum much like the one in Paris was offered.

The university did not always coexist happily with the city. In 1209, after a student was accused of killing a townswoman, there was a riot in which the populace seized and hanged two students. In response to this, some of the scholars gave up on Oxford as a bad job and fled to Cambridge, a much smaller town, to found yet another university. Back in Oxford, the worst

life Scotus produced an enormous quantity of work, mainly commentaries on standard theological and philosophical texts and discussions of commonly disputed questions. They represent the pinnacle of Scholastic thought, a dizzying combination of extreme cleverness and pedantic academic jargon. Even more than Aquinas, Scotus was essentially a philosopher rather than a theologian, and his work was academic, written for specialists. This is one reason his influence on later Christian thought has been less great than his talent might have suggested. Nevertheless, despite the difficulty of his writings, there is much in them that is of great value to theologians.

atrocity was the St. Scholastica Day massacre of 1355, which was sparked off by a student's throwing substandard wine into the face of the barman who had served it. Three days later, once the street battles had largely died down, hundreds of students were dead, the colleges had been looted, and the scholars had fled. The town was forced to pay reparations to the university for the next five centuries.

Despite all of this, Oxford quickly established a reputation as a major center of philosophical and theological thought. Its alumni included such thinkers as Roger Bacon, Duns Scotus and William of Ockham. While there was no particular sense that Oxford was a rival school to Paris, as Constantinople had been to Alexandria in the last days of the empire, we can see some slightly differing tendencies between the two centers of learning. In contrast to the mystical thought of Bonaventure or Bernard of Clairvaux and the speculative theology of Thomas Aquinas, the Oxford thinkers tended to be more preoccupied with language, everyday observation and general common sense. In an age of book learning, Bacon conducted scientific experiments; and Scotus and Ockham, although they violently disagreed with each other, both showed a concern for and sensitivity to the nuances of language and meaning that eluded the more far-reaching Aquinas.

These concerns have typified Oxford philosophy and theology ever since. And we can see this desire for commonsense, middle-of-the-road ideas coming out later in the English Reformation and the establishment of the Church of England as a middle way between Catholicism and Protestantism.

Thought

Much of the interest of Scotus's work comes from the remarkably free and trenchant criticism he pours on others. Even Thomas Aquinas himself is not immune to Scotus's penetrating dissection and ruthless exposition of mistakes. Because Scotus and his followers disagreed with Aquinas and other authorities, they were thought to be stupid, and "Duns"—or "dunce"—became synonymous with "idiot." However, not only was Scotus himself easily as clever as Aquinas, but the Scotists survived and their school of thought has proved a useful counterpart to Thomism, acting as a counterbalance to it from within Catholicism.

Some of Scotus's most acute criticism of Aquinas concerns his doctrine of God. We have seen how Aquinas thinks of God's prime attribute as being his simplicity, and from this simplicity he derives all of the divine perfections such as omnipotence and timelessness. Scotus, by contrast, thinks that God's most fundamental attribute is his infinity, and it is because he is infinite that God is omniscient, omnipotent and so on.

These different emphases on God's attributes reflect a more fundamental difference between Aquinas's and Scotus's understanding of the divine nature. We saw how for Aquinas the divine simplicity is essentially a negative quality: it is not that God *is* simple so much as that he *is not* composite. God transcends all qualities, so we cannot say what he is, only what he is not.

Scotus, on the other hand, thinks of the divine infinity in a much more positive way. God does not transcend good qualities like power and knowledge; he *possesses* them fully, to an unparalleled degree. Scotus thus disagrees with the Pseudo-Dionysian tradition of negative theology. This has important consequences for how we speak about God. We saw that Aquinas argues that whenever we say that God has a certain quality, we are speaking analogously. If we say God has perfect knowledge, then by "knowledge" we mean something like what we normally mean by "knowledge," but different. Scotus has no time for this sort of thing. He points out that the reason we say God has perfect knowledge is that we believe God to be supremely good, and we know from experience that knowledge is a good thing. But if what God has is not what we normally mean by "knowledge," then how do we know it is good? Why say that he has it at all?

And there is more. Analogous language is all very well, but it is meaningless unless it can be "cashed out" in nonanalogous language. Suppose we say that someone is like a lion, meaning that they are brave. That is an analogy; but it makes sense only because the person and the lion share a quality, namely bravery. In other words, when we use an analogy, it must be reducible to nonanalogous qualities. So Aquinas is wrong to say that we can speak of God *only* by analogy. If those analogies cannot be restated in nonanalogous terms, then they are meaningless. And if they *can* be restated in that way, then God does not in fact transcend earthly qualities, and we have no need of analogies in the first place.

The argument is devastating. And the dispute between Aquinas and Scotus illustrates one of the most fundamental problems facing theology. If, like Aquinas, we say God is so great that he transcends the universe and the categories that apply to it; if he is not a thing like other things but existence itself, through which all else exists; then can we say or know anything about him at all? Does the claim even make sense? Is it not, to all intents and purposes, no different from atheism? But if, like Scotus, we say that God is comprehensible, that he shares recognizable earthly qualities to a supreme degree, then is he really God? Is he not just the most powerful being in the universe, greater than all other beings but not fundamentally different from them?

Medieval Mysticism

The 12th and 13th centuries saw incredible developments in church structure and thought, with the appearance of chivalry, the great monastic and mendicant foundations, and Scholastic theology, along with the continued rise of the papacy. Yet this was not a sterile hardening period with no true spiritual devotion. On the contrary, the medieval period witnessed some of the most profound and moving religious experiences of all time.

All of the great theologians of the Middle Ages, including Anselm, Aquinas and Bernard of Clairvaux, were also spiritual writers of great depth. Yet even they were overshadowed by the extraordinary flowering of devotion and mysticism that was to bloom in monasteries and parish churches throughout the period.

One of the first great medieval mystics was Hildegard of Bingen, a German prioress who lived in the 12th century. Hildegard was a visionary and prophet who became enormously famous on account of her profound mystical teachings and her strange visions, which are now thought to have been associated with migraines. But she was also an incredibly versatile cultural figure. She composed music and poetry, painted, wrote important scientific and medical works as well as plays, and, in her spare time, even devised an imaginary language. She is also credited with the first-known written description of the female orgasm.

The 14th century saw major developments in mystical theology throughout Europe. In England, two opposed spiritual traditions jostled for elbow room. Richard Rolle, a Yorkshire hermit who lived for a while in a forest, wrote extremely popular spiritual works describing the positive, emotional experience of coming close to God. His writings, and those of the slightly later Walter Hilton, are in the tradition of "light" mysticism pioneered by Origen and in the East by Symeon the New Theologian. In contrast, *The Cloud of Unknowing*, an anonymous work by an

English parish priest, is firmly in the negative tradition of Gregory of Nyssa and Pseudo-Dionysius. It stresses how God is eternally hidden by a "cloud of unknowing," impenetrable to the intellect but accessible to love.

Transcending both traditions was Julian of Norwich, who despite the name was actually a woman. Julian was both a mystic and a speculative theologian. Her book *Revelations of Divine Love* describes a series of visions of Christ's passion and intermingles her theological reflections on them. The book is one of the warmest, most optimistic and sensible works of medieval theology.

At the same time an extraordinary spiritual tradition was developing in Germany, around the river Rhine. Meister Eckhart, a Dominican friar, taught a negative theology, a development of Pseudo-Dionysius. Indeed, his insistence that God transcends both unity and trinity, that we must push past "God" to find "the Godhead," and that the Godhead can be found within the heart of human beings has led to accusations of heresy and pantheism. However, the Meister was very influential, and the great tradition of the Rhineland mystics lived on in his disciples John Tauler and Henry Suso.

THE INQUISITION

In 1231 certain judges were granted the power to search out and try heretics in the name of the pope. Most of them were drawn from the Benedictine monasteries and Franciscan friaries, where it was hoped they would have attained the theological and spiritual discretion necessary for this solemn task. The Inquisition had begun.

In earlier centuries the church had sought merely to correct those it thought to be in error. Things began to change in the late 4th century, when a heretic named Priscillian was executed by the state for "sorcery," a capital offense. Most churchmen protested bitterly at this cruelty, and Ambrose of Milan, the most prominent bishop at the time, denounced it as a crime. However, by the Middle Ages it was becoming increasingly accepted that spiritual correction could be accompanied by physical chastisement. The Crusades were the most obvious example of this principle.

Like all ancient and medieval courts, the Inquisition regarded torture as an acceptable means of obtaining a confession from a suspect. Its judges did not have the power to execute people, but they could turn heretics over to the secular authorities for punishment, which invariably meant execution.

Nevertheless, despite these positive developments, all was not well within the Roman Catholic Church. The increasing power of the papacy and of lesser clerics created more scope for abuse of power. One of the best known descriptions of medieval life from this period is Geoffrey Chaucer's *The Canterbury Tales,* in which a group of pilgrims on their way to Canterbury tell each other stories to while away the time. Of the characters, figures like the worldly Friar, the devilish Summoner and the sinister Pardoner are among the most memorable, and they represent a powerful criticism of immorality and worldly standards among church officials and clerics. And this criticism would increasingly be echoed by theologians like Wyclif, rebels like the Hussites, and ultimately Luther and the Reformation.

John Wyclif

John Wyclif (also spelled Wycliffe) lived a century and a half before Luther, yet his doctrines not only anticipate those of the great Reformer, they sometimes exceed them. This cantankerous Oxford scholar is rightly remembered as "the morning star of the Reformation."

The 13th-century Inquisitors were, on the whole, fair-minded men with a genuine zeal for the truth who tried to carry out their awesome responsibilities with mercy and justice. Their later successors were far more notorious. The Spanish Inquisition was founded in 1478 to root out Islam and Judaism, and it achieved great success under the infamous Grand Inquisitor Torquemada. The bloody reputation of the Spanish Inquisition and its red-robed cardinals was forged over the next couple of decades as hundreds of heretics were tortured and executed. Those who recanted their heresy died on quick-burning fires, while those who remained obstinate to the last smoldered to death slowly.

The Spanish Inquisition was the most infamous example of the developing idea that the church had the power of life and death over its members. In 17th-century England, Catholics who refused to renounce allegiance to the pope were executed by King Henry VIII, and Protestants who refused to recant their faith were burned by Queen Mary. In Calvin's Geneva, meanwhile, anyone who broke the religious laws of the Reformed state could suffer any punishment, including death. It would be a long time before Christians of any denomination became more moderate in their thinking.

Life

Wyclif was born round about 1325 in Yorkshire. Nothing is known of his life until he arrived at Oxford, where he took his master's degree in 1358 and his doctorate in 1372. Clearly, 14th-century degree courses at Oxford lasted even longer than they do today. Despite becoming master of Balliol College, however, Wyclif was not a rich man; he relied on the living he earned as priest in not one but two parishes, neither of which he actually lived in. This, again, was common at the time.

But despite being perhaps not altogether blameless in this area himself, Wyclif was soon denouncing corruption and immorality in the church. He argued that authority—secular and religious—is dependent on God's grace. Someone in a state of sin has no right to any kind of authority, even if he is the pope.

Many people found Wyclif's ideas congenial, especially those who resented paying allegiance and money to a potentate in Avignon, where the papal court was at that time. John of Gaunt, one of the most powerful lords in England, summoned Wyclif to London to preach and had him serve as a personal adviser. Pope Gregory XI was not happy, however. In 1377 he issued a condemnation of Wyclif's ideas, ordering him to be arrested. Wyclif was defended by his university, which supported his doctrines; and the death of the pope in 1378 ended the affair. Gregory XI was succeeded by two claimants to the papal throne, Urban VI in Rome and Clement VII in Avignon. The ecclesiastical civil war that broke out, as both camps excommunicated each other and the Catholic world watched in horrified bemusement, showed just how pertinent Wyclif's concerns were.

Wyclif was now undermining the church's authority still further, claiming that since the source of all doctrine is the Bible, people should be able to read it for themselves without the need for translation or explanation from a priest. Inspired by Wyclif, teams of translators set to work producing a vernacular version of the Bible from the official Latin. The church authorities were horrified. They believed that if anyone was making an unauthorized translation of the Bible, they must be using it to teach doctrines not approved by the church. While parts of the Bible were occasionally allowed to be translated for the use of certain wealthy people, the idea of producing an English version of the whole thing for anybody to read was quite outrageous. The Bible had authority only within the context of the church.

The real crunch came in 1379, when Wyclif began to preach against the accepted understanding of the Eucharist. The storm was immediate. In 1380 Oxford University itself condemned Wyclif's teaching, and the following year he left the city for Lutterworth, one of his parishes. Here he continued to teach and write, becoming more and more bitter as time went on; he felt that the church had driven him from Oxford. Perhaps this is why he felt it necessary to declare that CARDI-

NAL stood for "Captain of the Apostates of the Realm of the Devil, Impudent and Nefarious Ally of Lucifer." Meanwhile, a council in London condemned his ideas in 1382; it was interrupted by an earthquake, which was interpreted as England's belching out the foul heresy.

Wyclif died in 1384, but his ideas lived on. He had plenty of followers in England, known as Lollards—originally an abusive term meaning "mumblers"; and he had even more in Bohemia, in the modern-day Czech Republic, where Jan Hus had been popularizing his ideas. However, the Lollards were brutally suppressed in England, where every attempt was made to erase the memory of Wyclif. The friars, whom Wyclif had attacked particularly bitterly, were especially instrumental in this. His writings were destroyed, his ideas were condemned at the Council of Constance in 1415, and in a rather grotesque bid to eradicate every trace of the man, his corpse was dug up in 1428 and burned.

Thought

Wyclif's thought was not a system of theology so much as a series of protests against what he saw as the abuses and errors of the Catholic Church.

Perhaps his most striking and influential point concerned the Scriptures. Wyclif argued that it was wrong that common people should have to rely on priests to interpret the Bible, since the Bible is the source of all truth. In fact the Bible should be available in the people's language, not the Latin of the learned classes, so that everyone can read it. Scripture, he argued, is the sole authority, and all truth can be found in it.

This was new. All Christians, of course, from the Fathers on, believed the Bible to be wholly true and inspired; but the idea that the Bible could be an *independent* source of truth apart from the church was a novelty, not found in the Fathers. It would be central to the Reformation.

However, the ideas that really got Wyclif into trouble concerned the Eucharist. The church taught that the bread and wine actually become the body and blood of Christ and cease being bread and wine, although they still look and taste the same. Wyclif denounced this as ridiculous. He did believe that Christ's body is present in the consecrated elements, but not that those elements *become* Christ's body, and he mocked priests who believed that they could "create" Christ's body on the eucharistic altar. It was these claims about the Eucharist that would prove especially influential among Hus and his followers in Bohemia.

Jan Hus

The life and death of Jan Hus herald, in tragic form, the end of the Middle Ages and the great theological project they had nurtured. To Hus and his followers, on

the eve of the Reformation, the Roman Catholic Church was going the way of the
Roman empire.

Life

Jan Hus was born in about 1369. He took his name, which means "goose," from
the town where he was born, Husinetz, in Bohemia, in the modern-day Czech Republic. He studied at Charles University in Prague, where he became a priest in
1400 and rector of the university two years later.

The university and the country were going through a rather tricky patch. The
university had been founded some decades earlier by Holy Roman Emperor
Charles IV, who hoped to create a cosmopolitan center of learning to rival Paris
and Oxford, where students from all parts of the empire could meet in scholarly
harmony. Unfortunately, by the time Hus became rector, the scholars had divided
into two camps: those from German-speaking areas and those, like Hus, who spoke
Czech.

The tension was symptomatic of the times. The power of the Catholic Church,
which had once unified the continent, now divided it. Since 1378 there had been
two rival popes, which meant that the kings of the emerging nation-states could
play them off against each other. The different nations of Europe were becoming
more and more clearly defined. Although Latin was still the language of scholars
and of the church, most people now spoke vernacular national tongues, and this
added to the growing divisions. The Middle Ages were coming to an end.

Into this difficult and uncertain situation came King Wenceslas IV of Bohemia.
Unlike the saintly Wenceslas of Christmas carol fame, who had ruled the country
five centuries earlier, Wenceslas was a weak and unpopular ruler, a drunkard who
was actually imprisoned twice during his reign. His sister was married to King
Richard II of England, however, and this meant that the writings and ideas of some
English thinkers became more widely known in Bohemia. Among them was John
Wyclif.

No one was more enthusiastic about Wyclif than Hus. Like Wyclif, Hus was
disillusioned with the official hierarchy of the Catholic Church; in particular, he
was disgusted by the power and riches claimed by the pope and his subordinates.

Hus was a very powerful and charismatic preacher. He was idolized by the
Czech scholars at the university, but the German speakers hated him. They were
certainly not happy about the radical ideas pouring—in the Czech language—
from the pulpit of the Bethlehem Chapel, an enormous church in Prague, capable
of seating a congregation of 3,000. The chapel was decorated with pictures showing the pope in all his finery next to a humble and poor Christ; even those who

could not understand Hus's sermons could hardly miss their message. And Hus was careful to put his principles into practice: at the chapel he set up a scheme to provide food and lodging for the poorest students at the university.

The Germans complained to church authorities about the teachings that Hus and his followers were spreading. Hus's enthusiasm for Wyclif, a condemned heretic, and his attacks on papal and clerical privileges were angering a lot of people. Both popes forbade the preaching of Wyclif's ideas at Prague. Wenceslas started getting nervous. Although he had earlier favored Hus and the Bohemians over the Germans, he now ordered the university to condemn Wyclif. Hus responded that he was more than happy to condemn any errors that might be found in Wyclif's works, though he would never condemn Wyclif himself. Wenceslas, weak and unsure of what to do, did nothing.

In 1409 a council met at Pisa to resolve the pope problem. Both popes were deposed and a new one was elected to replace them. Unfortunately, and rather predictably, neither of the old contenders accepted the ruling of the council, and they carried on just as before. So now there were *three* popes.

One of the first things the new pope did was to endorse the ban on Wyclif. Wyclif's books were burned, and Hus was forbidden from preaching. The result was chaos: Hus's supporters rioted on the streets of Prague, while Hus himself ignored the ban and continued to preach in the Bethlehem Chapel, becoming bolder every day. Wenceslas still supported him, and the church authorities could do nothing.

The situation reached a crisis point in 1411. One of the popes called for the people to contribute to a holy war he was planning. This crusade was not against infidels, however; it was against King Ladislaus of Naples, who was protecting one of the other popes. Hus, appalled that someone should actually go to war to secure for himself the power of the papacy, publicly denounced the plan. His preaching electrified the people of Prague; they rose up, burned the papal bull proclaiming the crusade, and heckled the preachers who supported it. In response the civil authorities beheaded three of the rebels—the first martyrs of the Hussite cause.

The whole business was proving a great embarrassment to Wenceslas, who did not wish to be known to the rest of Europe as the protector of heretics. He forced Hus to leave Prague, but his supporters did not calm down. The king tried calling synods and councils, but they had no effect. At his orders, the scholars of the university set out what Hus and his followers would have to do in order to end the conflict. They would have to agree that the pope is the head of the church and that the cardinals are its body and they must all be obeyed. But Hus refused to agree to this, because it suggested that the pope and the cardinals together *were* the church.

Hus pointed out that the head of the church is not the pope but Christ; and that every Christian is a member of the church, not just those in positions of power. The controversy continued, and Hus's ideas became better and better known throughout Europe.

The situation was finally dealt with by Wenceslas's brother King Sigismund of Luxembourg. Sigismund wanted to become Holy Roman emperor, but first he had to deal with the heresy outbreak. Despite his personal ambition, Sigismund seems to have been quite concerned for the cause of Christian truth. As emperor, he would found the Order of the Dragon, a knightly order dedicated to defending the Christian empire against the ravages of Islam. One of its most illustrious members was Vlad II of Walachia, whom Sigismund rewarded for his valor by making him ruler of Transylvania. As a member of Sigismund's Order, Vlad was sometimes called Dracul, meaning "Dragon," and his son, the sadistic Vlad the "Impaler," would also be known as "Little Dragon," or Dracula.

More important than these unsavory connections was the fact that in 1414 Sigismund called the Council of Constance to sort out the problems facing the Catholic Church. The first thing on the agenda was the papal schism: all three popes were forced to resign—not, it has to be said, without a good deal of reluctance—and a new, undisputed pope was elected.

This done, the council turned to the question of heresy. Sigismund had invited Hus to the council to try to clear up the Bohemian dispute, and Hus was happy to attend, especially since Sigismund provided him with letters of safe passage that guaranteed his personal security whatever might happen. Unfortunately, shortly after Hus arrived, he was thrown into a dungeon while the pope situation was sorted out. It looked as though the ambitious Sigismund's letters were not worth the paper they were written on.

When Hus was allowed to appear, he found that he was on trial for heresy. He was ordered to condemn Wyclif's works and recant his own errors. Hus replied that he thought very highly of Wyclif but would be happy to condemn any errors in his works that were pointed out to him; as for his own errors, he would not recant them because he had not committed any, although he would condemn any heretical statements that the council read out to him.

Hus did not expect this defense to work, and it didn't. He was ready for martyrdom and had in fact been careful to make his will before even leaving for the council. On July 6, 1415, he was solemnly condemned to be burned to death for heresy. As the decision was read out, Hus protested loudly, before falling to his knees and asking forgiveness for his enemies. His priestly vestments were removed, his priestly hairstyle was shaved off, and he was led away in a paper hat with the word *Heretic* on it.

As he was chained to a stake and kindling was heaped around him, he was asked to recant one more time. Hus replied: "God is my witness that I have never taught what false witnesses have accused me of. In the truth of the gospel which I have written, taught, and preached I will die today with gladness." He died quickly, suffocated by the smoke, and his ashes were thrown into the Rhine.

Thought

Hus was not an original theologian. He did not write a great deal, and most of what he did write was little more than a paraphrase of the works of Wyclif. It is not certain whether Hus had formed his own ideas before he read Wyclif, but he was certainly hugely influenced by the English Reformer. His skill lay in translating Wyclif's ideas into an enormously popular movement through his own charisma and commanding presence.

Hus's preaching ran along two lines. First, like Wyclif, he rejected any doctrine or practice that was not to be found in the Bible. In particular, he focused on the way the Eucharist was understood. Like Wyclif, he rejected the official teaching of the church that the bread and the wine actually become Christ's body and blood; he argued that the bread and wine remain what they are but become united to Christ's body and blood. This doctrine was quite similar to what Luther would teach a century later. Hus was also angry at the practice, common at this time, of distributing the bread to the congregation but keeping the wine back for the priests. He pointed out that this practice was entirely unscriptural, and indeed it became such a central issue for Hus and his followers that the Hussite warriors of the 1420s would ride to battle under a flag depicting a chalice.

Hus's second main concern was with abuses of power within the church. As the pictures in the Bethlehem Chapel illustrated, he was extremely unhappy with the power and privilege enjoyed by the pope. Not only did it contrast sharply with the poverty and humility of Christ, but the Bible instructs priests to have no possessions at all. In fact, although Hus believed the pope to be the rightful head of the church, he did not accept that simply being pope made anyone especially holy. He pointed out that nowhere in the Bible are we told that obeying the pope is necessary to salvation.

At the heart of Hus's teaching was a radical rejection of the power system that had developed in the church. He hated the idea that ecclesiastical authority should go hand in hand with political power; indeed, he realized that Christ had taught quite the opposite, that those in authority should be the most humble and self-giving. That was why he rejected the idea that the church consists of the pope and his cardinals, rather than of all the faithful; it was also why he was so appalled by the farcical efforts of different contenders to secure the papal throne for themselves. For Hus, true Christianity has nothing to do with where on the power scale you happen to be.

Influence

The story of Jan Hus reads almost like a dress rehearsal for that of Martin Luther a century later. Indeed, it was later said that Hus had told his executioner, "You are now going to burn a goose, but in a century you will have a swan which you can neither roast nor boil." Why did Hus fail where Luther would succeed? For one thing, Hus was not a great theologian: he wrote far less than Luther, and what he did write lacked the genius of the German Reformer. And the time simply was not right: in Hus's day there was not yet the widespread dissatisfaction with church practices with which Luther would later be able to connect.

But Hus is significant in that he shows just how confused theology and politics were becoming. During his lifetime, he was popular not just because of his theology but because of his nationality. And exactly the same thing would happen a century later; Reformers like Luther would tap into growing nationalist sentiments. Anything that looked like a blow against the international power of the pope was popular with the ruling classes and the working classes alike, who were beginning to resent that power and find instead a new sense of their own nationhood.

We can see that clearly if we consider what happened in Prague after 1415. Jan Hus was dead, but his movement lived on. To the Bohemians he was a national hero and a martyr, and his followers drew up a list of demands, known as the Four Articles of Prague. They wanted: both bread and wine to be distributed at the Eucharist; penances to be imposed fairly, regardless of who the sinner was; preachers to be allowed to preach even without the authorization of their local bishop; and priests to embrace total poverty.

Needless to say, the church was not about to grant all that, especially the last one. But the Hussites were not prepared to wait. In 1419 they vented their frustration on seven town councilors, in what historians refer to rather quaintly as the "Defenestration of Prague." Defenestration just means "out of the window," and that is exactly what happened to the unfortunate councilors, who were speared on the pikes of Hussites who waited in the street below. When King Wenceslas heard of the atrocity, he collapsed and died of a heart attack.

Sigismund, now Holy Roman emperor, decided to stamp out the Hussites through military action. A total of five crusades were launched against them throughout the 1420s and 1430s. But the Hussites had organized themselves into a powerful military force in their own right; under their brilliant commander the one-eyed Jan Zizka, the Hussite warriors defeated every force that came against them. Their combination of cunning tricks—such as putting their horses' shoes on backwards so that they could not be tracked—and incredible ferocity in battle gave them a fearsome reputation. In 1437, one army that was sent against them turned tail and fled simply at the sound of their battle song.

The Hussites were split, however, between those who thought that all wealth was wrong and a more conservative faction who thought that this only applied to priests. In 1434 they fought among themselves, and the conservatives won. They went on to make an agreement with the church authorities, who agreed to a toned-down version of the Four Articles of Prague. The extremist wing went underground and became known as the Bohemian Brethren, or the Moravians. They merged with the Lutheran movement in the 16th century but remained a powerful force within Protestantism. Their translation of the Bible into Czech, the Kralice Bible, is still used today.

4

THE REFORMATION

The Reformation period was marked by turbulence and uncertainty. The Catholic Church, which had provided an unshakable sense of unity throughout the Middle Ages, was now being rocked to its core by scandals, abuses, and the appearance of bold new theologians and reformers who were not afraid to challenge everything it stood for. This very uncertainty meant that new theological possibilities were opened up, to a degree that had not happened since the age of the church fathers. But it also led to division, misunderstanding and war. Theology and politics were hopelessly confused, and the consequences were not pretty.

The Renaissance

Europe was reawakening. Sailors and explorers were discovering new worlds. Artists were creating bold new works. Experimental science had been rediscovered, together with the works of antiquity, and incredible new technology was making information cheaply available to the masses. The Middle Ages were over. The modern age was beginning.

"Renaissance" means "rebirth," and while the Middle Ages were hardly a period of intellectual and cultural stagnation, there was a new excitement and inventiveness about the 14th to the 16th centuries. Much of this had to do with new geographical discoveries that came in the wake of Marco Polo's epochal expedition to China.

The explorers

Marco Polo was born in Venice in about 1254, the son of a merchant. When he was a teenager, he accompanied his father and uncle on a trading journey east, to strange lands where the older men had traveled years before, the first Europeans ever to do so. They traveled through the Middle East and across the Gobi Desert to the empire of the Mongols. Here they were received at the court of the legendary emperor Kubla Khan. From his mighty capital of Khanbalik the Great Khan ruled the largest land-based empire of all time, but he took time off building pleasure domes to greet the exotic travelers with lavish hospitality.

Marco stayed with the Great Kahn for five years, serving as a diplomat. He even spent three years as governor of the city of Yangzhou. Eventually, in 1292, all three Polos left China, accompanying a Mongol princess. They traveled through southeast Asia and southern India before arriving back in Venice in 1295. Legend claims that they brought with them the secret of pasta—long known to the Chinese—and introduced it to Italy.

Even more significant than this was Marco Polo's book about his exploits, which rapidly became the most influential travel book of all time. Generations were inspired by his vivid descriptions of the exotic places he had been and people he had met. Many doubted his word. Even today the rumor persists that he made the whole thing up. As Marco lay dying in 1324, his friends urged him to retract the parts of his tale that were untrue. He refused to renounce a single word, telling them only, "I never told the half of what I saw."

Explorers and travelers, their imaginations gripped by Marco Polo's book, vied with each other to find new routes to the mystic Orient. The Spanish and Portuguese in particular seemed possessed by a passion for exploration. The prize of a viable sea route to the riches of the East seemed within their grasp in 1486, when the Portuguese traveled right down the west coast of Africa and discovered the Cape of Good Hope, but the route thereby opened up was a long and treacherous one.

Christopher Columbus, a Genoan sailor, had the bright idea of reaching the East by sailing west. He understandably had some difficulty finding backers for his proposed voyage. This was not because people thought the world was flat—on the contrary, every educated person was well aware that the world was spherical, ever since ancient Greek philosophers and mathematicians had proven the fact. But they were also aware that the world was far too big to sail all the way around it to India from Spain.

As events turned out, Columbus's opponents were proved entirely correct. The world was indeed much larger than Columbus had claimed, and if America had not been in his way, he would have perished long before he reached his destination. Fortunately for him, in 1492 Columbus landed in the Bahamas, which he thought were a group of islands off the coast of east Asia. Once subsequent explorers had established that China did not in fact lie just beyond Panama, the race was on, and the mystical Orient was practically forgotten as every nation scrambled to carve up the new lands.

Classical art and scholarship

While new worlds were being discovered, old ones were being brought back to life. Artists had discovered the glories of classical sculpture, and people like Michaelangelo and Donatello were creating new masterpieces in the old style. Painters began to experiment with non-Christian themes, celebrating classical myths. They also brought startling new techniques to their work: the Flemish discovery of oil paints was one, the Italian discovery of the rules of perspective was another. Figures like Leonardo da Vinci encapsulate the Renaissance spirit—incredible artistry married to unstoppable inventiveness, both practical and whimsical.

But the rediscovery of classical art was nothing compared with the rediscovery of classical writing. New scholars appeared who cared about learning for its own sake, not simply for the sake of the church; they were interested in studying ancient authors, both Christian and pagan. Their leader was Erasmus of Rotterdam, the greatest scholar of the age, who pioneered the study of ancient Greek, by now an almost lost art in the West. Erasmus and his followers were "humanists," secular scholars who, although Christian, thought there was artistic and human value in all ancient writers. Like the artists, they thought of the Middle Ages as a sterile period and wanted to return culture to its roots in ancient Greece and Rome. This endeavor would spark not just a new age of learning but also the struggles of the Reformation.

The rise of science

Similarly, the ancient scientific ideals were reappearing as people realized that Aristotle—still the supreme secular authority—was as much a physical scientist as a speculative philosopher. In 1603 the Academy of Lynxes, the first scientific society, was founded in Italy. Men like Francis Bacon and Thomas Hobbes were not only asking questions about the physical world but going out and actually studying it. Instead of looking for answers in books, they performed experiments—to varying degrees of success. Bacon died of a cold after stuffing a chicken with snow to see what effect it had on decay.

Not all of this seemed good to the church at the time. The most notorious affair was that of Galileo Galilei, one of the greatest scientists of all time. Galileo was a vocal supporter of the theories of Nicholas Copernicus, who had argued that the earth revolved around the sun rather than vice versa, as most people since the ancient Greeks had believed. Unfortunately the Inquisition was not happy with this, and in 1633 they found Galileo guilty of heresy and prevented him from writing. The Inquisition pointed out that the Copernican doctrine contradicted the Bible, and they argued that if the earth really moved around the sun then the moon, which moves around the earth, would get left behind. Galileo knew perfectly well that this argument was daft, because he had invented the telescope and seen the moons of Jupiter, which stay in formation as their parent planet moves across the heavens. But many of his accusers refused even to look in the telescope, declaring it an instrument of Satan. Galileo was forced to recant publicly the notion that the earth moves; he is said apocryphally to have muttered immediately afterward, "Nevertheless, it *does* move!"

The information revolution

Yet all of these advances were dwarfed by the greatest revolution of all: the invention of printing. The method was developed in 1450 by a German silversmith named Johann Gutenberg, who discovered how to cast images of letters that could be rearranged quickly and efficiently to print anything one wanted. Before all texts had been copied by hand, and only large institutions such as monasteries, or rich individuals, could possess a library. Now, however, texts could be mass-produced quickly and cheaply. Not only could the humanists publish classical works and editions of the New Testament, but the Reformers could spread their radical new ideas throughout Europe.

Martin Luther

Martin Luther was a giant of history, probably the most significant European figure of the second millennium. His ideas and actions changed not just the church but the world.

Life

The man who would be called the "German Hercules" was born in Eisleben, a small village in the north of Germany, probably in 1483 (his mother remembered the time of night better than the year). His father, a miner with a sideline in canny business ventures, succeeded through sheer hard work in building up a sizable fortune and getting on first-name terms with the local aristocracy.

Luther received a good education, although he was not academically gifted: in the exams he took at the age of 18, he came in 30th out of 57 students. But he was conscientious and was sent to the University of Erfurt, one of the most respected in Germany. His father was hoping to cement his social standing by securing for his son a career as a lawyer. Luther, however, seems to have been unsure what he really wanted. At Erfurt he was confused by the full force of the Renaissance and the burgeoning humanist movement. He needed to find security and certainty.

His final break with the secular world came in 1505, when, at the age of 21, he was caught in a terrible thunderstorm. Convinced that his end was near, he prayed to St. Anne for deliverance, promising to become a monk if he was spared. The storm passed, and Luther's clothes had barely dried before he was applying to one of Erfurt's Augustinian monasteries. His father was furious, but Luther had made up his mind.

If Luther hoped to find spiritual consolation at the monastery, he was in for a shock. It came after his ordination as a priest in 1507, when he had to say his first Mass. He was overcome by the part of the liturgy where he had to address "the living, the true, the eternal God." Struck with horror by the thought of the awful majesty of God and his own presumption in addressing him, Luther stopped dead and had to be forced to continue with the service.

Luther's attitude of awestruck piety quickly transmuted into fear and self-loathing. Like Augustine before him, he had an unusually strong sense of his own sin-

THE CONQUISTADORS

Hardly had Columbus discovered the New World when more explorers arrived, each seeking to penetrate further into its exotic wildernesses than the last. By 1519, when Hernando Cortés set off to conquer the Aztecs, not only had Brazil and Amazonia been claimed for Portugal but the exploration of North America had begun. By 1550 both the Aztecs and the Incas had been defeated, and the conquest of Mexico, Texas, Florida and much of the southern part of North America had been completed.

The arrival of the conquistadors was a decidedly mixed blessing for the natives they encountered. The Aztecs had an advanced civilization, but it was a bloody one; their ruler Montezuma was a ruthless despot who enjoyed nothing more than ripping out the hearts of prisoners of war on the altars of his gods. But they stood no chance against Cortés and the Spanish. The ethereal capital city of Tenochtitlán, poised above a lake high in the mountains, was soon razed to the ground, its treasures plundered for European courts. Even worse were the diseases brought by the Europeans. It is thought that by the year 1600 only one native out of twenty-five remained. Most of the rest had succumbed to smallpox.

Theologians responded to the rapidly developing situation in different ways. Juan Gines de Sepúlveda, a prominent Spanish philosopher, argued that it was right and just to conquer the New World and enslave its population.

fulness. Unlike Augustine's case, however, this had nothing to do with an obsession with sex, something Luther was never particularly interested in. It was something darker, something to do with Luther's periodically gloomy and self-destructive nature. Throughout his life Luther suffered from attacks of severe depression, during which he was tormented by doubts of his salvation. Sometimes in the middle of a conversation he would be suddenly struck by an overwhelming sense of God's wrath and would have to leave the room to go and pray in anguish on his bed.

While he was at the monastery, this destructive sensibility took the form of a horrified realization that a just God would undoubtedly punish him awfully for the wretched life he was leading. He became obsessed with Romans 1:17, where Paul speaks of the righteousness of God. Luther learned from his scholastic studies that this was an "active" righteousness, an avenging justice, which would punish sins.

These people perpetuated barbaric practices such as human sacrifice and idolatry, and it was right to bring them to Christian truth.

Ideas such as this were opposed by Bartolomé de las Casas, who unlike Sepúlveda had actually gone to the New World and seen what was happening there. He devoted his life to trying to improve living conditions for the natives, eventually becoming bishop of Chiapas in Mexico.

These issues were taken seriously. In 1550 all further conquest was put on hold while a debate was held at Valladolid in Spain. There, in the first conference on human rights ever held, Sepúlveda and Casas slugged it out in impassioned debate. No winner was officially declared, so naturally both claimed victory. The important thing was that the exploration and conquest of new lands was forcing people to think seriously about issues of ethics and human rights and relate them to their Christian principles.

The conquistadors brought disease and violence, but as the example of Casas shows, they also brought Christian religion and virtues. The work of Casas and people like him led to Catholicism's becoming strongly established in South America, where it has remained until the present day. The violent history of the continent, combined with the popular strength of the Catholic Church, would produce innovative and engaging theology in the 20th century.

He did not find the idea very comforting.

> I, blameless monk that I was, felt that before God I was a sinner with an in-
> credibly guilty conscience. I could not be sure that God was satisfied by what
> I did to appease him. I did not love him. No—I *hated* the "righteous" God
> who punishes sinners. In my silence I did not say anything blasphemous, but
> still I complained, and I became angry with God.
> *Preface to Complete Works*

In 1510 Luther went on a pilgrimage to Rome. He found no answers here, even at
the Holy Staircase where Christ was said to have climbed up to Pilate, and which
was believed to have been moved from Jerusalem to Rome by St. Helena, the
mother of Constantine the Great. As was the custom, Luther crawled up the steps
on his knees, repeating the Lord's Prayer at each step, kissing the ground as he went.
The ritual was supposed to wipe clean the penitent's entire record of sin and allow
him to skip purgatory, but Luther felt nothing. When he finally reached the top, all
he could say was, "How do I know that all this is true?"

Back home, Luther's studies were becoming more advanced. Although not very
intellectual, he was diligent, and his hard work was rewarded in 1508 with the post
of professor of moral philosophy at Wittenberg. It was a new university in a tiny,
backward town in the north of Germany, and Luther's former colleagues at Erburg
not only disapproved of his teaching there but refused to recognize that the doc-
toral degree he completed at this obscure institution had any validity.

Nevertheless, it was here that Luther had the famous "tower experience" that
would change the world—an experience named after the garret university study
where Luther spent his days poring over the Scriptures. It is often referred to as
though it came in one blinding flash of light, like Paul's experience on the road to
Damascus. Luther himself said it happened in 1519, but it is often dated earlier
than this. In fact, like Augustine's conversion in the Milanese garden, Luther's tower
experience was merely the climactic moment in a gradual process that developed
over several years.

Luther had finally understood the passage in Romans that had tormented him
before.

> I meditated night and day on those words until at last, by the mercy of God,
> I noticed their context: "The righteousness of God is revealed in it, as it is
> written: 'The righteous person lives by faith.'" I began to understand that in
> this verse the "righteousness of God" means the way in which a righteous
> person lives through a gift of God—that is, by faith. I began to understand

that this verse means that the righteousness of God is revealed through the Gospel, but it is a passive righteousness—that is, it is that by which the merciful God makes us righteous by faith, as it is written: "The righteous person lives by faith." All at once I felt that I had been born again and entered into paradise itself through open gates. Immediately I saw the whole of scripture in a different light.

Preface to Complete Works

Luther realized that it did not matter how much he did; he would never put to rest the guilt that tormented him. Only God could do that. He had been saved not by works but by faith. God's righteousness is not an avenging justice; it is a gift to the faithful.

As Luther was forging this new sense of salvation by faith alone, a scandal was brewing. It concerned the sale of "indulgences," a concept that dated back to the 12th century when rich Christians were excused having to do penance for their sins if they contributed money for the Crusades. By Luther's day the system had become quite elaborate. It was believed that although someone who died in the faith of the church would be saved, they would first have to be purified in purgatory. The penalty of their sins had been neutralized by Christ and by baptism, but still the sins had corrupted their soul, and only after extensive—and highly unpleasant—purification to remove the effects of the sins would they be allowed into heaven. The average soul might spend thousands or even millions of years in purgatory. The saints, however, had been so penitent in life that they not only had gone straight to heaven but had even built up a "treasury of merit," a sort of storehouse of "extra" goodness that could be transferred to more sinful souls. An indulgence was a letter from the church that did exactly this, thereby excusing the buyer from a certain amount of time in purgatory. The church made an enormous amount of money out of these. Even more successful were indulgences for the dead. If someone was concerned about their dead relatives or friends supposedly sweating away their sins in purgatory, they could buy an indulgence on their behalf to shorten their sentence. A popular saying ran:

As soon as the coin in the coffer rings
The soul from purgatory springs.

Luther was roused against the practice by a man named Johann Tetzel who was charged with selling as many indulgences as possible on behalf of Prince Albert of Brandenburg. The prince, although only 23, was bishop of Magdeburg, bishop of Halberstadt and archbishop of Mainz all at the same time—a decidedly irregular situation for which he had to pay large revenues to the pope. He arranged with the pope that part of the proceeds from Tetzel's indulgences would be counted as payment of Albert's "bishopric tax."

The whole situation was clearly horribly corrupt, and Luther decided it was high time to have an academic debate on the wisdom of selling indulgences in the first place. "I'll knock a hole in his drum," he said when he heard about Tetzel, and he drew up a list of 95 short theses attacking indulgences, which he hoped to discuss with other academics. On All Souls' Day, 1517, Luther nailed his list to the door of the castle church in Wittenberg, which was used as a sort of community bulletin board.

"What I did toppled heaven and consumed earth by fire," he commented later. Instead of the minor academic debate he had planned, he had created a storm. Within a fortnight the whole of Germany was arguing about the Ninety-five Theses. Luther had inadvertently tapped into a deep unhappiness about the practices of the church. The authorities, of course, reacted vehemently, and Tetzel in particular denounced Luther to the pope. He had Luther's theses burned, and he published 106 theses of his own, which were delivered to Wittenberg and promptly burned by Luther's students.

Luther did not shy away from the debate he had started, and he wrote more to defend his theses, calling for widespread reform throughout the church. He wrote in German as well as Latin, and his colorful, uncompromising and often coarse language won him innumerable admirers. He won more through his preaching; Luther was an incredibly charismatic figure in person as well as in his books. When not in the grip of a fit of depression, he was charming, humorous, down to earth and altogether larger than life. His was a life-affirming theology, not a life-denying one; as he once remarked, "Sin greatly, and repent even more greatly." The role that Luther's personality played in the early Reformation is especially striking given his remarkable physical ugliness: he was a large, heavyset man, with lines of bristles on his cheeks where he was unable to shave because of the creases of his jowls. But his unhealthy appearance was offset by his penetrating eyes, whose dark light held and hypnotized those who saw him in the pulpit, the lecture hall or even the street.

In 1518 a "Disputation" was held at Heidelberg, where Luther appeared triumphantly before a packed hall of Augustinians and laid down the principles of his new theology. The affair was spiraling out of control. Tetzel, charged with embezzlement by the Catholic authorities and aghast at the disaster he had caused, was forced to remain indoors for fear of being lynched. The stress killed him within a year—despite a friendly letter of sympathy that Luther wrote to him. The pope ordered Luther to appear in Rome on charges of heresy, but Elector Frederick the

Wise, the ruler of Saxony, supported his new celebrity and kept him safely at home.

Frustrated, the pope sent Cardinal Cajetan, a leading theologian, to Augsburg to debate with Luther. Cajetan was a fair-minded man who had at least done Luther the courtesy of reading his books. But as far as he was concerned the only acceptable outcome of the meeting would be Luther's total recantation. Needless to say, he did not secure it. All he got from Luther was a declaration that the pope was subordinate to Scripture, at which Cajetan exploded and ordered Luther to leave and come back only when he was ready to recant. The meeting was over.

Finally, in 1520, the pope prepared a bull of excommunication. Hardly any town in Germany allowed it to be published. In Wittenberg a crowd of professors and students watched as with his own hands Luther placed the papal bull on the bonfire. It was a defining moment: nothing like it had ever happened before, not even at the height of Jan Hus's rebellion.

Like his predecessor Sigismund a century earlier, Emperor Charles V himself now moved to intervene. In 1521 he called a meeting before the parliament, or Diet, of the town of Worms. The Diet of Worms may have had the silliest name of any major church council, but it was a turning point in European history.

Luther—after stopping for a quick haircut and then fighting through a crowd of thousands—appeared before the packed chamber and the emperor. He was asked if the huge pile of books was his, something the emperor found hard to believe—since 1517 Luther had had three printers working overtime to keep up with his output. He was then asked: "Will you retract them? Yes or no!"

Luther replied in words that have echoed down the centuries:

> Unless I am convinced by scripture or by clear reason—for I do not trust the Pope or Church councils, since everyone knows that they can make mistakes and contradict themselves—I am bound by the scriptures I have quoted. My conscience is held captive by the Word of God. I cannot and will not take back anything, because it is neither safe nor right to go against conscience. Here I stand, I can do no other. God help me. Amen.

The emperor declared that if one monk stood against the whole of Christendom, then he must be wrong, for it was unthinkable that the entire church could have been wrong for the past 1,000 years. He condemned Luther as a heretic.

Luther was still protected by Frederick the Wise, who spirited him away and hid him in a castle for nearly a year. While his followers all over Germany, uncertain if he was even still alive, began to revolutionize church practices, Luther remained hidden in a tower, working on a new translation of the Bible from Erasmus's Greek edition into German. Like Wyclif before him, he believed that all individuals should have direct access to Scripture; and it must have been important, because Luther had a vision of the devil, which appeared in his room and tried to stop him. With commendable presence of mind, the Reformer seized his inkpot and hurled it at the apparition, leaving a stain on the wall that can still be seen today. He successfully completed his monumental translation, almost single-handedly revolutionizing German literature by setting a linguistic standard that would be followed for centuries.

But the Reformation movement was getting out of control, and Luther's followers were no longer content with trying to reform the Catholic Church. Throughout the German-speaking world they were breaking away from the church and setting up their own congregations. Nuns and monks were abandoning the monasteries. Even more significant, the German princes were supporting them, since they provided an excellent opportunity to defy the all-powerful pope. The decision of the Diet of Worms was simply ignored.

In Wittenberg one of Luther's followers, a priest named Carlstadt, was performing the Eucharist in normal clothes, abolishing infant baptism and church music, inciting mobs to burn religious images, and even getting married. Things were getting dangerous. Luther, who was something of a social conservative, therefore returned to Wittenberg to regain control of the movement. He had now realized that there was no longer a place for him in the Catholic Church, but that did not mean the abandoning of order and common sense. A new church was being forged, the Lutheran Church, a rival to the Roman Catholic Church, rather like the Eastern Orthodox Church—except that unlike the easterners this new church would coexist with the Catholics in Europe. Luther had never intended for this to happen, but now that it had, it needed proper leadership.

Luther was alarmed at the social uprising that was now becoming associated with his religious revolution. In 1525 peasants all over Germany rose up in revolution before being swiftly and brutally suppressed by the authorities. Luther wrote several works against the peasants, and the princes used them to justify their bloody response to the uprising. It was not the most edifying episode in Luther's life.

In 1524 the movement had suffered another blow when Erasmus of Rotterdam, the greatest scholar of the age and the man who had made the Reformation possible with his editions of the New Testament and the Greek fathers, came out in opposition to Luther. Erasmus approved of reform but not of splitting with the church, and he objected to Luther's denial of free will. Luther commented bitterly to his friends, "Whenever I pray, I pray for a curse on Erasmus" (*Table Talk* 668); but in public he responded with *On the Bondage of the Will*, written in 1525, which reaffirmed the Augustinian doctrine that we do not save ourselves, but God works through us to save us. We have no say in whether we are saved or not.

As he was distancing himself from the humanists, Luther was also putting more clear water between himself and Roman Catholicism. His declaration that Jan Hus had been a follower of the truth who was unjustly burned did not make for peaceful relations with Rome, and Luther cemented the break in a significant way in 1525. Katherine was a nun who had abandoned her vocation in response to Luther's denunciations of monastic life and his message that celibacy should not be required of God's ministers, but who had failed to find a husband. She therefore married Luther himself, despite the fact that he too was a monk and a priest. Luther was rather reluctant at first, professing himself not infatuated by the girl, but the marriage was a happy one, perhaps partly because Katherine made some of the best home-brewed beer he had ever drunk. Luther was also very close to his six children, who played in the chaotic mess of his study as he worked, together with 11 other nephews, nieces and assorted orphans. The home was always open to people in need, although some visitors found it too noisy. In fact, Katherine had to turn away some of her husband's guests because the family was too poor to help them all. Luther refused to accept any earnings from his books, because they had been published for Christ's sake, so they all had to live on his meagre university salary.

Now that the new Reformation—or Protestant—churches were established, Luther began to spend most of his time dealing with internal divisions between the different branches of the movement. The biggest challenge came from those based in Switzerland, who, under Ulrich Zwingli in Zürich and Oecolampadius in Basel, had been creating a religious movement much like Luther's but independent of it. Zwingli's program of reform, like that of Wyclif and Hus, included sweeping aside the Catholic understanding of the Mass. The Catholic Church taught the doctrine of "transubstantiation," which means that the bread and wine cease being bread and wine—although they still look and taste the same—and become the body and blood of Christ. Zwingli rejected this, holding that the Eucharist is simply a memorial and that Christ is accessible to the individual believer directly. Luther, for his part, believed that the bread and wine remain bread and wine *and* become body and blood as well—a doctrine known as "consubstantiation." The Swiss and German Reformers quickly fell out over the matter, and it looked as if the Reformation might be collapsing under its own weight. However, at the Marburg Colloquy in 1529, they managed to put aside their differences and agreed to disagree. They could not overcome their divisions, but they did part on good terms—even though Luther, fired up as usual, refused to shake Zwingli's hand, an act that brought tears to the eyes of the Swiss Reformer.

Another significant event was the Diet of Augsburg, called by Emperor

Charles V to allow the Reformers to state their case. Luther was not allowed to attend, but his sidekick Philipp Melanchthon was. Melanchthon, a younger man who taught Greek at Wittenberg, was a mild-mannered moderate who agreed with Luther in all matters but tended to be more tactful in expression. He was also extremely clever, and although the Diet rejected his views, the tract he wrote for the occasion, the Augsburg Confession, would become the classical statement of Lutheran theology.

Through all this, Luther continued to teach at Wittenberg University and to preach. He was not a well man, and the stress of dealing with constant controversy, of playing a major role on the world stage, must have played a part in his premature aging. Fortunately, Frederick the Wise was succeeded by his son, the equally virtuous John the Magnanimous, and he not only protected Luther but increased his allowance. This allowed Luther some peace, but he still spent his last years traveling constantly, attending councils and conferences, giving advice, writing and preaching, dogged by increasing ill health. He suffered terribly from gallstones and lost the sight of one eye.

At last, exhausted from his never-ending work, Luther suffered a heart attack in 1546. By a strange coincidence, he was passing through the town of Eisleben, where he had been born 62 years earlier. He knew that his long-expected end had come, but there was time for his sons and friends to arrive at his bedside. His companions asked him, "Reverend father, do you stand by Christ and the doctrine you have preached?" "Yes," replied the Reformer, and breathed his last. He was buried in the Wittenberg church where it had all begun 30 years before.

Thought

Luther's thought revolved around two great themes, the authority of Scripture and salvation by faith alone, and one figure, Christ. Everything he wrote and did flowed from these interconnected principles.

Scripture. As far as Luther was concerned, there was only one source for theology: the Bible. Human reason and church tradition are acceptable tools, as long as they are put to the service of the Bible. They do not provide any alternative source of theological knowledge or practice.

Why did Luther think this? In part he was inspired by the humanists, who were calling for European culture, including Christianity, to return to its roots. Men like the great scholar Erasmus believed that Christians needed to be more aware of where their faith had come from, and Erasmus's epochal edition of the Greek New Testament, published in 1516, as well as his editions of the church fathers, was intended to hurry this process along. We should never forget that Luther was a child of the Renaissance. His stress on "Scripture alone" was in part an extension of this humanist principle, allied to the Augustinian and Scholastic reverence for the Bible that he learned in the monastery of Erfurt.

The upshot of this is that Scripture should be interpreted only by itself—a modern version of Origen's and Augustine's principles of biblical exegesis, although Luther rejected the allegorical method and thought that the whole of Origen's work was worth less than one word of Christ (*Table Talk* 767). Also, anything that is not in the Bible is not acceptable Christian doctrine or practice. Luther therefore rejects indulgences, pilgrimages, the interpretation of the Mass as a sacrifice, the special status of priests, the use of relics, praying to saints and the immaculate conception of Mary. In other words, the whole paraphernalia of the Catholic Church that had been built up over the preceding 1,000 years is swept away. This also includes the intellectual traditions of the Middle Ages: Luther wholeheartedly rejects Aristotelianism and Scholasticism and brands thinkers like Aquinas and Scotus idiots who imported alien philosophy into the gospel.

Luther's belief in the supremacy of Scripture will seem familiar to modern Protestants and evangelicals, but Luther did not use the Bible quite as many of his spiritual descendants do today. Although he denied that the pope or the church had any authority over and against the Bible, he was aware that the content of the canon had been decided by the church. This meant that he could cast a critical eye over the canon and judge it according to the true supreme authority, Christ himself. So the printed page of the Bible has no authority in itself, not even if we take it as God's Word; it has authority only inasmuch as it points to Christ.

> Christ is the Lord, not the servant, the Lord of the Sabbath, of law and of all things. The scriptures must be understood in favour of Christ, not against him. For that reason they must either refer to him or must not be held to be true scriptures.

For this reason, Luther's translation of the New Testament consigned the books of Hebrews, James and Revelation to a sort of appendix, because in his opinion they failed to meet this strict criterion. James, in particular, Luther had little time for, since he recognized that the book contradicted his doctrine of salvation by faith alone.

Scripture, then, is not an independent authority but is authoritative only as a lens through which we see Christ. Yet it is, ultimately, the only such lens in existence. The Catholics' insistence that the church was the only institution authorized to interpret Scripture was an attempt to subordinate Scripture to human tradition. Similarly, the radical Reformers' belief that every individual could interpret the Bible according to their own experience simply made their own whims the final authority. Against both extremes, Luther insisted that Scripture can be interpreted only by other parts of Scripture, because Scripture speaks to us with the voice of Christ.

Salvation by faith. The insight that struck Luther as he sat in his tower room wrestling with Romans remained the heart of his theology, from which all other principles flowed. It was a very simple insight. We are saved not by works—by what we do—but by faith. And by "faith" Luther did not mean intellectual agreement with a set of propositions, a kind of mental work by which we save ourselves. He meant a state of complete trust in God, a surrendering of the whole person to God's love.

> It astounds me that anyone can be offended by something as obvious as this! Just tell me this. Is Christ's death and resurrection something that we do, or not? It is obviously not our work, nor is it the work of the law. Now it is Christ's death and resurrection alone which saves and frees us from sin, as Paul writes in Romans 4: "He died for our sin and arose for our righteousness." Tell me more! What is the work by which we take hold of Christ's death and resurrection? It cannot be an external act but only the eternal faith in the heart that alone, indeed all alone, takes hold of this death and resurrection when it is preached through the gospel. Then why all this ranting and raving, this making of heretics and burning of them, when it is clear at its very core, proving that faith alone takes hold of Christ's death and resurrection, without any works, and that his death and resurrection are our life and righteousness?
> *On Translating*

Luther attacked all of the abuses of the Catholic Church because he thought they contradicted this principle: indulgences were a way of buying salvation; pilgrimages were a way of earning it; the veneration of relics and saints was a way of trying to put it in a box and own it; and the special status of priests was a way of putting salvation in the control of the church, of regulating people's access to God. All this, for Luther, was nonsense and superstition. A person is saved on the basis of personal faith in Christ, not because of anything they do or anything that the church gives them. That means that everyone is a priest, if a priest is someone with direct access to God.

Luther's conception of faith is complemented by his notion of sin. He thinks of sin as self-obsession, or, as he puts it, "curvedness"—the unnatural bending of the person in on itself instead of outward toward others. And he regards this as the universal state of all humanity. Luther is even more negative in his assessment of human nature than Augustine. He holds that it is completely impossible to perform any good act by oneself. Aristotle had argued that the best way to become a good person is to do good acts, since one will get into the habit this way, just as the best way to become a good pianist is to practice playing the piano. This is why parents try to bring up their children with good habits. Christian Aristotelians such as Aquinas agreed with this commonsense view. But Luther is having none of it; the state of sin is impossible to escape. It is part of the human condition and there is nothing we can do about it.

But, like Augustine, Luther emphasizes not the pathological perversion of human nature but God's grace in redeeming it. Through faith, the sinner can unfold his horizons, opening himself up to God and, through him, to others. He is no longer closed in on himself.

Luther's account of sin is a profound and compelling one, but it has been heavily criticized in recent years, especially by feminist theologians. It is true that many people are inordinately selfish. But it is also true that many others—especially women—are too selfless. They are like the caricature of a 1950s housewife who runs herself into the ground in an effort to serve her husband and children. For people like this, regard for others can reach pathological and self-destructive levels; and Luther's declaration that God's grace leads us from selfishness toward selflessness can only exacerbate the problem. Instead, there should be a balance between regard for self and regard for others.

Luther's conception of faith and the gift of God's righteousness was not of course new. Despite Luther's criticisms, the medieval theologians shared it too. What was new was the claim that salvation comes through faith alone, and the raising of this principle as the linchpin of the Christian faith. Luther appealed to Augustine's theology, especially his attacks on the Pelagians—but he appealed even more to the Bible, and especially to the letters of Paul. He believed that when Paul speaks in Romans about the righteousness of God and salvation by faith, he means a personal, individual relationship between God and the believer. This is a relationship that results in good works, but not one that is based on them. This interpretation of Paul is disputed by modern New Testament scholars; what is certain, however, is that while Paul speaks of "salvation by faith" he never speaks explicitly of "salvation by faith alone." Luther was well aware of this, of course, but argued that his interpretation was what Paul had meant. His Catholic opponents appealed, not unreasonably, to the letter of James, which explicitly contradicts the principle (Jas 2:24), and to the ethical exhortations throughout the Gospels and Paul's letters themselves. If we do not have to do anything to ensure our salvation, then why does the Bible tell us to do anything at all?

Christ. The third controlling principle of Luther's theology is the one on which the other two depend and the one through which they are linked: Christ. The Scriptures are true and the sole source of authority because they are the Scriptures of Christ. And salvation is through faith alone because Christ has achieved our salvation through his death and resurrection. Thus Christ is no mere historical figure. He is Christianity—and it is Christ himself, not simply some doctrine about him, that is preached by Scripture and the church.

> Even if an angel were to come down from heaven and appear in front of me, it would not make me believe any more. I have the bond and seal of my Saviour, Jesus Christ. I have his Word, Spirit, and sacrament. It is on these that I depend, and I need no new revelations.
> *Table Talk* 236

Indeed, on one occasion Luther did see a vision of Christ—but knowing that the true Christ appears only through the Scriptures and the faith of the individual, he knew that it was just the devil up to his old tricks again.

In the final analysis, Luther's faith is faith not in a system, or in a religion, but in a person. He was not a mystic, and he never had much time for the methods of Pseudo-Dionysius and the rest. Yet this emotional, personal faith has much in common with the medieval mysticism of people like Bonaventure, Julian of Norwich and the Rhineland mystics—one of whom, John Tauler, Luther regarded as one of the greatest theologians of all time. And Luther's emphasis on the personal relationship with Christ enjoyed by the individual Christian would develop into Pietism in later Protestantism. Quite apart from this, his conviction that all matters of Christian doctrine must be grounded directly in the person of Christ would be a central feature of all Protestant theology. It would be taken up and systematized by the greatest figure in the second generation of the Reformation movement, John Calvin.

John Calvin

Calvin was possibly the most important Protestant theologian of all time. From the disparate, disorganized heritage of Luther and Zwingli, he forged a systematic vision of the Christian faith and life that still profoundly influences modern Western society.

Life

John Calvin was born in 1509 in Noyon, France. His father was a prosperous lawyer, and John followed him into the profession. He studied at the University of

Paris, where he became thoroughly imbued with the principles of the Renaissance, humanism and scholarship.

As his studies progressed, Calvin found himself drawn toward Protestantism. He had been brought up as a Catholic, but several family members had gravitated toward Luther's movement, and Calvin, as a liberal-minded humanist, naturally felt sympathetic toward the Protestants who were being persecuted by the French authorities. He was a serious-minded young man, inclined to scholarly and contemplative activities. He would spend his evenings alone in his room, reading until the small hours, and always got up early to think about what he had learned the previous night. As a result he became remarkably learned but not very healthy.

The French persecutions eventually caused him to leave Paris in 1534. He went to learn Hebrew in Switzerland instead, and there he published his *Institutes of the Christian Religion*, a short book outlining the fundamentals of the Protestant faith. With this work and several others, Calvin hoped to show that Protestants were reasonable people, not rabble-rousing demagogues.

In 1536 he decided to move to Strasbourg. On the way he passed through Geneva, where he was waylaid by Guillaume Farel, a former disciple of the Swiss Reformer Zwingli. Farel recognized the young traveler's scholarly and administrative talents and begged him to stay and help with the creation of a new Protestant church in the city. Calvin had intended to spend only one night in Geneva, but Farel insisted that if he did not stay to do God's will then he would suffer the divine wrath. The thought of this terrified Calvin, who prudently decided to do as he was urged and allowed himself to be made professor of sacred literature.

The new professor quickly took a leading role in setting up the new church, successfully persuading most of the town to renounce the pope in 1537. However, old habits die hard, and Calvin tried to bring about reform too quickly. Many people still wanted to follow Catholic rituals and customs, and others took Reformation ideas to extremes, becoming enthusiasts of the kind that had prompted Luther to return from hiding to Wittenberg. Calvin found the city riven by dissension and factions, and he declared that it was impossible to administer the Eucharist to such a congregation.

The tension grew so great that Calvin was forced to leave Geneva in 1538. He finally made his way to Strasbourg, where he worked as a pastor to Protestant refugees from France. After three years, the city council of Geneva begged him to return, since the city lacked strong leadership, having also lost Farel. Calvin declared that he would never return, since he loved his new work—until one of his friends at Strasbourg pointed out that now he was behaving like Jonah. Once again, Calvin reluctantly bowed to what seemed to be God's will and returned to Switzerland.

This time his stay in Geneva was to be permanent, and under his leadership the city was transformed into a theocracy to rival the Byzantine empire.

Calvin expected nothing of the Genevans that he did not also require of himself. He lived a decidedly austere life. A small, thin, pale man with a long beard, he ate

GENEVA

Geneva was an old, not especially important city on the shores of Lake Léman. Throughout the Dark Ages and Middle Ages it changed hands with dizzying regularity, belonging first to one nation and then to another; but by the 12th century it was essentially independent, under the control of its bishop.

Geneva was becoming increasingly wealthy and important, and its merchants grew to resent the power of the church. This was one of the reasons the bishops were expelled in 1533, and two years later the town accepted the new movement of the Reformation, as preached by Guillaume Farel.

However, the city was quite isolated from the main centers of Protestantism, partly because its inhabitants spoke French rather than German, the language of Luther and his disciples. It was not clear what direction the new regime would take. Fortunately, a young Protestant humanist named John Calvin happened to be passing through Geneva in 1536 on his way to Strasbourg, and Farel wisely waylaid him and had him stay to help out. Calvin quickly alienated much of the populace and was forced to abandon the project, but he returned in 1541 and set about completing it. The plan was to transform Geneva into a state run on Protestant scriptural ideals.

The first step was to establish a proper system of ministers and to write some doctrinal bases for the city's faith. This done, Calvin saw to it that the council began enacting legislation in line with Reformation doctrine. This meant applying the moral exhortations of the Bible literally and systematically. Calvin shared Luther's emphasis on the sufficiency of Scripture for all theology and added to it a conviction that all commands in Scripture must be obeyed fully and to the letter. He therefore oversaw the first wholesale attempt ever undertaken to establish a society along biblical moral principles. Indeed Calvin's Geneva was one of the most audacious experiments in the total union of church and state ever carried out. Clergy played an important role on the city council and could not only pass laws but enforce them and punish those who disobeyed.

only one meal a day and slept very little. He was also a severe workaholic; a year before his death, when his friends advised him to take it easy, he angrily stated that he had no intention of letting God find him idle. In addition to his administrative and preaching duties, which were considerable, he devoted much time to revising

The most notorious example of this theocracy in action was the execution of a colorful Spaniard named Servetus. A skilled physician and unorthodox theologian, Servetus rather ambitiously hoped to "deconvert" Calvin and tried to join forces with members of the city council who disliked the Reformer. He was promptly arrested, found guilty of heresy and sedition, and burned at the stake by the very council he had tried to subvert. Calvin was not personally responsible for this and was not happy about it: he thought that Servetus should be executed more humanely, by sword rather than fire. But he certainly thought execution was a reasonable punishment for such heresy. In this Calvin was at one with everyone else of the time; and indeed other Protestant leaders, including Luther's mild-mannered friend Melanchthon, wrote to him expressing their support for what had been done. All things considered, it is really quite extraordinary that Servetus was the only person to be executed for heresy under Calvin's regime.

Many people denounced the system as popery by a different name. They felt, not unreasonably, that they had escaped one all-embracing Catholicism only to fall captive to another. Others, however, welcomed the regime. Protestants fleeing persecution all over Europe flocked to Geneva, which was becoming known as "the Protestant Rome." By the 1550s up to half the city's population was made up of foreign immigrants; when they left again, they spread Calvin's ideas and practices throughout Europe. Many of them trained at Calvin's academy, the first Protestant university.

The growth in population meant that Geneva was swiftly becoming a major economic center. And its status as the central city of the Reformation gave it unrivaled intellectual prominence. After the 16th century, Calvin's theocracy did calm down a little, and eventually it gave way to a more gentle, liberal and intellectual regime. In the 18th century Geneva would become a major center of the Enlightenment, boasting such luminaries as Voltaire and Rousseau.

and expanding his *Institutes of the Christian Religion,* which had been transformed from a short outline of faith into a massive, detailed and highly structured exposition of it. At the same time Calvin produced vast numbers of biblical commentaries of a remarkably high quality, which were praised even by his theological opponents; and, like all good Reformers, set about translating some of the Bible into the vernacular. Indeed, his works helped to establish and stabilize the French language in a way almost comparable to Luther's influence on German.

Calvin died in 1564. At his own request, his grave was marked only by a plain stone, and today its location has been forgotten.

Thought

In almost every way Calvin was wildly different from Luther, a man he admired but never met. Where Luther was passionate, charismatic and prone to exaggeration, Calvin was quiet and thoughtful, with a far more stable character. His writings give no hint of profound personal struggles of the kind that plagued Luther. He was also a generation younger than the German Reformer, and he inherited the central tenets of Protestantism rather than helping to forge them. Where Luther was a fiery prophet, Calvin was a logical systematizer. His great work, the *Institutes of the Christian Religion,* remains the most important and influential work of Protestant dogmatics ever written.

Calvin's theology was, in essence, the same as Luther's, especially in his insistence on Scripture alone as the basis of theology and practice. But in systematizing and restating the Protestant faith, he gave it quite different emphases. He believed more or less the same things as Luther, but not in quite the same way. These different emphases would mean that Calvinism—the Reformed Church—would become quite distinct from Lutheranism.

Sin. Calvin has an awful lot to say about sin, which, like Irenaeus, he thinks of essentially as disobedience. It all stems from Adam's original disobedience, and it is because of that first sin that humanity is now in such a woeful condition:

> The whole man, from the top of the head to the sole of the foot, is so flooded, as it were, that no part remains without sin, and so everything that comes from him is considered sin.
> *Institutes* 2.1.9

This is the famous doctrine of "total depravity": original sin has corrupted us to such an extent that it is *impossible* to do anything pleasing to a holy God. The soul is so steeped in sin that any action, however apparently good, is in fact a sin.

Does this make sense? Surely we would not say that Mother Teresa was no better than Adolf Hitler? But that might seem to follow, if all acts are morally equal. But in fact that is not what Calvin is saying. He does not mean to suggest that nobody ever does any good acts or that all acts are morally equal. Neither does he mean that it makes no difference to God or others what you do. On the contrary, the importance of leading a good life is central to his theology. What he does mean to say is that whatever goodness may be in our actions does not come from ourselves. It comes from the grace of God working through us. And that grace is not restricted to Christians; Calvin accepts that some non-Christians clearly lead better lives than others, and so they too are channels of God's grace, although in their case it is not the kind of grace that saves. Indeed, it is only the constant action of God's grace that prevents us all from giving in to our sinful lusts and going mad.

The doctrine is very reminiscent of Augustine, whom Calvin quotes approvingly as often as possible, but it goes further. Augustine never taught total depravity, merely the inescapability of original sin. However, Calvin's doctrine has the same basic import as Augustine's theology, which is that humanity in its natural state is essentially opposed to God. God alone can save humanity—and this is what Calvin, just like Augustine, is really interested in.

Christ and salvation. Like Luther, Calvin places Christ at the center of his theology: everything in Christian doctrine and practice must flow directly from the person of Christ. From a practical point of view, this means rejecting later innovations of the church, like the seven sacraments and the power of the pope.

Like Luther, Calvin argues for the classical, Chalcedonian understanding of Christ; but his understanding of how Christ saves us is quite distinctive. It is rooted in medieval theology and draws on Luther, but achieves a clarity and emphasis that is quite new.

> Christ, while suspended on [the cross], subjects himself to the curse. And it was necessary that this be done, in order that the whole curse, which was waiting for us—or rather lying upon us—because of our sins, might be taken from us by being transferred to him.
> *Institutes* 2.16.6

The idea here is very simple. Humanity deserved punishment for its sins. When Christ died, he took humanity's place: God was punishing Christ instead of humanity. The punishment has therefore been meted out, justice is satisfied, and humanity can go free.

The doctrine is obviously an objective account of the atonement and is a development of Anselm's similar teaching; but it has been reworked to match the different legal system that Calvin knew. Anselm had thought that Christ's death was a gift given to God so that humanity did not need to be punished. The law in Calvin's day, however, did not recognize the possibility of making a payment to avert punishment; therefore he has Christ actually being punished in the place of humanity. The essence of the doctrine is *substitution* rather than *satisfaction.*

Like Anselm and the other medieval theologians, then, Calvin's understanding of the atonement is centered on the death of Christ, rather than his life, as it was for Irenaeus and the church fathers. Calvin does stress that Christ's resurrection is as important as his death, but more emphasis is laid on the latter—and this has been the case in the Reformed tradition ever since.

It is important to recognize that Calvin's doctrine of the atonement was a development of what had come before him, given that it has undoubtedly proved the most successful part of his thought. Today Christians all over the world, and in every denomination and tradition, believe that Christ was punished in their place. Many are even unaware that any alternative Christian doctrine of the atonement has ever existed. This may be partly due to the fact that the legal system in which Calvin was trained has largely remained in place in the Western world, so the doctrine is easily understandable in a way that Irenaeus's or Anselm's is not. And the doctrine has its merits: it drives home the fact that salvation is an unearned gift, won entirely through the suffering of Christ. Yet it is not without its problems.

For one thing, Calvin is quite clear that humanity's sins merit eternal damnation. Those who are not saved will never escape the fires of hell. This being the case, we might reasonably ask why Christ, if he took our place, was not condemned to an eternity of hellfire. Crucifixion, however horrible, hardly compares with what lies in store for unrepentant sinners; how then can the penalty have been paid?

Perhaps more fundamentally, we may ask why we punish criminals in general. Is it out of a desire for revenge? Is it in order to try to improve them, to stop them from offending again? Or is it because we believe in some kind of objective justice? Hopefully it is not for the first reason, and surely God does not punish us for that reason either. The second seems more promising; as we have seen, Origen believed that suffering, including the fires of hell, is sent by God to purge away our sin and is therefore temporary. But if that is the case, then punishing one person for another's crime would be pointless—it would be like a clean person having a bath on behalf of a dirty one. And if God punishes Christ to satisfy an objective justice, does this mean that "justice" is higher than God? We seem to have moved from Anselm's notion of God's *being satisfied* to one of God's *doing the satisfying.* Moreover, surely it can never be just to punish one person in the place of another. Many theologians reject Calvin's doctrine as fundamentally immoral.

The basic point of these objections is this: the whole thing goes completely over our heads; we are not involved at all. It does not leave us fundamentally changed. This, as we have seen, is the weak point of all objective theories of the atonement. It is this that gives such strength to subjective ones like Abelard's—although, of course, they have problems of their own. Calvin, however, is ready for the objection, and he is extremely keen to stress the subjective element in all of this. The key to this is faith and the role of the Holy Spirit.

Faith, for Calvin, is central to Christian life, and by "faith" he means not simply an intellectual agreement with a set of propositions—although this is part of it— but a fundamental turning of the heart toward God, through Christ. That means not simply that we take Christ as our example, as Abelard may have meant; neither does it mean merely that Christ acts upon us. In fact, through faith we are united to Christ. Calvin writes:

> [The Bible says] that God "has chosen us in him before the foundation of the world," not because we deserved it, but "according to the good pleasure of his will"; so that in him "we have redemption through his blood, even the forgiveness of sins"; so that peace has been made "through the blood of his cross"; so that we are reconciled by his blood; so that, protected by him, we are saved from the danger of death; so that, grafted into him in this way, we can share in eternal life, and hope to be let into the kingdom of God. And this is not all. Because we share in him, although we are still foolish, he is our wisdom; although we are still sinners, he is our righteousness; although we are unclean, he is our purity; although we are weak, defenceless, and vulnerable to Satan, we have the power which has been given to him in heaven and in earth, to crush Satan under our feet, and storm the gates of hell; although we still carry about us a body of death, he is our life. In short, everything he has belongs to us too, we have everything in him, and he has nothing in us. On this foundation, I say, we must be built, if we are to grow up into a holy temple in the Lord.
> *Institutes* 3.15.5

It is striking how similar the passage is to the thought of some of the Byzantine theologians. Like them, Calvin stresses the importance of union with Christ. But unlike them, he does not think of this primarily in mystical or eschatological terms, as the summit of the mystical experience or as the goal of humanity. He conceives it in soteriological terms—that is, as part of what it is to be saved—and ethical terms. Union with Christ is something that happens right now, and it is the root of life for all Christians all of the time. *We* are not the ones who live; it is Christ living through us. Like the Byzantine theologians, Calvin is heavily reliant on the theology of Paul, as presented in Romans 6—8.

Calvin gives his own distinctive spin to the notion, however, by his emphasis on the agency of God in all of this. Because of total depravity, human beings are incapable of uniting to Christ through faith themselves, and it takes place only through the action of the Holy Spirit on the believer. There is thus a trinitarian pattern to salvation as Calvin presents it, and indeed he always has a strong sense of the role of the Holy Spirit. To put it rather crudely, the Holy Spirit acts in Calvin's theology rather like the glue that holds together doctrines as diverse as the total depravity of human beings, salvation through faith alone, the role of Christ as our substitution and the centrality of ethics to the Christian life. It is through the action of the Spirit that human beings can do good, and it is through the action of the Spirit that they can come to have faith and be saved by Christ. Thus although Calvin thinks of salvation as coming about in objective terms, he stresses that it cannot work unless its subjective aspect is allowed full play—but he does so in quite a different way from Abelard. There is no Pelagianism here; on the contrary, everything that happens, both objective and within the believer's heart, does so only because God does it.

In fact, the action of the Holy Spirit is quite irresistible. This is the doctrine of predestination, and it is the most characteristic element of Calvin's thought.

Predestination. Luther, like Augustine, had believed that because of original sin human beings no longer have control over their destiny. They are saved solely through the will of God and are therefore predestined by God to salvation. Calvin firmly upholds this notion.

If we are saved, he argues, it is certainly not through our own efforts. Therefore anything we do can make no difference to whether we will be saved or not. So if we are saved, it can only be because God has eternally ordained that we will be saved. He has predestined us.

There is an obvious objection. Assuming that not everyone will be saved, it would seem to follow that God has predestined some unfortunates to damnation and that nothing they do can change his decision. Luther shied away from saying something as unpleasant as this. Calvin, however, is more consistent. He teaches "double predestination": the eternal decree that some people will be saved and the eternal decree that everyone else will be damned.

Calvin is unable to explain why God should have brought about such a thing— why should he want anybody to be damned? This, for Calvin, is the central mystery of the Christian faith, and he speaks of it as "the decree to be shuddered at." Others have gone further and accused the doctrine—and, by extension, Calvin himself— of unbecoming cruelty. In fact, it is really no more unpleasant to say that God has predestined certain people for damnation than it is to believe that some people will be damned at all. And if we dislike the doctrine, that is in itself no reason to criticize Calvin, who believed it because he thought it was true, not because he liked it, which he didn't. The question is not, do we like the sound of this doctrine? It is, does this doctrine make sense? In other words, is it consistent with itself and with the wider theological position that it is part of?

The doctrine of double predestination is perfectly consistent, at least with itself, but it does have some consequences that not everyone will be happy with. For one thing, it means that not everyone has the same ability to respond to the gospel of salvation, because some people have been predestined not to do so. So the preaching of the church is limited in its scope.

> The covenant of life is not preached equally to all, and among those to whom it is preached, does not always meet with the same reception. This diversity displays the unsearchable depth of the divine judgment, and is without doubt subordinate to God's purpose of eternal election.
> *Institutes* 3.21.1

Even worse, it seems that Christ did not die for everybody. God decreed that some people would not be saved; clearly then, Christ did not die for their sins, because otherwise his death would not have been fully effective in securing salvation. So some people's sins were not transferred to Christ. The doctrine that Christ died only for the elect is known as "limited atonement," and it is not clear that Calvin himself taught it. However, his later followers certainly did, and it follows quite clearly from his theologies of predestination and salvation. And all of this seems hard to reconcile with the biblical claim that Christ died for the sins of the world, as well as with the Christian faith that the benefits of Christ's death are available to all who want them. The Calvinist response, of course, is that God has decreed that only certain people *will* want them.

Another objection to the doctrine of predestination might be that it is ethically paralyzing. If everything is predetermined, then why bother? If I am elect, I am elect; if not, there is nothing I can do about it, so why try to lead a good life? Indeed, if I am elect, then nothing I can do could deelect me! This idea would produce the doctrine in later Calvinism of the "infallibility of the elect"—the notion that the elect can do nothing wrong. Needless to say, such a doctrine is decidedly open to opportunistic abuse.

We have seen repeatedly, however, that Calvin himself is at great pains to avoid this charge. There are few theologians who match him for the frequency and earnestness of his injunctions to good behavior.

The Christian life. Calvin's answer to the claim that his theology leaves no ground for moral behavior would be similar to that of other Christians who stress that we play no part in our salvation. It is that living right is not a prerequisite for salvation, as Pelagius thought; it is a response to salvation. Indeed, as we have seen, the role of the Holy Spirit in effecting a union between the believer and Christ means that living correctly is virtually a part of what it is to be saved. If we are not living correctly, then Christ cannot be in our heart. And this is not at all inconsistent with the doctrine of total depravity. As we have seen, that doctrine does not mean that it is impossible for us to do good; it means that whatever good we do comes from God rather than from ourselves. It is a theological doctrine rather than an ethical one. Calvin's emphasis, like Augustine's, is always on the goodness of God and his grace in saving us, rather than our own miserable nature, and the fact that God does act through us and does save us means that a very serious ethical charge is laid at our door.

> We do not belong to ourselves; therefore, neither does our own reason or will to rule our acts and thoughts. We do not belong to ourselves; therefore, let us not try to do what the carnal nature wants. We do not belong to ourselves; therefore, as far as possible, let us forget ourselves and the things that are ours. On the other hand, we belong to God; let us, therefore, live and die to him. We belong to God; therefore, let his wisdom and will govern all our actions. We belong to God; so let us direct every part of our life to him, the only legitimate goal.
> *Institutes* 3.7.1

Calvin set very high ethical standards for himself and for the city of Geneva. It may be that not every moral person is one of the elect; but it is certain that anyone who does not live morally cannot be elect.

Influence

Karl Marx famously declared that he was "not a Marxist." Often a great thinker founds a school of thought but finds that his ideas get subtly changed. We saw that at the start of this book, when the Platonists became more dogmatic than Plato himself ever had been. And we have seen here some hints that it is a serious problem too with Calvin, the founder of Calvinism. Throughout the Reformed world, including the Netherlands, Scotland, and some elements in England and America, Calvinism became a rigidly defined system of thought. Traditionally it has been summarized in "five points," memorized by the acronym TULIP: Total depravity, Unconditional election (we are not saved by anything we do), Limited atonement, Irresistible grace (we are predestined by God to salvation or damnation) and the Perseverance of the saints (the elect can never be deelected).

It should be clear that this theology is something of a development and simplification of Calvin himself, but the lines are very hard to draw—especially given that most Calvinists, both past and present, would consider themselves first and foremost biblical Christians rather than followers of a 16th-century Frenchman. Where does Calvin stop and Calvinism begin? Calvin was a serious-minded and compassionate man who spent many years trying to reason with the freethinker Servetus before he was put to death; but Calvinist theology has at some points in its development been not unfairly accused of losing sight of this compassionate basis. In the hands of lesser thinkers, Calvin's legacy would produce puritanical rigidity in ethics and morbid guilt trips in psychology. That has led to Calvin's being himself associated with these consequences, which is not necessarily fair. At the same time, of course, his theology had positive consequences, such as the famous Protestant work ethic. These consequences are still with us today, for Calvinism would prove to be the most durable Protestant faith, underlying Puritanism, much Anglicanism and the faith of the founding fathers of the United States.

The Later Reformation

If Martin Luther had known what he was starting on All Souls' Day, 1517, he might never have nailed that list to the church door.

Luther tapped into a great swell of bad feeling about the Catholic Church, which had already broken out in the protests of Wyclif and Hus over a century before. The Dominican preacher Girolamo Savonarola had also fiercely denounced ecclesiastical misconduct in Florence, eventually being hanged for rabble-rousing and false prophecy in 1498.

In many ways, then, the Reformation was long overdue. Once Luther had opened the debate, an immense wave of change swept over the European church, both within and without the Catholic Church. The reforms that took place within Catholicism are often called the Counter-Reformation, as though they were a kind of response to Protestantism; in fact, all the reforms were part of the same movement. Some Reformers were able to carry out their program within the church; others, like Luther and Zwingli, his contemporary in Zürich, were rejected and forced to start their own churches. They succeeded in doing this in part because political rulers realized that if they supported the new movement, it would be a blow against the power of the pope. Indeed, the term *Protestant* comes from the protest of the German princes against the suppression of Lutheranism in 1529. And they were also aided by the new power of the printing press, which allowed their ideas to spread rapidly.

The divided churches

Within a matter of decades, the unquestioned monopoly of the Catholic Church had been replaced throughout Europe by three major churches struggling for elbow room: the Catholic Church, the Lutheran churches, which were confined mainly to German-speaking regions, and the Calvinist or Reformed churches, which were more widespread. A notable success of the latter was Scotland, which became largely Calvinist through the efforts of John Knox, a graduate of Calvin's academy

THE COUNCIL OF TRENT

For the first time in many centuries, the heretics seemed to be having the upper hand. For once their criticisms were justified and their ideas sensible. The Protestant Reformation had split Western Christianity into two while the popes could only sit and watch aghast.

It was time to do something about it. In 1545 the leaders of the Catholic Church met at Trent in Italy. Plans for a council had been brewing for over a decade; Pope Paul III had had to overcome considerable opposition to get things off the ground. The purpose of the council was to plan the reform of both doctrine and church practices in the light of the Reformers' criticisms. It was an immense task, and the sessions of the council lasted on and off for almost twenty years. The bold spirit in which the members embraced it was demonstrated by the fact that Protestant leaders were invited to attend the council—although they were not allowed to speak or play any part.

If these silent onlookers hoped for significant concessions from Rome that might lead to the reconciliation of Catholics and Protestants, they were disappointed. As far as doctrine went, the council saw its task as stating clearly the faith of the Catholic Church and budging not an inch in any direction. On the central doctrine of Lutheranism, the council decreed that faith is indeed necessary to salvation, but it is not sufficient. Salvation comes through works as well as through faith, as James 2:24 states. What of Romans 3:28, which seems to state that faith alone is necessary? The council answers that what this means is that faith is the starting point of salvation. We will not get anywhere if we do not have faith; but if that faith is not accompanied by good works it will be useless.

in Geneva. This was quite apart from less organized movements in the radical wing of the Reformation, which took its principles to extremes, such as the Anabaptists, who insisted on rebaptizing converts from Catholicism. Groups like these foreshadowed the Pietism of later years.

Each church was forced to define itself in contrast to the others, and so after the initial period of great creativity marked by major theologians like Luther, Melanchthon and Calvin, there followed a long and confused period in which enormous

Equally significant was the declaration of the council that while Scripture is indeed authoritative in all matters, it can be reliably interpreted only by the Catholic Church. So tradition and the "magisterium" or teaching role of the church are equal in authority to the Bible. The council therefore condemned those who rejected as unscriptural the doctrines of purgatory and of transubstantiation, and it maintained that there are indeed seven sacraments, not two as the Reformers claimed.

Nevertheless, the council was prepared to admit that the Reformers' criticisms of church practices did have some merit. Efforts were made to ensure that all clergy were properly educated, and there was a clamping down on people's being bishops of several places at once, like Prince Albert of Brandenburg, who had sparked off Luther's protest in the first place. In general, abuses of church privileges were thoroughly cleaned up. But the council affirmed the importance of monasticism and refused to consider the possibility of married priests.

The decrees of the Council of Trent were finally ratified and promulgated by Pope Pius IV in 1564. The decrees of the council played a similar role in the later Reformation period to that of Nicaea in the later stages of the Arian conflict in the 4th century; it set a standard of faith and practice that defined the Roman Catholic position as opposed to its opponents. It was the centerpiece of the Catholic Counter-Reformation. In fact, Trent would become the standard of Roman Catholicism even in later times. All subsequent Catholic councils, including both Vatican councils, would present themselves as explaining its decrees, not adding to them, just as the councils of the Orthodox Church have been seen as footnotes to the Council of Nicaea.

numbers of very minor theologians wrote increasingly entrenched and systematic presentations of their respective churches' theologies.

The Catholic Church, for its part, had to tread a careful line between failing to do anything about the genuine abuses in its ranks and seeming to give in to the Reformers' criticisms. The Council of Trent, held between 1545 and 1563, sought to do this. And the 16th century saw several major new movements within Catholicism. One was the extraordinary flowering of profound mysticism in Spain, spearheaded by John of the Cross and Teresa of Ávila; another was the founding of the Society of Jesus by Ignatius Loyola.

Ignatius was a Spanish soldier who became interested in religion in 1521, after reading a life of Jesus while convalescing in bed after a battle. He founded the Society of Jesus, or the Jesuits, along military lines in 1540. The idea was a tightly organized society that would educate children, provide spiritual direction and send missions overseas. It excelled at all these things and also proved a powerful force in the fight against Protestantism. However, the Jesuits were not a force for reform: on the contrary, they were opposed to the very idea. Ignatius's attitude is summed up in his Rule 13: "I will believe that the white that I see is black, if the hierarchical Church says so." With this attitude the Jesuits fought passionately for the conversion of all mistaken people, which meant heretics, Protestants and the inhabitants of distant countries.

Beyond Europe

Mission, in particular, was an important tool in the struggles of the churches. It seemed to many Catholics that the discovery of the New World had been providentially timed to coincide with the mass apostasy of much of the old one. Enormous efforts were made to bring Catholicism to America and also to the Far East, both with great success. The Jesuit missionary Francis Xavier arrived in Japan in 1549 and proved especially successful there, although Christianity was banned and driven underground there within a century. King Philip II of Spain, meanwhile, was very keen to prove his loyalty to the pope and was responsible for the conquest and conversion of much of South America. Many Protestants, feeling for their part that God had provided a convenient new continent as a home for their purified Christianity, looked to North America—ultimately with even greater success.

The wars of religion

Meanwhile, in Europe the struggles were intensifying. War broke out in France in 1562 as rival families struggled for control of the country; unhappily, religion got mixed up in it, and for the first time Catholics and Protestants were at war. The worst atrocity was the St. Bartholomew Massacre of 1572, when in just a couple of days over 20,000 French Protestants, known as Huguenots, were slaughtered by Catholic troops. Throughout Europe, forces were mobilized. It was clear to Protestants that the Catholic Church was not simply an error-stricken anachronism. It was the army of Satan.

At the same time, Dutch Calvinists were rebelling against Spanish Catholic rule of their country. Nationalism overcame religious differences, and in 1576 the Dutch Catholics and Protestants united to overthrow the Spanish; but the Catholics soon made peace with Spain and went their own way. The Netherlands were left as a stronghold of the Reformed faith.

The culmination came in 1618 with the Thirty Years' War, as the Protestant states of Germany and the Catholic ones launched attacks against each other, dragging most of the rest of the continent into what was really the first all-encompassing European war. The scale of the destruction was something no one had ever seen before.

The Church of England

In the face of all this, one country succeeded in navigating the Reformation with barely a hitch: England. King Henry VIII needed to divorce his wife in order to produce a male heir, but the Catholic Church refused to let him do this. Henry therefore decreed that the church in England was now under his own control, not that of the pope. What had been achieved in other countries through endless preaching and struggle happened in England through royal decree, in a series of measures in the 1530s. The king simply took control of the existing Catholic structures, demolished the monasteries and executed anyone who, like Sir Thomas More, refused to renounce their allegiance to the pope. Henry's advisers, Thomas Cranmer and Thomas Cromwell, were sympathetic to Lutheranism, and the new Church of England was formed along broadly Protestant lines. However, because there were no rival churches in the country, the Church of England never became as strident and definitive about its beliefs as did the continental churches.

Despite a brief blip in the 1550s, when Queen Mary tried to reestablish Roman Catholicism and executed enormous numbers of Protestants, the Church of England remained secure. In the late 16th and 17th centuries, under men like Richard Hooker, the Church of England would forge a distinctive theological approach, taking what they regarded as the best from both Catholicism and Protestantism.

Puritanism

On Boxing Day, 1620, a ship named the *Mayflower* arrived at Plymouth, Massachusetts. Its passengers were hoping to start a new society based on what they believed to be the decrees of God. They were Puritans.

Puritanism evolved from the dissatisfaction of many people in the Church of England with the way things were going. They felt that the way the church drew on Catholic ideas and practices was unacceptable, and they pressed for a more Calvinist approach in doctrine and in morality. By the 1560s some of these extreme Protestants were already splitting off from the Church of England and holding their own meetings. It was a popular movement, not an academic or intellectual one, and enjoyed much support among working-class people.

The Puritans believed that human beings are completely sinful and that this can be overcome only by extreme hard work and penitence. They stressed the importance of personal repentance and conversion as a condition of church membership. The word *puritanical* has therefore sometimes come to have a wider, negative meaning, apart from its reference to Puritans proper. It suggests extreme misery, dourness and disapproval of anything remotely fun.

Puritanism was something of an exaggeration of certain elements of Calvinism, and more moderate elements in England were not happy about its rise. In the early 17th century Puritans began to suffer persecution from the authorities, especially from William Laud, archbishop of Canterbury in the 1630s. Laud (who, judging by contemporary portraits, looked remarkably like Mr. Toad from *The Wind in the Willows*) had especially little time for fanatical Puritans who broke into churches and vandalized banners or who destroyed clerical vestments, believing them to be instruments of popery—and he punished them accordingly. It was in response to this that Puritans began to emigrate: some to the Netherlands, a bastion of the Reformed faith; and others to the New World, hoping to rid themselves of the apostasy of Anglicanism and set up a true Calvinist society—a sort of new Geneva on a larger scale. Those who set off in 1620 from Plymouth in England were the first, and there were many more to follow.

The situation blew up in England in the 1640s at the outbreak of the English Civil War, a pitched struggle between supporters of King Charles I and the forces of Parliament. In a way this was the last of the European wars of religion, because the Royalist forces tended toward Catholicism while the Parliamentarians were Puritans. The defeat of the king saw the triumph of Puritanism in the Church of England, and an attempt was made to reform England along Puritan lines—even banning the celebration of Christmas. Archbishop Laud was rewarded for his former zeal in stamping out Puritanism by being beheaded for treason in 1645.

However, the restoration of the monarchy in 1660 spelled the end of the movement as far as the established church was concerned. From then on, Puritanism spilled over into new churches—such as the Methodists and the Baptists—or abroad, to America. There the settlers of 1620 and those who followed later had successfully set up a new Calvinist state. The colony was small but grew gradually, as more people arrived and joined forces with other colonies in the region. However, the expansion of the colony eventually spelled the end of Puritan government. In 1692 the colony was changed from a theocracy to a secular form of government, and the Puritans ceased to be a major political force.

They remained a powerful cultural force, however. The Puritan version of Protestantism would greatly influence all subsequent North American theology and spirituality, particularly the Pietist movement. Even today, the ideals of Puritanism—hard work, high moral standards, and individual repentance and confession—remain central to much of American society, and politicians and other public figures are expected to live up to them. And still today, the original settlers of 1620 are venerated as the Pilgrims and remembered each year at Thanksgiving. It is striking to reflect that American society can be traced back to a group who considered 17th-century England to be insufficiently fanatical in matters of religion, and in a way it is even more significant that America still commemorates the fact today.

Pietism

By the middle of the 17th century, European Christianity was facing something of a crisis. The creativity and excitement of the early Reformation had long since given way to a dry and deathly dull scholasticism, as representatives of the major churches devoted their time to producing long and tedious *summas* of their various faiths. And the devastation of the wars of religion was still fresh in people's memories. Catholicism, Lutheranism and Calvinism alike seemed to have little to offer the ordinary person.

The rise of Pietism was a reaction to all of this. The movement was triggered by Philip Spener, a Lutheran from Alsace, whose *Pious Wishes* of 1675 called for a new emphasis on personal devotion and a changed life. Spener admired Luther but believed that the Reformation was only half finished; he hated the new intellectualist orthodoxies and argued that doctrine is less important than personal faith and moral living.

Pietism became popular throughout Germany and then throughout the rest of Protestant Europe. The Pietist gospel revolved around the issues of repentance, individual conversion and living a new life; the Lutheran stress on salvation by faith alone was downplayed. It was deeply influenced by Puritanism but lacked its concern for correct doctrine.

Pietism would be enormously influential. It prepared the ground not only for the great 18th-century revivals in England and North America, under people like George Whitefield and John Wesley, but also for 18th-century rationalist religion, which had a similarly low regard for the doctrinal differences between faiths. Ultimately it would blossom in the thought of Friedrich Schleiermacher, the greatest of the 19th-century theologians, as a guiding force in the development of modern Protestant theology.

John Wesley

For two and a half centuries after Calvin, no great theologians arose to rethink the Christian message. The rivalry between the churches meant that professional theologians were too busy writing dull, repetitive dogmatic treatises and polemical pamphlets for each other's benefit to do anything creative. But the potential for mass publication opened up by the printing press and the rise in general literacy meant that the way was now open for a new kind of Christian theology. The great movements of the post-Reformation era, such as Puritanism and Pietism, were popular movements, and their leaders were not academics, monks or theologians but powerful preachers, able to move the hearts of thousands through their sermons and devotional writings. None was greater than John Wesley.

Life

Wesley, who was born in 1703, was the fifteenth child of an intemperate and rather unsuccessful Anglican clergyman. Much of his passion for religion was inherited from his mother, Susanna, a warmly devoted if rather strict woman with a very strong sense of the nearness of God.

Although they were Anglicans, both of John Wesley's parents came from Puritan backgrounds. So it was unsurprising that their son shared the Puritan passion for hard work and self-improvement, which took him to Oxford—by now an intellectual backwater full of comfortable, red-nosed clerics. In this unchallenging climate, Wesley's ability soon became obvious, and in 1726 he became a fellow himself, lecturing on Greek and philosophy. He maintained the pious habits his mother had taught him and would spend many (presumably) happy hours with his younger brother Charles, reading each other edifying spiritual works.

After being ordained in 1728, John, together with Charles, set up a small society of their friends in Oxford. It was run along the lines of a religious society—a common phenomenon among Puritans and Pietists who, finding their spiritual needs not met by the Church of England, sought to supplement church services by meeting regularly for devotion and moral exhortation. The Wesleys' group was regarded as something of a joke by many students, and because of their strict habits they came to be known as the Methodists.

In 1735 the two brothers were invited to join the rapidly growing colony of Georgia as pastors and missionaries. John did not have a good voyage, being terrified by the storms they encountered; but he was very impressed by the calmness of a group of Germans on the ship. They were Moravians, members of a group that traced its roots back to the 15th-century theological rebellion of Jan Hus and that had since become a major Pietist religious society in Europe.

In Georgia, John spoke to the Moravian pastor, who asked him if he knew Christ. When Wesley replied that he knew he was the Savior of the world, the Moravian pressed him: "Do you *know*, yourself?" Wesley answered, "I do," but wrote in his journal, "I fear they were vain words." The Moravian, for his part, wrote in his own journal, "I noticed that true grace dwelt and reigned in him."

The Wesley brothers spent two fairly disastrous years in Georgia, during which they learned that ordinary people do not care for ministers who try to turn them into a religious society. John was involved in a particularly unfortunate relationship with a young woman whom he almost married; when he decided that it would interfere with his vocation, she married someone else, and Wesley, believing her to be leading a life of immorality, refused to admit her to the Eucharist.

On his return to England (hastened partly by imminent legal action over his treatment of the young woman), John Wesley was plunged into a crisis of faith. His "Methodist" group at Oxford, his strict routine of Bible reading and devotion, and his ministry in America had all been attempts to purify himself and lead a holy life; but he felt a failure. Like Augustine and Luther before him, he simply felt too sinful. And as with them, the realization that he could not make himself holy at all came like a divine revelation. It occurred on May 24, 1738:

> In the evening I went very unwillingly to a society in Aldersgate Street, where one was reading Luther's preface to the Epistle to the Romans. About a quarter before nine, while he was describing the change which God works in the heart through faith in Christ, I felt my heart strangely warmed. I felt I did trust in Christ, Christ alone, for salvation; and an assurance was given me that He had taken away my sins, even mine, and saved me from the law of sin and death.
> *Journal 2*

Wesley realized that salvation comes through faith in Christ, and this faith is not intellectual agreement with a set of propositions *about* Christ; it is a personal relationship *with* Christ. That was what the Moravian minister had been trying to show him in Georgia. And Wesley also realized that with this personal relationship in place, the holy life he had been trying to achieve would follow naturally. But holiness was not about ordering one's habits and trying to purify oneself, as he had been doing; it was about helping others. Wesley was transformed from an uptight, self-obsessed Puritan into a genuinely loving, other-regarding person.

After a period spent with the Moravian community of Herrnhut in Germany, Wesley went to Bristol to help his friend George Whitefield, who had also recently returned from Georgia and had a conversion experience similar to Wesley's. Whitefield was one of the greatest preachers of all time, a man of incredible passion who could reduce an open-air crowd of thousands to tears and who was said to have driven fifteen people insane with one of his early sermons in Gloucester. Wesley rapidly became almost his rival. Huge crowds flocked to hear him, and his sermons were frequently punctuated with shrieks and wailing from the crowd, as his hearers, caught up in the emotion of the message, collapsed in fits, thrashing and sobbing, only to be restored to calmness and peace by the unrelenting flow of words.

Wesley was fast becoming the leader of the revivals, a great movement sweeping both Britain and America. But it was not random, directionless enthusiasm: Wesley ensured that the movement had a sensible structure and leadership, with its own meeting places and leaders. He built up a coterie of highly skilled helpers, including his brother Charles, who wrote over 9,000 hymns for the movement, many of which remain extremely popular today. It was becoming a church within a church, and needless to say, the authorities of the Church of England were not entirely happy about it. Wesley's followers were known, once again, as Methodists, and accusations of "enthusiasm" were hurled by everyone from bishops to screaming mobs, who often charged Wesley bodily, only to be turned back by his hypnotic gaze and calm words.

The success of the movement owed a great deal to Wesley's personal charisma and commitment. Even his followers sometimes called him "Pope John." A small, neatly dressed man, he had the orator's gift of capturing the attention of every individual in his audience and seeming to speak to them alone. And he spoke to a lot of people: from the early 1740s onward, he spent his life traveling the length of Britain on horseback, sometimes over 100 kilometers a day and up to 8,000 a year. He invariably preached four or five times every day. It is little wonder that his marriage was a terrible failure, since his wife had no love for such a lifestyle and Wesley was unprepared to change it in the slightest, even when she followed after him, shouting abuse. They drifted apart to such an extent that he did not learn of her death until after her funeral.

Indeed, even after his evangelical conversion, Wesley remained something of an obsessive rigorist, anxious never to waste a single moment of the day or change his routine for anything. Samuel Johnson remarked that Wesley was an interesting person to talk to but he never seemed to stay for very long; he always had to dash off to be somewhere else. Throughout his life, Wesley kept a remarkably detailed journal in which he noted with tiresome precision the numbers and relative strengths of the temptations he experienced each day, together with the degree of success with which he had resisted them. This rather pedantic casuistry would remain a feature of some later evangelical traditions.

Wesley remained immersed in his work until the end. He kept up his horse riding and preaching until well into his seventies and threw himself into social issues, campaigning vigorously for prisoners' rights and the abolition of slavery and also denouncing the rebellion against the British Crown of the American colonies where he had once worked. He attributed his enormous energy, health and eternal good looks to the fact that for decades he had always got up at four in the morning and preached at five. The fact that anyone was prepared to hear a sermon at such a time is itself testament to his remarkable popularity and powers of speaking. He died in 1791, at the age of eighty-eight, but the movement he founded was still going strong.

Although Wesley always regarded himself as an Anglican clergyman, the Methodists had soon become an independent church, the most important and influential of the "Nonconformist" English-speaking organizations. Today it has 70 million members, who still commemorate 24 May as the date of John Wesley's conversion. But his influence goes beyond them; evangelicals of all denominations claim Wesley as one of their great heroes, as do members of the Pentecostalist movement.

Thought

Even the wilder performers of rock music would have raised a makeup-caked eyebrow at one of Wesley's performances. People shrieked, fainted, thrashed about or laughed hysterically, spellbound by the preacher's glittering eye and beguiled by the caress of his words.

What was this message that had such extraordinary effects? It revolved around salvation and how the individual can find peace with God—the issue that had plagued Wesley before 1738. Wesley never applied his formidable mind to the traditional issues of Christian theology, such as the nature of the Trinity or of Christ. His opinions on these matters were traditional and orthodox, and he saw no need to repeat what others had said perfectly well. But he did feel that not enough had been said on the "way to heaven," as he called it.

The "way to heaven" lies through faith in Christ. Wesley wholeheartedly agreed with Luther that salvation is by faith alone, not by works; and he added to this an insistence that "faith" means a radical existential attitude toward the person of Christ:

> Christian faith is then, not only an assent to the whole gospel of Christ, but also a full reliance on the blood of Christ; a trust in the merits of his life, death, and resurrection; a recumbency upon him as our atonement and our life, as given for us, and living in us; and, in consequence hereof, a closing with him, and cleaving to him, as our "wisdom, righteousness, sanctification, and redemption," or, in one word, our salvation.
> "Sermon I"

The same point had been stressed by the Reformers, especially Melanchthon and Calvin, but the idea had been rather forgotten in the intervening period of dogmatic orthodoxy.

Although Wesley's theology had its roots in the thought of Calvin, it was a kind of "nice" Calvinism with the more unpleasant parts toned down or removed. Wesley stressed the sinfulness of humanity but did not believe that all actions performed before conversion are sins. More fundamentally, and in contrast to the stricter Whitefield, he denied predestination and declared repeatedly that every person is free to accept God's grace. It is not a freedom we deserve, but it is one that God graciously gives us. He vehemently rejected as blasphemous the Calvinist notion that Christ died only for the elect. It was Wesley's particular genius to clear away the scholastic pedantry and harshness from the Reformation message and restate it clearly and compassionately in tones that shook the world.

5

THE MODERN ERA

✍

No sooner had the conflict of the Reformation period settled down than Christian thinkers were faced with more challenges—challenges that would shake their very assumptions to the core. Theologians had been forced to deal with rival or alien systems of thought before, but the rise of modern science raised issues on a hitherto unprecedented scale. Christians had to reevaluate not only the traditional doctrines of the church but their understanding of the nature of Christianity itself. The fact that theologians arose who were more than equal to the challenge makes this period one of the most fascinating—and important—in the history of the church.

The Enlightenment

Like the Renaissance, the Enlightenment was an all-encompassing trend of thought that is very hard to define. In many ways, it is still going on.

The natural sciences

The Enlightenment grew out of the scientific and philosophical advances that were made in the 16th and 17th centuries. In the hands of men like Carolus Linnaeus, the biologist, and above all Sir Isaac Newton, the brilliant mathematician and physicist, the natural sciences were becoming a major intellectual and cultural force. People were looking at the world with new eyes—the eyes of reason, not those of faith.

The scientists believed in God, certainly, but they believed in him as a sort of last-ditch scientific hypothesis to be appealed to when nothing else could be found. He was a "God of the gaps," used to plug the holes in scientific knowledge. And as science progressed and the gaps shrank, there was less and less space for God. There is a story of Pierre-Simon Laplace, the great mathematician and astronomer, presenting Napoleon with an edition of his books. The emperor asked what place God had in Laplace's system, to which the scientist answered, "Sire, I have no need of that hypothesis." The story is entirely apocryphal, but it illustrates exactly what was going on.

The humanities

It was happening in the study of history as well as in science. In his monumental *The Decline and Fall of the Roman Empire*, the first part of which was published in 1776, the historian—and unbeliever—Edward Gibbon tried to explain why Christianity had proved so successful in late antiquity. He suggested that it was because the Christians were especially devout; their doctrine of future bliss, the stories of Christian miracles and their own virtuous lives were all very popular; and in the church they possessed a strong social structure that the empire was increasingly unable to provide. In other words, he explained the success of Christianity in historical, non-supernatural terms. Since everyone from Justin Martyr on had always taken it for granted that the success of Christianity was entirely due to its truth, and to the hand of God, this was an extremely radical position for Gibbon to take. He was explaining history—and the history of Christianity at that!—in a way that not only did not mention God but did not seem to leave him any role at all. But this methodology of explaining natural events solely in terms of other natural events is fundamental to all subsequent history as well as science.

The new philosophies

The new hope in the power of unaided human reason reached its zenith with the philosophy of rationalism taught by René Descartes and Gottfried von Leibniz. The rationalist philosophers believed that true ideas are intrinsically different from false ones, so it is theoretically possible to tell whether something is true or not simply by examining the idea, without having to go outside and check whether it matches reality. This meant that one could produce an elaborate system of metaphysics, religion and science simply by thinking extremely hard.

At the other extreme, English-speaking philosophers such as John Locke and David Hume denounced this sort of thing as silly and argued that knowledge comes only through experience. We cannot tell whether something is true unless we go and see for ourselves. This philosophy of empiricism underlay the amazing advances in science that were being made at the time.

The important thing from our point of view is that the rationalists and empiricists alike had little time for the idea of revelation. The notion that beliefs should be taken on faith, on the basis of authority, had no place in the Age of Reason. That is true even for thinkers like Locke and Leibniz, who were well known as theologians as well as philosophers. Ultimately it is up to *us* to determine what is true, either through the unaided power of reason or through scientific investigation.

Reason and religion

The same ideas were spread by cultural figures like Voltaire, the central spokesman for the French Enlightenment. His slogan was "Crush infamy!" Through his plays, novels, pamphlets and letters he sought to do exactly that, freeing humanity from a slavish following of old verities and the power of the church. Christianity was all right for servants, but enlightened people like himself knew that traditional doctrines like the Trinity and the divinity of Christ were just incoherent dogmas, forced on gullible people by reactionary powers. Reason tells us that God exists, but not much else. The Age of Reason was also the Age of Skepticism.

These ideas became known as "deism" and were extremely influential in the 18th century. The deists believed that God had created the world but had set it up with excellent physical laws and had never needed to intervene since. It was the "watchmaker" idea of God. They rejected notions of revelation and dogma and hoped to live by rationally deduced moral laws. Their faith was the religious version of the general optimism and belief in the continual improvement and perfectibility of humanity.

Deism seems hopelessly naive to us today. But on one level it was an attempt to engage with a new problem that had never occurred to theologians before and that would become an overriding issue in the centuries to come—the relation between Christianity and other faiths. For the first time, cultured people were becoming aware that other religions, such as Islam and Buddhism, were not simply forces of darkness but had worthy ideals and conceptions of God. They were realizing, in short, that Christianity is just one religion among others—and a very historically conditioned one at that. The deists believed that their stripped-down version of Christianity was a kind of common core of religion, what you would get if you took any religion and removed the encrustations of tradition.

Similar points were made by Jean-Jacques Rousseau, another French cultural icon of the 18th century, who rather went against the progressive grain by arguing that humanity had once lived in idyllic simplicity that had become disrupted by civilization. But he also believed in a "primitive religion" that had become corrupted and weighed down by centuries of development.

People like the deists and Rousseau were, in essence, trying to deal with another new issue: how the ideals of Christianity relate to its history. The work of historians like Gibbon was showing that Christian doctrine had not been laid down in some once-for-all divine moment and that it was not all clearly there in the Bible, which is what people had tended to assume. It was becoming clear that Christian doctrine had developed gradually over a period of centuries. So why on earth should anyone believe it? These problems of history would be stated in their most worrying form by Lessing, and they would become one of the primary issues of theology in the 19th and 20th centuries.

Gotthold Lessing

Playwright, historian and critic, Lessing was one of the most prominent figures of the German Enlightenment. His theological ideas are a distillation of the problems that the Enlightenment threw up for Christianity and that are still addressed by theologians today.

Life

Born in Kamenz in 1729, Gotthold Lessing was the son of a Lutheran pastor, at whose insistence he studied theology and medicine. Lessing, however, was more interested in literature, and he wrote his first play at the age of 19. The production was a failure, and Lessing had to flee to Berlin to escape his creditors. However, the experience did not discourage him, and he continued writing. His plays and critical essays soon established him as a leading cultural figure, which he remained until his death in 1781.

Thought

As a historian, Lessing realized that many theological issues are really historical ones. In particular, he saw that the Bible can be approached as a historical source like any other. To illustrate this, in the 1770s he published a series of extracts of the work of Hermann Reimarus, an obscure professor of Asian languages who had died a few years before. Reimarus had argued that Jesus had believed the end of the world was imminent; after his death his disciples claimed that he would return soon; but when this failed to happen they changed the message. Christianity was thus based on a mistake and a deception.

Lessing did not endorse Reimarus's views and claimed he had published them in the hope of provoking people to defend Christianity as powerfully as Reimarus had attacked it; but he did want to show some of the problems involved with basing a religion on ancient history. Lessing was acutely aware of the great differences between people of different ages. He wrote, "There is a broad, ugly ditch of history that I cannot jump across." If Jesus was a 1st-century Palestinian Jew, then perhaps Reimarus was right to say that his message was so rooted in that context that it seems garbled or simply mistaken to us now.

But the problems run deeper than this. Lessing believed that the truths of religion are eternal and necessary and can, in theory, be discovered by the exercise of enlightened reason. They are totally different from historical truth, which is contingent—any historical event *could* have turned out differently. For example, William the Conqueror might have lost the Battle of Hastings if he had not been so lucky. So how can we base religion on historical events? Suppose Pilate had decided not to crucify Jesus after all. What would have happened to the Christian gospel then? Lessing concluded, "The accidental truths of history can never become the proof of the necessary truths of reason."

In Lessing's eyes, the historical religions, Christianity, Judaism and so on, play an important but limited role in the development of humanity. They teach ethical values. But they will one day be superseded when people learn that value and morality are based not on supposed historical fact but on reason. Lessing's last play, *Nathan the Wise*, portrays the Jewish character Nathan as embodying these virtues of serene, enlightened rationality.

Different religions are therefore of equal value, since they are all historically limited and will one day become obsolete. Lessing argued forcibly for religious tolerance. In *Nathan the Wise*, Nathan tells a story of a man who owned a valuable gold ring. Uncertain which of his three sons to give it to, he had two identical copies made, so he could give a ring to each son. Later, the sons argued over who had the original, but it was impossible to tell the rings apart. Nathan comments that instead of fighting over who was their father's true heir, they should each have tried to act as though he was and lived a good, harmonious life. Similarly, arguing over which religion is the true one is futile; none can be proved right or wrong. However, by living as though our religion is true, in a rational and ethical way, we can overcome religious boundaries and follow the true, eternal dictates of reason.

Reflections

Lessing was very much a man of his time. His belief in a true religion, discoverable by serene reason, and a future age when everyone would live in enlightened harmony, now seems quaint. But the problem of the relationship between religion and history is still central to theological debate today. Lessing sought to separate them, and in so doing it seems that he wrenched Christianity away from its roots and basis. If Christianity is not centered on the life and death of the historical figure of Christ, then it loses its distinctiveness. A central task of theology since Lessing has been to try to show how Christianity can be firmly rooted in these historical events without becoming outdated, incomprehensible or uncertain.

Immanuel Kant

Immanuel Kant was the greatest product of the Enlightenment, a man of truly staggering genius. He is generally considered the greatest philosopher of modern times—

perhaps of all time—and his intellectual legacy is still being explored today.

Life

Kant led an incredibly dull life. He was born in Königsberg in 1724 and died there

ROMANTICISM

The Romantic movement was one of the most important cultural forces of the late 18th and early 19th centuries. It was a reaction to the Age of Reason—the serene and enlightened ideals of Lessing and Kant, the stately, ordered science of Newton and the elegant coffee shops of civilized Europe. The Romantics yearned for something more interesting.

They were deeply influenced by Jean-Jacques Rousseau, whose idea of the "noble savage" uncorrupted by civilization seemed a powerful antidote to the ever more refined European high society. He argued—in direct contradiction to Christian ideas of the time—that human beings are naturally good and are only made bad by social institutions. Rousseau's ideas struck a deep chord with many people.

Essentially Romanticism was a celebration of emotion over reason and of nature over civilization. The movement was spearheaded by people like Friedrich Leopold, Baron von Hardenberg, whose name, one might think, was romantic enough; but he preferred to be known as Novalis. Novalis's famous Hymns to the Night, *a cycle of prose poems dedicated to his fiancée who had died suddenly at the age of fifteen, remains the very epitome of Romantic literature: evocative, mysterious, fantastic and irrational.*

Novalis also set a standard by dying of consumption in 1801 at the age of twenty-nine. The image of the pale young man feebly calling for his laudanum as he pens feverish verse on his pillow to his dead sweetheart remains the absolute stereotype of the Romantic poet. It may be a caricature, but this ideal of experiencing the full emotions of life to such a degree that one would die young, worn out and not regretting a moment of it, resurfaced in the lives and work of the great figures of English Romanticism: Percy Bysshe Shelley, John Keats and Lord Byron.

And there was more to it than poetry. Painters abandoned the structured subjects and styles of the time and sought to portray tempestuous seas and craggy mountains. Composers, similarly, gave up the formal style of Wolf-

in 1804, having spent almost all of the intervening period as a professor at Königsberg University. Despite his renown as a geographer, he never visited any of the places he lectured on. He never married (something he regarded with great distaste) or had a pet, he hated virtually all music and art (except poetry), and he fol-

gang Amadeus Mozart and learned instead the stormy and unpredictable rhythms of Ludwig von Beethoven.

The whole sweep of Romanticism was encapsulated and transcended by the greatest cultural icon of the age, Johann Wolfgang von Goethe. Goethe's Sorrows of Young Werther, a gloriously self-indulgent book published in 1774 after an unhappy love affair, was entirely in the Romantic strain; but his later work, particularly the epochal Faust, published after his death in 1832, transcended the irrationality of Romanticism to embrace a more holistic understanding of humanity and religion. However, Goethe shared with the true Romantics a distaste for the arid rationality of Voltaire and Kant, and the status he enjoyed in his last decades as a sort of semi-divine sage worshiped by literati of every kind set the seal on the death of the Age of Reason.

In a way Romanticism was to the Enlightenment what Pietism was to the sterility of the post-Reformation period, and naturally it had its religious side. Where Enlightenment thinkers had believed that godliness and true religion are found through the perfect functioning of the mind, Romantics placed them in the exercise of the emotions. In a way, however, they tended to agree with their Enlightenment forebears that traditional doctrines like the Trinity and original sin had no place in modern Christianity. Theirs was a religion of the heart and of nature, not of doctrine. It might have seemed to many that traditional orthodoxy was, if not dead, then definitely on its way out.

However, despite this, the insights of Romanticism played a major role in the formulation of the work of Friedrich Schleiermacher, the first great theologian since Calvin and the man who kick-started modern theology. For two and a half centuries the development of Christian thought had been the work of popular preachers and ordinary people; it is somewhat ironic that the anti-intellectualist movement of Romanticism was partly responsible for placing it back in the hands of professionals and academics.

lowed the same routine every day like clockwork. Kant's habits were so regular that the citizens of Königsberg would set their clocks as he passed their houses on his daily walk; and the one time he stayed home to reread a particularly interesting book (by Rousseau), everyone in the city was late.

Despite this, and his eccentric habits such as working at his desk in his night-gown or keeping his socks up with a strange contraption involving elastic stretching from his trouser pockets, Kant was much loved. He was a warm and witty man who regularly entertained many guests at lunch, providing copious amounts of wine. Students had to arrive an hour early for his lectures if they wanted to find a seat.

Thought

Kant's masterpiece was his *Critique of Pure Reason*, which appeared in 1781. This magisterial and frequently incomprehensible work swept aside the pretensions of rational philosophy and metaphysics. In essence, Kant's basic point was that human reason is incapable of making any sense unless it confines its attentions to the content of human experience—but the very fact that we are human, with preprogrammed physical and mental equipment for experiencing the world, means that that experience is not pure and objective but is partly our own creation.

This had enormous consequences for metaphysics and the theory of knowledge. It was the end of the rationalist philosophy of Leibniz and his followers, who had tried to speculate about things beyond human experience; and it was the end of the empiricist philosophy of Locke and *his* followers, who had not realized that there is no such thing as a pure experience unaltered by the mind that experiences it. And Kant's revolution also had serious consequences for religion. It meant that reason cannot address issues such as the existence and nature of God, which lie outside our experience. Before Kant, everyone from Aquinas to Descartes had thought it quite easy to prove God's existence like a mathematical theorem; after Kant, almost no one has tried to do this anymore, although many still defend "proofs" that suggest that God *probably* exists.

Kant thought that religion is not really a matter of *knowing* at all. It is a matter of *doing.* The religious life is the moral life, and Kant thought that religious ceremonies that do not achieve anything practical are a complete waste of time. Despite being rector of his university, he always contrived to be "indisposed" whenever his presence was required at any official religious ceremony. He believed, furthermore, that ethical principles can be rationally determined and do not need the dictates of religion to establish them; but he also thought that the best—indeed the only—way to lead a religious life is to follow those ethical principles. This is how God is honored. Just like Lessing, Kant thought that the differences between the religions really mask underlying similarities. Doctrine is, in essence, irrelevant, and the mark of a good religion is the usefullness and validity of its ethics.

Reflections

Kant was a Lutheran from a Pietist background, and we can see the influence of this nonrationalist, ethical, personal sort of faith in his views on religion. Those views would prove extremely influential. Although the idea that religion is essentially about living right would be vehemently rejected by Schleiermacher, the true founder of modern theology and himself deeply influenced by Kant, it would be central to 19th-century theology. It is still extremely widespread today, since it has an inspiring sound to it and helps explain how religion and science can coexist. It is comforting to say that science is about facts while religion is about values.

Yet the approach has serious problems too. Perhaps the most serious is that, as a matter of fact, it does not describe how religions really work. Religious people, whether we like it or not, do make substantial claims about the world and about God; they do not simply act in a certain way, they believe that certain things are true. And furthermore, these truth claims are not all about some kind of parallel religious universe, a separate sphere distinct from that with which science concerns itself. For example, implicit in the belief that God exists and created the universe is a corollary that the universe therefore has a purpose of some kind and that it cannot really be understood without taking God into account. But these ideas are decidedly at odds with the preconceptions and methods of most modern science. Whether we like it or not, incidents such as the condemnation of Galileo in the 17th century and the arguments over Darwin in the 19th are not isolated incidents when people failed to realize that religion and science deal with separate issues. Science and religion do operate according to different value systems, and they do make conflicting claims about the world. And in modern times, this has meant that Christians have had either to retreat and reject the findings of modern science or to try to modify their faith and deal constructively with the new challenges that it throws up.

Friedrich Schleiermacher

At the head of modern theology stands Friedrich Schleiermacher. At a time when Christianity seemed to many to be in its death throes, impaled on the cold reason of the Enlightenment, Schleiermacher saved it from an ignominious retreat into irrational Pietism. His work allowed Christians to engage constructively with the forces of reason and skepticism and even recruit them to their cause, turning the atheists' weapons against themselves. In short, if anyone is to blame for the existence of this book, it is Schleiermacher.

TÜBINGEN

Tübingen was founded in the Middle Ages and later became one of the most important cities in the German state of Wurttemberg. Its university was to become among the most renowned in the German-speaking world. There, amid ancient castles and churches, Philipp Melanchthon, the most brilliant disciple of Martin Luther, taught in the 16th century. But it was in the 19th century that Tübingen would attain its real theological significance.

In 1826 Ferdinand Baur joined the theological faculty at Tübingen University. Baur was a disciple of the great philosopher G. W. F. Hegel, who had himself studied at Tübingen. Like Reimarus and Lessing before him, Baur believed that the Bible should be studied like any other historical document. For example, texts like the creation story in the Old Testament could be discussed in the same way that scholars were used to discussing ancient Greek or Roman myths. Baur used literary-critical techniques to argue that most of the books of the New Testament were not in fact written by their traditional authors and that many of them were actually written much later than had commonly been thought. Some of Baur's views were a little overenthusiastic by modern standards, but his groundbreaking work laid the way open for later generations of biblical scholars. For decades Tübingen would remain the mecca to which they would come.

The Tübingen scholars were not theologians in the sense of people who reflect on Christian doctrine. They tended to be either Hegelian intellectuals or not Christians at all. But their work posed a challenge to Christian thought as great as the more dramatic revolution that was occurring at the same time

Life

Schleiermacher was born in 1768 in Breslaw, the son of a Prussian army chaplain. When he was nine, his father came into contact with Pietism and experienced a devotional reawakening. Schleiermacher became determined that his son should be protected from the atheistic skepticism of the Age of Reason and sent him, at the age of 15, to a boarding school run by the Moravian Brethren, the pious evangelical sect that traced its roots back to Jan Hus and that had been a major influence on John Wesley.

The warmth of the Moravians' devotions made a great impression on Schleier-

*in the geological and life sciences. For example, until this time few people—
even atheists—had doubted that the stories about Jesus in the Gospels were
true. Even if, like the Deists, they did not believe in miracles, they thought
the "miraculous" events had really happened but had been misinterpreted.
When Jesus walked on the water, for example, he was actually standing on
submerged rocks; and when he fed the five thousand, he actually inspired
everybody to produce their own packed lunches and share them around.
Credulous bystanders, it was thought, had mistaken these ordinary events
for miracles. But in 1835 a scholar at Tübingen named David Strauss swept
all that away when his* Life of Jesus *argued that none of these things happened at all. The stories in the Gospels were created by the early Christians
as reflections on profound spiritual truths, and we actually know very little
of the historical Jesus at all. Strauss lost his job and his livelihood for daring
to suggest such a thing, but it would never be possible for scholarly Christians to read the Bible in the same way again. The way was open for the
work of Albert Schweitzer and his colleagues in the early 20th century.*

*Today the kinds of critical techniques that were pioneered at Tübingen are
taught throughout the world; biblical scholarship would be unthinkable
without them. Tübingen remains at the forefront of critical theology. Its
most famous modern representative is Hans Küng, not a biblical scholar at
all but a Roman Catholic theologian disowned by his own church for his liberal views on papal infallibility. In the figure of Küng and others like him, the
critical, questioning stance of Tübingen seems assured of a long future.*

macher, especially their belief that true religion is concerned not with outward form, or with doctrines, but with an inner, personal experience of Christ. However, not all was well. Although Schleiermacher admired the Moravians' religious devotion, he found it hard to emulate. He later wrote:

> In vain I aspired after those supernatural experiences ... of the reality of which
> ... every lesson and every hymn, yes, every glance at the Brethren, so attractive
> while under their influence, persuaded me. Yet me they seemed ever to flee.
> *The Life of Schleiermacher As Unfolded in His Autobiography and Letters* I.7, trans.
> Frederica Rowan

Worse, the Moravians did nothing to nurture their pupil's increasingly questioning mind. As a 10-year-old child Schleiermacher had been unable to sleep, tormented by doubts about the Calvinist doctrine of the atonement; and during his teens his worries increased. He heard of the new, scientific methods of Bible study and dogmatics that were being pioneered by scholars at the university in Tübingen and by others, and he wanted to find out more, but the Moravians could not help. Like Pietism in general, they reacted to modern scholarship by ignoring it. Schleiermacher expressed his worries in letters home, but his father was unhelpful. He advised his son to avoid the "tree of knowledge," adding tersely, "You do not intend to be a vain theologian" (*Life* I.45).

Starved of critical engagement, Schleiermacher's intellectual worries increased until he found himself unable to accept what he was taught. Eventually he decided to confide in his father. He wrote him a sensitive and moving letter:

> Alas! dearest father, if you believe that without this faith no one can attain to salvation in the next world, nor to tranquillity in this—and such, I know, is your belief—oh! then pray to God to grant it to me, for to me it is now lost. I cannot believe that he who called himself the Son of Man was the true, eternal God; I cannot believe that his death was a vicarious atonement.
> *Life* I.46

His father's angry and bewildered reply grieved Schleiermacher greatly. His father was unable to understand such "wickedness of heart" (*Life* I.50), even accusing his son of disturbing the rest of his dead mother with his willful impiety, and informed him that although he still loved his son, he was honor-bound to disown him.

The Moravians were no more helpful. Schleiermacher was desperate to have his doubts answered and refuted, but he reported, "The labourers refuse to enter upon any argument with me or to undertake to refute me, and with my friends I am strictly forbidden to speak upon the subject" (*Life* I.55). It was made clear that he was no longer welcome in the Moravian community.

Despite his father's intemperate words, he remained in contact with his son and supported him in everything he did, although they never saw each other again. Schleiermacher left the Moravians and went to study at the University of Halle, where, following his father's advice, he made an intensive study of the works of Kant, at that time causing a storm throughout the intellectual world. In 1790, despite his intellectual doubts, he became a Reformed minister and found a job as private tutor to the children of a Prussian count. He greatly enjoyed the warm, intellectually curious atmosphere of this aristocratic family and their friends. Indeed, throughout his life Schleiermacher thrived on the company of friends. He once wrote to one of them:

> I cannot thrive in solitude. In truth, I am the least independent of mortals;
> indeed, I sometimes doubt whether I be really an individual. I stretch out all
> my roots and leaves in search of affection; it is necessary for me to feel myself
> in immediate contact with it, and when I am unable to drink in full draughts
> of it, I at once dry up and wither.
> *Life* I.188

Schleiermacher was a warm, sociable person who enjoyed many very close friendships throughout his life. Some of these were begun when, in 1796, he moved to Berlin as a hospital chaplain. Here he threw himself into the world of high culture, meeting the leading figures of Romanticism, including the poet and philosopher Friedrich Schlegel. Schleiermacher and Schlegel shared rooms for a while and began an ambitious project to translate Plato into German. He also met a married woman who became his closest confidante, much to the delight of the city's gossips. However, Schleiermacher fell in love with another married woman, who refused to dissolve her unhappy marriage for Schleiermacher's sake. Schleiermacher seems in general to have been particularly fond of female company. Some of his closest friendships were with women, including his sister. He believed that women have a greater capacity than men for love and religious sense, and he even remarked that he would have preferred to have been born a woman.

It was during this period, in 1799, that Schleiermacher published the book that made him famous. Tired of the Enlightenment's attacks on religion as outmoded superstition, he planned a brilliant counterattack to put religion back into intellectual discussion. *On Religion: Speeches to Its Cultured Despisers* achieved this and more: it set out a completely new approach to religion, brilliantly sidestepping the old, futile arguments of the Enlightenment and setting the stage for modern theology. The genius of the work lay in Schleiermacher's insight that religion need not be one human activity among others, to be accepted or rejected, like sport or politics; rather, it lies at the heart of all human endeavor. The "cultured despisers," by rejecting religion in favor of rational, enlightened humanism, were shooting themselves in the foot. To be religious, argued Schleiermacher, is part of what it is to be human. It is impossible to accomplish anything without it:

> Because you do not deal with life in a living way, your conception bears the
> stamp of perishableness, and is altogether meagre. True science is complete vision; true practice is culture and art self-produced; true religion is sense and taste
> for the infinite. To wish to have true science or true practice without religion, or
> to imagine it is possessed, is obstinate, arrogant delusion, and culpable error.
> *Speeches on Religion* 2

The book was hugely popular, and Schleiermacher became the new darling of the Romantic movement. Even Johann Wolfgang von Goethe approved of his book and treated Schleiermacher like an old acquaintance when he later met him. Excited by the stir he had caused, Schleiermacher exclaimed to a friend, "What may I still not become in this sublunary sphere!" (*Life* 1.209). He had succeeded in his aim of rehabilitating religion as one of the main topics of intellectual debate, and his newfound fame helped his career too: in 1802 he became a professor at Halle University as well as a university preacher. There he lectured on an enormous variety of subjects, including a completely new one of his own invention: hermeneutics, the discipline of critically deciphering texts from the past. The elevation of this activity into a science created a tool that would be of enormous service not just to theology but to classical and literary studies too.

Schleiermacher continued to write, and his work shows the gradual maturation of his thought as he continued to grapple with the problems he had first encountered as an adolescent at the Moravian community. But he was being forced to deal with political events in Prussia as well. In 1806 Napoleon invaded the country, demolishing the Prussian military with ease. Schleiermacher watched as his city fell to the French, commenting morosely, "Napoleon must have a special hatred for Halle" (*Life* 2.70). Enemy troops were billeted in Schleiermacher's own house, although he suffered nothing worse than the loss of large numbers of shirts and most of his spoons; and his church was put to use as a granary.

These events inflamed Schleiermacher's patriotism. Unwilling to live under French rule, he moved back to Berlin, where he became minister of Trinity Church and threw himself into political activities. Some of these were more legitimate than others. He worked as an adviser on education to the government; at the same time he was involved in underground resistance movements, traveling the country in attempts to provoke an uprising against the French. He became editor of a newspaper, *Prussian Times*, which urged constitutional reform and opposition to the French. This got him into trouble with the authorities, and he was even ordered to leave the country, an order he ignored. The *Prussian Times* was accordingly dissolved in 1814.

At the same time, Schleiermacher was one of the leading lights of the new University of Berlin, becoming dean of theology in 1810 and rector of the university in 1815. As such, he was able to promote theology as a scientific discipline to stand alongside other subjects. His *Brief Outline of the Study of Theology*, a standard syllabus proposal, became an influential manifesto of what the subject should be. Of far more importance, however, was *The Christian Faith*. Written in 1821 and revised in 1830, this book set forth Schleiermacher's mature vision as a theologian, building on the basic insights presented in the *Speeches* years before. It is this work that establishes beyond all doubt Schleiermacher's place in the theological pantheon: it is the model for all systematic theologies since. In it he attempts nothing less than the total revision of the whole of Christian doctrine, to re-present it in a new, contemporary way. The *Speeches* provided the agenda for a new conception of religion; *The Christian Faith* sets forth that new conception. On the basis of this work, Schleiermacher is quite rightly remembered as the father of modern theology.

In addition to his pioneering work as a theologian, Schleiermacher finished his monumental translation of Plato, begun many years previously with Schlegel, which established his academic reputation beyond all doubt. Somehow he found time in 1809 to marry, at last, Henriette von Willich, the widow of an old friend.

Despite all this, it was as a pastor that Schleiermacher achieved greatest fame. He was a brilliant, charismatic speaker. One of his greatest sermons was preached in 1813, as Prussia prepared to attack Napoleon, fleeing from defeat in Russia. Bishop Eilert was among the listeners, and later wrote:

> There, in this holy place and at this solemn hour, stood the physically so small and insignificant man, his noble countenance beaming with intellect, and his clear, sonorous, penetrating voice ringing through the overflowing church. Speaking from his heart in pious enthusiasm, his every word penetrated to the heart, and the clear, full, mighty stream of his eloquence carried everyone along with it. His bold, frank declaration of the causes of our deep fall . . . struck down like thunder and lightning, and the subsequent elevation of the heart to God on the wings of solemn devotion was like harp-tones from a higher world. The discourse proceeded in an uninterrupted stream, and every word was *from* the times and *for* the times. And when, at last, with the full fire of enthusiasm, he addressed the noble youths already equipped for battle, and next, turning to their mothers, the greater number of whom were present, he concluded with the words: "Blessed is the womb that has borne such a son, blessed the breast that has nourished such a babe,"—a thrill of deep emotion ran through the assembly, and amid loud sobs and weeping, Schleiermacher pronounced the conclusive Amen.
> *Life* 2.203

He had become one of the leading intellectual and cultural icons of Germany. One of his proudest achievements was to be awarded the Order of the Red Eagle by the king of Prussia in 1831. People flocked from all over the country to hear his sermons and lectures or to attend his confirmation classes; it was said that he had no students, only disciples.

Schleiermacher died in 1834. Among his last words to his wife were: "I charge you to greet all my friends, and to tell them how sincerely I have loved them" (*Life* 2.337). His coffin, carried by twelve of his students, was followed through the streets of Berlin by a line of mourners over a mile long, among whom were the king and crown prince; and thousands crowded the streets to watch.

In his *Brief Outline* Schleiermacher had written: "Imagine the concern for religion and the scientific spirit united, for the sake of theory and practice, in the highest degree and in the most perfect balance, and you have the idea of a 'prince of the church'" (*Brief Outline* 9). In his life and work, Schleiermacher himself fulfilled these criteria perfectly. His questioning mind, together with his unswerving devotional piety, led him to insights and ideas that opened up previously unimagined possibilities for Christian thought.

Thought

Religion. The first of Schleiermacher's ideas to be published, his views on the nature of religion, are still the best-known aspect of his thought. We have seen that with his *On Religion: Speeches to Its Cultured Despisers* he introduced a new conception of religion, forcing it into the consciousness of enlightened humanists. How did he manage this?

Schleiermacher's position is essentially a development of—and a reaction against—Kant. We have seen how Kant demolished the rationalist systems of metaphysics that had hitherto formed the basis of theology: for Kant, God cannot be an object of *theoretical* reason or knowledge, because he lies outside our experience. Religion is therefore to be placed in the sphere of *practical* reason: it is concerned with morality or ethics. Schleiermacher agreed with the first of these positions but rejected the second.

In the *Speeches* Schleiermacher distinguishes between two components of human life: knowledge and action. He agrees with Kant that true religion is not a matter of knowledge. As he later put it:

> If piety *is* that knowledge, then the amount of such knowledge in a man must be the measure of his piety. . . . Accordingly, on the hypothesis in question, the most perfect master of Christian Dogmatics would always be likewise the most pious Christian.
>
> *Christian Faith,* p. 9

And no one would argue with Schleiermacher's point there! But religion is not really about action either, because acts of great evil as well as great good have been done in the name of religion. If we are to have any criteria for telling which actions really reflect true religion, then the heart of religion must lie elsewhere. Schleiermacher concludes: "Piety cannot be an instinct craving for a mess of metaphysical and ethical crumbs" (*Speeches* 2). Instead, he argues, there is a third component to human life, in addition to knowledge and action. This he calls feeling, and it is here that religion is to be located.

This notion has frequently been misunderstood. By "feeling," Schleiermacher does not mean a vague emotion, as when one feels pleasure. It is not irrational; rather, it is what underlies the possibility of reason. "Feeling" makes possible both emotion and knowledge, as the basis of all human experience. He describes it, in strikingly modern terms, as "self-consciousness" (*Christian Faith*, p. 5). But if we are conscious of our selves, then we are also aware of our own limitations and therefore aware of our dependence on something beyond us. Schleiermacher accordingly declares: "The common element in all howsoever diverse expressions of piety . . . is this: the consciousness of being absolutely dependent, or, which is the same thing, of being in relation with God" (*Christian Faith*, p. 12).

By locating religion in the realm of this self-conscious feeling, Schleiermacher accomplishes several extraordinary things at once. First, he protects religion against the advance of Enlightenment rationalism. We have seen that as science made great strides forward, it increasingly displaced religion as the explanation for the world. But for Schleiermacher, religion and science perform totally different functions to begin with. Science is part of "knowing" and religion is part of "feeling." They are quite distinct. Religion is not about knowledge of the scientific kind. No atheistic arguments can topple God, and no advances in scientific knowledge, even if they succeed in explaining the entire universe perfectly, can remove the need for him. We do not deduce God rationally; we experience him as part of our self-consciousness, and nothing can ever take that away.

This is shown in Schleiermacher's treatment of miracles. Unlike his Enlightenment predecessors, he does not divide events into two groups, those with natural causes and those directly caused by God, inexplicable by science. On the contrary, everything has natural causes, and he is quite happy to accept that science can explain every event. To say that an event is a miracle is not to say that science cannot explain it; it is to say that in it one sees the power of God. So an event may be miraculous to one person but not to another, depending on whether it speaks to their religious sensitivity. Schleiermacher writes:

Miracle is simply the religious name for event. Every event, even the most natural and unusual, becomes a miracle, as soon as the religious view of it can be the dominant. To me all is miracle. . . . The more religious you are, the more miracle would you see everywhere.

Speeches 2

Paradoxically, when we accept the natural causes of every event, it is possible to see God everywhere. Similarly, *revelation* does not refer to a special way of knowing, a special communication of God to human beings. Every insight, every piece of knowledge can be called revelation, if one understands it in the light of one's consciousness of God.

These points should make it clear that Schleiermacher does not close religion off in its own little realm, separate from the rest of the world, as the Moravians did. On the contrary, he puts it firmly at the center of life. The consciousness of God that is "feeling" is not just mystical experiences that favored individuals like Pseudo-Dionysius may enjoy from time to time. On the contrary, it is part of everybody's everyday experience. To be human is to be self-aware, and to be self-aware is to be conscious of one's dependence on God. This feeling accompanies every action and every piece of knowledge, and nothing is possible without it.

Thus Schleiermacher attacks the "cultured despisers" of religion with their own weapons. They wish to divest themselves of superstition and fulfill their potential as human beings. Very well, says Schleiermacher, but to do that they must acknowledge the importance of religion, because feeling—the realm of religion—is central to every human act. By rejecting religion, they reject their own human potential. True humanism must embrace religion, not ignore it.

Some critics have overplayed this element of Schleiermacher's thought. They accuse him of focusing his attention not on God but on the Christian. Instead of analyzing our own feeling of self-consciousness, we ought to be thinking about God. This is the essence of Karl Barth's radical rejection of Schleiermacher. But the charge is unfair, because, for Schleiermacher, to be aware of one's self *is* to be aware of God. That is not because God exists as part of us; on the contrary, it is because our own finitude points away from ourselves. To be aware of one's self, for Schleiermacher, is to be aware of one's self *in relation to God.* And that relation is one of complete dependence, an idea reminiscent of Irenaeus and Aquinas. Schleiermacher's theology is, indeed, centered on God. But the route to God necessarily lies through one's own self-consciousness. To put it another way, if we ask what God is like, we must begin with our experience of God.

Clearly there is more to religion than just consciousness of dependence on God: there are systems of doctrine and ethics. These are what the "cultured despisers" rejected as antiquated or incomprehensible. Schleiermacher agrees that this is often the case. He accepts their importance but only in a secondary way: they are an expression of the all-important feeling of consciousness. "Christian doctrines," he writes, "are accounts of the Christian religious affections set forth in speech" (*Christian Faith*, p. 76). As such, they may well become out of tune with those affections. If the world moves on, then what was in a past age a useful reflection of religious feeling may become an unhelpful fossil, an incomprehensible relic of time long gone; and Schleiermacher felt that this was exactly what had happened to the classical formulations of Christian doctrine, such as the Chalcedonian Creed. It was right to discard them and try to find new ways to express religious feeling, expressions that could be understood by ordinary people without having to learn Greek.

Christianity. All religion, then, centers on this consciousness of dependence on God. But different religions are conscious of it in different ways. In *The Christian Faith* Schleiermacher focuses on the unique way in which Christians experience this universal feeling. He writes: "Christianity is a monotheistic faith . . . and is essentially distinguished from other such faiths by the fact that in it everything is related to the redemption accomplished by Jesus of Nazareth" (*Christian Faith*, p. 52).

This may, at first glance, seem fairly innocuous. But when Schleiermacher says that *everything* is related to the redemption brought by Christ, he really means it. Throughout the rest of his book, every doctrine is considered in the light of this statement. The entire edifice of Christian doctrine is dismantled, and no stone—however sacred—is left unturned. For Schleiermacher, any doctrine is authentically Christian if and only if it can be shown to flow directly from the consciousness of salvation in Christ that is common to every Christian.

Some doctrines reflect this experience only indirectly. An example is the virgin birth: it is perfectly possible to be conscious of Christ's redemption without holding any particular theory about how he was conceived. The doctrine of the Trinity and all doctrines concerning the end times and the return of Christ fall into the same class. Doctrines like these are not essential to Christianity, because they do not directly express the believer's conscious relationship to Christ; and their difficulty or unlikeliness may even put people off Christianity altogether.

The doctrines that remain are taken apart and rebuilt from scratch. Each is related to the consciousness of dependence on God through the salvation of Christ. Thus the traditional attributes of God—his omnipotence, omniscience and so on—are not treated as separate facts describing an external object, God. They are treated instead as complementary ways of describing God's action on the self through Christ. The idea is a little like Gregory Palamas's belief that when we describe God we are talking only of his activity, not his nature, which is unknowable. Schleiermacher, however, places the emphasis firmly on our experience of that activity, rather than on the activity itself. We experience God as that which acts upon us; thus the traditional attributes are nothing other than different ways of describing the range and effect of that perfect activity.

Similarly, the doctrine of humankind's sinfulness reappears as an expression of the self's awareness of its imperfect consciousness of God's redemption through Christ. To talk of sin is simply to talk of the negative, painful side to our consciousness of God: the awareness of our own limitations. Conversely, to talk of redemption is to talk of the positive side, the positive activity of God upon the self, through Christ.

Schleiermacher's theology, then, is avowedly christocentric: everything is related to Christ. No longer do we have a set of distinct doctrines about different subjects; instead, every doctrine reflects the same experience in different ways. In his radical Christocentricism, Schleiermacher was following the example of Luther and Calvin. He was returning to some of the fundamental principles of the early Reformation that had been rather forgotten in the decades of dogmatic bickering that had followed. But even the Reformers never dismantled the whole system of Christian belief to put it back together in relation to this one principle. In doing this, Schleiermacher set the tone for all subsequent Protestant theology—although, as we shall see, later thinkers took it to lengths Schleiermacher could never have imagined.

Another effect of this emphasis on the experience of salvation in Christ is that Schleiermacher neatly sidesteps the debates that were raging around issues of tradition and authority. We do not believe in Christ because of what the Bible tells us. On the contrary, we experience Christ ourselves, and on the basis of that experience we turn to the Bible.

Christ. It should be clear that in Schleiermacher's eyes the doctrine of Christ is the pivot on which the whole of Christian theology revolves. It is no surprise to find that more space is devoted to this doctrine in *The Christian Faith* than to any other. And Schleiermacher's ideas on this subject are among his most influential in modern Christian thinking.

We have seen how in earlier ages theologians like Cyril of Alexandria, faced with the fact of Christ's divinity, grappled to show how he could at the same time be human. Schleiermacher takes the opposite approach—beginning with Christ's humanity, he aims to show in what sense he can be called divine. Yet Schleiermacher begins not with the historical, human figure of Jesus but with the Christian's feeling of salvation through him. This means that Christ's role as Savior is the foundation on which Schleiermacher's Christology is built. In that sense he begins with neither Christ's humanity nor his divinity. Rather, both humanity and divinity are derived from that irreducible fact of the believer's consciousness of salvation.

Christology, then, like all other doctrines, must begin with personal experience. Our doctrine of Christ must be based solely on our consciousness of redemption through him. Schleiermacher therefore argues that we should not distinguish between who Christ is and what he does—the two traditional divisions of Christology.

What, then, is special about Christ, and—Schleiermacher suggests this is the same question—how does he save us? Schleiermacher finds the answer in the essence of religion, the consciousness of God. Christ possessed this to a perfect degree. In a famous definition, Schleiermacher writes:

> The Redeemer, then, is like all men in virtue of the identity of human nature, but distinguished from them all by the constant potency of his God-consciousness, which was a veritable existence of God in him.
> *Christian Faith*, p. 385

Much is squeezed into this short sentence. First, it is clear that Schleiermacher experiences no difficulty in affirming Christ's humanity. The founder of the discipline of hermeneutics is well aware of Christ's historical existence at a particular place and time, as a human being like any other. How, then, can this historical individual be God? The answer lies in Schleiermacher's profound analysis of the religious consciousness that he believed lay at the heart of all life. Since through this experience we know God as the infinite power that acts on us, God's primary attribute is his perfect, unending activity. That, in fact, is what God is. God can therefore be said to exist *where* he is perfectly active. And since our religious consciousness is an awareness of God's activity, God can be said to be present in a person who has that consciousness perfectly. Christ, then, was a human being with a supreme awareness of his relation to God, an awareness that permeated his every thought and action. Schleiermacher writes, "To ascribe to Christ an absolutely powerful God-consciousness, and to attribute to him an existence of God in him, are exactly the same thing" (*Christian Faith*, p. 387).

Paradoxically, then, Christ is divine because he possesses an essential human quality to a perfect degree. So is he a sort of religious Mozart, a merely human genius who might in principle be emulated by others with an equally strong sense of their relation to the divine? Schleiermacher answers that Christ is still unique because of the role his supreme God-consciousness has played in history. That God-consciousness not only defines the person of Christ but also brings about our salis through union with Christt that we share in that consciousness.

...er is not a Pelagian, believing that Christ acts as an example of how

of God at every moment. Christ actually imparts that awareness to his

...rough a mystical communion with all its members.

...rt's music is of finite value, because it is limited in appeal to a certain place and time. It lasts but will not last forever. There may one day be a time when nobody appreciates Shakespeare any more. But what Christ achieved will never cease to be relevant. As Schleiermacher puts it:

> In admitting that what is peculiar to the Redeemer's kind of activity belongs to a general aspect of human nature, we by no means wish to reduce this activity, and the personal dignity by which it is conditioned, to the same measure as that of others. . . . For no one has yet succeeded, in any sphere of science or art, and no one will ever succeed, in establishing himself as head, universally animating and sufficient for the whole human race.
>
> *Christian Faith*, p. 386

Reflections

Schleiermacher blazed a new trail for others to follow. He succeeded in creating a new vision of Christianity, one that completely bypassed the old divisions between reason and revelation, natural and supernatural, science and religion. By basing religion around the self, around the believer's own experience of God, he saved it from the obscure, baroque and arid metaphysical systems of the Age of Reason just as Kant brought those systems crashing to the ground. And what's more, he founded a new tradition of Christian theology: ever since Schleiermacher, the most creative academic theology has been in the hands of German speakers. The German Protestant tradition over the two centuries following him has been almost equal to the Greek tradition in the first four centuries of Christianity.

Schleiermacher was certainly a man of his times. His belief that the essence of religion lies in feeling, not in systems of doctrine, clearly allies him with the Romantic movement. Yet as we have seen, he did not think of feeling as an antirational, sentimental emotion; it is a pervasive, precognitive consciousness of the self existing in relation to God. His theology can justifiably be called existentialist, a prefiguring of what was to come. But he never slipped into the navel-gazing self-absorption of some later existentialists. Schleiermacher firmly believed that all religious experience and the systems of doctrine that are based on it happen at the level of the group rather than the individual. The motivating force of his life, his love of friendship, played an important role in his theology.

Yet there are problems with Schleiermacher's work, and just as his influence lives on today, so too do the difficulties.

Schleiermacher's analysis of the religious experience at the heart of existence is one of the greatest strengths of his thought—but it is also a major weak point. Was he right to think that all human beings are aware of their own self, dependent on God? Schleiermacher thought he was. But readers who are not themselves religious may disagree.

By grounding all doctrine in the believer's direct experience of God, Schleiermacher hoped to avoid the difficulties of traditional metaphysics. Yet in so doing he also lost its strength: the ability to make objective claims about God. If talk of God's power or goodness is really just a description of how we experience him, can we say that God is really, objectively powerful or good? Can we say anything about him at all? Are we not, in the end, just talking about ourselves?

Schleiermacher hoped to strip Christianity of those doctrines that he felt did not communicate the essence of the religion. But can we really say that the Trinity—relegated to an appendix of *The Christian Faith*—is not an important doctrine? Schleiermacher's greatest critic, Karl Barth, made it central to his theology, and it has remained central to Protestant theology ever since. And what of eschatology? Christianity began as an eschatological religion, waiting expectantly for the return of its Lord. Can this element of it really be shrugged aside as not reflecting the believer's experience of Christ?

The most difficult problems, however, concern Schleiermacher's Christology, the centerpiece of his theology. As we have seen, he believed Christ possessed an awareness of his close relation to God that permeated his every thought and action. In light of this, it is unsurprising that Schleiermacher greatly preferred John's Gospel to the other Gospels. In John, Jesus is presented as a serene, perfectly self-assured figure, profoundly and constantly aware of his own relation to God as Son to Father.

However, most New Testament scholars agree that this portrait is largely a theological construct. The Synoptic Gospels, which present a much more human Jesus, capable of tiredness and suffering, are closer to the true, historical Jesus. This is the Jesus who could, at the point of death, cry out in despair that God had abandoned him. But that is unthinkable for Schleiermacher's Christology, which depends on Jesus' unbroken sense of closeness to God, and Schleiermacher argued that Jesus never really felt despair or alienation. Paradoxically, although Schleiermacher begins with Jesus' humanity, he ends up with a picture of Jesus that makes him practically inhuman. In the hands of Albert Schweitzer at the turn of the 20th century, this criticism would prove fatal to the theological tradition that Schleiermacher founded.

This is in fact a problem for any theologian who denies the classical idea of Christ as God come down to earth. The situation is very simple. One can regard Christ's saving power as coming from his *nature* or his *character*. Think back to the Christology of Irenaeus and Athanasius. For them, the very fact that Christ is God become man is what saves us. In theory, it does not really matter what kind of character Christ had or how he felt or behaved; his divine nature is the important thing.

Schleiermacher, however, denies that Christ possessed a special, preexistent divine nature. He sees Christ's saving power as coming from his character—what he was like as a person. He is thus compelled to describe that character in superhuman terms, in a way that goes beyond what the real Jesus was probably like, and in a way that makes him curiously unsympathetic and incomprehensible as a character.

This, in a nutshell, is one of the most fundamental problems of Christology. There are two basic ways we can construct a doctrine of the atonement. First, we can take the classical route of appealing to Christ's divine nature: it is because Christ is divine that he saves us, perhaps by becoming incarnate (as with Irenaeus and Athanasius) or by doing something that only God could do (as with Anselm or Calvin). But the notion of Christ's divinity is unacceptable to many people today, even supposing that it makes sense in the first place. Like Schleiermacher and many of his modern followers, we can appeal instead to Christ's character as a human being supremely conscious of God's presence. But this notion simply seems to be too weak to support a decent account of salvation. Even supposing that John's Gospel does present a complete portrait of the real Jesus, is it really enough to save us? How did Jesus become so perfectly aware of his relationship to God? How do we become mystically united to this historical person? And is sharing in his sense of the divine really what we mean by salvation?

Many people will find Schleiermacher's view of salvation, as well as his doctrine of Christ's person, simply too thin. Some of his later critics certainly did. Yet his achievement in providing this alternative vision remains indisputable. He showed that it is worthwhile to make the attempt to recast Christian ideas in a totally, even shockingly, new way. And he was not alone: as Schleiermacher was rebuilding Christianity from the ground up, another radically original thinker, Søren Kierkegaard, was doing the same thing in a very different way.

Søren Kierkegaard

Søren Kierkegaard was one of the most unusual thinkers of the 19th century. Original and iconoclastic, he remained virtually unknown during his lifetime but became extremely influential in the 20th century.

Life

Kierkegaard was born in Copenhagen in 1813. His father had been a serf, named after the churchyard (*kierkegaard* in Danish) where he had worked, but who had subsequently done extremely well for himself. Nevertheless he had a very gloomy, morbid character; he was convinced that he and his whole family were under some kind of curse, divine retribution for the time when, as a child working in the freezing cold as a shepherd, he had once sworn at God. He impressed on his children the centrality of suffering to life and religion. Søren would later comment,

> As a child I was strictly and earnestly brought up to Christianity, humanly speaking, insanely brought up: even in my earliest childhood I had been overstrained by impressions which were laid upon me by the melancholy old man who was himself oppressed by them—a child, insanely travestied as a melancholy old man.
>
> *The Viewpoint of My Authorship*

Søren inherited much of this outlook from his father and was an unhealthy, unliked boy; at school he was bullied by those stronger than him, and he took his revenge by reducing less quick-witted students to tears with his viciously sarcastic tongue.

At the University of Copenhagen Kierkegaard did much better, at least outwardly: spending money lavishly, dressing well and attending all manner of parties and society events. He also became engaged to a girl named Regine Olsen. Unfortunately, it was all show: underneath, Kierkegaard felt deeply unhappy and unfulfilled and believed that his artistic melancholy prevented him from finding happiness with Regine. Since breaking off an engagement could be a very serious matter at this time, he decided to act as outrageously as possible to his fiancée so that she would be quite justified in breaking it herself. Unfortunately she saw through the act, and eventually he was forced to end the engagement himself and spend some time avoiding her determined efforts to win him back.

This experience, together with the death of his father in 1838, impressed on Kierkegaard the seriousness of his calling, which was to write. He completed his theological training, despite his preference for philosophy, obtained a master's degree in philosophy, and settled down to spend the rest of his days living comfortably on his sizable inheritance, churning out book after book. He became a well-known figure in Copenhagen, easily spotted in his fine clothes and expensive carriage. An obvious intellectual, he spoke ten languages even though the only foreign country he ever visited was Germany. The local press delighted in caricaturing his instantly recognizable figure with its long thin legs, curved back, tall hat and long cane.

Thought

Kierkegaard was fed up with the state of contemporary philosophy and religion. Philosophers like Kant and G. W. F. Hegel spent their time developing systems, trying to objectively describe the world and humanity's place in it. Kierkegaard felt that this was rather a waste of time. What we should be doing instead is focusing on what it is like to be a human being in the world, looking at the choices that confront us in life and how we are to make them. This is partly reflected in the curious style of Kierkegaard's books, which are novelistic, aphoristic, full of poetry and narrative; many of them were published under false names, adding to their generally puzzling, unclear nature.

So Kierkegaard never discusses the existence of God or what God is like in himself. He is too well aware of Kant's revolution to do that. Instead, God features in his works as part of the world of experience that the individual inhabits. God and the world alike are characters in the story that is told and lived by the individual.

Christian faith, then, is not about a set of propositions that are believed; it is about a life that is lived. This is not a regression to the dry ethicalism of Kant, who sought to define objective moral rules that are rationally deduced and universally applied. It is an account of what it is like actually to live in the face of God and the world.

Kierkegaard believes that life is a matter of confronting, and deciding between, radical choices. For example, he describes several types of life one can choose to lead. There is the aesthetic life, the life of sensuality, rather like the way Kierkegaard himself lived while a student. But that kind of life leads only to hollow emptiness, because it cannot satisfy the eternal aspect of human nature. This is why we may choose instead to lead an ethical life, renouncing what brings shallow happiness—just as Kierkegaard did when he broke off his engagement and devoted himself to writing. The ethical life is a self-denying but positive one that seeks to improve the self and the world.

Yet even this must give way to the life of faith, which is what happens when the individual realizes that the self-determination of the ethical life is always subject to the overriding commands of God. Kierkegaard uses the example of Abraham, who was called by God to sacrifice his son—not something normally called for by conventional ethics. Because Abraham had the faith to obey God, his son was spared. Similarly, if we follow the call of faith, we may find that the demands of the ethical life are suspended. Kierkegaard himself realized this one day when he happened to pass his former fiancée on the way out of church and she nodded at him in a friendly way. Kierkegaard was struck by the idea that perhaps marriage was not, after all, incompatible with the life he had chosen: that if he had had true faith in the past, he would have married Regine *and* followed the ethical life. But of course, it was only through many years' experience that he could learn this. The life of ethical self-denial can be overridden by the life of faith, but it cannot be skipped.

So faith, for Kierkegaard, is something paradoxical, embracing the contradictions of life and existence rather than trying to order them logically, which is what Hegel, at that time by far the most famous, influential and unassailable philosopher in the world, sought to do. Kierkegaard also hated the way the church tends to assimilate itself to the world, either politically and socially, like the well-to-do Lutheran bishops, or intellectually, like those who integrated Christianity with Hegelian philosophy.

When Kierkegaard died in 1855, at the age of forty-two, he was virtually unknown outside Denmark. His iconoclastic, highly individual philosophy can be seen as anticipating later "outsiders" like Friedrich Nietzsche and Albert Schweitzer, but it was not until the 20th century that his importance was generally recognized. Today he is acknowledged as the father of existentialism, one of the most important intellectual movements of the 20th century, and he is remembered as one of the outstanding religious thinkers of the 19th.

Geology and Biology

In 1860 a debate was held in the new University Museum at Oxford. The subject was Charles Darwin's theory, published just a few months earlier, on biological evolution through natural selection. Among the speakers were Samuel Wilberforce, the bishop of Oxford—known as "Soapy Sam" on account of his rhetorical ability and ecclesiastical ambition—and Thomas Huxley, a biologist and one of Darwin's greatest admirers.

Wilberforce, it is said, turned to Huxley and, to the laughter of the audience, demanded to know whether the scientist traced his descent from an ape on his grandfather's or his grandmother's side. Huxley muttered to a friend, "The Lord hath delivered him into mine hand," and, standing, replied that he would much rather trace his descent back to a humble ape than to a man who used his intellectual gifts to stifle free debate and meddle in matters he knew nothing about. The meeting dissolved in uproar, and the battle lines between science and religion were drawn.

In fact, the tale is apocryphal: the debate did take place, but no one really knows what either Wilberforce or Huxley said to the other, and in reality it seems that the bishop had the upper hand. It is an anecdote told by scientists who like to believe in the victory of witty, rational men of science over domineering, authoritarian clergy. But it does illustrate the serious and emotional issues that were emerging from the interaction of science and theology at the time.

The earth sciences

The issues had been simmering for half a century before the great debate because of major advances made in geology. Geology developed as a science in its own right only in the late 18th century; before that it had consisted mostly of learned amateurs writing long descriptions of gems and fossils. By 1800, scientists like James Hutton and William Smith were pioneering new understandings of the earth's history and the processes that formed it. They understood that different kinds of rock had been formed by different natural processes and that different layers or strata of rock had been laid down at different times in history. It was becoming clear that the earth must be a lot older than had hitherto been suspected. It was certainly older than the few thousand years suggested by a literal reading of the Old Testament. The most famous biblical chronology was that of Irish archbishop James Ussher, who in 1654, after much scholarly research and calculation, had declared that the world was created on October 21, in 4004 B.C.

The new discoveries of the geologists were a major revolution. The scientists of the Age of Reason, above all Sir Isaac Newton, had described a mechanical universe operating as smoothly and timelessly as an intricate clock created by God and set in motion. But now scientists were learning that the world is not a timeless piece of machinery but something that changes over time: something, in fact, that changes as a result of its own history, being acted on by forces from within. It was no longer necessary to invoke God to explain why the world looked the way it did.

The fossils

The issue was complicated by the presence of fossils in the geological record. These were clearly the remains of creatures that no longer existed. Before the work of the geologists, it had been a simple matter to dismiss fossils as creatures that had been wiped out in the flood of Genesis 6; but if different strata had been formed at different times, then the creatures in them had obviously not all died at the same time. In fact, the different strata were all characterized by different sets of fossils. It looked as though the earth had been inhabited by different kinds of creatures at different periods, each species somehow disappearing and being replaced by others.

Different theories were advanced to explain this. One of the most popular was that of the great biologist Baron Georges Cuvier, who believed that each geological period had ended with a massive catastrophe, wiping out all life, which God then replaced with a new ecosystem. This "catastrophism" was opposed by evolutionists, who believed that the new creatures had somehow developed gradually out of the old ones.

Darwinism

Charles Darwin, when he published his epochal *On the Origin of the Species* in 1859, was certainly not saying anything new in arguing for the theory of evolution. What was new was his powerful and persuasive explanation of *how* the process of evolution works—the theory of "natural selection." He pointed out that creatures are similar to their parents but not identical; there is apparently random minor variation in each generation. And he argued that those individuals that happen to be well suited to their environment will survive, prosper and give birth to new individuals sharing their characteristics, while those less suited will die out. So any new characteristic with which an individual is born is likely to be passed on if it is useful. In this way species evolve and develop in a process that is not random, or determined by God, but follows natural laws.

It is not surprising that some in the church reacted with horror. On the one hand, of course, much of this seemed to contradict the account of creation found in the opening chapters of Genesis. Some scientists had thought that the catastrophic theory was quite compatible with the creation account—each "age" might be equivalent to one of the "days" of the biblical account—but the evolutionary theory was harder to reconcile in this way.

At another level, the theory of evolution contradicted fundamental Christian notions about humanity and sin. Darwin applied his theory not just to the natural world but to humanity itself—the aspect of the controversy that so exercised Wilberforce and Huxley at Oxford. In 1871 he expanded on his ideas in *The Descent of Man*, in which he argued that human beings evolved naturally from lower creatures. So not only does life itself follow natural laws, but the human mind and soul are not some supernatural element breathed into the body by God. They evolved from nothing. The ideas of the original righteousness of Adam, the fall and original sin which had held sway over Western thought since Augustine were directly challenged.

Even more fundamentally, however, Darwin's theories left a shrinking place for God. In the Enlightenment scientists had described a world that functioned according to laws laid down by God: God had set everything up and then left it to its own devices. This was deism. But now it seemed that the world in its present state was not directly created by God. The diversity of life itself could be explained by reference to quite simple natural laws. God still had a place as the original Creator, perhaps, and Darwin believed in him; but he was becoming less and less useful or important as a scientific hypothesis. As in Laplace's legendary comment, there was simply no need for him.

The theories of Darwin—and the wider implications of science, which, to the popular mind, he represented—were thus seen to pose a threat to Christianity even greater than the work of the Tübingen scholars. And the church reacted to his work much as it did to biblical criticism. Some Protestant theologians enthusiastically accepted his ideas and worked on ways to integrate them into their theology. They were, after all, quite compatible with the liberal theology of Albrecht Ritschl and Adolf von Harnack. But other churchmen—especially in Britain and America— took a much less sympathetic view. The modern evangelical movement, including its more extreme fundamentalist manifestations, arose largely in response to both Darwin and Tübingen. And the Roman Catholic Church simply pronounced Darwin wrong, thereby refusing to enter the debate at all.

Today, of course, a broad consensus in science supports the basic truth of Darwin's ideas; although they have been extensively modified over the decades, they remain central to modern biology. Few mainstream theologians would challenge evolution either, and large numbers of Christians are untroubled by the theory. Yet the battles of evolutionary theory versus creationism are still being fought in some places, especially in the English-speaking world, and there are those who still regard the theory of evolution as a fundamental attack on the heart of Christianity.

Evangelicalism

Evangelical is an enormously vague term, sometimes used to refer to any Protestants; in Germany it is synonymous with *Lutheran.* Here it is being used in a narrower sense to mean the largely English-speaking movement that had its roots in the 18th-century revivals of Wesley and Whitefield and in what was known as the Second Great Awakening of the early 19th century. This was a kind of repeat performance of Wesley's revivals and occurred throughout North America between the 1790s and 1840s. A great feeling swept through the Protestant churches there of the importance of individual faith, personal devotion, the conversion of the heart—all the things Wesley had believed in so firmly. The American Methodist and Baptist churches grew at an enormous pace.

Yet this new surge of Pietism was facing forces quite different from those Wesley knew, and ones it was ill equipped to deal with. There was no place in Pietism for critical biblical scholarship and historical criticism—as the young Schleiermacher had learned with the Moravians. Evangelicalism developed as a radical rejection of these sciences and in conscious opposition to liberal theology in all its forms. The evangelicals were extremely doctrinaire, stressing the essential nature of certain doctrines inherited from the toned-down version of Calvinism promulgated by Wesley. The sternest of the evangelicals, however, toned it up again.

The Princeton school

The most prominent of these were a group of scholars at Princeton Seminary: Charles Hodge, his son A. A. Hodge and, most of all, Benjamin Warfield. These thinkers emphasized above all else the infallibility of the Bible. This in itself may seem no different from what Christians in all ages had believed—but that was before the rise of critical scholarship. Wyclif and Luther had innovated by stressing the Bible's status as an independent authority from the church, a notion that had been unthinkable before; Warfield and his colleagues now described the Bible as an authority independent from science, both natural and textual. The methods and findings of the Tübingen scholars were to be simply ruled out of court. And the same was true of the natural sciences where these conflicted with biblical teaching. In his youth Warfield had been very interested in natural history and read and thoroughly approved of Darwin's books; but he repudiated all that when he became a theologian.

It is important to recognize that the position of Warfield and his colleagues on the Bible differed from that of, say, Augustine or Aquinas, primarily in its context rather than its substance. It was a conscious rejection of all alternative sources of authority, from the pope to Darwin.

The Fundamentals

The defining moment in evangelicalism came between 1910 and 1915, when a series of pamphlets called *The Fundamentals* was published. These booklets, some of which were written by Warfield himself, laid down a set of particular doctrines as "fundamental" to the Christian faith. Those who denied them, it seemed, were not really true Christians at all. The fundamentals included the divine inspiration and total infallibility of the Bible, the deity of Christ and his virgin birth, his substitutionary death in our place as punishment for our sins, and his bodily resurrection afterward. They therefore represent a sort of postscientific Calvinism. The name *fundamentalism*, as an unkind word for the more extreme versions of evangelicalism, comes from the title of these pamphlets; *fundamentalist* is often applied to those who not only hold these doctrines but who refuse to associate with those who do not.

Evangelicalism today

Evangelicalism prospered, however, and has proved to be an enormously powerful force within Christianity, transcending its origins as a reactionary, negative movement. It has been able to draw on the profound spiritual resources of Methodism and other nonconformist traditions and of the Protestant Reformers, sometimes recognizing little difference between their doctrines and its own. It is characterized above all by a reverence for Scripture and devotion to the divine person of Christ, understood in terms of a personal relationship between Christ and the individual believer. This is often expressed by an emphasis on the individual conversion experience, when the believer realizes in faith that Christ has been punished for her sin and in faith allows him into her heart and life with dramatic personal consequences. The influence of Calvin and Pietism is very strong.

Today evangelicalism is one of the most successful forms of Christianity in the world. George Gallup Jr. regularly conducts polls that show that between a third and a half of all American adults regard themselves as evangelical Christians. While such polls must always be viewed with some skepticism—especially when notoriously vague terms like *evangelical* or *born again* are used—evangelicalism is certainly the most widespread version of Protestantism. Indeed, to many outside the church, at least in the Western world, the word *Christian* means someone like that amiable caricature of evangelicals, Ned Flanders from *The Simpsons*. But evangelicalism is in fact a very broad and varied movement, in both attitude and doctrine. Some groups have retained, to varying degrees, the reluctance to deal with other Christian traditions that characterized early evangelicalism and that it inherited from Puritanism. The most extreme of these are often called fundamentalists, and indeed groups exist that consider *fundamentalist* an honorable term and are happy to apply it to themselves, rejecting all contact with more liberal Protestants, let alone Catholics.

These, however, are in the minority among evangelicals; far more widespread are the more moderate "conservative evangelicals." The "conservative" part of their name refers to doctrine rather than politics (American evangelicalism is often associated with Republican politics, but in Britain and Australia it is frequently quite left of center in political terms). These groups place considerable emphasis on orthodox, classical doctrine; this is closely connected to their reverence for the Bible and for the traditional Protestant ways of interpreting it, and they are opposed to the liberal tendency to reinterpret or discard these traditions. Conservative evangelicalism probably represents the mainstream of evangelicalism, and it possesses vast spiritual resources of every kind, especially a very strong tradition of biblical devotion. The movement is equally strong on evangelism, the task of presenting Christianity to non-Christians. One of the most famous representatives of this kind of evangelicalism is the American evangelist Billy Graham, who represented the American religious mainstream to such an extent as to act publicly as a mentor to several U.S. presidents. Apart from him, the best-known authors from the conservative evangelical tradition in the 20th century include, in America, J. I. Packer, and in Britain, John Stott and F. F. Bruce. Bruce was an important biblical scholar, and his work, and that of others like him, shows that mainstream evangelicalism can engage with other Christian traditions and with secular scholarship while remaining true to its fundamental doctrines and convictions. Clearly, conservative need not mean reactionary.

The strength and appeal of this form of evangelicalism can be seen in the notable popularity of the Alpha Course, a ten-week introduction to evangelical Christianity which was developed in the early 1990s by Nicky Gumbel, a minister at Holy Trinity Brompton, a major evangelical church in London. Today the Alpha Course is used throughout the world as an evangelism tool by members of most Protestant denominations and a growing number of Roman Catholic churches. It is an extraordinary demonstration of the great appeal and power of evangelical Christianity and of its ability to transcend traditional denominational and doctrinal boundaries. However, some nonevangelical churches, while impressed by the success of the Alpha Course, dislike its doctrinal rigidity and have tried to put together alternative versions that reflect different Christian traditions.

This dissatisfaction with the sometimes rather rigid evangelical orthodoxy is also reflected by some elements within evangelicalism itself. They make up what we might consider to be the left wing of evangelicalism—those who are keen to maintain the strengths and heritage of traditional evangelicalism while moving beyond it and engaging with liberalism. For them, the most valuable insight of evangelicalism is its emphasis on faith and a relationship with a personal Savior. Christianity, in their view, includes uncertainty as well as certainty, a notion reminiscent of Kierkegaard. Writers and ministers in this group—which is predominantly British—represent some of the very latest developments with evangelicalism, and their future is uncertain, as is their exact place on the theological spectrum. Many conservative evangelicals would not regard them as evangelicals at all, because they are not so committed to what conservatives regard as essential evangelical doctrines. Dissatisfied with this absolutist attitude, some liberal evangelicals prefer to think of themselves as "postevangelicals," from the title of the 1995 book by one of their leading spokesmen, Dave Tomlinson. The movement is striking because it represents a growing current of criticism—some of it quite vehement—against the dominant evangelical tradition from within its own ranks. But it has so far been essentially a pastoral movement rather than a theological one, and it remains to be seen how much of a positive and enduring contribution it will make to theological debate.

If evangelicalism is the quintessential theology of the English-speaking world today, then its opposite number, liberalism, has been the centerpiece of German theology. As modern evangelicalism was taking shape in the late 19th century, so too was modern liberalism, under the guidance of Ritschl.

Albrecht Ritschl

Albrecht Ritschl is a central figure of 19th-century thought. He developed the insights of Kant and Schleiermacher and forged the mighty edifice of 19th-century liberalism—much of which, despite the demolition job of Schweitzer, Barth and Niebuhr, is still standing.

Life

Born in Berlin in 1822, Albrecht Ritschl was the son of a bishop of the Prussian Reformed Union Church. He seems to have lived a largely blameless and incident-free life, studying at Tübingen until 1864, when he became professor of theology at Göttingen; he remained there until his death in 1889. It was there that he made his name as the premier theologian of the age, becoming known as *the* Göttingen Theologian. His disciples included most of the great names of the second generation of liberal theology, such as Adolf von Harnack and Ernst Troeltsch; his critics represented all shades of Christian opinion.

Thought

Ritschl's theology owes much to that of Schleiermacher. Like him, Ritschl believes that God must be known through humanity; and, like him, Ritschl thinks that God is known above all through the human community of the church.

Schleiermacher made the experience of redemption through Christ the linchpin of his thought. Ritschl takes a similar line, taking justification as the determining feature of all Christian doctrine. He focuses not so much on the nature of religion, as Schleiermacher did, as on its purpose. Human beings, having failed to live up to God's purpose for them, need to be reconciled to God. The purpose of religion is to make this possible.

Schleiermacher had thought of redemption as occurring through a personal experience of Christ, who passes his God-consciousness to the believer. Ritschl, however, rejects the possibility of any kind of mysticism. There is no place in his thought for the personal feeling that was distinctive of Schleiermacher. Ritschl focuses on the concrete facts of history. For him, reconciliation occurs through the historical community of the church. When Jesus talked about the "kingdom of God," Ritschl suggests, he meant a human community, existing historically in this world in a spirit of love and morality. By participating in this community, we can live up to God's standards.

Ritschl, then, thinks of Christianity as essentially a matter of living a good life. In this respect, he represents something of a regression back past Schleiermacher, who strenuously opposed this idea, to Kant. He agrees with Schleiermacher, however, that the old doctrinal formulations of the Trinity and Christ's natures are outdated and no use to modern believers. He argues that religious statements are statements not of fact but of value. So to say that Christ is divine, for example, is not to make a factual claim; it is to say that he has divine value for us, because God is known through him.

Influence

Ritschl's version of Christianity was enormously influential and still is today. The idea of Christianity as essentially living a good life, of Jesus as a great moral teacher, is still very popular. It is a vision of Christianity with all the difficult bits taken out—strange metaphysics like the Trinity or even stranger 1st-century Jewish apocalyptic visions of the end of the world. This is its strength; it is also, of course, its weakness. Ritschl and his followers are open to the charge of having missed all the distinctive parts of Christianity and turned it into a carbon copy of contemporary moral philosophy such as that of Jeremy Bentham or John Stuart Mill. Ritschl's Jesus, moreover, is a rather insipid, watered-down version of the real thing. In the end, criticisms such as these would prove fatal to liberal theology. A more lasting way of dealing with the issues of the modern world was being worked out by a very different theologian, Cardinal Newman.

John Henry Newman

John Henry Newman was a colossus of 19th-century Christianity. His career took him from an evangelical conviction that the pope is the antichrist to becoming a Roman Catholic cardinal. The issues he grappled with and his answers to them remain both enduring and inspiring; and his official Roman status as "Venerable," bestowed in 1991, may yet be upgraded to full sainthood.

Life

John Henry Newman was born in London in 1801, the son of a banker. His mother's family were French Huguenots, strict Calvinists whose rigorous evangelical faith was deeply imprinted onto the young Newman. At the age of 15 he underwent something of an evangelical conversion and vowed to dedicate his life to celibacy.

In 1826 Newman won a fellowship at Oriel College, Oxford, and there he came into contact with what would later be called the Oxford Movement. His Calvinism

THE OXFORD MOVEMENT

In July 1833, John Keble preached a sermon to Oxford University on the subject of "national apostasy." He was protesting against proposed legislation to reduce the number of Anglican bishops, but the issues he raised went much deeper. Was the Church of England simply a state department, to be ruled by the whim of members of Parliament? Or was it something more?

Oxford University was just beginning to awaken from the long, complacent drowsiness of the 18th century, when nobody had ever bothered to take exams; and for a brief period Oriel College was spearheading academic and intellectual reform. Its leading light was Keble. There is a story that while bursar of Oriel, Keble once made an error in the books that nearly cost the college almost 2,000 pounds; subsequent examination revealed that he had accidentally added the date to a list of expenses. But what he lacked in financial acumen he more than made up for in religious zeal; like many devout Englishmen of the time he was in the habit of whipping himself when he felt the promptings of sin, and he was deeply concerned for the spiritual state of the church. His sermon of 1833 prompted several of his colleagues to do something about it. They included John Henry Newman, Richard Froude and Edward Pusey, also fellows at Oriel, and William Palmer of Worcester College. Together these earnest young men launched what would become known as the Oxford Movement, which would transform the Church of England.

They felt that the church could be renewed only by returning to its roots, as exemplified in the theology and practices of the church fathers. This meant finding a middle way—the via media central to Newman's thought—between the stripped-down Christianity of Protestantism and the elaborate ritualism of Catholicism. In this they were following the lead of Anglicans of previous centuries such as Thomas Cranmer and Richard Hooker. Froude in particular was especially hostile to the Protestant Reformers and pioneered the idea that Catholicism could be a broader concept than Roman Catholicism. The Church of England could be thought of as a Catholic church, and indeed if it remained true to early Christianity then it would be more Catholic in this sense than the church presided over by the pope.

The reformers published their ideas in a wide variety of forms, chiefly the famous Tracts for the Times, which gave their movement the name Tractarianism. With his brilliant mind and devout piety, Newman was their obvious leader, but he became increasingly doubtful about the possibility of steering a course between Catholicism and Protestantism. After the furor caused by Tract 90, in which he argued that there was nothing in the Thirty-nine Articles—the official doctrine of the Church of England—contrary to the Council of Trent, Newman largely retired from public life. His conversion to Roman Catholicism in 1845, followed by that of thousands of his admirers, was a severe blow to the Church of England and to the Oxford Movement in particular.

Edward Pusey offered a more stable approach. He was the sort of person for whom the adjective staunch was invented: staunchly Anglican and staunchly conservative in theology, he was one of the very few Englishmen who had taken the trouble to go to Germany and see what was happening at Tübingen and other centers of biblical scholarship. What he saw there shocked him, not least because he realized how totally unprepared for it the Church of England was. But he was far too staunch to follow Newman to Rome. His answer was to encourage a new emphasis on liturgy and mystery, a sacramental theology that emphasized the rites of baptism and Communion and encouraged personal and corporate holiness.

The Oxford Movement was enormously influential. Throughout England, priests began venerating the bread and wine, wearing vestments and even using lighted candles on church altars—all perfectly standard practices today, but greeted with widespread horror and outrage in the 1840s and 1850s. Priests found themselves prosecuted for teaching the Real Presence of Christ in the Eucharist, and their churches were wrecked by rampaging mobs desperate to eradicate all traces of "popery" and "romishness." But the movement was too strong to be set back by such minor matters. By the time Pusey died in 1882, the Church of England had been transformed. Ritual, liturgy, mystery, devotion and beauty remain central to its thought and practice today.

began slowly to erode. His association with the other members of the movement and in particular a trip to Italy in 1832 impressed upon him the need for the Church of England to regain some of the dignity and glory of Catholicism.

In 1828 Newman was appointed vicar of the university church. Throughout the 1830s his reputation grew as a charismatic and inspiring speaker, the natural leader of the reform movement that was growing in Oxford. He might have been thought of as England's answer to Schleiermacher, had any Anglicans heard of the German theologian. Newman wrote many *Tracts for the Times*, including the first in 1833, and the last, Tract 90, in 1841. This tract caused a huge stir, because in it Newman interpreted the Thirty-nine Articles, the official doctrinal basis of the Church of England, in a Catholic way—despite their highly Calvinist nature.

Newman's ideal was the *via media*, the middle way. He believed that the Catholic Church had betrayed the Christian faith by adding to it over the centuries, but at the same time the Protestant churches had stripped too much away. The Church of England should be a halfway house between the two extremes, avoiding both excesses and remaining true to the historical roots of Christianity itself.

With this in mind, Newman pioneered academic study of the church fathers, hoping to glean inspiration from them. But he was shocked by what he discovered. It began to seem that the notion of the middle way had been tried before—and had failed. As he studied the Arian controversy and the christological heresies that had preceded the Council of Chalcedon, he was struck by the similarities of what he was reading to modern church history. It seemed to him that the heretics of the Patristic age were no different from the Protestants of the Reformation:

> The principles and proceedings of the Church now were those of the Church then; the principles and proceedings of heretics then were those of Protestants now. . . . The shadow of the fifth century was on the sixteenth. It was like a spirit rising from the troubled waters of the old world with the shape and lineaments of the new.
>
> *Apologia pro vita sua* 3

If the Arians were mistaken to split off from the church, then were the Reformers not just as mistaken? Was not the middle way simply a barren attempt at compromise, an equally culpable abandonment of the one true church? Ironically, Newman's determination to provide the Church of England with the means to renew itself had driven him to the conviction that the Church of England, like all schismatic sects, was a lost cause.

In 1842, following the furor over Tract 90, Newman retired from public life to a retreat at Littlemore, where he and some followers lived a quasi-monastic existence. In 1845 the inevitable happened and Newman was received into the Roman Catholic Church. The news rocked the country: the Church of England's rising star had abandoned the established church. There was at this time no Roman Catholic Church structure in England, and the "Romish" Church still suffered from widespread prejudice and distrust dating back to the time of Queen Mary.

Newman was ordained as a Catholic priest and played an important role in the reestablishment of the Catholic Church in England in 1850. The public greeted this event with great hostility, and Newman wrote and spoke vigorously in support of his new church.

However, he was not by nature a public person. Newman's lifelong dedication to celibacy was just one aspect of his ascetic, monklike personality, which was reflected physically in his person: despite his long life, he was never very well. He was so cadaverously thin that he sometimes had difficulty sleeping because he was too bony to get comfortable. Newman was simply not very interested in material things; he regarded the physical world as a fairly insubstantial veil over the spiritual world, and God was far more real to him than any of the people he saw around him. This was a very Platonic outlook on life, enhanced but not caused by his immersion in the works of the church fathers. He was essentially a mystic whose religion was based on an ongoing encounter with an infinitely engaging Personality. It is quite revealing that Newman's favorite church father was Gregory of Nazianzus; he shared with Gregory a melancholy character, intrinsically given to solitude and poetry, but still with a hankering after public life and influence. It was in this spirit that he was instrumental in setting up Catholic oratories in London and Birmingham, and in 1851 he was pleased to be offered the post of rector of a new Catholic university in Dublin, which would take him further out of the limelight.

Newman remained a prominent figure in the academic world, and in 1864 he returned to public consciousness after he was attacked by Charles Kingsley, an Anglican priest and author, over what Kingsley believed to be Newman's claim that lying was acceptable for Catholic priests. The rather childish series of letters between the two resulted in Newman's *Apologia pro vita sua* (Apology for His Life), a spiritual autobiography rather like Augustine's *Confessions,* although much less morbid.

Newman also maintained the critical, moderating stance he had demonstrated as an Anglican. When the First Vatican Council proposed to lay down as a dogma of faith the infallibility of the pope, Newman opposed it—not because he disagreed with the doctrine but because he thought it right to wait and reflect on it before decreeing it positively as an article of faith.

Nevertheless, in 1879, despite the fact that he was not a bishop, Newman was made a cardinal. This swift promotion, unprecedented in modern times, met with the enthusiastic approval of the British public. It was a vindication of his status as the leading religious thinker in the English-speaking world, a status he retained unchallenged until his death in 1890.

Thought

It was while he was at Littlemore, shortly before his conversion to Roman Catholicism, that Newman wrote his most important theological work, *The Development of Christian Doctrine*. He wrote it in an attempt to deal with his own earlier objection to Roman Catholicism—the undeniable fact that a great deal of Catholic doctrine was found neither in the Bible nor in the church fathers. We have seen in this book

THE FIRST VATICAN COUNCIL

To Pope Pius IX it seemed that everything about the modern world was campaigning against the Roman Catholic Church. The rationalism and faith in unaided human progress that still remained from the Enlightenment; political and theological liberalism; biblical scholarship, the rapid rise of modern science—all seemed to be threatening the faith of the church. In 1864 he published the Syllabus of Errors, *a long list of "modern" beliefs, all of which he roundly condemned. The general tone of the document was summed up in the final and most damnable "error" of all, number 80: "The Roman pontiff can, and ought to, reconcile himself and come to terms with progress, liberalism and modern civilization."*

The pope was determined to ensure that the condemnation was ratified by the whole church, and in 1869 the First Vatican Council was called to carry this out. Over eight hundred Catholic leaders from all around the world attended. Although it was of course dominated by Europeans, this was the first Catholic Church council to involve non-Europeans. Even Orthodox leaders were invited, but they did not come—hardly surprising given what the main decree of the council would be.

The council vigorously upheld the teachings of the Council of Trent and affirmed the pope's condemnation of the Syllabus of Errors. *It upheld his teaching in that document that reason is decidedly inferior to revelation and that revelation is to be found solely through the Roman Catholic Church.*

how Christian doctrine has developed throughout history; and Newman was well aware of this fact and the problem it represents. Why, for example, should we believe the doctrine of the Trinity if it did not really exist as we know it until Augustine? Why should we believe in the divinity and humanity of Christ if that was not settled until Chalcedon? And many doctrines associated with Roman Catholicism in particular, such as transubstantiation or the immaculate conception of the Virgin Mary, were not worked out until much later than that. It hardly seems reasonable that we should have to believe something that was first stated by some 13th-century theologian; surely Christianity is supposed to be about Christ and the teachings of the New Testament.

Newman suggested that doctrine was not handed down in one divine act, like the giving of the law to Moses, remaining unchangeable forever; but neither was it

There was no hint of ecumenicalism here!

But the most important decision of the council concerned the pope himself. It declared that the pope is the supreme leader of the church and that this fact can never be reversed or altered. And it decreed:

> *When the Roman pontiff speaks ex cathedra, that is, when, in the exercise of his office as shepherd and teacher of all Christians, in virtue of his supreme apostolic authority, he defines a doctrine concerning faith or morals to be held by the whole church, he possesses, by the divine assistance promised to him in blessed Peter, that infallibility which the divine Redeemer willed his church to enjoy in defining doctrine concerning faith or morals.*

The notion of papal infallibility had for a long time been largely assumed; now for the first time it was not only explicit but made an article of faith. Many Catholics refused to accept it and formed the sect known as the Old Catholics, so called because they clung to the pre-Vatican I faith. They recognized that the council represented an unthinking conservatism, a complete rejection of modernism and a trenchant reactionism that threatened to keep the church stuck in the Middle Ages, increasingly irrelevant to the modern world. It would be nearly a century before the Catholic Church would finally deal with these problems in a constructive and creative way, at the Second Vatican Council.

simply human reflection on personal experience, liable to change according to circumstance, as Schleiermacher claimed. Instead he proposed that doctrine develops and evolves, just as a seed grows into a tree.

Newman was in his own way grappling with the issue already identified as central to post-Enlightenment theology: the relation of doctrine to history. Newman realized that the Protestant faith in "Scripture alone" was essentially a rejection of the idea that history is of any importance: everything Christians believe is supposedly derived from a timeless revelation, and all historical development since then is irrelevant and misguided. As a major historian of Christian thought, Newman could hardly accept that. He realized that any idea is a complex thing that appears different to different people and naturally changes as it is publicly discussed and assimilated. But provided that its evolution remains true to the original idea, it is a legitimate development rather than a corruption. The doctrines introduced by the Catholic Church, rejected by Protestants, were therefore not arbitrary human innovations but natural developments of the doctrines that had always been explicitly upheld.

When he realized this, Newman abandoned work on the book. There was no need to write anything further.

Newman's pioneering work on the development of doctrine was enormously significant, because it was one of the first real attempts to describe the nature of doctrine rather than its content—a task that has since been central to theology. But Newman was not really a theologian, someone who actually does the developing of doctrines, like most of the people we have considered in this book. He was more like Wesley—a very prominent religious figure who lived rather than taught theology. Newman's importance lies in the fact that he showed the possibility of a moderate path through the various wild religious extremes of the 19th century: German intellectual liberalism, Protestant popular fundamentalism, Catholic reactionism. First as an Anglican and then as a Catholic, Newman pioneered a moderate, sensitive traditionalism that combined intelligence and scholarship with penetrating spirituality. In this respect his influence was really much greater in the 20th century than the 19th: his ideas have continued to inspire moderate Anglicanism, and he has been cited as one of the main inspirations behind the epochal Second Vatican Council of the 1960s.

Albert Schweitzer

Many theologians have written about love for humanity and devotion to others. Schweitzer, perhaps more than any of them, actually lived that life. He has found a place in the popular mind as a supreme example of a life dedicated to the service of others. But his altruistic life contrasts sharply with his nihilistic theology, a theology that recognized the bankruptcy of the 19th-century liberal project and cleared the way for the new directions of the 20th century.

Life

Albert Schweitzer was born in 1875 in Kaysersburg, Alsace, at that time part of Germany. Yet another son of a Lutheran pastor, he studied philosophy and theology at Strasbourg. Here, at the age of 19, he made the decision that would determine the plan of his life. As he lay in bed one morning, his thoughts turned to his own good fortune compared with so many others in the world:

> While outside the birds sang I reflected on this thought and before I had gotten up I came to the conviction that until I was 30 I could consider myself justified in devoting myself to scholarship and the arts, but after that I would devote myself directly to serving humanity.
> *Out of My Life and Thought* 9

Schweitzer never deviated from this plan. First he set about making a name for himself in "scholarship and the arts." He gained a doctorate in philosophy in 1899, and he began an intense career of writing and preaching. His workload was so great that he would work all through the night, drinking black coffee with his feet in a bowl of cold water to keep himself awake. His first love, however, was music. A child prodigy at the organ, he continued to perform throughout his life. One of his first books, published in 1905, was about Bach; he and others in Strasbourg devoted much energy to finding new ways of playing Bach's music that were at once authentic and challenging. It is striking how many theologians have also shown a talent for music or the composition of hymns, from Gregory the Great to Abelard and Aquinas. Together with Hildegard of Bingen, Schweitzer is one of the few figures in this book whose work can be found in the record shop as well as the bookshop.

At the same time, however, Schweitzer was thinking about how he would devote himself to humanity once he had finished with scholarship. In 1904 he learned of an urgent need for physicians in the French African territories, and the next year he enrolled in medical school, abandoning his brilliant career as a writer, preacher and musician. Friends and family, as well as the theological and medical faculties, were horrified, but Schweitzer would not be dissuaded from his new desire to work with his hands instead of with words. After eight years of training, he was stunned to be turned down by the missionary society because of his theological views. Eventually he was allowed to go, provided that he worked only as a doctor and didn't do any preaching.

Accordingly, in 1913 Schweitzer left for French Equatorial Africa to found a hospital on the Ogouwe River. His work was interrupted by World War I; as a German in French territory he was imprisoned in France and was unable to return to Africa until 1924. There he continued to write on theology and ethics. His hospital became famous, as did the principle of "reverence for life" upon which it was founded. Schweitzer himself, with his unruly shock of white hair and enormous mustache, became a 20th-century icon of altruism and Christian charity until his death in 1965. One of the greatest honors of his life was the award of the Nobel Peace Prize of 1952.

Thought

Schweitzer was an extraordinary man, and the most extraordinary thing about him was that he was so prominent in so many different fields. Musicians know him as an important organist and Bach theorist; theologians know him as a major biblical scholar; and the world knows him as probably the 20th century's most famous philanthropist and doctor. But there is one element that links his interests: authenticity. In Strasbourg he had sought to find new ways of interpreting Bach's music that could be both authentic and contemporary, and it was at this time that he became interested in tackling Christianity in a similar way.

Schweitzer read the New Testament much as Gotthold Lessing had done, as a collection of historical sources of varying trustworthiness, and was astonished at what he found. He published his findings in *The Quest of the Historical Jesus* in 1906, a survey of "lives of Jesus" from Hermann Reimarus onward. Schleiermacher, Ritschl and the rest had believed that Jesus was an "amiable carpenter" who, serene and enlightened, had preached a warm message of tolerance and rational ethics. Their Jesus had given his life to found the kingdom of God, an ethical community of believers on earth. But that was not what Schweitzer saw when he read the Gospels. He wrote:

> The Jesus of Nazareth who came forward publicly as the Messiah, who preached the ethic of the Kingdom of God, who founded the Kingdom of Heaven upon earth, and died to give His work its final consecration, never had any existence. He is a figure designed by rationalism, endowed with life by liberalism, and clothed by modern theology in an historical garb.
> *Quest*, p. 396

On the contrary, Schweitzer found, the real Jesus was an eschatological prophet. Jesus wasn't interested in founding a rational, enlightened society here on earth. His work and preaching revolved instead around the coming kingdom, when he believed that God would intervene dramatically in human history and bring all earthly affairs to an end. Jesus' death was an attempt to hasten this event, and its failure prompted his last utterance, a cry of despair from the cross.

Schweitzer's central point was not so much that Jesus was mistaken, although he did believe this. Rather, it was that Jesus is essentially incomprehensible to the modern mind: "The historical Jesus will be to our time a stranger and an enigma" (*Quest*, p. 397). How can people today even understand, let alone sympathize with, a Jewish apocalyptic prophet who died two millennia ago? Jesus preached the coming kingdom of God. Can that phrase mean anything to people today? Can they really take it seriously?

Ritschl and other liberals had completely failed to understand Jesus. In fact, they had re-created him in their own image as a sort of early liberal utilitarian. Schweitzer commented, "There is no historical task which so reveals a man's true self as the writing of a life of Jesus" (*Quest*, p. 4). His contemporary George Tyrrell famously remarked that Jesus' modern biographers had "looked into the deep well of history, and saw there only the reflection of their own faces."

With *The Quest of the Historical Jesus* Schweitzer pulled the rug out from under the feet of liberalism. The serene Jesus of Schleiermacher and Ritschl was gone, and with him their worldly, community-based religion. Unfortunately, Schweitzer had little to put in its place. Like Kant, he believed that Christianity was essentially a system of ethics. He argued that it was still possible to follow the "spirit of Jesus," although what he meant by this was far from clear. It is hardly surprising that he concluded, "Those who are fond of talking about negative theology can find their account here. There is nothing more negative than the result of the critical study of Jesus" (*Quest*, p. 396).

Reflections

Today Schweitzer's reputation has come under fire. It is hard, now, to sympathize with the paternalistic authoritarianism with which he ran his hospital. Schweitzer was very much a man of his generation, unable to appreciate that Africans could have a worthwhile culture or leadership ability of their own. And he was well aware that his Christian vision was inherently contradictory: as the follower of an incomprehensible, world-rejecting Christ, Schweitzer tried to embrace the world and humanity. His ethics, centered on the ultimately futile attempt to overcome the inherent selfishness and competitiveness of the world, share a sense of bleak helplessness with Friedrich Nietzsche. Indeed his portrait of Jesus as a tragic hero, crushed by his own attempt to bring history to a crisis, is remarkably Nietzschean. Jesus, wrote Schweitzer, lays hold of the wheel of the world to set it moving on that last revolution which is to bring all ordinary history to a close. It refuses to turn, and He throws Himself upon it. Then it does turn; and crushes Him. Instead of bringing in the eschatological conditions, He has destroyed them. The wheel rolls onward, and the mangled body of the one immeasurably great Man, who was strong enough to think of Himself as the spiritual ruler of mankind and to bend history to His purpose, is hanging upon it still.

Quest, p. 396

There is much in Schweitzer's writing that, like this passage, is poetic and noble; but its beauty is rugged, austere and essentially hopeless. He destroyed the foundations of 19th-century liberalism but could present no coherent alternative. That task was left to his younger contemporary Karl Barth.

6

THE 20TH CENTURY

Someone watching the theological scene at the close of the 19th century could never have guessed what was going to come next. Science and biblical criticism seemed to have wiped out traditional, metaphysical Christianity; the only options left were unthinking fundamentalism and a weak, watery liberalism. But the 20th century saw an extraordinary resurgence of interest in classical theology of the kind pioneered by the church fathers and perfected by the medieval theologians. The unique horrors of the 20th century, and the collapse of society's faith in reason and progress that had marked the earlier modern period meant that the rational theology of the preceding two centuries no longer seemed relevant. At the same time, the waning of Christianity in Europe and its rapid growth in other parts of the world means that theology took on a far more international, and varied, nature.

The task of theology today, as in every age, is to restate the Christian message in terms that contemporary people can understand. The work of 20th-century theologians, who wrote in a time of uncertainty, when to some the world seemed to have lost faith in both reason and religion, offers an unparalleled resource for that ongoing task.

Karl Barth

In the closing years of the 19th century, a small boy was climbing the stairs of a church tower in Pratteln, on the outskirts of Basel, Switzerland. He reached for the handrail to steady himself, but in the darkness he accidentally pulled the bellrope and was horrified to hear the huge bell above him ring out across the whole town.

The boy was Karl Barth, and he would later liken his effect on modern theology to his experience in the Pratteln bell tower. Searching for a support to his Christian faith, he instead unleashed a deafening alarm that shattered the calm of the Christian world.

Life

There was little about Barth's early life to hint at the great place he would occupy in the history of Christian thought. He seemed much like any other young German-speaking theologian. He even looked utterly nondescript: his thin-faced, forgettable appearance seems to blend into the background of every photograph. Born in Basel in 1886, he studied in Germany during the final flowering of liberal theology. His father, a conservative theologian, insisted that his son study Reformed theology at Bern, but Karl also attended schools in Berlin, Tübingen and Marburg. There, like many others, he became a disciple of men like Adolf von Harnack and Wilhelm Herrmann, the greatest names in liberalism of the time.

After completing his studies, Barth was ordained as a Reformed minister, and in 1912 he took up his first parish of Safenwil, a small farming town in Switzerland. In this unlikely environment the earnest young liberal found the theological edifice he had been taught starting to crumble.

Problems began when Barth started systematically studying the Bible in order to prepare his sermons. In its pages he did not find the doctrines of liberal theology with its this-worldly message of progress and reason. On the contrary, he found a voice from beyond the world—a mysterious God who could not be searched out by human reason or religion. The God of the Bible, by contrast, *spoke out*, actively, unpredictably. The Bible, as Barth was now reading it, was an exciting, fast-moving account of God: who he is and what he does, how he acts in the world and how he turns around the lives of human beings. Barth could find in the Bible none of the navel-gazing obsession with self and society that he had been taught by liberal theologians.

Matters came to a head in 1914. A few days after World War I broke out, an open letter was published in Germany supporting the country's involvement in the hostilities. It was signed by ninety-three leading intellectuals—including the liberal theologians under whom Barth had studied. As the Kaiser stood on his balcony delivering speeches written by Harnack, Barth washed his hands of liberal theology and the moral bankruptcy he now saw associated with it.

It was time to find a new, biblical approach. The world had to be reawakened to the uncompromising God of the Bible, and Barth set out what he had found in a *Commentary on Romans*, published in 1919 to very moderate success. Dissatisfied with his work, Barth rewrote it extensively for the second edition. Published in 1922, the new version fell, as Barth put it, like a bomb in the playground of the theologians—or like a bell accidentally rung from a high steeple.

In page upon page of extraordinary rhetoric, Barth proclaimed the Godness of God:

God, the pure and absolute boundary and beginning of all that we are and have and do; God, who is distinguished qualitatively from men and from everything human, and must never be identified with anything which we name, or experience, or conceive, or worship, as God; God, who confronts all human disturbance with an unconditional command "Halt," and all human rest with an equally unconditional "Advance"; God, the "Yes" in our "No" and the "No" in our "Yes," the First and the Last, and, consequently, the Unknown, who is never a known thing in the midst of other known things; God, the Lord, the Creator, the Redeemer—this is the Living God.

Romans, p. 330

What Barth sought to convey through this kind of writing was the sheer, unconditional *agency* of God. The 19th-century liberals had been wrong to think that we could find God by contemplating our own experience or using our own reason. God cannot *be found* at all: he is not passive. He must *find us:* he is active. To the whole of human endeavor God simply says "No." He offers, instead, an even greater "Yes" of his own.

In 1921 Barth was offered a chair in theology at Göttingen, and with some misgivings he abandoned the life of a parish minister for that of a professor—although he never really felt suited to either. As his reputation grew, he moved to Münster in 1925 and Bonn in 1930. He found himself at the center of a new movement of theologians keen to break with the humanistic religion of the 19th century and establish a new sense of the great gulf between humankind and God. Because of this emphasis, the movement became known as "dialectical theology." Other members included Rudolf Bultmann and Emil Brunner.

As a university professor, Barth felt it necessary to address the field of systematic theology. The first volume of *Christian Dogmatics* appeared in 1927—to the horror of some of the other dialectical theologians. The book took seriously such things as the doctrine of the Trinity, which had surely been done away with by liberal theologians decades before! Some felt that Barth was betraying the critical principles of his early work. He, conversely, thought that they were clinging to the remnants of liberalism and rationalism. The group fell apart, and each went his own way.

Still, Barth became unhappy with some of his own ideas. The *Christian Dogmatics* was never continued; in its place he began a new work, the *Church Dogmatics.* The first half of the first volume was published in 1932. The project would take Barth the rest of his life.

As he worked on it, the controversies continued. Barth had burst onto the theological scene as a powerful and angry critic, and he always remained essentially confrontational. Convinced of his own rightness, he was incapable of compromise on the smallest matter. He was often overhasty in attacking others. One work, *Rudolf Bultmann: An Attempt to Understand Him,* offered little more than a caricature of Bultmann's real views. A particularly unhappy controversy was that with his former theological ally Emil Brunner; Barth's response to Brunner's ideas was simply entitled *No!* (See below for an account of the differences between the two men.) Still, Barth could recognize some worth in his opponents' views, and he likened himself and Brunner to the elephant and the whale. Both are God's creatures, but they can never meet.

Barth became increasingly distracted from theological controversy, however, by political developments in Germany. He was disgusted with the rise of the Nazi Party but truly horrified by the reaction of the church. The Catholic Church, instead of opposing Hitler, made a truce with him—which Hitler later brushed aside. Worse, a popular movement known as the "German Christians" arose in the Protestant churches. These people preached a strange mixture of Christianity and Nazism, seeing Jesus as an Aryan superman overcoming the dark forces of Judaism, and marched "with the swastika on our breasts and the cross in our hearts."

To Barth this simply proved what happens when the church allows itself to be influenced by anything other than God's revelation in Christ. He vehemently opposed the German Christian movement and played an important role in the establishing of an alternative. The "Confessing Church" was born in 1934, based on a statement known as the Barmen Theological Declaration, which firmly rejected the idea that Christians owe any allegiance to anything that contradicts Christ. The statement was largely the work of Barth. Always politically concerned, he once declared, "We must hold the Bible in one hand and the newspaper in the other."

In 1935, as a result of this opposition to the Nazis—and his refusal to salute Hitler at the start of his lectures—Barth was sacked from his job at Bonn University. Two days later he was offered one at Basel, so he returned to his native town, where he remained for the rest of his life. There he devoted himself to his work, producing a prodigious quantity of books, articles and pamphlets. His life settled into a steady routine of reading, writing and teaching. His tastes were simple: most of his leisure time was spent reading detective novels, smoking his omnipresent pipe and listening to Mozart.

Barth had first encountered Mozart as a small boy when he heard his father picking out a tune on the piano, and his devotion to the composer never flagged. Indeed it bordered on the spiritual. He once remarked, "If I ever get to heaven, I shall first ask after Mozart, and only then after Augustine and Thomas, Luther and

Calvin and Schleiermacher" (*Karl Barth—His Life*, p. 409). On one occasion, attending a concert of Mozart, he had a mystical experience in which he felt he saw the composer standing by the piano. Mozart's music was the one human endeavor that Barth was prepared to admit could bring us closer to God—something that greatly puzzled him.

Barth remained in Switzerland after the war, but he devoted much thought to the problem of Germany's reconstruction. Lecturing in the ruins of Bonn University in 1946, in the rubble he came across a bust of Schleiermacher, which he rescued and had restored to a place of honor. He was attacked by many after the war for refusing to speak out against Communism as he had against Nazism. Barth's belief that anti-communism was potentially a greater threat than Communism itself reflected his generally left-wing politics, the result of ministering to working people back in Safenwil.

Throughout this time, work on the mighty *Church Dogmatics* continued, and Barth began to realize, as the work's scope became ever wider, that he could never hope to complete it. It would, like Mozart's *Requiem*, be an unfinished masterpiece.

As the volume of his work increased, Barth became something of a patriarch, widely recognized as the world's greatest living Christian writer. Although a Protestant, he was asked to attend the Second Vatican Council, but he was prevented by ill health. He made good the deficiency in 1966 by inviting himself to Rome to meet Catholicism's foremost theologians. There he discussed theology with Pope Pius XII, who called him the greatest theologian since Aquinas.

The visit showed that Barth must have mellowed a little in his old age, since he had always shown great antipathy toward Catholicism before. Indeed, Barth seems to have been anxious at this stage in his life to bury some of his long-standing hatchets. In the same year, 1966, his old adversary Brunner died. Barth had sent him a message:

> Tell him, *Yes*, that the time when I thought that I had to say "No" to him is now long past, since we all live only by virtue of the fact that a great and merciful God says his gracious Yes to all of us.
> *Karl Barth—His Life*, pp. 476-77

These were the last words that Brunner ever heard. And in 1968 Barth himself died. The *Church Dogmatics*, still unfinished, now ran to something like 6 million words—a whole shelf of theological exploration. His other works, added together, would fill another shelf. Yet he was always aware that his message was, at heart, a simple one. In the 1950s and 1960s he had sometimes preached in Basel Prison. On one occasion he told the prisoners:

Some of you have perhaps heard it said that in the last forty years I have written a great many books and that some of them have been very fat ones. Let me, however, frankly and openly and even gladly confess that the four words, "My grace is enough," say much more and say it better than the whole pile of paper with which I have surrounded myself. When my books have long since been superseded and forgotten, then these words will still shine on in all their eternal richness.

Barth, p. 99

Thought

It was said of the great philosopher Bertrand Russell that it was impossible to criticize him, because he was so clever that he would invariably have thought of your criticism already and dealt with it. There is a similar sort of problem facing anyone aiming to give an account of Barth's theology: his writings were so voluminous and so wide ranging that he can never really be summarized or pinned down to any particular position, even the ones normally taken as most characteristic of his thought. Anyone familiar with how Barth is normally represented tends to be surprised when they come to read the *Church Dogmatics*, simply because he tackles every subject in such a rounded way that he seems to have anticipated absolutely everything.

Still, there are some themes in Barth's work that are more or less constant. If there is such a thing as "Barthianism," we can say that these themes are what it consists of—provided we remember that Barth isn't tied down by "Barthianism" any more than Calvin is by "Calvinism"!

God. Barth's theology stems more than anything else from the profound sense of the otherness of God that he described in *Romans.* God, for Barth, is immeasurably beyond human beings and has nothing in common with them. Barth vehemently rejects the claim of Aquinas that although God is so great that we cannot say anything truly of him, we can nevertheless use analogical language of him, drawing analogies between human beings and God—a doctrine sometimes called the *analogia entis* or "analogy of being." Barth says, "I regard the *analogia entis* as the invention of Antichrist, and I believe that, because of it, it is impossible ever to become a Roman Catholic" (*Church Dogmatics* I/I, p. xiii).

Because of the great gulf between God and humanity, it is impossible to know him unless he makes himself known. Throughout his life, Barth remained implacably opposed to any hint of natural theology—the idea that something of God can be known apart from revelation. This was the cause of his disagreement with Brunner, who argued that some limited knowledge of God is available to everyone and that in particular we may know that we are sinful because of the workings of the

conscience. Barth rejects this. Even knowledge of our own sinfulness must be revealed through Christ.

In this Barth was influenced by Kierkegaard's claim that God is not an object to
be discovered but a subject to do the discovering. But Barth rejected Kierkegaard's
emphasis on personal experience and subjectivity. Indeed, the reason he abandoned
his *Christian Dogmatics* was that he felt it was too influenced by existentialism.

Of course Barth also rejects Schleiermacher's belief that there is a feeling of God
shared by all humanity. Although Barth conceded Schleiermacher's greatness, he
could see little good in him:

> Until better instructed, I can see no way from Schleiermacher . . . to the
> chronicles, prophets, and wise ones of Israel, to those who narrate the story
> of the life, death, and resurrection of Jesus Christ, to the word of the apos-
> tles—no way to the God of Abraham, Isaac, and Jacob and the Father of
> Jesus Christ, no way to the great tradition of the Christian church. For the
> present I can see nothing here but a choice. And for me there can be no ques-
> tion as to how that choice is to be made.
>
> *Friedrich Schleiermacher: Pioneer of Modern Theology*, ed. Keith Clements, p. 63

All of this makes Barth seem rather negative, and in his first *Romans* era incarnation
he was. But this is just the preliminaries—the clearing of the ground, as it were—
for the positive emphases of Barth's theology. Like Augustine and Calvin before
him, Barth is far more interested in the positive workings of God's grace than in
the inability of humanity to sort itself out.

Revelation. To all of humanity's works, God simply says "No!" But at the same
time there is a "Yes!" We cannot reach up to God, but God has reached down to
us. Through his revelation we can, after all, know God. Barth's message is ultimately
positive; in his terminology, God's unconditional "No" to humanity's efforts is ultimately transcended by his even greater "Yes."

Barth's theology, then, is one of *revelation.* That revelation comes exclusively
through Christ, the Word of God. It is mediated through the Bible and the teaching
of the church. So the Bible and church teaching can also be called the Word of God,
although in a secondary way.

This means that Barth has little interest in the historical circumstances surrounding the writing and compiling of the Bible or the formation of doctrine. He treats the
Bible as essentially authoritative, God's Word, but only in a secondary sense. The Bible
is the vehicle for God's Word and Spirit, not a replacement for them.

And what is the content of this revelation? It is nothing other than God himself:
his self-giving reveals him as perfectly free and loving. More than this, it reveals him

as Trinity: "*God* reveals Himself. He reveals Himself *through Himself.* He reveals *Himself.* God, the Revealer, is identical with His act in revelation and also identical with its effect" (*Church Dogmatics* I/I, p. 296).

The fact of the Trinity is thus a primary fact about God, and Barth tackles it near the beginning of the *Church Dogmatics* because he thinks we cannot understand anything else about God until we take this fact into account. This contrasts sharply with Schleiermacher, who left the Trinity until the end of his work *The Christian Faith.* For Barth, doctrines like the Trinity, the nature of God and the incarnation form an organic whole. They cannot be compartmentalized separately from each other. All doctrines must be understood in the light of the Trinity and the incarnation, and they interpret each other.

In fact, Barth saw his task as rescuing these classical Christian doctrines from their demolition by 19th-century liberalism. Instead of discarding these doctrines as old-fashioned or incomprehensible, we must accept them as God's revelation to the church and try to understand them. Because of this attempt to rehabilitate orthodox doctrine, Barth's theology is often known as "neo-orthodoxy."

In this endeavor Barth was greatly influenced by Anselm, especially his slogan "faith seeking understanding." Barth realized that this means that theology can be rational, but it is not the kind of rationality that tries to relate Christian doctrine to something outside itself, mere human rationality. That was the rationality of Lessing and Ritschl—and look what kind of Christianity they ended up with. On the contrary, theology needs to come to grips with a rationality of its own, a rationality that comes from Christ and the witness to him recorded in the Bible. That is the rationality of God, not of humankind, and it is a far greater kind of rationality, for God's Word—his *Logos*—is rationality itself.

Christ and salvation. Schleiermacher had argued that Christ is at the center of all Christian doctrine. On this, if on little else, Barth agrees with him. All our knowledge of God comes through Christ. Christ is nothing other than God come down to humanity.

It should be clear that Barth has little time for the Christology "from below" of the liberals. He holds to the classical formulation of Chalcedon, interpreting it in a dynamic, deliberately fluctuating way:

> It is impossible to listen at one and the same time to the two statements that Jesus of Nazareth is the Son of God and that the Son of God is Jesus of Nazareth. One hears either the one or one hears nothing. When one is heard, the other can be heard only indirectly, in faith.
> *Church Dogmatics* 4/I, p. 180

Barth points out that the New Testament uses a variety of names and expressions for Christ, and he suggests that only thus can we capture the dynamic way in which he mediates between God and humankind. In fact, the way Christ does this goes right to the very heart of Barth's theology. We have seen how Barth is keen to emphasize the greatness and majesty of God, and critics have asked how it is possible to reconcile this outlook with a proper understanding of the suffering of Christ. If God is so great, how could he ever be powerless? Barth tackles the problem head-on: he suggests that it is a mark of God's greatness—indeed, the greatest thing about him—that he is willing to risk everything and put himself, vulnerable and helpless, in the hands of his creatures.

> It is in the light of the fact of His humiliation that on this first aspect all the predicates of His Godhead must be filled out and interpreted. Their positive meaning is lit up only by the fact that in this act He is this God and therefore the true God, distinguished from all false gods by the fact that they are not capable of this act, that they have not in fact accomplished it, that their supposed glory and honour and eternity and omnipotence not only do not include but exclude their self-humiliation. False gods are all reflections of a false and all too human self-exaltation. They are all lords who cannot and will not be servants, who are therefore no true lords, whose being is not a truly divine being.
> *Church Dogmatics* 4/1, p. 130

In Christ we see the traditional, worldly understanding of power dramatically reversed. God is at his most powerful when he is at his most helpless, because his is a kind of power that has nothing to do with force. Just as God is the cause and goal of the whole world, yet it is impossible to know him through the world, so too he is the most powerful agent in the world, yet he is also the most helpless. He works through the power of love, not the power of coercion.

Here, then, we see a powerful restatement of one of the most fundamental paradoxes of Christianity, woven into a new understanding of the nature of God. It is an important anticipation of the theology of Jürgen Moltmann.

God's purpose in becoming powerless in Christ is of course to save, and Barth expresses this in traditional, objective terminology. However, he also acknowledges the influence of subjective views of the atonement by emphasizing its effect on our lives: "The very heart of the atonement is the overcoming of sin: sin in its character as the rebellion of man against God, and in its character as the ground of man's hopeless destiny in death" (*Church Dogmatics* 4/1, p. 253). In this respect Barth is very close to the spirit of Calvin. We saw earlier that the great

Reformer sought to bind an objective account of salvation with an emphasis on how it affects the believer and leads to a change in behavior, and this too is at the heart of Barth's theology.

Reflections

Barth's influence on Christian theology remains immense. This is perhaps curious given the fact that few theologians today claim to agree with him. Many consciously react against him; many more are influenced by him even if they do not know it.

For one thing, Barth's great emphasis on the agency of God as the seeker rather than the one who is sought has made a major impression on subsequent theology. It has been especially striking to see the effect of this on Roman Catholic theologians, given that Barth worked it out—in part—in conscious opposition to the *analogia entis,* which he regarded as one of the fundamental errors of Catholicism. One important and interesting example is Hans Urs von Balthasar, who met Barth at Basel. In his work *The Glory of the Lord* von Balthasar sought to describe the agency of God in terms drawn from Byzantine theology and the Greek Fathers. For him, that agency is best understood in terms of Beauty—of the supreme Beauty of God striking the believer, who can only react by basking in it. It is an idea that has its roots in the thought of Plotinus; the big difference, of course, is that for von Balthasar the divine beauty is known through Christ and is therefore found within the world rather than by turning away from it.

Barth also put the Trinity and Christology at the center of Christian thought, and they continue to remain there. As we shall see, the 20th century witnessed a "rediscovery of the Trinity," and much of this is due to Barth. The same is even more dramatically true of Christology. Theologians such as Jürgen Moltmann have taken Barth's insistence that all our knowledge of God comes through Christ to new lengths.

At the same time, there has been great reaction against Barth. Even those theologians who do "come out" as Barthians generally do so only in a qualified sense, eager, perhaps, to escape from his considerable shadow. There are several points on which Barth has traditionally been criticized, and while the criticism is not always justified, it does help to define the shape of his theology and show how it has affected subsequent thinking.

For one thing, Barth's attitude toward history is often seen as very deficient. He seems to show no interest in how the Bible was written and put together or how doctrines were formulated by the Fathers—for him they are givens, revelation that must be interpreted. We may ask, as Newman did, *why* we should regard the doctrine of the Trinity, for example, as the definitive and primary revelation about God when we know that the doctrine developed only gradually throughout the first four centuries of Christianity. Barth comments at one point, when speaking of his treatment of the Trinity, "There seem to be no compelling reasons why we should so distrust the Church of the 4th century and its dogma that we abandon the question as to the meaning of this dogma" (*Church Dogmatics* I/I, p. 378). That, really, is all that Barth has to say on the matter, and for many it will not suffice.

Even worse, Barth's lack of a sense of the place of history is shown up by the fact that he has almost nothing to say about the historical Jesus. At one point he writes,

> The atonement is history. To know it, we must know it as such. To think of it, we must think of it as such. To speak of it, we must tell it as history. To try to grasp it as supra-historical or non-historical is not to grasp it at all. *Church Dogmatics* 4/I, p. 157

Yet it seems that Barth failed to heed his own warning. He says very little about the historical Jesus and even declares himself uninterested in the "Quest" that Schweitzer wrote about. We have seen that the 18th century questioned the link between religion and history, and much of the 19th century was spent trying to show how the one could be based on the other. Barth seems to reject the whole enterprise, cutting Christianity adrift from its historical foundations.

This lack of interest in history is connected to Barth's great emphasis on the fact that there can be no knowledge of God apart from Christ. Instead of the *analogia entis*—the analogy of being of Aquinas—Barth suggests an *analogia fidei*, an analogy of faith. The relation between humankind and God is based on faith, not nature. Here again we see the strong link between Barth and the early Reformers. But if this is so, it seems impossible to talk about God to anyone who does not already know him. We can come to know him only through a miracle on God's side. There is no role whatsoever for apologetics, the task of presenting Christianity to those outside it.

Because of this, many have seen Barth as a sort of theological bully. Because Barth rejects the idea of natural theology so vehemently, he is in principle unable to argue for his position, and indeed he makes no apparent attempt to do so. We can either accept his ideas or not; there is little argument about them. He simply presents them—or, as Paul Tillich put it, throws them at us like rocks. Because he does not argue for his ideas, the unsympathetic reader may feel little inclination to agree with them.

And this can have a profoundly negative effect, of a kind that Barth would not have wanted. Where Schleiermacher tried to bind religion and culture together, to show the "cultured despisers" of religion that in fact they could not do without it, Barth does the opposite. Secular culture and faith in God, according to him, can never meet. To embrace one is to reject the other. Failure to do this, argues Barth, results in the kind of travesty of Christianity preached by the German Christian movement, where Christianity is so diluted by cultural ideas that it becomes unrecognizable. So for those of Barth's readers who do in fact side with culture, there seems to be little role for God. Barth has made God so separate from the world that God seems at risk of disappearing altogether.

And this did, to a certain extent, come about. Barth's influence can be seen behind the "religionless Christianity" of Dietrich Bonhoeffer and even the "death of God" movement of the 1960s. Barth sought to untether God from the world, to raise him to the heights he felt God should occupy. Some of his successors let go of the string. It was with this sort of problem firmly in mind that some of Barth's colleagues and successors sought to find a more constructive approach to the relations between theology, history and culture. The most important was Barth's former ally, Bultmann.

Rudolf Bultmann

Rudolf Bultmann occupies an uneasy place in modern theology. He was never a systematic theologian and never wrote a work of dogmatics. In fact, he was a major figure in New Testament scholarship. Like a modern-day Origen, he presented all his theological ideas as results of his biblical studies.

And those theological ideas are often hard to pin down. Associated with the dialectical theology of the 1920s, Bultmann was closely allied to Karl Barth. Yet his later work often seems to have more in common with the 19th-century liberal theology that dialectical theology was supposed to replace. That, at least, was how Barth saw it, and the result was a long-standing disagreement between Barth and Bultmann.

Life

Bultmann's life was that of a career scholar and revolved around religion right from the start. The son, grandson and great-grandson of Lutheran ministers, he was born in 1884 in Oldenburg. Like Barth, he studied theology at Tübingen, Berlin and Marburg, where he came under the influence of Wilhelm Herrmann, one of the foremost proponents of liberal theology. Unlike Barth, he remained at Marburg for the rest of his life, first as student and then as professor.

Bultmann made his name with his *History of the Synoptic Tradition* of 1921. In this work Bultmann developed the new technique of "form criticism," a method of studying the Bible that focused on how its stories tend to fall into certain categories or genres. By studying these genres, critics could chart the development of the material as it was passed on by word of mouth before being written in the surviving texts. Bultmann noted that the picture of Jesus in the New Testament is largely a theological construct. We do not, in fact, know much about Jesus; we certainly do not know him to be the moral reformer preached by liberal theology.

At the same time, Bultmann was becoming aware of the emphasis in the New Testament on eschatology, the imminent arrival of the kingdom of God and the end of the world. The liberals had ignored this central element of early Christianity, since it had no place in their gospel of social progress and this-worldly morality. Like Schweitzer before him, then, Bultmann found the historical foundations of liberal theology slipping away.

Bultmann became associated with Barth, with whom he had much in common. But he was never happy with Barth's apparent uninterest in questions of history and critical scholarship and with his rather naive approach to the Bible. Like Barth, Bultmann was a prominent member of the Confessing Church, which opposed Hitler in the 1930s. Although Bultmann was not, as a rule, as interested in politics as Barth, his opposition to Nazism certainly went beyond the merely theological. In 1933 he told an audience that civil disobedience was now an urgent duty:

> If Adolf Hitler, in a very gratifying decree, exhorted us not to change the old names of streets and squares, then the new Marburg town council should be ashamed of itself that, at its first session, it could find no more urgent a duty in the new situation than to give new names to some of our streets and squares.
>
> *Existence and Faith*, p. 164

Theologically, however, Barth and Bultmann drifted apart, and Bultmann formed a more fruitful partnership with Martin Heidegger, the existentialist philosopher, who taught with him at Marburg in the 1920s. Bultmann felt that the insights of existentialism were powerful tools for restating the New Testament message in terms that made sense to modern people, and he set about forging a new Christian existentialism.

At the heart of this project was the conviction that the message of the New Testament not only could but should be restated in different terms. In 1941 Bultmann set forth his ideas in an essay, *New Testament and Mythology*, which had almost as much effect as Barth's *Romans* had twenty years earlier. It presented a new program: "demythologizing," the task of stripping from Christianity the outdated worldview in

EXISTENTIALISM

Existentialism comes in many forms, but is always concerned with the self—the subjective individual—and what it is like to be such an individual. Existentialists develop special concepts and terminology to describe that experience as accurately as possible.

Existentialism developed partly from the paradoxical philosophy of Søren Kierkegaard, who sought to describe what existence is like from the inside rather than create an objective system claiming to describe it from the outside. In the early 20th century it was also greatly influenced by the "phenomenology" of Franz Brettano and Edmund Husserl, who similarly tried to rid philosophy of its pretensions to objectivity.

Martin Heidegger, the most important (and difficult) existentialist philosopher of the 20th century, focused on the self's "being in the world," a precarious state in which the self is confronted by its limitations, especially its mortality. Faced with this, the self tends understandably to try not to think about it, becoming obsessed with material things or with other people. But this brings only unhappiness, which Heidegger calls "inauthentic" existence. "Authentic" existence is achieved when the self faces up to its situation and learns to accept its limitations.

Heidegger's ideas were developed and simplified by the French existentialists, primarily Jean-Paul Sartre and his associates Simone de Beauvoir and the novelist Albert Camus. In the cafés of the Parisian Left Bank in the 1950s they forged a humanistic, left-wing, atheistic and highly enjoyable existentialist philosophy. For Sartre there is no God and the universe has no meaning; he describes existence as a predicament in which the individual must come to terms with the essential absurdity of the world. In a rejection of Aristotelian metaphysics and all similar attempts to impose objective order on the world, he declares that there is no essence, there is only existence. The kind of predicament Sartre spoke of was described most famously in Waiting for Godot *by Samuel Beckett, in which the two main characters spend the whole play hanging about in a surreal hinterland as they wait for a Godlike figure who never shows up. Their situation is a strange combination of comedy and tragedy.*

Clearly existentialism was never a definite set of beliefs, like Platonism or Aristotelianism; it was a tendency or way of doing philosophy that could come in many different forms. While Sartre-style existentialism was explicitly anti-Christian, there was no reason other versions should not be allied successfully with Christianity; and indeed the basic idea of existentialism has much in common with some forms of Christianity. In a way Augustine was the first existentialist, and if the work of Sartre was a negation of that of the medieval mystics, then that very fact gave it a kind of paradoxical similarity to them. Many 20th-century theologians sought to use the insights and terminology of existentialism to express their theological ideas. The best-known were Rudolf Bultmann and Paul Tillich, but they were by no means the only ones; even Karl Barth flirted with existentialism at one stage. An easier, more readily comprehensible existentialist theology was propounded by the British theologian John Macquarrie.

However, in recent years existentialism has been much less influential in both philosophy and theology. From a philosophical point of view, the movement was hopelessly solipsistic—stuck irretrievably in the first person. Its rejection of objectivity was its weakness as well as its strength, since it had surrendered any claim to describe the world as it actually is—which is surely what philosophy is all about. In any case, the idea that "existence" is equivalent to "human existence" betrays a decidedly anthropocentric viewpoint. Similarly, from a theological point of view existentialism was unable to deal satisfactorily with the ways individuals relate to each other. The rediscovery of the classical doctrine of the Trinity that characterized much 20th-century theology was accompanied by a renewed sense of the importance of relations for understanding personhood. Similarly, recent advances in scholarship suggested a new emphasis on the corporate, social nature of salvation in the thought of biblical authors such as Paul. All of this has meant a gradual abandonment of existential ideas and terminology and a search for something to replace them.

which it had first appeared and restating it in language that made sense to modern people. Bultmann became an enormously controversial figure, especially in Germany and America, where some churches went so far as to hold trials for heresy of those suspected of sympathizing with him.

Like the other dialectical theologians, Bultmann not only was enormously energetic, producing vast quantities of books and articles, but maintained the activity for a remarkably long time, even after his retirement. He died in 1976.

Thought

Demythologizing. "Demythologizing" became a kind of slogan and remains the best-known aspect of Bultmann's thought. At first glance, it seems similar to the attitude of the liberal theologians of the 19th century. Following Ritschl, they tended to dismiss many traditional Christian doctrines, such as the Trinity and the incarnation, as outdated, incomprehensible, and in any case products of Greek thought, not authentic Christian faith. And indeed Barth thought that Bultmann was essentially reverting to old-fashioned liberalism, and Barth reacted against this tendency by striving to uphold these old doctrines in their traditional form.

However, Bultmann's aim was really to *rescue* these doctrines, or what he saw as their essential point, not to discard them. His point was a simple one. Today people tend to have a "scientific" worldview. This means that they try to explain the world scientifically, by reference to natural events and processes. The world, which is physical in nature, can be explained and understood by rational experimentation and prediction. Any event can be fully explained by referring to other events, with no need to appeal to the supernatural. That is the way of thinking we saw being forged in the Enlightenment by scientists like Laplace and historians like Gibbon. By contrast, when the New Testament was written and Christian doctrines were originally formulated, people had a very different view of the world, what Bultmann calls a "mythological" one. They understood the world in supernatural terms and explained it by telling stories of gods, angels and demons. They regarded the physical world as an arena where these stories could be played out, suspended between heaven (which was above it) and hell (which was below).

Modern subscribers to the scientific worldview cannot accept this way of seeing things, which is essentially alien to them:

> Let us think simply of the newspapers. Have you read anywhere in them that political or social or economic events are performed by supernatural powers such as God, angels or demons? Such events are always ascribed to natural

powers, or to good or bad will on the part of men, or to human wisdom or stupidity.
Jesus Christ and Mythology, 3:1

This is why the 19th-century liberals rejected many traditional doctrines, and others continue to do so—because they were products of the mythological worldview that few modern people can accept. But Bultmann's point is that the faith of the first Christians, although presented in mythological language, need not be tied to that worldview. It can be translated into terms acceptable to the modern, scientific one. The kernel of theological truth can be extracted from the husk of now incomprehensible mythology and restated for a modern audience.

A perfect example of how this can be done is the eschatology that Bultmann found throughout the New Testament. The first Christians expected Christ to return any day, riding clouds of glory. To many people today such a belief seems quaint: we do not believe heaven to be above us, nor do we expect the world to end soon, any more than we think clouds can be used for transport. But that does not mean we should ignore this doctrine as the 19th-century liberals did. On the contrary, the doctrine reflects a belief in the immediate power of God, a belief that we cannot guarantee our security by working hard and trusting in material things. The material order is subject to the decree of God, and it is he who judges and saves. That is the conviction that the mythological language was intended to convey. Beliefs such as these can continue to exercise great power over us without the mythological baggage in which they originally came packaged. Bultmann writes:

> Shall we retain the ethical preaching of Jesus and abandon his eschatological preaching? Shall we reduce his preaching of the Kingdom of God to the so-called social gospel? Or is there a third possibility? We must ask whether the eschatological preaching and the mythological sayings as a whole contain a still deeper meaning which is concealed under the cover of mythology. If that is so, let us abandon the mythological conceptions precisely because we want to retain their deeper meaning.
>
> *Jesus Christ and Mythology*, 1:2

Knowing God. What, then, is the message that Bultmann believes must be extracted from the New Testament? The most important element is God. In the New Testament, Bultmann found a belief in a God who stands over and against the material order, who sustains that order and can tear it down whenever he chooses. Like Barth, he found an emphasis on the greatness of God, who is exalted far above and beyond humanity. Thus Bultmann, together with Barth, is considered a dialectical theologian, one who stresses the great distance between God and humanity.

However, Bultmann uses this idea in a very different way from Barth. Where Barth focused his attention on God and tried to describe him in rhetorical rather than purely descriptive terms, Bultmann argues that God is so great that we cannot know him or speak of him sensibly at all. Like Barth, Bultmann stresses that God is not an object—he is the ultimate *subject*. He is not an existing thing; he is the basis for the existence of everything. Bultmann is thus clearly in the tradition of Pseudo-Dionysius and Thomas Aquinas, and like Aquinas he recognizes that this view of God raises serious problems for theology, the task of which is to speak of God. Where Aquinas solved the problem by appealing to analogical language, Bultmann uses a very different tactic:

> If "speaking of God" is understood as *"speaking about God,"* then such speaking has no meaning whatever, for its subject, God, is lost in the very moment it takes place. Whenever the idea, God, comes to mind, it connotes that God is the Almighty; in other words, God is the reality determining all else. . . . Every "speaking *about*" presupposes a standpoint external to that which is being talked about. But there cannot be any standpoint which is external to God. Therefore it is not legitimate to speak about God in general statements, in universal truths which are valid without references to the concrete, existential position of the speaker.
>
> *What Does It Mean to Speak of God?* I

In other words, instead of trying to make objective statements about God, we should speak about our own subjective experience. Because our existence is dependent on God, understanding ourselves will allow us to understand him.

In this respect, then, Bultmann seems very reminiscent of Schleiermacher—another reason Barth profoundly disagreed with him. But Schleiermacher did not have the benefit of existentialist philosophy, which Bultmann encountered in the person of Heidegger, his colleague at Marburg. Bultmann used Heidegger's basic system to set forth the New Testament message as he understood it in its "demythologized" form.

Existentialism. Of all 20th-century theologians, none embraced existentialism more enthusiastically than Bultmann—who was at the same time highly conscious of the pitfalls of such an approach. He was greatly influenced by his friend Martin Heidegger, and particularly by Heidegger's descriptions of "authentic" and "inauthentic" existence, which Bultmann believed could be valuably used in describing Christian experience.

For Bultmann, what the New Testament conveys in its mythological language about sin and judgment is the experience of inauthentic existence, the denial of responsibility and the self's true nature. And authentic existence, or salvation, cannot be attained simply by accepting one's nature, as Heidegger thought; it comes through Christ, as we identify ourselves with his death on the cross.

So Bultmann regards the power of Christ and the atonement as lying in their *significance* for us. In this he is reminiscent of Abelard. But Bultmann uses existentialist terminology to draw this idea out further.

Faith and history. Bultmann distinguishes between the *historical* and the *historic,* an idea he takes from Heidegger. "Historical" events are simply normal events that occur at a certain point. "Historic" events, however, are those that have great significance and continue to influence people in the present. For example, the Boer War and World War I were both historical events. But World War I was also a historic event in a way that the Boer War was not, because of the effect it had on the way people thought and the effect it still has, on theology as well as on other cultural activities.

In fact, historic events and people need not be entirely historical. Robin Hood or King Arthur might be an example, a highly inspiring and idealistic figure of extreme historical dubiousness. A more interesting case is Alexander the Great, a figure of great historic significance and certainly a historical figure, but one about whom few details are known. A person or event might, then, loom large from a historic point of view but remain obscure and mysterious to conventional historical analysis.

Bultmann regards Jesus as falling into a similar category to Alexander the Great. His New Testament studies led him to conclude that relatively little is known of Jesus. And what is known of him conflicts, to a certain extent, with the subsequent Christian proclamation. Jesus announced the coming kingdom of God, but the authors of the New Testament largely ignored this message and instead preached about Jesus himself.

This may seem worrying if we think it important to follow the teaching of the historical Jesus, but Bultmann's point is that this is not what matters. Jesus' importance lies in his historic significance—what he means to us now—not in his historical existence as a distant figure from the past. It lies in the repeated proclamation of his story and the power of that story to change our lives. Thus Bultmann does not consider it helpful to ask whether, say, the resurrection "really" happened. As a historical event it is valueless, even granting the dubious possibility that it ever happened. As a historic event, however, it is of enormous importance.

Reflections

Many people have found Bultmann's work remarkably attractive and helpful. His status as a major New Testament scholar means that his work is intellectually respectable, grounded in sound historical scholarship in a way that is not true of many theologians—particularly his sparring partner, Karl Barth. He represents a constructive approach to Christianity that avoids the pitfalls of Barth's absolutism and liberalism's relativism.

But there are continuing worries over his work. It is, for example, unclear whether demythologizing is really a viable program. Is it not simply subordinating the Bible's message to contemporary culture? That was how Barth saw it. Bultmann responded that he was simply removing the mythological framework of the Bible's message and retaining the message itself. But of course this presupposes that it is possible to distinguish clearly between the message and the framework or worldview in which it is presented. What one person considers a discardable framework might be someone else's essential message. And surely to translate a message is to change it.

In any case, it has to be said that Bultmann's existential account of the New Testament's message is not enormously convincing, especially in the light of later biblical scholarship. Paul and John, in whom he thought he saw the basic ideas of Heidegger's existentialism, were in fact saying quite different things. Paul, in particular, was not very concerned with the individual's experience; instead he focused on what happened to *groups* such as the Jews and the Gentiles. Where the 19th-century liberals imposed their own ethical views on Jesus, it seems that Bultmann simply imposed his on Paul and John.

What this goes to show, of course, is that demythologizing is an ongoing operation. It must be done afresh for each new generation. Bultmann's restatement of the New Testament, helpful in his day, no longer convinces; and the language of existentialism itself now sounds old-fashioned. Most people would probably agree that the goal of presenting traditional ideas in new, more relevant ways is a worthy one, even if they may not agree with the details of Bultmann's methods.

Perhaps more problematic is Bultmann's treatment of history. Despite his status as a New Testament scholar, Bultmann seems to agree with Barth on the relative unimportance of history. Like him, he seems to regard the message of the Bible as somehow more important than the subject of that message, Jesus himself. The fact that he makes this problematic move reflects the seriousness with which he takes the problems of tying religious faith to a poorly known set of historical events— the problems identified by Enlightenment thinkers like Lessing—and the problems that I have identified as among the central issues of modern theology.

However, Bultmann's approach seems more balanced than Barth's. Where Barth seems uninterested in any historical questions, Bultmann tries to ground his theol-

ogy in the historical beliefs of the earliest Christian communities. Since these beliefs grew directly from the historical person of Jesus and the events surrounding
his death, they are not totally detached from history. They are *about* history but not
based on it.

Still, many of Bultmann's successors became unhappy with his treatment of history, and there has been something of a movement toward trying to base theology
more securely on history. The best-known proponent of this approach is Wolfhart
Pannenberg. And as Bultmann was working out his alternative to Barth's theology,
another theologian was doing the same thing in a very different way: Bonhoeffer.

Dietrich Bonhoeffer

The name of Dietrich Bonhoeffer will probably be familiar to more readers than that
of any other 20th-century theologian. His life was a rare display of courage in the
face of tyranny, and his execution by the Nazis established his place among the martyrs of the church. At the same time, his thought has made a great impact outside the
cloisters of academic theology; in fact, it has not been particularly influential within
them. In his life, death and thought, Bonhoeffer was a theologian for the people.

Life

It comes as something of a relief to find a German theologian who was not the son
of a Lutheran pastor. In fact, Bonhoeffer's father was a psychology professor, and he
and most of his eight children were agnostics. This may go a long way toward explaining Bonhoeffer's concern to make Christianity relevant to a secular world, a world
"come of age" that no longer accepted the old certainties of God and revelation.

He was born in 1906 in Breslau, just early enough to be deeply affected by the
death of one of his brothers in World War I. He was also just old enough to be
taught the basics of liberal theology by its last master, Adolf von Harnack, when
he studied at Berlin. But Harnack's day was nearly over, and Bonhoeffer quickly
came under the influence of Karl Barth, the harbinger of a new way of doing theology, whose controversy with Harnack was shaking the theological world to its
foundations. When he eventually met Barth, Bonhoeffer was struck by this extraordinary man:

> There is even more to Barth than his books. . . . I am even more impressed
> by his conversation than by his writings and lectures. Here you really see the
> whole man. I have never seen anything like it before nor thought anything like
> it possible.
> *Bonhoeffer,* p. 45

Bonhoeffer was a brilliant student but was not happy with the prospect of an academic life, and he trained for the ministry instead. His training took him to Barcelona, Rome and the United States, where he found his theological horizons being forcibly widened. He was struck by the fact that Americans appeared to have little respect for Luther and the German theological tradition in general. In particular, he became friends with the American theologian Reinhold Niebuhr, whose political theology made a great impression on him.

In 1931, back from America, Bonhoeffer became a lecturer in Berlin. He combined his teaching and writing with pastoral work, throwing himself into the ecumenical movement. Problems arose, however, with the emergence of National Socialism. Bonhoeffer, who had several Jewish friends, was implacably opposed to the Nazis from the very beginning and spoke out against the strange combination of Nazism and Christianity known as the German Christian movement. Unable to work as a pastor in Germany, he took up a parish in London, catering to the German community there. Perhaps a little harshly, given his own Swiss nationality and relative safety, Karl Barth wrote to him:

> You ought to . . . concentrate on one thing alone, that you are a German and that your Church's house is on fire, that you know enough and also know how to say it well enough, to be capable of bringing help, and that fundamentally you ought to return to your post by the next ship! Or let us say, the ship after next.
> *Bonhoeffer,* p. 67

In 1934 Barth helped establish the Confessing Church as an alternative to the official, Nazi-run Reich Church. Acting on Barth's advice, Bonhoeffer returned to Germany to work for the new church. He became the leader of an illegal seminary in Finkenwalde. There, in cramped conditions, financed mainly by Bonhoeffer's own university salary, an almost monastic community came into being. Bonhoeffer saw to it that the seminary's emphasis was on spirituality, meditation and prayer rather than on academic matters. In addition to the students who passed through the house, a small group of core members, known as the House of Brethren, remained there as an informal leadership coterie.

Bonhoeffer was becoming unhappy with the Confessing Church, which he believed did not go far enough in its opposition to the Nazis. In 1938 ministers were required to swear allegiance to Hitler; the Confessing Church did not oppose this, since it was not regarded as an intrusion into theology. Although theologically opposed to the infiltration of Christianity by Nazi ideas, the church was not politically opposed to the Nazis. This has often been regarded as a fundamental flaw in

Karl Barth's thought: his main objection to the German Christians almost seemed to be the fact that they allowed secular culture to influence their theology, rather than the fact that they supported a racist and inhumane political regime. This worried Bonhoeffer, and in 1939, trying to decide what he should do, he visited the United States again. The American theologians begged him to stay with them, but Bonhoeffer had realized where his place was. He wrote to Niebuhr:

> It was a mistake for me to come to America. I have to live through this difficult period in our nation's history with Christians in Germany. I will have no right to participate in the reconstruction of Christian life in Germany after the war if I do not share the tribulations of this time with my people. . . . Christians in Germany are faced with the fearful alternatives either of willing their country's defeat so that Christian civilization may survive, or of willing its victory and destroying our civilization. I know which of the two alternatives I have to choose but I cannot make the choice from a position of safety.
> *Bonhoeffer*, pp. 98-99

On his return, Bonhoeffer became involved with opposition to the Nazis within Germany. His high profile in the international ecumenical movement made him the perfect intermediary between the underground conspirators and sympathetic people abroad. However, the authorities began to put him under surveillance. In April 1943 Bonhoeffer was arrested by the Gestapo and taken to Tagel Prison.

Conditions there were difficult at first. Kept in solitary confinement and harshly interrogated, Bonhoeffer came close to despair, wondering if it was his duty to commit suicide for fear of breaking and betraying his friends. Luckily, the warders soon warmed to the minor celebrity in their charge, and Bonhoeffer was allowed books, papers and visitors.

The time in prison dragged on as Bonhoeffer's trial was delayed again and again. He spent the time reading and writing notes, poems and letters to his friends. Later the posthumous *Letters and Papers from Prison* became popular as a moving collection of work documenting the last years of a man condemned to die for his Christian beliefs. As a result, the innovative and daring theological ideas jotted down by Bonhoeffer during this time in these letters became his best-known work.

Bonhoeffer's case suddenly became much more important and urgent in the eyes of the authorities in July 1944, when an attempt at a coup against the Nazis was finally carried out by senior officials in the German army. By a series of incredible fortunes, Hitler escaped the bomb that was left for him with no worse injuries than partial deafness and the destruction of a pair of trousers. Recrimination was swift, and the conspirators were quickly executed. Those only marginally connected to the plot, including Bonhoeffer, found themselves being interrogated more seriously. A plan to smuggle Bonhoeffer out of prison disguised as a mechanic was abandoned as his friends and family members were arrested and he feared for their safety. In February 1945 Bonhoeffer was transferred to the concentration camp at Buchenwald.

Time was running out for the Nazis, and the decision was taken not to let the prisoners survive their captors. On April 9, as the Russian army closed in on Germany, Bonhoeffer and his comrades were hanged. His brother was shot a week later. Two weeks after that, Hitler was dead.

Thought

Bonhoeffer died when he was thirty-nine. Barth, when he was that age, had not even begun to think about the *Church Dogmatics*. Thus all we have of Bonhoeffer is his early work and the beginnings of ideas for new directions sketched out in his letters from prison. As with some of the early Fathers, it is necessary to fill in some of the gaps of his thought or even to dare to reconstruct what he might have written if he had lived.

Perhaps the key to Bonhoeffer's thought is the fact that although he died over twenty years before Barth and Bultmann, he was a generation younger than they. This meant two things: first, he was greatly influenced by them; but second, his world was very different, and he was confronting an entirely different way of thinking. Although he was just old enough to have been taught by Harnack, his thinking did not begin, as Barth's and Bultmann's had, with the premises of liberal theology. Instead it began with the insights of dialectical theology itself—but a dialectical theology worked out in the context of a world that was beginning to abandon religious faith altogether. Bonhoeffer is, in a way, the first post-Christian theologian.

His most interesting ideas, and certainly those that became best known after his death, were set out in a few brief passages in letters written from prison during the last year of his life. In them Bonhoeffer's concern for practical matters shines through on every page. It is not enough simply to provide a coherent account of Christianity, as Barth was attempting in his *Church Dogmatics*. On the contrary, our task must be to *live* a Christian life and understand how Christianity can be relevant to the modern world—a concern that shows the influence of his friend Reinhold Niebuhr. Bonhoeffer therefore muses at length on the kind of world that theology must address. It is a world in which religion is losing its power.

> The time when people could be told everything by means of words, whether theological or pious, is over, and so is the time of inwardness and con-

science—and that means the time of religion in general. We are moving toward a completely religionless time; people as they are now simply cannot be religious any more.

Letters and Papers from Prison, p. 279

We saw earlier how, as science progressed during the Age of Reason, the idea of God as the direct cause of events became less and less useful. "The God of the gaps" was being squeezed out. Bonhoeffer recognizes that this is now true not simply in physics and biology but in religion as well. This idea of God as the final answer to otherwise unanswerable problems is simply losing its usefulness.

> Man has learnt to deal with himself in all questions of importance without recourse to the "working hypothesis" called God. In questions of science, art, and ethics this has become an understood thing at which one now hardly dares to tilt. But for the last hundred years or so it has also become increasingly true of religious questions; it is becoming evident that everything gets along without "God"—and, in fact, just as well as before.
>
> *Letters and Papers from Prison,* pp. 325-26

Such is the secular nature of the modern world that people no longer feel the need to talk about God even when dealing with the most profound problems of existence.

> Efforts are made to prove to a world thus come of age that it cannot live without the tutelage of "God." Even though there has been surrender on all secular problems, there still remain the so-called "ultimate questions"—death, guilt—to which only "God" can give an answer, and because of which we need God and the church and the pastor. . . . But what if one day they no longer exist as such, if they too can be answered "without God"?
>
> *Letters and Papers from Prison,* p. 326

Clearly, Bonhoeffer was greatly affected by Barth's denouncing of "religion" as humanity's futile attempt to draw close to God. But he goes further than Barth in several important ways. Instead of simply regarding religion as humankind's hubris and folly, he realizes that it is becoming meaningless even to human beings. Barth said that religion will not help us find God. Bonhoeffer says that it will not even help us talk usefully to other people.

Barth's response was to reject the this-worldly religion of liberalism, replacing it with an enormous gulf between God and the world. Bonhoeffer takes exactly the opposite approach. He thinks that the Barth-style disjunction between God and the world is responsible for the mess religion is in. The distant God is the God of the gaps, the *deus ex machina* brought in as an explanation when all else fails. The result, argues Bonhoeffer, is a marginalization of God.

> If in fact the frontiers of knowledge are being pushed further and further back (and that is bound to be the case), then God is being pushed back with them, and is therefore continually in retreat. We are to find God in what we know, not in what we don't know; God wants us to realise his presence, not in unsolved problems but in those that are solved.
> *Letters and Papers from Prison*, p. 312

So we must look for God *within* the world.

> It always seems to me that we are trying anxiously in this way to reserve some space for God; I should like to speak of God not on the boundaries but at the centre, not in weakness but in strength; and therefore not in death and guilt but in man's life and goodness.
> *Letters and Papers from Prison*, p. 282

In a way, then, Bonhoeffer represents something of a reversion to Schleiermacher, who sought to show that religion is at the heart of everyday human life, not something for esoteric, superstitious mystics. But Bonhoeffer combines this approach with Barth's emphasis on *God,* not religion. It is God who is at the heart of everyday life, rather than the human activity of religion. Similarly, Bonhoeffer approves of Bultmann's program of demythologizing but regards it as not going far enough. Instead of creating a false distinction between mythological aspects of religion and its central elements, we must somehow find a way past religion as a whole.

This is what Bonhoeffer means when he talks about "religionless Christianity," a much misunderstood phrase. He certainly doesn't mean Christianity without God; neither does he mean Christianity without ministers and rituals. We should always remember that Bonhoeffer not only was a minister himself but ran a seminary that operated much like a monastery. What he means is a new conception of Christianity that avoids distinguishing between everyday life and religious activities. We shouldn't live normally for six days a week and spend Sunday thinking about God; we should put God at the heart of everything we do, every day.

God, then, is not "out there" somewhere. There is not a part of human life labeled "religion" which deals with God. The modern world has no need for religion or that kind of God. God is at the center of human life. Being a Christian means joining in the experience of the world:

Christianity puts us into many different dimensions of life at the same time; we make room in ourselves, to some extent, for God and the world. We rejoice with those who rejoice, and weep with those who weep.
Letters and Papers from Prison, pp. 310-11

Thus Bonhoeffer rejects all otherworldly interpretations of Christianity, the tendency to emphasize what will happen to us after we die rather than what goes on in this world:

The decisive factor is said to be that in Christianity the hope of resurrection is proclaimed, and that that means the emergence of a genuine religion of redemption, the main emphasis now being on the far side of the boundary drawn by death. But it seems to me that this is just where the mistake and the danger lie. Redemption now means redemption from cares, distress, fears and longings, from sin and death, in a better world beyond the grave. But is this really the essential character of the proclamation of Christ in the Gospels and by Paul? I should say it is not. The difference between the Christian hope of resurrection and the mythological hope is that the former sends a man back to his life on earth in a wholly new way which is even more sharply defined than it is in the Old Testament. . . . This world must not be prematurely written off; in this the Old and New Testaments are at one. Redemption myths arise from human boundary-experiences, but Christ takes hold of a man at the centre of his life.
Letters and Papers from Prison, pp. 336-37

Who, then, is the God who joins us at the center of life? Bonhoeffer rejects not only Barth's world-transcending God but also his triumphalist one.

Here is the decisive difference between Christianity and all religions. Man's religiosity makes him look in his distress to the power of God in the world: God is the *deus ex machina*. The Bible directs man to God's powerlessness and suffering; only the suffering God can help.
Letters and Papers from Prison, p. 361

It is at this point, perhaps, that Bonhoeffer's language becomes most profoundly paradoxical, on a level with Barth's. He writes:

God would have us know that we must live as men who manage our lives without him. The God who is with us is the God who forsakes us (Mark 15:34). . . . Before God and with God we live without God. God lets himself be pushed out of the world on to the cross. He is weak and powerless in the

world, and that is precisely the way, the only way, in which he is with us and helps us. Matthew 8:17 makes it quite clear that Christ helps us, not by virtue of his omnipotence, but by virtue of his weakness and suffering.
Letters and Papers from Prison, pp. 360-61

Despite the profoundly un-Barthian sentiments, dwelling on God's weakness rather than his greatness, there is a Barthian structure of thought beneath the surface here. Bonhoeffer's thinking, like Barth's, is highly christocentric. His description of God is based on the helplessness *of Christ*. But he goes beyond Barth in arguing that *all* our knowledge of God must be based on our knowledge of Christ. This has radical consequences for our view of God:

Of this man we say, "This is God for us." This does not mean that we know, say, at an earlier stage quite apart from Jesus Christ, what and who God is, and then apply it to Christ. We have a direct statement of identity; whatever we can say here is prompted by a look at him, or, better, is compelled by this man.
Christology, p. 106

The ideas hinted at here would be fully worked out twenty years later by Jürgen Moltmann.

Bonhoeffer's work is fascinating, as it gives us a glimpse of theology in transition. Some of Barth's central ideas—the worthlessness of religion, the centrality of Christ for Christian doctrine—are enthusiastically taken up and pursued to radical new conclusions—religionless Christianity, God in the heart of human life, and God as weak, present only in absence—that appear very un-Barthian.

These ideas, sketched out by Bonhoeffer in his prison cell, became popularly known when his letters were published after his death. They became widely discussed in the English-speaking world as a result of their presentation in John Robinson's phenomenally popular *Honest to God*, published in 1963. Their influence can be seen in popular religious movements of the 1960s and 1970s, particularly the death of God movement, process theology and the work of Moltmann. Bonhoeffer's lively style, his personal courage and the remarkably contemporary setting of his theology ensure his popularity throughout the generations.

Reinhold Niebuhr

The early 20th century saw liberalism, the splendid creation of 19th-century theology, come crashing to the ground. We have already seen two of those responsible for undermining it: Schweitzer, who showed it to have no historical basis, and Barth, who demolished its theological presuppositions. However, there was a third voice of protest, one that many readers may find more persuasive. That voice belonged to Reinhold Niebuhr, the foremost American theologian of the 20th century.

Life

It was probably inevitable that at least one of the Niebuhr children would become a theologian. As things turned out, two of them did. Their father—who had emigrated from Germany to the United States as a young man, joined an Evangelical Free church and become a pastor—taught them theology, including Harnack's version of liberalism, and Greek from an early age. Instead of being put off by this, Reinhold, who was born in 1892 in Missouri, knew as a child that he wanted to follow in his father's footsteps, and he trained at a seminary near St. Louis run by his father's denomination. In 1913, at the age of twenty, the newly ordained minister was installed as pastor of his home church, replacing his own father, who had just died.

Niebuhr spent a further two years of study at Yale's School of Religion before taking charge of the Bethel Evangelical Church in Detroit. It was here, amidst the industrial squalor and racial tensions of the rapidly growing city where Henry Ford's innovative new production techniques had recently been implemented, that his distinctive theological voice was forged:

> We went through one of the big automobile factories today. . . . The heat was terrific. The men seemed weary. Here manual labor is a drudgery and toil is slavery. The men cannot possibly find any satisfaction in their work. They simply work to make a living. Their sweat and their dull pain are part of the price paid for the fine cars we all run.
>
> *Leaves from the Notebook of a Tamed Cynic*, pp. 99-100

Concerned for the welfare of the workers of Detroit, Niebuhr became involved in the social gospel movement, which campaigned for social reform in the name of Christian values. Although regarded by many as a vehicle for socialism, the movement was inspired in part by liberal theology and its ideal of the kingdom of God as a harmonious society on earth.

But Niebuhr found himself becoming dissatisfied with ideals such as this. For one thing, most of the workers in the car factories were not churchgoers. They certainly weren't intellectual theological liberals. Liberalism, in fact, was a religion of the middle classes, of those who exploited the workers. Its utopian dream of a harmonious society was completely out of touch with reality. More specifically, while it preached a simple ethic for individuals, it had nothing to say to groups. It could offer no solution to the problem of the increasing gulf between rich and poor, bourgeoisie and workers. In fact, as the religion of the intellectual middle classes, it simply reinforced this gulf.

Niebuhr was, in a way, facing a similar problem to that tackled by Schleier-macher over a century earlier. But instead of encountering "cultured despisers" who needed to be shown that religion was an essential part of human life, Niebuhr was faced with ordinary people for whom the bourgeois religion of Schleiermacher and his successors was irrelevant.

Niebuhr expressed his dissatisfaction in *Does Civilization Need Religion?* in 1927, and the following year he took up a teaching position at Union Seminary in New York. His outspoken Marxist ideals, expressed in many articles and lectures as well as his book, were making him famous; and his dynamic teaching and preaching at the seminary only enhanced his reputation. There, in 1932, he wrote his most im-portant book, *Moral Man and Immoral Society*, which stepped up the attack on liberal-ism as socially inert and Protestant values in general as conducive to class exploita-tion. His awestruck students responded by running a red flag up the seminary flagpole in 1934.

It was not just because of his writing that the FBI was compiling an ever-ex-panding file on Niebuhr. In the same year that he produced *Moral Man and Immoral Society*, he ran for Congress as a Socialist. More fruitfully, he helped set up numer-ous trusts and societies, including the Fellowship of Socialist Christians; he was also on the committee of the League for Independent Political Action, together with the philosopher and educational reformer John Dewey. At the same time he founded and edited the journal *Radical Religion*, which later became *Christianity and Society*, as well as another one, *Christianity and Crisis*. No one could accuse Reinhold Niebuhr of failing to stick to his principles, any more than they could call him lazy.

As the years passed, Niebuhr became more and more prominent in American society as well as international Christian circles. He worked for the U.S. State De-partment and the Council on Foreign Relations as well as the World Council of Churches and—toning down his politics a shade—became involved in the Demo-cratic Party. At the same time his brother H. Richard Niebuhr was also becoming famous as a theological social critic.

Niebuhr's enormously energetic lifestyle came to an end in 1952, when a stroke left him partially paralyzed. Now forced to confine himself to something ap-proaching a normal workload, Niebuhr gave up active political and social work in favor of writing and continued to turn out enormous numbers of articles, reviews and books, on history as well as theology. His status as one of the most prominent American intellectuals of the 20th century was reflected not simply in his appear-ances on the cover of *Time* magazine but also in his being awarded the U.S. Presi-dential Medal of Freedom in 1964. After his death in 1971, the corner of Broadway where Union Seminary stands was named Reinhold Niebuhr Place.

Thought

Niebuhr did not consider himself a theologian. And a theologican in the sense of someone concerned primarily with dogmatic issues he was not. His main contri- bution was to Christian ethics, in the broadest sense possible—what Christianity has to say about how we live, not simply to the individual but to society as a whole. He felt that this issue was central to the task of making Christianity relevant to the modern world:

> The fact is that more men in our modern era are irreligious because religion has failed to make civilization ethical than because it has failed to maintain its intellectual respectability. For every person who disavows religion because some ancient and unrevised dogma outrages his intelligence, several become irreligious because the social impotence of religion outrages their conscience.
> *Does Civilization Need Religion?* p. 12

The attempts of Schleiermacher and his liberal successors to make Christianity in- tellectually credible, then, were something of a waste of time. Similarly, the conti- nental dialectical theology of Barth and Bultmann seemed entirely taken up with the task of restating Christian doctrines in one way or another. What good was that to the ordinary working person?

For Niebuhr, the starting point of any Christian thinking must be humanity it- self. Human nature is what we are most familiar with, and in addressing it we may hope to say something relevant and useful to people. In this way, then, Niebuhr is quite close to the liberal tradition and sharply different from Barth, whose focus was always wholly on God.

Nevertheless, Niebuhr did not agree with liberalism's optimism about human nature and the progress of civilization. His years in Detroit saw to that. He had a very deep sense of sin. His analysis of the human condition is a pessimistic one, based as it is on a recognition that human beings, although finite and limited, are frustrated by their limitations and try to overreach them:

> Man is insecure and involved in natural contingency; he seeks to overcome his insecurity by a will-to-power which overreaches the limits of human crea- tureliness. Man is ignorant and involved in the limitations of a finite mind; but he pretends that he is not limited. . . . All of his intellectual and cultural pursuits, therefore, become infected with the sin of pride.
> *The Nature and Destiny of Man,* 1:178-79

So Niebuhr regards sin as, essentially, pride and the attempt to set oneself up as greater than one really is. This is firmly in the Calvinist tradition that Niebuhr inherited from his evangelical background. However, Niebuhr also recognizes an alternative form that sin may take: instead of falsely ennobling themselves, human beings sometimes falsely debase themselves and try to lose themselves in the world. In this case, sin takes the form not of pride but of sensuality.

And sin is a social phenomenon, not simply an individual one. Niebuhr stresses that institutions are actually more capable of sin than individuals are:

> In every human group there is less reason to guide and check impulse, less capacity for self-transcendence, less ability to comprehend the needs of others and therefore more unrestrained egoism than the individuals, who compose the group, reveal in their personal relationships.
> *Moral Man and Immoral Society*, pp. xi-xii

This, of course, reflects Niebuhr's socialism and his strong sense of class injustice. It is also a powerful, sociologically aware reinterpretation of the Pauline account of sin as an oppressive force that controls people, rather than simply bad things that people do—as in Romans 6—7.

In contrast to true Marxists, Niebuhr does not believe it possible for the sinful cycle to be broken by human means. In his eyes, the Sermon on the Mount is a discourse on the impossibility of leading a truly ethical life. At best, all we can hope to bring about in society by our own means is a system of checks on power, so that oppression is kept to a minimum. But religion, with its emphasis on love and self-sacrifice, can break down the sinful cycle in society. Religion lifts people out of themselves, giving them a new perspective and breaking down the power of the ego.

Niebuhr's approach is sometimes called "Christian realism," since he combines a pessimistic analysis of the human condition with this idealistic stress on the power of religion to overcome it. It is notable, too, that he talks of religion as such, describing Christianity as a religion like others—again a liberal idea, and one that Barth built his whole theology around opposing.

Religion is powerful because of its mythic qualities. In his account of the role of myth in religion, Niebuhr seeks to avoid what he regards as two contrary errors: repeating tired old doctrines that are rooted in outmoded worldviews and discarding anything distinctively Christian because it offends against the latest intellectual fad. Instead we must accept myths for what they are—the expression of profound truths in prescientific form. The task of theology is to unpack these myths a little, to rationalize them or create a coherent system. This is essential if religion is not to degenerate into anarchy. However, Niebuhr does not endorse Bultmann's pro-

gram of demythologization, whereby the eternal truth of each myth can be stripped
of its mythic clothing and re-presented as a rational fact. On the contrary, Niebuhr
regards myth, and mythic religion, as ultimately transcending reason: "Every authentic religious myth contains paradoxes of the relation between the finite and the
eternal which cannot be completely rationalized without destroying the genius of
true religion" (*An Interpretation of Christian Ethics*, p. 24).

This, then, is why Niebuhr does not regard himself as a dogmatic theologian,
for theology, if taken too far, loses the essential paradox and mystery of religion. It
refuses to accept religious myths and ideals on their own terms, just as the 19th-
century liberals reinterpreted Jesus not as a Jewish eschatological prophet but as a
benevolent social reformer like themselves.

Niebuhr also rejects the dogmatic attitude as applied to ethics. Just as there are
two extremes to be avoided in dealing with myth, so there are in ethics: on the one
hand, a legalistic insistence on upholding the letter of the law, even when it is in-
appropriate, and on the other, a total rejection of the rule of law. Instead Niebuhr
seeks to uphold the primacy of the law of love, as taught by Christ. This, argues
Niebuhr, is clearly opposed to self-absorbed lawlessness; but it also transcends ordinary human laws, which are limited in application because of their temporary,
historical nature.

> There are many norms of conduct, validated by experience, between the con-
> ditions of man's creatureliness and the law of love, which is the final norm of
> man's freedom, but they must be held with some degree of tentativity and be
> finally subordinated to the law of love. Otherwise the norm of yesterday be-
> comes the false standard of today; and lawlessness is generated among those
> who are most conscious of, or most affected by, the historical changes in the
> human situation.
> *Faith and History*, p. 185

The upshot of this is that Niebuhr advocates a relativist ethic. Instead of trying to
follow unbreakable moral rules, the Christian should try to apply the law of love
in each situation as it comes up. Every situation is unique and requires a unique
response based on the law of love.

Niebuhr's practical approach to theology provides a valuable counterpoint to
the dominance of the German-speaking tradition in the 20th century and the
rather rarefied or abstract tendency into which it can sometimes lapse. Paradoxically, that abstract, Germanic theology would be represented most strongly by Niebuhr's colleague and only rival as the supreme American theologian, Paul Tillich.

Paul Tillich

Paul Tillich was one of the strangest theologians of the 20th century. He belonged to the same generation as Barth and Bultmann, but the structure of his work shows virtually no sign of their influence. His thought was something of a throwback to the 19th century, yet it was couched in the most modern technical terminology. And he was the most prominent American dogmatic theologian of the 20th century, yet his German accent was so strong that many of his students could not understand him.

Life

The first part of Paul Tillich's life showed no hint of what was to happen to him later. He was born in 1886 in Starzeddel, at that time in Germany but now in Poland. Needless to say, he was the son of a Lutheran pastor; and after studying philosophy and theology he was himself ordained in 1912.

Everything changed in 1914. Tillich was sent to the trenches as an army chaplain, and for four years he was immersed in the horrors of World War I. He realized that the liberal theology and humanist philosophy he had been taught were unable to deal with the reality he was facing; he spent as much time digging graves as he did preaching sermons.

However, he did not believe that theology had to cease being academic if it was going to speak to this situation. In 1919 he returned to the University of Berlin, and five years after that he was at the University of Marburg, where he became immersed in the new theology of Karl Barth. More important, however, was Martin Heidegger, whom he met here. Like Bultmann, Tillich was enormously impressed with Heidegger's existentialism, which he felt to be a powerful development of early 19th-century philosophy, especially that of the German idealists and of Kierkegaard.

But Tillich's reactions to his wartime experiences were not solely intellectual. He began to lead something of a rebellious lifestyle, throwing himself into the famously decadent society of Weimar Germany. He always loved nightclubs and parties, and surrounding himself with friends: in this respect, he was firmly in the tradition of Martin Luther. More notoriously, he particularly enjoyed the company of women—despite the fact that he had been married since 1914. The many affairs he conducted throughout his life, to varying degrees of consummation, would cause something of a scandal after his death when his wife published his biography. Much of this had something to do with Tillich's mother's death when he was seventeen. He had been so traumatized by this that he had repressed the event and refused ever to speak of her again. It may be that this was one of the reasons he idealized all women ever after and seemed to be chasing some kind of perfection that he could never find.

In the early 1930s Tillich railed against the German Protestant churches' apparently favorable attitude to the burgeoning National Socialist movement. In 1932 he wrote a book titled *The Church and the Third Reich*, which contained "Ten Theses" condemning Protestantism for capitulating to Nazism. He was deliberately imitating Luther's Ninety-five Theses against indulgences. Tillich courageously sent the book to Hitler; he was rewarded in 1933, when the Nazi leader became chancellor of Germany, with summary dismissal from his teaching post at the University of Frankfurt. Luckily, Reinhold Niebuhr was in Germany at the time and invited Tillich to the Union Theological Seminary in New York. So despite the fact that he spoke little English and knew nothing of American culture, Tillich and his family emigrated.

Tillich spent twenty years at the seminary in New York, after which he was given the rare honor of a university professorship at Harvard University. He soon mastered English sufficiently to write in the language, although he retained a strong German accent. He was soon by far the most prominent academic theologian in America—since Niebuhr was never very happy being thought of in these terms—and his belief that the task of theology was to mediate between culture and religion meant that he was producing a constant stream of writings on all manner of subjects. His *Systematic Theology*, which was published in three volumes between 1951 and 1963, was one of the most important Christian works of the 20th century.

Paul Tillich died in Chicago in 1965. His ashes were scattered in a park named after him in Indiana, landscaped with trees, lakes and excerpts from his own writings.

Thought

Tillich's thought revolves around the conviction that theology has to engage with contemporary culture. In this he is the polar opposite of Karl Barth. For Tillich, all theology is essentially apologetics. In fact, he suggests that religion and culture are really two sides of the same coin, incapable of existing without each other—an idea very much in the spirit of the theology of Schleiermacher. Tillich presents his theology as a series of answers to the questions posed by modern life. His answers, however, are couched firmly in the language of modern thought—namely existentialism.

God. Like Kierkegaard, Tillich begins with the insight that life is all about contradictions and paradoxes that cannot be collapsed or resolved. In particular, life is governed by the interplay between "being" and "nonbeing." Tillich suggests that all existing things, including ourselves, exist only within a framework, a system, in relation to other beings. But to exist in such a state is potentially not to exist, and so we find ourselves fighting to impose our own existence against the forces of nonbeing.

One effect of this is that we are aware of our own finite nature. But in striving to exist, we are in a sense pushing past that finitude and looking toward infinity.

All of this is the fundamental question that is posed by life. And for Tillich the answer that Christianity gives to it is, of course, God. God is the power of existence, the force of Being that enables us to overcome nonbeing. He is the infinite that we know of through our own finitude. Here, then, Tillich is expressly opposed to Barth. Barth refused to accept that human beings can have any sense of God without God's giving it to them—even the sense that they need God. For Tillich, by contrast, God is the answer to a question that faces us from the sheer fact of existence itself, and we find him precisely because we are aware of our need for him.

What does it mean to say that God is "Being"? Tillich is using the language of existentialism to express an idea that we have seen recurring throughout Christian history:

> The being of God is being-itself. The being of God cannot be understood as the existence of a being alongside others or above others. If God is *a* being, he is subject to the categories of finitude, especially to space and substance. Even if he is called the "highest being" in the sense of the "most perfect" and the "most powerful" being, this situation is not changed. When applied to God, superlatives become diminutives.
> *Systematic Theology*, 1:235

Tillich says that his point is the same as that of Aquinas, that God is not one being among others but that which makes existence itself possible. He appeals to Aquinas's claim that in God there is no distinction between existence and essence. But all the same, Tillich's doctrine of God seems even more abstract than Aquinas's. We saw how despite his claim that we cannot say anything about God, Aquinas goes on to make quite a number of substantive claims about him. It seems that Aquinas does think of God as substantial in some way, even though the categories of existence followed by normal objects do not apply to him. For Tillich, however, this does not seem to be the case, and indeed his existentialist outlook is inherently opposed to the notion of describing God or anything else objectively. God, like the world, has meaning only insofar as he impinges upon our own existence and experience.

This can be seen a little more clearly if we consider Tillich's concept of religious symbol. The great doctrines of Christianity are "symbols," for example, the idea of God as Creator or the idea of Christ as Redeemer. Tillich thinks of these not as doctrines stating some kind of proposition, as, say, Calvinists might; rather, they are *images* that express an underlying existential attitude. The symbol of "God the Creator" expresses the idea that God is being-itself, pushing us beyond the destructive power of nonbeing and enabling us to transcend our finitude. Tillich can therefore talk about "God above God," meaning the reality that underlies the symbol, and in this regard he is strikingly similar to Meister Eckhart and the Rhineland mystics. Indeed Tillich draws heavily on this kind of mystical theology in explaining why the symbols of traditional theism must be transcended—they are simply inadequate to express the reality of God. But Tillich expressly says that to call God "being-itself" is not a further symbol; it means simply what it says. It could be said with some justification that Tillich has made God so abstract that he hardly seems real at all.

Sin and salvation. For Tillich, sin and salvation are two sides of the same coin. This reflects his essential belief that the polar opposites of life can never be reconciled, that they always exist in tension with each other. This is very reminiscent of Kierkegaard.

"Sin" and "salvation" are symbols. They express our experience of life as estrangement and love, which can never be separated from each other. Tillich describes the situation like this:

> Man as he exists is not what he essentially is and ought to be. He is estranged from his true being. The profundity of the term "estrangement" lies in the implication that one belongs essentially to that from which one is estranged. Man is not a stranger to his true being, for he belongs to it. He is judged by it but cannot be completely separated, even if he is hostile to it. Man's hostility to God proves indisputably that he belongs to him. Where there is the possibility of hate, there and there alone is the possibility of love.
> *Systematic Theology,* 2:44

The tension between being and nonbeing is what causes our estrangement from ourselves and its inevitable psychological consequences: guilt, loneliness and meaninglessness. Here Tillich is deliberately opposing the common idea of *sins* in the plural, as deliberate acts for which we deserve to be punished. This has been the dominant view in the Protestant tradition. He appeals instead to the idea in Romans 6—7, where sin appears as a sort of cosmic force that oppresses us, God's response to which is not forgiveness so much as rescuing.

Tillich thinks of this rescuing as the appearance of what he calls the New Being: a new way of living, described as "essentially being under the conditions of existence, conquering the gap between essence and existence" (*Systematic Theology*, 2:118). This comes through the person of Christ, who is, of course, another symbol.

Christ. Tillich is insistent that the overcoming of estrangement would be meaningless if it had not been fully enacted in an individual life. This means that the historical reality of Christ is essential to the working out of salvation. But Tillich is careful not to make salvation dependent on potentially disprovable historical claims. Despite the centrality of the historical reality of Jesus, Tillich thinks of the New Being as being dispensed through the medium of the New Testament. That is, instead of thinking simply of Christ we should think of "the Christ-event," which refers to Jesus, the whole train of events of his life, death and its aftermath; the realization of the New Being in his followers; and the writing of the New Testament documents.

So is our faith based on the report of Christ rather than on Christ himself? We saw that Bultmann suggested an idea like this and that he has come in for much criticism for it. Tillich aims to avoid this criticism by showing how the picture of Christ in the New Testament is true to the historical Jesus, even though modern biblical criticism like Bultmann's suggests that it may not be as accurate as we would like. He uses the analogy of art, pointing out that a portrait may be slavishly realistic like a photograph; alternatively it may be abstract, expressing only the painter's thoughts and retaining nothing of the subject's peculiarities. But there is a third possibility, the *expressionistic* portrait, which portrays the subject realistically but seeks to use this representation to express deeper truths about their character. In the same way, the depiction of Jesus in the New Testament is not slavishly exact, and on the purely historical level it is open to revision by critical scholars. But it does express accurately the appearance of New Being that began with Jesus, and it is through this depiction that we share in the New Being ourselves.

What all of this means is that Tillich retains a delicate balance between objective and subjective reality. There would be no salvation without the historical figure of Jesus, but that figure would have no significance without the faith community that arose around him, interpreted him and transmitted his message to the future. Tillich expresses this in terms of the name Jesus Christ, which encapsulates the conviction that Jesus, the historical human being, is the Christ, the one sent by God who brings New Being. This is Tillich's understanding of the Chalcedonian description of Christ's two natures. And it means that salvation is real and really changes us—but it must be continually renewed in faith.

Reflections

Tillich has been greatly criticized for detaching Christianity from its historical foundations. Is his answer to Lessing's questions really decisive? Does he not shift the "Christ-event" away from Christ himself to the early church?

More fundamentally, what exactly is it that the Christ-event is meant to do? When Tillich speaks of the New Being and its overcoming of existential estrangement, it seems that he is simply replacing the old set of religious symbols with some new ones. How literally are we supposed to take this language, and what, when you come right down to it, does it all *mean?*

This is symptomatic of the sometimes exasperatingly abstract nature of Tillich's work as a whole. Despite the great differences between his thought and that of Barth, they are similar in that both can sometimes seem to be spinning off into a world of words and images of their own invention that do not really connect with reality. This perhaps is more unfair to Tillich than it is to Barth, since Tillich was at least concerned to avoid doing this, whereas for Barth it is practically a theological virtue. In Tillich's case it is caused in part by his belief that theology is about apologetics rather than dogmatics: it is about answering the questions of secular life rather than reflecting on and developing the questions that it asks itself. This means that Tillich's thought can sometimes seem to lack a real doctrinal structure.

Some of these problems—if that is what they are—came to the fore in England in 1963, when John Robinson, then the Anglican bishop of Woolwich, published a small book called *Honest to God.* The book was a popular study of some of Tillich's and Bonhoeffer's leading ideas and focused in particular on a nonrealist idea of God as Being and Christ as a human being who was fully transformed by his relation to this Being. The book was an astonishing bestseller, but the Church of England was no more prepared for this sort of thing than it had been prepared for German biblical criticism. There was a massive public outcry that an Anglican bishop could say such things, and Robinson was popularly caricatured as an atheist who had betrayed his flock.

Most of this reaction was hysterical and excessive, and indeed to a theologically aware reader today Robinson's ideas seem pretty tame. But some of the reaction does reflect a genuine potential dissatisfaction with the theology of Tillich that lay behind them. By reinterpreting Christian "symbols" as the answers to existential questions, did Tillich interpret away the distinctiveness of Christianity? The answer to this question is very far from clear, not least because it was one of which Tillich himself was perfectly aware and which he was very keen to avoid. Many of those who ask it have probably never read Tillich's books themselves, which, despite their reliance on the language and concepts of existentialism, are penetrating, insightful and frequently remarkably profound.

Karl Rahner

In an age dominated by great speculative Protestant thinkers, Karl Rahner took their best ideas to forge a distinctive Roman Catholic theology, at once traditional and creative.

Life

Karl Rahner always maintained that he had led an extremely ordinary and uninteresting life. Nevertheless, there must have been something a little unusual about him even at an early age. He was born in Freiburg, Germany, in 1904, one of seven children of a fairly normal Catholic family. He seemed an average child, not notably academically gifted or outgoing. But in 1922, at the age of eighteen, he decided to join the Jesuits—for reasons that in his old age he could not remember. He assumed that that too had been a fairly ordinary thing to do.

Rahner was ordained as a priest in 1932 and remained a Jesuit all his life. He was equally an academic, however, and spent his formative years in several universities, including a period at the University of Freiburg, where, like practically every other theologian of the period, he met Martin Heidegger and was enormously impressed with his work. By 1937 he was teaching theology, and he did so for most of the rest of his life.

Rahner was educated in the kind of Catholic theology and philosophy that became dominant after the First Vatican Council: a rigid Thomism that looked back to the Scholastic reformulations of Aquinas's thought rather than forward to try to relate those insights to modern philosophy and science. Rahner had no time for this attempt to hide from modernity. He always regarded himself as a Thomist, but from the beginning his aim was to reinterpret this tradition in ways that made sense to the modern world.

Naturally, the Catholic Church did not always take kindly to this. In 1950 Rahner was prevented from publishing a book about the assumption of the Virgin Mary, which had just been proclaimed as infallible dogma by the pope. Rahner did not deny the doctrine, but he reinterpreted it in a way not approved of by the church. Twelve years later Rahner was summarily informed that from then on all his work would be checked in advance by a Vatican official. Rahner simply replied that in that case he would not write anymore, and he did not seem very bothered by the edict. Fortunately others protested on his behalf, and later that year he was made "peritus," or theological adviser, at the Second Vatican Council—and he was responsible for a great deal of what was said at that epochal council. Rahner had been transformed from a marginal, not very respectable figure into the most out-standing official theologian of the Catholic Church.

Despite his self-proclaimed ordinariness and unforthcoming character, Rahner impressed those who knew him as a very warm and thoughtful man with an almost childlike delight in the world. He had a notable weakness for fast cars, carnivals and ice cream, although presumably not all at the same time; and once in a New York department store he was forced to buy an enormous number of bottles of perfume after he had innocently opened them all to sample them. Beyond this, his students detected a genuine holiness and even saintliness in his unprepossessing figure. After his death in 1984, some of them found themselves praying not only *for* him but *to* him on their own behalf.

Thought

At a time when theologians were publishing immense works of systematic theol-ogy, Rahner firmly resisted all pretensions to "systems." In fact, he rather disingen-uously insisted that he was only an amateur theologian—a dilettante or dabbler in theological matters. If that is so, then he certainly did a lot of dabbling; he may not have written a systematic theology, but he did produce the *Theological Investigations*, hundreds of essays on a huge variety of topics, published in twenty-two volumes from 1954 onward. While they present a formidable appearance, occupying even more shelf space than Barth's *Church Dogmatics*, their short, piecemeal nature makes them infinitely more accessible. And in them we can see Rahner returning fre-quently to certain themes and ideas, which form the core of his theology.

Humanity and God. At the heart of Rahner's thought lies the conviction that hu-man life is impossible without God. This in itself may not seem very original. But Rahner really means it quite literally. He argues that everything we do involves an awareness of God—that it is impossible to do anything, perceive anything, experi-ence anything without at some level also experiencing God.

This is certainly a striking claim, and one that at first glance seems obviously false. What exactly can Rahner mean by it? The idea is subtle, and Rahner illus-trates it with a number of different images. For example, God is essential to every-day experience in the same way that light is. We cannot see anything unless there is light present, and we are always aware of the light—yet not consciously, at least not normally. We cannot see light in the same way that we see objects; rather, we see the light by looking at the objects it illuminates. The Impressionist painter Claude Monet could claim that his medium was light, and so it was, for his works express the play of light on objects beautifully. Yet of course he never simply painted light;

he painted objects *in* the light.

In the same way, we cannot experience anything without God's making it possible. We may be quite unconscious of this fact; we may even not believe in God at all. But we are still experiencing him at some level. Rahner also uses the image of the horizon against which we see things. We may not notice the horizon, but it is there, and we do see it even if we do not realize the fact.

Another way of putting the same thing is to appeal to a certain mystery at the edge of existence. The constant but unspoken presence of the mysterious infinite is what allows us to deal with the immediately obvious, nonmysterious finite. To put

THE SECOND VATICAN COUNCIL

In 1959 Pope John XXIII was elected to the seat of St. Peter. It quickly became obvious that there was a new regime at the Vatican: the new pope was keen to move beyond the reactionary dogmatism that had been the Catholic Church's official response to the modern world for a century and a half. Within three months of taking office, he announced plans for a new church council and established a new secretariat "for promoting Christian unity" to prepare for it. This council was going to be like no other.

The Second Vatican Council opened in 1962 with twenty-five hundred participants—more than at any other church council in history. It closed in 1965. Those three years saw the Catholic Church undergoing a profound change of outlook.

On one level, there was a serious shakeup of liturgical practice. The Mass could now be celebrated in the language of the people as well as in Latin; the priest no longer turned away from the congregation when consecrating the elements. Changes like these signified a greater openness within the church, a rejection of the notion that the priesthood is a kind of secret society that works mysterious magic.

Even more significant, however, was the new openness to those outside the church. The council accepted that although the Catholic Church is the one legitimate Christian church, Christ may be found outside its boundaries. It would be unreasonable to condemn pious Christians whose only fault is to have been born into other churches, and the council stated that in previous

it another way again, humanity intrinsically strives toward its own divinization—an Eastern Orthodox idea which it is striking to find in a Roman Catholic writer. Rahner thus writes:

The experience of God must not be conceived of as though it were *one* particular experience *among* others at the same level, as for instance an experience of pain at the physiological level can be regarded as at the same level as an optical reaction. The experience of God constitutes, rather, . . . the ultimate depths and the radical essence of *every* spiritual and personal experience (of love, faithfulness, hope and so on), and thereby precisely constitutes also the ultimate unity and totality of experience, in which the person as spiritual

centuries mistakes had been made on both sides of the divide. The way was thus opened up for serious dialogue and mutual engagement with the Protestant churches. Even more striking was the council's approval of the Orthodox Church, which it regarded as essentially the Eastern wing of the Catholic Church; it stressed that each individual church in the East must maintain its own traditions while remaining in communion with the church at large. And Orthodox priests really are priests—their ordination is valid—which is not true of Protestants, even Anglicans.

The council also adopted a new, positive attitude to other religions. Buddhism, Judaism and Islam were all singled out as faiths that teach a great deal that is true and good. Their followers are not simply potential converts to Catholicism; on the contrary, they may have much to teach Christians.

While the Second Vatican Council upheld the teachings of earlier Catholic councils, including Trent and Vatican I, it obviously reflected a wholly new attitude—openness and willingness to deal positively with the challenges thrown up by the modern world, rather than turning away from them. It was an event of fundamental importance to the ecumenical movement, which seeks to build links between the different churches. However, the popes who have followed the council, especially John Paul II, have tended to try to push the church in a more conservative direction again. The full implications of Vatican II remain to be worked out and implemented.

possesses himself and is made over to himself.
Theological Investigations, 11:154

As with Tillich, the idea is similar in a way to Irenaeus's and Aquinas's belief that
God at once transcends the universe and is paradoxically close to it. The fact that
God is the given by which we experience the world means that we can never experience him in the same way we experience normal objects, any more than we can
see light. But at the same time it means that he is always there, always available to
us, whether we know it or not.

It is clear that Rahner's ideas here have much in common with Schleiermacher's
fundamental claim that religion is an irreducible part of life, essential to feeling,
which accompanies all thought and action. But for Rahner, like Tillich, what is fundamental to life is not religion but God. There is therefore a more existential approach here, putting existence on a more personal, relational footing. And of course
there are parallels with Bonhoeffer's vision of "religionless Christianity." Like Bonhoeffer, Rahner believes that God is met in the ordinary world, in the realm of ordinary experience. What we would normally call religious experiences, the experiences of great mystics, are not some strange, unusual experiences that are unlike the
rest of life; they are an intensifying of a kind of experience that we have all the time.

Christ and the church. Something similar can be said about Christ. Rahner's
thoughts in this area are, again, similar to Schleiermacher's. Like Schleiermacher, he
begins not with Christ's divinity but with his humanity. He argues that this is the
better way to approach the issue, because there is a tendency among many Christians to assume that Christ's divinity is somehow more important than his humanity. Everyone knows that Christ is supposed to be divine, but there is less appreciation of why and how he is like us, and this of course is heretical in tendency if not
in formulation.

So given that Christ is human, how can we also express the fact that he is divine?
Rahner argues that there is a problem here only if we think that *human* and *divine* are
somehow opposites, one expressing a limited nature and another an unlimited one.
In fact, human nature has an unlimited aspect: the very presence of mystery in everyday experience, the consciousness of God. If a human being were to realize this
side of their nature totally and perfectly, then in their humanity they would be so
open to God that they would be themselves divine. And this is what Jesus was like.
His humanity and divinity are not separable qualities; he is divine inasmuch as he
is supremely human.

It is the transmission of this perfect sensibility of God to us that lies at the heart
of salvation. Through Christ, God is no longer simply the horizon against which

we experience the world; he himself somehow comes closer and is more directly perceived. Rahner describes what happens in very similar terms to Karl Barth: he emphasizes that what God gives us through Christ is nothing other than himself. But Rahner has a much wider conception than Barth of the arena in which this divine self-giving occurs. Instead of a single, remarkable, divine self-communication in Christ, Rahner thinks of Christ as the high point of a process of grace that is as long as history itself. He thinks of the whole of history as being the working out of God's grace, and he suggests that all of God's actions, including the creation of the universe and the incarnation, are really different aspects of the one divine desire to love. In this respect again he is very like Irenaeus; and like Irenaeus, Rahner lacks the idea that the incarnation was somehow dependent on humanity's having sinned in the first place. The incarnation would always have been part of God's plan for the world, whatever human beings did. This sense of the universal significance of Christ and the role of the whole of history in the working of divine grace antici-pates ideas more commonly associated with Wolfhart Pannenberg.

But Rahner focuses grace not only on Christ but also on the church. In this re-spect he is an avowedly Catholic thinker, anxious to uphold and reinterpret the tra-dition of Augustine and Aquinas. Rahner is clear that the Catholic Church was de-liberately founded by Jesus—which is not to say that Jesus personally set out the form that the church would take, envisioning in detail the ecclesiastical structure, the sacraments and so on. Rather, Jesus intended that his message, the self-revela-tion of God, be received and spread by a community of believers, a community originating in him and developing in the future. Christianity is not a matter of the individual's subjective consciousness of God; it has objective truth and commits the individual to social life. The Catholic Church is what emerged from this intent of Jesus, and it is his authentic successor in spreading his message.

What this means is that the decrees of the Catholic Church, even if they cannot be traced back to Jesus himself or even the New Testament, must be taken very se-riously as the authentic expression of the faith of Jesus. In this way Rahner manages to combine traditional loyalty to the Catholic Church with a sensitivity to the ob-vious fact that its official teachings have developed dramatically over the centuries.

Anonymous Christians. But Rahner tempers this traditional understanding of the role of the church with a liberal approach to those who are outside it. He is con-cerned to forge a constructive approach to the problem of other religions: is there any hope for those in different traditions of faith?

There are essentially three approaches one can take. The first is the traditional Catholic—and Calvinist—answer, which is that faith in Christ is necessary to salvation and followers of other religions will not be saved. This may be logically neat but is not very helpful from a pastoral point of view, and in Rahner's eyes it contradicts the teaching of the New Testament that God wills the salvation of everyone.

An alternative is to affirm the exact opposite and say that all religions lead equally to God and that the faithful follower of any religion can hope to be saved. This is the approach of the British theologian John Hick, who calls for what he terms a "Copernican revolution" in religion: one that sees all religions as aiming at God, rather than placing Christianity at the center and evaluating other faiths' approximation to it. But of course this answer has difficulty with the notion of objective truth; all religions contradict each other in very important ways, and to say that these differences don't matter, or are somehow less significant than the "important" parts of religion that one has identified, is rather patronizing, not to mention incoherent.

Rahner opts for a middle way between these two extremes, one that aims to preserve the optimism of the second with the logic of the first. He accepts that faith is essential to salvation, that it is only through Christ that we can be saved. This is as fundamental to the New Testament as the idea that God wills the salvation of all. But Rahner appeals again to his claim that human existence presupposes the experience of God. How we react to that experience—whether we acknowledge God's presence, put our faith in him and try to lead our life accordingly—is independent of what faith tradition we have been brought up in. As we have seen, the whole world is the arena for the outpouring of God's grace, and so it is possible for anyone to respond to that grace. Everyone who does so is a Christian, even if she or he is not a member of the church or has never heard of Christ. Such people are "anonymous Christians." They are Christians without even knowing it.

The idea is extremely similar to Justin Martyr's doctrine of the "seed of the Logos," and it is striking to see this doctrine, which was based on ancient philosophy and cosmology, rehabilitated by a 20th-century Roman Catholic using insights drawn from existentialism and Kant. Even more striking is that Rahner interprets it in a Thomistic way. It is simply his version of the idea that grace completes nature rather than overriding or contradicting it, which we saw to be fundamental to the thought of Aquinas.

We saw that Justin is quite clear that the "seed of the Logos" possessed by non-Christians, while real and valuable, is decidedly inferior to the fullness of the Logos possessed by the church—and Rahner stresses the same thing. It is no good rejecting Christianity and saying that we are responding to the experience of God in our own way. Christ is the supreme manifestation and source of the experience of and response to God; and if we reject him and his church we can hardly claim to be following it in another way. It is better to see a "tribute band" than no band at all, but no one who claims to be a fan of a famous band will prefer to see the imitators when they have the option of seeing the real thing.

Reflections

Rahner's notion of the omnipresent experience of God, always glimpsed but never fully realized, strikes many people as either extremely profound or remarkably silly. It seems strange to say that even atheists really believe in God even if they do not know it. It must be left to each reader to decide whether Rahner's claim is true to life.

More notorious is the concept of the "anonymous Christian," which is certainly the best-known aspect of Rahner's thought. The main criticism that is leveled against Rahner here is that the idea is extraordinarily patronizing. It seems to suggest that a faithful Hindu, for example, may really be a Christian even if he does not know it and even if he vehemently denies it himself. However, Rahner certainly accepts that Christianity may have much to learn from other religions; he does not simply see other religions as imperfect versions of Christianity. More important, it should be remembered that his notion of the "anonymous Christian" is intended as the solution to a theological problem and not as an aid to interfaith dialogue. It is not suggested that Christians go about telling adherents of other faiths that they may be Christians underneath. Rather, the suggestion helps us to reconcile faith in God's saving will with belief in the uniqueness of Christ. Rahner also offers it as a pastoral aid to Christians who are deeply worried about close relatives or friends. It is for their own comforting, not for telling other people.

Process Theology

Where 19th-century theology had tended to do away with those parts of Christianity that its formulators did not like, theologians in the 20th century from Barth on generally sought to come to terms with traditional doctrines and restate them for modern ears. Some, however, have felt that this is a rather desperate atttempt—and none more so than the process theologians.

Process theology takes its name from the philosophical ideas of Alfred North Whitehead, Bertrand Russell's collaborator who, in the 1920s, proposed doing away with traditional metaphysics, which was all about "substances," and replacing it with the idea of *processes*. Instead of thinking about objects that persist through a number of changes, we should think in terms of huge numbers of very short *events* that succeed each other. So change is fundamental to the universe, rather than something that merely happens to the things in it.

The process theologians include J. B. Cobb and Whitehead's former pupil Charles Hartshorne, who apply these ideas to God. The essence of their theology is that there are two ways of looking at God's relation to time and the universe. We saw that Aquinas described God as outside time, looking down on history as we might look down from a tall tower. The process theologians suggest that it is more constructive to think of God as *inside* time, just as we are. He is not a "substance" acting on the world: like everything else, he is a series of events within the world. It still makes sense, on this view, to talk about God's transcending the universe, but only in the very abstract sense that he exists throughout it.

So process theology thinks of God as caught up in the world of change and event, just like everything else. God is not unchanging; he can suffer; and he does not, in any metaphysically significant way, transcend the universe, which means that his power and knowledge within it are limited. God is the greatest being in existence, but his power is that of persuasion rather than coercion. He acts for good at all times, but even he finds it an uphill struggle when dealing with human free will. Process theology thus has a valuable contribution to make to discussions of the problem of evil.

The strength of process theology lies partly in its appeal to the Bible. Its supporters point out that in the Bible, and especially in the Old Testament, God is an active character who *does* things. And while everything always works out as he wants it to, he often seems to take roundabout routes to achieve it. The Bible describes God as "almighty"—but to interpret this as "strictly omnipotent" is, so it is claimed, a later import from Greek philosophy. The classical doctrine of God, as exemplified by Aquinas, of a perfect, unchanging, omnipotent being has far more to do with Plato than with the Bible.

Nevertheless, process theology has been criticized as untrue to the conviction, expressed by innumerable Christian theologians, that God's power lies in the way he transcends the universe. It contradicts the fundamental hope of Christianity that while things may not necessarily look that way, God has everything in hand. For this reason process theology, although a significant force in the 1960s and 1970s, is no longer at the top of the theological agenda.

Liberation Theology

Liberation theology has been one of the most striking developments in Christian thought in recent decades. It can be thought of as the response of the developing world to the doctrinal obsessions of Western theology.

Liberation theology developed in South America in the 1960s and 1970s, in response to the terrible conditions endured by the poor of that continent. Missionaries and priests working with the poor found that the doctrinal theology they had inherited from the Catholic Church did not address their situation, and they clamored for something different.

New theologians like Juan Luis Segundo and above all the Peruvian Gustavo Gutiérrez began to emphasize practice over doctrine. They argued that Christian thought can be developed only on the basis of experience, the experience of liberation of the poor. In their eyes, the Bible reveals a God of action who identifies with the lot of the poor and the suffering and works to set them free. We can understand this only by identifying with it ourselves, committing ourselves to overthrowing oppression and liberating those who suffer. Liberation theologians therefore seek to move beyond the traditional concerns with *orthodoxy*, which literally means "right belief," and instead set out the concept of *orthopraxy* or "right practice."

The South American liberation theologians were almost all Roman Catholic, and in the 1980s they came under attack from the Vatican for their affinities with Marxism. But as Gutiérrez was at pains to point out, liberation theology has no truck with the materialism and atheism of . It looks for social justice and transformation in this world, not a future one—but it looks to the transcendent God to bring it about. Liberation theology is thus influenced by the new understanding of eschatology pioneered by Jürgen Moltmann. It has also been inspired by approaches to the Bible pioneered in the 20th century: Barth's emphasis on letting the Bible speak to us rather than vice versa, and the stream of *narrative theology*, according to which Christianity is a matter not of abstract doctrines but of a story. To the liberation theologians, it is a story of salvation and liberation.

The inspiring message of liberation theology struck a chord throughout the world. In particular, in North America J. Deotis Roberts and James Cone pioneered *black theology*, which speaks of the "blackness" of Christ and even of God. What this means is that God identifies with oppressed minorities of all kinds, but in modern times this means, above all, identification with the oppressed black population of the United States. God is actively on their side and opposed to those who oppress them. Blackness is thus a sort of symbol of being oppressed, and we see a similar approach to femaleness in some feminist theologians. These theologies, and their counterparts in Asia and South Africa, are often more extreme and revolutionary than those of the South American liberation theologians, because they also draw on their Protestant heritage and are not subject to the controlling influence of Catholicism. *Contextual theology*, the South African version of liberation theology, proved especially powerful in the struggle against apartheid, a struggle that in many ways mirrors the stand of the German Confessing Church against Nazism in the 1930s.

PENTECOSTALISM

In April 1906 a man named William Seymour began preaching at 312 Azusa Street, Los Angeles, California. The venue was a former African Methodist Episcopal church, and the preacher was a former student of Charles Parham, a seminary teacher whose students, given an assignment to study what the Bible said about the blessings of the Holy Spirit, had suddenly begun to experience those blessings themselves.

Parham believed that his students were receiving a "second blessing" of the Holy Spirit, a sort of supplement to the "first blessing" that comes at baptism. The surest sign of the blessing was "speaking in tongues," talking in what sounded like a nonsense language. The phenomenon is mentioned in 1 Corinthians 12 as one of the gifts of the Spirit, and Parham soon experienced it himself and became convinced that a new movement of the Holy Spirit was afoot.

That movement burst forth at William Seymour's meetings. Three services were held every day of the week, and at them the huge congregation would shriek and wail in a feverish excitement. Before long there were miracles too, until the walls of the church were covered with the crutches of those who had been cured.

Perhaps the most striking thing about these meetings was the way they overcame the racial barriers that were prevalent at the time. William Seymour was a black man, but he had been allowed to attend Parham's largely white Bible classes. Most of the worshipers at Azusa Street were black too, but there were plenty of white faces in the crowd. As Frank Bartleman, the most important chronicler of these events, put it, "the color line has been washed away in the Blood."

Jürgen Moltmann

Jürgen Moltmann is one of the most important theologians writing today. Together with Wolfhart Pannenberg, he has developed the insights of 19th- and 20th-century theology in strikingly creative ways and opened whole new avenues of possibility for the future of Christian thought.

Life

Jürgen Moltmann was born in 1926 and studied at several German universities

The dramatic ministries of Parham and Seymour are usually taken to mark the beginning of the Pentecostal movement. The movement takes its name from the Day of Pentecost, when, according to the opening chapters of Acts, the Holy Spirit descended on the apostles and gave them the ability to preach to huge crowds in unfamiliar languages. In fact, of course, Pentecostalism had roots much further back than Parham: it grew out of 19th-century evangelicalism and ultimately traced its heritage to John Wesley and the revivals of the 18th and early 19th centuries. There had been dramatic signs of the "second blessing" even before Parham and Seymour, but it was only in the 20th century that the movement really spread throughout America. By the 1950s it had begun to penetrate the mainstream churches—Lutherans, Anglicans and Roman Catholics. Because of its transdenominational nature, this new wave of Pentecostalism, sometimes called neo-Pentecostalism or the charismatic renewal, has been much less doctrinally uniform than the earlier Pentecostals; in particular, the strict theology of "two blessings" is much more relaxed, and it is no longer normally claimed that those who lack the gift of tongues lack the Holy Spirit.

In general, Pentecostalism and the charismatic movement have had little direct influence on theology, because of their dogmatic vagueness. From a purely doctrinal point of view, the movement's theology is very similar to that of evangelicalism, apart from the extra emphasis on the role on the Holy Spirit. However, the sheer scale of the movement means that it does raise issues for theologians. There are an estimated 100 million members of the charismatic movement today, and that alone means that theologians need to pay special attention to the nature and role of the Holy Spirit in the church.

before shooting to theological prominence in 1964 with *Theology of Hope.* The book's translation into English in 1967 marked the appearance of a new kind of theology, a theology that arose from the ashes of modernism and the "death of God" of the 1960s and that sought to avoid both world-denying Barthianism and navel-gazing existentialism. The subsequent appearance of *The Crucified God* in 1972 and *The Church in the Power of the Spirit* in 1975 completed the trilogy. Since 1967 Moltmann has been professor of systematic theology at the University of Tübingen.

Thought

The three titles of Moltmann's early trilogy are the key to his thought, a profoundly trinitarian theology that revolves around "the crucified God." Moltmann represents the pinnacle of the Protestant trend that I have traced from Luther and Calvin through Schleiermacher to Barth—the insistence that all Christian doctrine must revolve around Christ. In Moltmann this idea reaches a peak that none of those earlier theologians could have imagined.

The centrality of the cross. We have seen how medieval theologians such as Thomas Aquinas sought to explain the relationship between the two sources of knowledge of God: reason and revelation. Aquinas argued that reason is a valid source of knowledge, but it is "completed," or surpassed, by revelation. So we can know of God's existence by looking at the world around us, but revelation then moves beyond this and tells us that God is a Trinity and that he became incarnate in Christ. In other words, we begin with a certain notion of God and then have this notion modified by the Christian message. We learn that God the Creator is also God the Redeemer.

Moltmann turns this on its head. He argues that Christ is the starting point for our understanding of God. In other words, instead of starting with an idea of God and then modifying it by reference to Christ, we simply point to Christ and say, "That is what God is like."

In saying this Moltmann is taking his cue from Karl Barth, who, as we have seen, profoundly rejects natural theology, the idea that we can have any knowledge of God apart from revelation. But Moltmann uses the idea quite differently from Barth. For Barth it meant that God is profoundly different from the world, exalted to an unimaginable degree. Moltmann, by contrast, points out that the most obvious characteristic of Christ is that he suffers and dies. So if we are really serious about treating Christ as our window into God's nature, then we must accept that this is true of God too. And not only that: if Christ is our *primary* source of information on God, then it means that suffering is God's *prime* quality. It is in suffering that God is most Godlike. As Moltmann puts it, "Christ's surrender of himself to a Godforsaken death reveals the secret of the cross and with it the secret of God himself. It is the open secret of the Trinity" (*The Church in the Power of the Spirit*, p. 95).

This is a direct reversion of the traditional assumption that it is a problem somehow to talk about God as suffering. In fact, traditionally it is heresy to describe the divine nature itself as suffering; only the Second Person of the Trinity suffers, and he does so only "as" human, his divine nature somehow standing aloof from it all. Moltmann is having none of this. For him, God intrinsically suffers.

This, of course, radically distances him from Barth, who stresses the differences between God and humanity. It is not for nothing that Moltmann's theology is sometimes called "cross theology."

This emphasis makes Moltmann's thought rather like liberation theology, and indeed Moltmann does use it as a profound response to human suffering. In response to those who say that God does nothing to relieve human suffering, Moltmann can point out that God is not a detached observer. He himself suffers right along with us.

Moltmann holds this stress on the divinity of Christ being manifested through his suffering together with a wholly trinitarian outlook. In this respect he is very much in line with Barth. Christ is not simplistically identified with God; rather, he is the Second Person of the Trinity, and all three members suffer, although in different ways. Moltmann understands this to be a consequence of the close relations between the Persons as well as between each of the Persons and the world. Here he is dwelling on the trinitarian theology of the Cappadocian fathers, who described the differences between the Father, Son and Holy Spirit as consisting solely in their mutual relations. For Moltmann, what this essentially means is that each member of the Trinity exists not in isolation but in a state of fundamental openness to each other and to the world. In other words, God is love—and he takes upon himself what we suffer.

But there is more. Christ did not just die; he was also raised up. There is a fundamental paradox here, a dialectic that goes to the heart of human experience and the heart of God. It is the distinction between the "now" and the "not yet." And the fact that God has raised the One who died is why Moltmann's theology is also known as "theology of hope." God is not just the God of suffering, he is also the God of resurrection—and Moltmann ties this in with the New Testament emphasis on eschatology, the coming end of the world.

Theology of hope. How is this possible? Didn't Schweitzer show that Jesus was an eschatological prophet, a deluded fanatic who is incomprehensible and rather repulsive to modern sensibilities? Moltmann thinks not. In fact, he thinks that the eschatological message of Jesus and the first Christians is more relevant today than ever. Instead of being a liability to Christianity, its eschatological message is what makes it relevant. It is a real message, not one to be demythologized as Bultmann thought, but proclaimed in its reality. So Moltmann does for eschatology what Barth did for the Trinity. He rescues what had been a marginalized embarrassment to Christian doctrine and makes it the centerpiece of his theology:

The eschatological is not one element of Christianity, but it is the medium

of Christian faith as such, the key in which everything in it is set, the glow
that suffuses everything here in the dawn of an expected new day. For Christian faith lives from the raising of the crucified Christ, and strains after the
promises of the universal future of Christ. Eschatology is the passionate suffering and passionate longing kindled by the Messiah. Hence eschatology
cannot really be only a part of Christian doctrine. Rather, the eschatological
outlook is characteristic of all Christian proclamation, of every Christian existence and of the whole Church.
Theology of Hope, p. 16

This is all grounded firmly in Christ, and specifically in Christ's death and resurrection. The Christian message is a message of hope because the Christ who died
was raised again. The same will happen to the world—it will be transformed and
raised up. Moltmann conceives of salvation in universal terms, the extension to the
whole of creation of what God has done in Christ. So for Moltmann the universe
itself, and its destiny, is all understood christologically.

Reflections

Moltmann's theology is among the most powerful and inspiring of the second half
of the 20th century. It builds on the insights of Barth and Bonhoeffer but goes beyond them in its profound insights into the nature of God and salvation. At the
same time, Moltmann seeks to describe a Christian vision that tackles contemporary problems but does so creatively, not becoming mired in the thought structure
and jargon of contemporary—and therefore temporary—culture, as Tillich did.
However, there are certain problems with it.

The central problem concerns Moltmann's claim that *all* our knowledge of God
comes from Christ. It has been pointed out that if this is so then there is nothing
shocking about the cross. That is, if the first thing we learn about God is that he
suffers, then there is nothing interesting about the claim "God suffers." There is
something more arresting about the claim if we already have some idea of who or
what God is—the Creator of the universe. To be told that the Creator also suffers
is certainly arresting. This at least is the more biblical way of thinking; consider the
book of Romans, which begins in chapter 1 with the claim that everyone knows
about God and moves on to the cross only in chapter 5.

To put it another way, if God intrinsically suffers *anyway*, then the cross does not
achieve anything new. If the cross is a window into God's inmost nature, then it is
not a force that acts on God and somehow changes his relationship to the world.
Paradoxically, by seeking to place the cross at the very center of his theology, Molt-

mann may have robbed it of some of its power.

We might also ask just how powerful Moltmann's message of hope is to those who suffer. He tells us that God himself enters into our suffering and takes it upon himself. But is this really an answer? If I feel ill, I do not want the doctor to say, "Oh yes, I have the same symptoms too. I wonder what it is." I want him to cure me. Sympathy is all very well, but it does not achieve anything. Moltmann's answer, of course, is that the Christ who dies is the Christ who rises; and eschatology gives us a vision of hope for the future. But that does not explain why we are suffering now. Surely an omnipotent God would be able to arrange matters so that no suffering right now is required? The problem is hardly a new one—and if we think that Moltmann does not provide a logically watertight answer, we can hardly blame him for that. But we may still wonder how much real comfort his answer might provide for those who suffer.

Feminist Theology

The reader cannot have failed to notice that nearly all the names mentioned in this book are male. Today this is recognized as a serious problem. There have of course been many female saints, and some of the greatest names in theology, including Gregory of Nyssa, Jerome and Augustine, have been closely associated with pious women. But it is quite clear that throughout Christian history women have taken a decidedly back-seat role. Even today no females are allowed on Mount Athos, the holy mountain of Greek Orthodoxy—unless they are cats.

And this is not simply a historical accident but something that has been aided and abetted by Christian theology itself. Christian theologians have always been quick to notice that Adam would never have sinned if Eve had not egged him on and that Eve was in any case a sort of "Adam, version" created for his benefit. The view is especially associated with Aquinas, but even in recent times it was maintained by Barth, and both of these theologians are particular bogeymen in the eyes of modern feminists. The other major woman in the Bible is of course the Virgin Mary, who plays only a supporting role to the male Jesus and whose virtue consists of being self-effacing and obedient. These two images of women—Eve the sinner and Mary the saintly mother—have played central roles in Christian thought ever since Irenaeus. And of course not only was Jesus a man, and all the apostles were men, but God himself is virtually always represented as male in the Bible. These ideas, together with the assumptions of ancient philosophy that men are naturally superior to women, lie behind the continued refusal of the Roman Catholic and Orthodox churches to consider the possibility that women might ever be ordained.

In the late 20th century and the early 21st feminist theologians have protested bitterly at all this. They have exposed Christianity as preaching a dominating God, one who oppresses marginalized groups like women, racial minorities, the working classes and so on. They have criticized the notion of many Christian thinkers, especially in the Protestant tradition, that sin is essentially pride and have argued that as far as women go a bit *more* pride would be a good idea. They have bitterly attacked the idea that women should model themselves after the humble, obedient, virginal Mother of God.

In this respect feminist theology is closely allied to liberation theology. But it has followed a significant constructive agenda. On the one hand, feminist biblical scholars and historians have sought to unearth and reclaim the forgotten women in Christian history, such as Hildegard of Bingen and Julian of Norwich. And on the other, they have set about creating a new feminist theology.

The most central and well-known aspect of this concerns God. Why has God

POSTMODERNISM

Postmodernism has been the most important intellectual movement to emerge since World War II. Unfortunately, no one is quite sure exactly what it is—least of all the postmodernists themselves.

It is not a single movement but a general term for a wide variety of trends and claims that have occurred across all disciplines in recent decades. Their adherents are united, however, in their belief that the "modern" period is at an end, and with it all the old certainties.

The "modern" period, in this context, means the Renaissance and above all the Enlightenment. It means the Age of Reason, when intellectuals believed in human progress and the ability of human reason to solve all problems, when the world was an ordered place and people knew what was what.

Now this has all changed. In the wake of two world wars and the Holocaust and under the shadow of the possibility of nuclear war, the 20th century saw the old certainties stripped away. The existentialists showed that human existence is a matter of stark choices in an objectively meaningless world.

The essence of postmodernism, in response to all this, is that there are no certainties anymore, and there never really were in the first place. Jacques Derrida, probably the best-known thinker to be called a postmodernist, describes

always been thought of as male? Why should he not also be described as female? Some theologians have therefore experimented with the idea of a female God. God can be Mother as well as Father. The traditional Trinity of Father, Son and Holy Spirit is replaced by one of Mother, Lover and Friend. Those who advocate such changes respond to criticism that their language is neither biblical nor traditional by arguing that it is a modern way of expressing the biblical insights that God is a loving Creator. Much is made of the fact that *ruach*, the Hebrew word for "spirit," is feminine, although this argument is fairly limited given that the same could be said of the Greek *hamartia*, meaning "sin"! Some theologians therefore claim that the whole issue is unresolvable and that using parental terms for God is inherently misguided anyway because it perpetuates the idea of God as somehow dominant. Rosemary Radford Ruether, the most prominent feminist theologian, argues that there is no acceptable name for God at all at the moment.

However, the approach is by no means new. In the Middle Ages the idea of Jesus

the fundamental mistake of Western thought in the past as what he calls "logocentrism"—the elevation of one idea or principle to a level of unassailable certainty. Modernism's logos was reason, and before that it was God

Instead of succumbing to logocentrism, postmodernists insist, we must realize that there are no absolutes—or if there are, we cannot know them. Postmodernism is often associated with relativism, the belief that there is no such thing as truth and that every point of view is equally valid. But one certainly does not have to be a relativist to be a postmodernist, and it is far from clear whether relativism is really coherent or even consistently expressible at all.

Instead of making such sweeping claims about the nature of truth, many postmodernists prefer to focus on difficulties of communication. They point out that words do not have fixed meanings: the meaning of any word is determined at least partly by its context and its relation to other words. There is no fixed link between a word and what it refers to; indeed, words refer only to other words, as you can see if you look in a dictionary. There is no objective meaning that is transferred from an author of a text to the readers of the text: each reader must construct their own meaning. In effect, everyone creates their own text from the author's words. This idea is often ex-as a Mother was common among spiritual writers, who derived profound mysticism from the notion of being nourished by the blood flowing from his side just as an infant feeds on its mother's milk. This idea of the femaleness of Jesus is taken up by some modern theologians. While Jesus was obviously a man, it can be said that his maleness was of a kind that subverted traditional patriarchy: instead of dominating others he served them, and instead of shunning "sinful" women he welcomed them. His death was the death of patriarchy, and after his resurrection (which was first revealed to his female followers) God's grace was poured out on all people irrespective of gender or race. Galatians 3:28 states that in Christ there is no such thing as Jew or Gentile, slave or master, male or female.

Wolfhart Pannenberg

Wolfhart Pannenberg's work is a distillation and reflection of the great insights of 20th-century theology, but it also seeks to correct the one-sidedness of these traditions.

Life

Pannenberg has led the outwardly uneventful life of the career scholar. Born in

---

pressed in the use of irony. Postmodernist writers, artists and filmmakers stretch and deliberately break the conventions of their genres, pointing out that conventions are just that and have no objective reality. Through techniques like painting impossible objects, telling inconsistent narratives or having their characters discuss the film they are in, postmodernists invite the reader or viewer to interpret the text in their own way, and they delight in showing up their own falsity or artificiality.

The relevance of all this to theology is clear. The claim that there are no certain authorities, that a text has no objective reality, that meaning varies from person to person and even from sentence to sentence—all of this requires a rethinking of traditional Christian ideas. Nevertheless, it is debatable how much of an effect postmodernism has really had on recent theology. While its ideas are obviously anathema to, say, traditional Roman Catholicism of the Vatican I variety, the ideas of unassailable authority and a wholly objective God have hardly been unquestioned in modern theology since at least Schleiermacher. And modern biblical criticism has long since dispelled the myth of a determinative, unambiguous text. So the criticisms of postmodernism are not, perhaps, as unexpected and shocking to

1928 in Stettin, Germany, he studied at several universities after World War II—including Basel, under Karl Barth. In 1961 he edited a book titled *Revelation as History*, in which he and a group of other young theologians rejected the basic assumptions of Barth's and Bultmann's theologies and sought to place theology on a new footing. Pannenberg thus emerged not only as the leader of this "Pannenberg Circle" but as an important and distinctive new voice in Protestant thought. Since then he has taught at several universities and has been an institution at the University of Munich since 1968. His *Systematic Theology*, published in three volumes in the 1990s, was one of the most eagerly anticipated Christian publishing events in that decade and was received as the most important work of dogmatics since Tillich, or perhaps even since Barth.

Thought

The essence of Pannenberg's theology can be summed up in one word: history. Throughout his work he has argued that this is what theology is all about. His thought is the most sustained attempt yet to deal creatively with the challenge posed to traditional theology by Lessing, and it offers bold new directions for escaping the impasse that the Enlightenment continues to cause Christian thought.

theologians as they might appear at first glance.

In effect, it might almost be said that if the Enlightenment criticized religion for failing to live up to the exacting objective standards of contemporary culture, culture has now realized that religion was right all along in maintaining that such standards are impossible. At any rate, modern theologians certainly engage with postmodern thinkers and are happy to use their insights in their work—but they hardly allow their agendas to be determined by postmodernism.

Besides, no one really knows how important postmodernism will turn out to be in the long run. Postmodern is an enormously overused word, and one that (in a suitably ironic postmodern way) never means the same thing twice. And the influence of postmodern ideas is often overstated. If you ask most scientists whether they think their work is purely metaphorical and they are not discovering objective facts about the world, they are likely to give a fairly definite answer. The Age of Reason is still alive and well in many more quarters than one might think. Whether postmodernism really is the dawning of a new intellectual and cultural age or simply a passing trendy fad, only time will tell.

This emphasis on history means breaking significantly with much modern theology. Pannenberg rejects the approach of Schleiermacher, because it bases theology on personal experience, basing faith, in effect, on faith. The same is true of the individualistic existentialism of Tillich. Even more radical is Pannenberg's rejection of Bultmann. He argues that Bultmann's distinction between "the historical" and "the historic" is not an attempt to deal with the problems of history but an avoidance of them—it is a fancy way of saying that history is not important. What matters for Bultmann is not what happened but what we like to imagine happened; and that is no basis for Christian faith.

Pannenberg is happier with Barth's insistence on the objective nature of revelation as something given by God—the self-revelation of God. But he does not like Barth's emphasis on the "Word" as the vehicle and content of this revelation. That seems to seal revelation off from history, making it a special, one-time supernatural happening that cannot be investigated like a normal historical event.

What Pannenberg proposes instead is much more ambitious. He suggests that we think of the *whole* of history as revelation. That is, there is no radical difference between ordinary events and miraculous ones: on the contrary, it is through the ordinary that God works, as Schleiermacher and Bonhoeffer both insisted. But we must have faith to appreciate this fact. History makes sense only through its interpretation, and without someone to appreciate it, it would be meaningless. So does this mean that faith is just a matter of subjective interpretation? Is God's action not objective and real? Not at all. The situation is rather like appreciating art. A work of art, however great, would be nothing without people to appreciate it; beauty is in the eye of the beholder. But at the same time, it makes sense to evaluate artworks and to describe some as especially great. In the same way, if there were no one to reflect on history and see God's hand in it, then there would be nothing to see. But in fact we do reflect on history, and we do see God's hand in it, and we are right to do so.

In a way Pannenberg's thought is a development of the religionless Christianity of Bonhoeffer. It is a radical rejection of the great dividing line that Barth drew between God and the world. It is a conviction that God is to be found *in* the world. Pannenberg insists that history *as a whole* is to be understood as revelation.

But at the same time there are certain events in history that are especially revelatory. Think, for example, of the exodus, which the Jews have interpreted as the supreme demonstration of God's saving will on their behalf. Here the hand of God was most evident, but through a historical event—the escape of a group of slaves from Egypt. And Pannenberg suggests that faith is based on events of this kind. That is, we do not have faith first and then interpret history on the basis of it; we look at history and derive faith from it.

But surely this is impossible. Didn't Lessing show that? How can religion be based on historical events that may or may not have happened? Pannenberg answers that no historical event is absolutely certain, like a mathematical theorem—but there are certainly degrees of probability. It is not *absolutely* certain that Napoleon existed, but we would be pretty daft to deny it. In the case of Jesus, there is a lower degree of probability, from the point of view of dispassionate historical analysis. We cannot be as certain of what Jesus was like or what he did as we can about Napoleon. But that does not mean that it is irrational to believe certain things about him. We trust in the uncertain every time we leave our house, and we choose to believe that our spouse loves us even when we cannot be certain of the fact. This is faith. The demand of Enlightenment thinkers like Lessing and Hume that religious truths should have the same kind of certainty as mathematical truths is simply silly.

This means that Pannenberg is happy to incorporate the findings of critical scholarship into his work. This again distinguishes him from both Barth and Bultmann. Barth was supremely uninterested in biblical scholarship, since what mattered to him was the transcendental, ahistorical Word. And Bultmann was of course interested in biblical scholarship, being a leading proponent of it; but the effect of this was to detach his theology from history by focusing on how we react to supposed past events rather than on those events themselves.

For Pannenberg, by contrast, what actually happened is of supreme importance, and he is happy to accept that we cannot be certain what happened, but we can critically weigh the evidence and choose to believe it. The best example is the resurrection of Jesus. Pannenberg believes that the evidence supports the Christian belief in this as an actual historical event. Where many New Testament scholars have suggested that the story of the empty tomb is a reflection of the faith of the early church, Pannenberg insists that the story—and the reality behind it—are the *foundation* of that faith.

What that reality is, however, is unclear, and Pannenberg's emphasis on this point distinguishes his approach from what some theologians, such as Bultmann and Tillich, would regard as rather naive. The idea of Jesus' bodily resurrection is symbolic, although exactly what it symbolizes is very unclear. Pannenberg stresses that we must understand it in terms of the worldview of Jesus himself and his disciples, the worldview of ancient Jewish apocalyptic. In his emphasis here Pannenberg is quite similar to Moltmann. Jesus' resurrection is, at heart, about our own resurrection at the end of time. It is a foretaste of the culmination of history. As Pannenberg writes:

All theological questions and answers are meaningful only within the framework of the history which God has with humanity and through humanity with his whole creation—the history moving toward a future still hidden from the world but already revealed in Jesus Christ.
Basic Questions in Theology, 1:15

So it all comes back to history again, the whole sweep of history. We cannot properly understand a book until we get to the end of it, and similarly life will always be confusing until history comes to an end and we see what it all meant. But we have been given a sneak preview of that end in the resurrection of Jesus. So Christology is grounded in history, and history is grounded in Christology. This profound sense of the universal significance of Christ is almost a modern restatement of the theology of Irenaeus.

Pannenberg's work represents a real engagement with the issues and methods of modern culture. If Barth is a radical rejection of contemporary culture and Tillich is an overreliance on it, then Pannenberg is a critical but sympathetic engagement with it. He uses the insights and methods of history while still criticizing them; his belief that history makes sense only in the realm of faith represents a profound understanding of the relationship between history and religion. History is based on faith, as well as vice versa. Pannenberg has not only answered Lessing's question, he has turned it upside down.

African Christianity

Christian theology was virtually invented in Africa; few other places can claim theologians of the stature of Tertullian, Origen and Augustine. But after the 5th century, with the collapse of the Roman empire, the continent largely dropped out of the Christian consciousness. The invasion of the Muslims in the 7th century, reducing the Monophysite and Nestorian churches to embattled minorities, completed the transformation. Coptic Christianity survived only in Ethiopia, which had originally been converted by missionaries sent by Athanasius in the 4th century.

It was European expansion and conquest in modern times that brought Christianity back to most of the continent, beginning with the explorers of the 15th century who sailed down the western coast in an attempt to reach the Orient. Along the way they preached the gospel to the local people they passed. Later, in the 18th century, Christianity was spread by slaves who had worked in Europe, been freed and chose to return to Africa. Systematic evangelization began in the late 18th century, as Pietist and evangelical groups such as the Moravians felt it their duty to spread the gospel to the "dark continent." Enormous efforts were made to take their version of Christianity into the little-known interior of Africa, with great success.

Today African Christianity coexists to varying degrees with Islam. In some countries, such as the Sudan, Christianity is in danger of being eradicated. But in others it has proved enormously popular. It exists mainly in three forms—Roman Catholicism, which is broadly similar to Catholicism in other countries; Protestant denominations found in other countries, such as Anglicanism; and the African initiated churches, or AICs. The AICs are churches founded out of African missions with little or no help from outside sources. They vary enormously, from churches very like their Western Protestant equivalents to extraordinary mixtures of Christianity and traditional local religions or cults. Members of the AICs often share the deeply spiritualist outlook of their non-Christian neighbors but still reject traditional pagan practices as witchcraft and try to differentiate themselves as much as possible, sometimes wearing different clothes or observing dietary regulations.

There is, then, something of a highly supernaturalist approach to Christianity in Africa, with strong charismatic, informal tendencies, and this applies to the mainstream Protestant churches as well. Pentecostalism is a powerful force in these churches. Doctrinally they are often highly conservative and evangelical, a legacy from the evangelical missionaries of the 19th century. This has sometimes led to tensions, because many of the African churches are Anglican (or Episcopalian), in communion with the Church of England, and when the African clergy and bishops have met up with their English and American counterparts, the conservative views of the former have been known to clash with the more liberal outlook of the latter, especially over such matters as women and homosexuality.

Nevertheless, there have been over the past century important developments within African theology. One of the most curious was apartheid theology, which provided a theological rationale for the racism of South Africa. The country's Dutch heritage meant that Calvinism was the dominant tradition there, and the apartheid theologians argued that separation of different races was part of God's predestined plan for humanity. They accepted that there was a unity of all the elect, of whatever race, but that this does not override the barriers God has set up within nature.

It hardly needs to be said that apartheid theology is not exactly fashionable today and that many Christians strongly opposed it during its heyday. The 1960s saw the rise of South African confessing theology, which was consciously inspired by the Confessing Church of Barth and Bonhoeffer that stood up to the influence of Nazism in German Christianity in the 1930s. Thinkers in this tradition seek to create a theology that celebrates black culture and empowers it, and in this respect it has much in common with liberation theology. Indeed, African black theology is very similar to the North American version, seeing blackness as a symbol for the poor and downtrodden with whom God identifies. It is often known as *contextual theology*, meaning it tries to forge a theology that speaks to the context of modern South Africans.

A more distinctive theology has risen in recent years since the publication in 1985 of the Kairos Document by the Institute for Contextual Theology. The document aimed to find new ways to oppose apartheid theology and suggested a new "prophetic theology" that might manage to do this. The notion of *kairos* means moments of opportunity that may be seized prophetically by socially minded Christians. It is a theology that brings a message of hope to the oppressed rather than wasting time trying to appease or persuade the oppressors. Prophetic theology is thus a kind of alliance of liberation theology with the charismatic tradition and has strong evangelical ties. Its best-known representative is Desmond Tutu, the former Anglican archbishop of Capetown.

Asian Christianity

In Asia, Christians have been forced to confront totally different issues from their colleagues in Europe. Asian Christianity has always been a minority faith, struggling to define itself in relation to older, more established religions. Today the solutions that different individuals and communities have found are of more than academic interest to the West, where Christianity is once again becoming a minority faith.

Christianity was introduced into China in the 5th and 6th centuries—not by Catholics or Orthodox but by the Nestorian Church, which, after splitting off from Orthodoxy in the 5th century, began to spread eastward. One of the heroes of this early period was a Nestorian monk named Olopen, who in the 7th century was a revered visitor to the court of Emperor Tang Taizhong. The Nestorian Church seems to have been mistaken for a kind of Buddhist sect and was known as Jinjaio; it suffered when Buddhism was banned by Wu Zhong, and it largely—although not completely—died out.

The 16th and 17th centuries saw renewed attempts to introduce Christianity to the East, especially by Catholic missionaries, above all the Jesuits. In China none of these attempts was very successful, and in 1616 Catholicism was banned and all the missionaries sent home. Japan, by contrast, was more welcoming, at least initially. The great Jesuit missionary Francis Xavier arrived at Kagoshima in 1549, and the "Kirishitan" faith proved very popular as the Japanese welcomed the introduction of Western ideas. By the end of the century there were 300,000 Christians in Japan. Nevertheless, it was far from uncontroversial, and the Christians suffered periodic persecution, the worst incident coming in 1597, when twenty-six Japanese and foreign Christians were crucified in Nagasaki.

In 1614 Christianity was banned throughout Japan. Fifty-one more Christians were martyred at Nagasaki in 1622, and two years later fifty were burned alive at Edo. By the end of the 1630s Japan had expelled all the missionaries and closed its doors to the West completely. Christianity was driven underground, but it survived.

In contemporary times Christianity has found that the best way to survive in Asian cultures is to change to match those cultures—exactly as it did in late antiquity in the Mediterranean world. In India, which has a strong Anglican tradition as a legacy of British rule in addition to the much older Nestorian Church, Christian priests and worshipers alike remove their shoes before entering a church and are careful never to turn their backs to the altar, just as in a Hindu temple.

A more dramatic example of this approach was discovered in the 1850s and 1860s, when Japan finally ended its self-imposed exile from the outside world. To the amazement of foreign missionaries, around sixty thousand Christians were found who had kept the faith alive since the persecutions of the Kirishitan period. But their faith had undergone some serious changes. Lacking any written texts, it had been passed on secretly by word of mouth, and now the Kakure Kirishitan or Hidden Christians had lost all ecclesiastical structure, the doctrine of the Trinity and all the sacraments except for baptism and penance. Their images of Christ depicted a chubby, serene figure suspiciously similar to the Buddha. Most strikingly of all, only half of them were willing to rejoin the Catholic Church when contact was reestablished. The rest declared that the Kakure Kirishitan faith was the only authentic version of Christianity and remained separated from the church. They still exist, but in ever-dwindling numbers.

Meanwhile, mainstream Christianity was reintroduced to Asia in the late 19th century and quickly found once again that only by adapting itself to the native culture could it hope to survive. In China the Indigenizing movement made this its explicit aim, drawing on ideas from European liberal theology to present an understanding of Christianity that stressed its similarities to Confucianism. However, in the early 20th century many Chinese theologians rebelled against this, just as Barth was rebelling against liberalism in Europe.

In 1920 the Apologetic Group was formed in Beijing, with the aim of presenting Christianity not as a kind of variation on Chinese culture but as the solution to the problems raised by culture. For theologians like T. C. Chao, the leading spokesman of this group, Christianity's virtues lay in its differences from traditional Chinese culture. Chao stressed the centrality of the personality of Christ, a human being who becomes suffused with God's love, the concretizing of God and the source of the possibility of reintegration of the human personality. Clearly European theological ideas were an important influence here. Others, however, stressed the political implications of Christianity. Lei-ch'uan, who taught at Yenching University in the 1920s and 1930s, pointed out that Jesus was a political and social reformer who identified with the poor and called for the abolition of private property. While there are obvious similarities to the Communism that would shortly take hold of China, these ideas are a striking anticipation of South American liberation theology.

Nevertheless, all these liberal or radical interpretations of Christianity have proved less influential in China, and other Asian countries, than a Barth-style affirmation of traditional doctrine and practice. This is found especially in Ming-tao Wang, who in his long life exercised enormous influence over the Chinese churches in the 20th century. He strongly criticized liberals for basing their Christology on the personality of Jesus as portrayed in the Gospels while ignoring the suggestions of his divinity found in the same texts, and he stressed the importance of the miraculous, especially the resurrection; here we see certain similarities to Wolfhart Pannenberg. And like Jürgen Moltmann, Wang also stressed eschatology, denouncing utopian attempts to make Christianity into a socialist movement. For him, salvation from the evils of the world happens at the individual level, not the social level, and is complete only with the future return of Christ.

EPILOGUE

This book has traced not the history of Christianity itself but the history of Christian *thought*, of Christians who have tried to reflect on the meaning of their faith and its relation to the cultural world in which they lived. And indeed, at first glance it is amazing just how different many of them are. What would St. Paul—the first and greatest Christian theologian—have thought if he could have known the extraordinary range of thinkers who would come after him, all claiming to various degrees to represent his religion? What would he have made of figures as diverse as Symeon the New Theologian, John Calvin, Tertullian, Søren Kierkegaard and Jan Hus? Would he even be able to understand their theologies, let alone judge between them?

Yet on a closer inspection, what are perhaps more remarkable than these people's differences are their similarities. Despite their very different historical circumstances and philosophical dispositions, they are all, first and foremost, *Christian* theologians. Whether Orthodox, Roman Catholic or Protestant, whether Platonist, Aristotelian or Darwinist, and whether ancient, medieval or modern, all of these thinkers ultimately draw their theology above all from the Bible and a common core of reflection upon it. From Justin Martyr to Wolfhart Pannenberg, each of these writers is concerned with the same faith. It may be surprisingly hard to state exactly what that faith is when it has taken so many different forms, but perhaps the common core is that they all have faith not in a set of doctrines but in a person, Jesus Christ, who is preached through the Bible, and that they are convinced that through him we are saved and know God. That means that there is a common standard of criticism that we can apply to them all despite their differences: How adequately do they handle that basic faith? How true are they to what we think is the heart of Christianity, and how convincingly do they draw out its consequences and relate them to the needs of their age?

Undertaking such an evaluation is of course always going to be a subjective matter, because much depends on our own point of view. If one person thinks that the Bible is the supreme authority in matters of faith while another sets great store by church tradition, then they may well prefer different theologians and have good grounds for thinking some theologians more authentically Christian than others. It is through this process of critical evaluation that the way is opened up for new theologies and theologians.

It is easy to lose sight, in examining the doctrines of the great theologians, of the fact that they do not exist in a kind of intellectual parallel universe, talking only to each other and to philosophers or other cultural figures. Every one of the figures in this book was a member of a Christian community, and indeed most of them were religious leaders of one kind or another. Their theology is an attempt to express the life of their communities in written form. In this book we have on the whole met only the greatest theologians, the most famous and influential. But behind and around them stand legions of lesser thinkers, each of whom, in his or her way, made their own contributions to the development of Christian thought. And surrounding them all are the Christian communities to which they belonged.

One of the things I have tried to show clearly in this book is the way that everyone who writes theology is rooted in their own traditions but is able to transcend them. Each of the figures who appears in this book inherited not just the Christian faith but a particular understanding of that faith, and their theology was a digestion and re-presentation of it as a response to the particular problems they were facing. At the same time they introduced innovations of their own, ensuring that the tradition that their successors inherited was not quite the same. Over the centuries the traditions change, split and branch off, and head in unexpected new directions.

What directions might they take in the future?

If there is one lesson to be drawn from the preceding pages, it is that it is impossible to tell. Origen could never have guessed at the state-sponsored glories of Byzantine theology that would come after him; Aquinas could have had no inkling of the revolution of the Reformation; and Ritschl and Schweitzer certainly did not think that 20th-century theology would take the course it did.

Today more than ever, Christian thought stands at a crossroads. For the first time since the 4th century, the Christian faith is a minority concern in Europe, even as it becomes ever more popular in Africa. But popularity and intellectual innovation do not necessarily go together; the German tradition continues to dominate the theological world, and it remains to be seen whether African theological traditions will grow to rival it. Asia, in particular, looks more poised to loom large in the theological scene in the near future. The English-speaking world remains hugely influenced by its Christian past, even as Christianity itself dwindles in influence, but it has never produced innovative and original theology on a scale like that of the German-speaking nations. What it does excel at is popular movements like Pentecostalism and evangelicalism. Perhaps the future of English-speaking theology lies in that sphere, rather than with the heirs of the Oxford Movement.

But it is impossible to predict what forms any of this might take. Is there any life left in the great Barthian tradition that so dominated the 20th century? Will theologians of the future continue to draw their inspiration from classical theology, or will they try to find something new? Only two things are certain: as long as Christianity continues to exist, theologians will seek to rewrite and re-present its claims in contemporary language; and they have a tradition of unparalleled richness and diversity to draw on to help them.

Glossary

anthropology: The study of human beings. In a Christian context, the doctrine of human nature. Theologians who have made important contributions to this area include Irenaeus, Origen, Augustine, Gregory Palamas, Schleiermacher, Kierkegaard, Niebuhr and Rahner.

apologetics: The task of presenting Christianity sympathetically to nonbelievers.

apophatic theology: A branch of mysticism that emphasizes the fact that God cannot be known. It is associated especially with Gregory of Nyssa and Pseudo-Dionysius.

apostasy: The act of betrayal—more specifically, religious betrayal, denying one's faith. The original Christian apostate was Judas Iscariot, who betrayed Christ, and such betrayal has always been regarded with special horror by Christians. The existence of apostasy has traditionally caused problems for Christian theology, especially in its early centuries when the church was persecuted: Had apostates really been Christians before their fall? What about those who repented of their apostasy and sought to return to the church?

atonement: A central doctrine of Christianity, the notion that through Christ fallen humanity has been or can be reconciled to God. Exactly how this happens, however, is open to debate, and different theologians have proposed different theories of the atonement to explain it. Some of the best known are associated with Irenaeus, Anselm, Abelard and Calvin.

Caesaropapism: The tendency in some forms of Christianity to unite church and state to such a degree that the head of state is also head of the church. It is most associated with the Byzantine empire, but it can also be seen in old Russia and, in different forms, in Calvin's Geneva, the Puritans in early North America, and the Church of England. It sometimes overlaps with Erastianism, the subjugation of the church to the state.

Christology: The doctrine of Christ. There are two parts to the doctrine: who Christ was, and what he did; but the word is often used to refer only to the former. Establishing exactly who Christ was and is and in particular how he relates to God and humanity has always been a central task of Christianity. Important theologians to deal with it include Tertullian, Origen, Athanasius, Cyril, Maximus the Confessor, Anselm, Schleiermacher and Rahner. The Council of Chalcedon represents the classical statement of the church on the subject, and the Second and Third Councils of Constantinople are also important.

cosmological argument: Any line of reasoning that aims to prove God's existence from the nature of the world—as opposed to one that aims to prove his existence from his own nature (the ontological argument). Today this is the most common method of arguing for God's existence, although its proponents rarely suggest that it definitely *proves* God's existence—rather, it gives us good reason for believing in God. The most important theologian to have relied on cosmological arguments is Aquinas.

council: A meeting of bishops or other high-ranking church leaders to settle some problem. Where the problem is doctrinal, because of the rise of some heresy, the council may well issue a creed of some kind. When the members of the council have been drawn from the whole Christian church, it is known as an ecumenical council; according to the Orthodox Church there have been seven ecumenical councils, but the Western churches recognize only the first four.

creed: A list of statements describing clearly what the author or speaker believes. Creeds have traditionally been used, consciously or otherwise, to establish the differences between insiders and outsiders. For example, the Nicene Creed was written to clarify the differences between Arians and non-Arians and to exclude the former from church membership. Many of the great creeds have been issued by councils that met for that very purpose. The most important creeds in Christian history include the Nicene Creed, first set out at the Council of Nicaea, although better known in the form established at the Council of Chalcedon. This creed is recited in churches around the world, as is the Apostles' Creed, a simpler traditional statement of belief that evolved in the early centuries of the church. There is also the Athanasian Creed, which states the doctrine of the Trinity; despite the name, this creed was actually written some centuries after Athanasius.

damnation: The doctrine that some people will not be saved but will suffer eternal punishment for their sins. Most Christians throughout history have believed this, but modern theologians usually have difficulty with it, since it seems to contradict the notion that God is love.

dialectical theology: The name given to the new theological approach of Barth and Bultmann in the early 20th century—so called because it stresses the differences between God and humanity.

docetism: The doctrine that Christ was not really human but only appeared to be (from the Greek word meaning "seeming"). Docetism is rejected by the church as heretical, but it was one of the earliest doctrines of Christ and has proved very resilient—although usually in a fairly subtle form, such as the notion that Christ's divinity is more important than his humanity or that he is not really like us. One theologian sometimes accused of this kind of docetism is Schleiermacher.

Eastern Orthodoxy: The Eastern wing of the Catholic Church, which gradually separated from the Roman Catholic Church throughout the early Middle Ages. It differs from Roman Catholicism in its emphasis on tradition rather than the authority of the church, with its ultimate authority resting in the seven ecumenical councils. It also has a much more egalitarian structure: the head of the church is the bishop of Constantinople, but he is the first among equals. Orthodox theology stresses mystery and beauty rather than rational dogma. It also tends to be much more resilient to change than Western theology, and the Orthodox Church may well have the greatest claim to be the closest in theology and practice to the early church. The most important theologians of Eastern Orthodoxy are the Cappadocian fathers and Gregory Palamas.

ecclesiology: The doctrine of the church. Theologians with a strong ecclesiology tend to emphasize the importance of the church in formulating doctrine and the importance of belonging to the church as a condition of salvation. Strong ecclesiologies are associated with Roman Catholicism and weak ones with Protestantism. Major formulators of Catholic ecclesiology include Augustine and Aquinas.

ecumenical: Concerned with all the Christian churches. The ecumenical movement aims to encourage dialogue and cooperation between the different churches, recognizing that each tradition has valuable insights to share with the others. This is not an easy matter because the whole reason that there are different churches in the first place is that they disagreed vehemently over something at some point in history. One of the most important steps forward in ecumenism was the Second Vatican Council.

eschatology: The doctrine of the end of the world (from the Greek word meaning "end"). There is a strong eschatological element in the New Testament, from Jesus' preaching of the kingdom of God to the expectation found in books like I Thessalonians that Christ would return very soon. The book of Revelation describes the events of the end times in graphic detail. Classical theology continues to affirm that Christ will reappear in glory at the end of history and judge humanity. However, the continued nonappearance of Christ has led many theologians either to downplay this doctrine or to reinterpret it entirely. Theologians in this camp include Ritschl, Bultmann and Tillich. Others, however, including Schweitzer and Moltmann, have sought to reestablish eschatology as a central theme of Christianity.

ethics: How we lead our lives—or more specifically, how we try to lead our lives in the "right" way. This has always been a central concern of Christianity, as in other religions. Some theologians, notably Kant and Ritschl, have argued that this is in fact what Christianity is. Other theologians to give a special prominence to ethics in their thought include Abelard, Calvin, Schweitzer, Bonhoeffer and Niebuhr.

Eucharist: The central act of worship in Christianity, also known as Communion, or (in Roman Catholicism) the Mass. The priest blesses bread and wine, which are then consumed by the congregation. The service follows the pattern of the Last Supper as recorded in the Gospels and I Corinthians, when Jesus blessed bread and wine and described them as his body and blood. Exactly what this means is a matter of great debate. To Roman Catholics, the bread and the wine actually become Christ's body and blood at the moment when the priest repeats Christ's words. Most Protestants reject this as superstition, and many claim instead that the bread and wine stay that way and serve only as memorials of Christ's sacrifice. In particular, they reject the Catholic belief that the Eucharist is itself a sacrifice offered by the priest. Protestants argue that this diminishes the centrality of Christ's sacrifice. Catholics reply that it is not an independent sacrifice but a sharing and re-presentation of what Christ did. Important theologians to have written on the Eucharist include Augustine, Aquinas, Luther and Calvin.

evangelism: The task of preaching Christianity to those outside the church. The word *evangelism* should not be confused with *evangelicalism*, which is a particular kind of Christianity—although, to add to the confusion, evangelicals are traditionally especially concerned with evangelism.

faith: This can mean many things: simple belief in God; belief in a certain set of statements, such as the Nicene Creed; or, more profoundly, an attitude of trust and dependency on God. It is an especially important notion to Protestants, who since Luther have stressed that it is only through faith that we can be saved. Important theologians to have dealt especially with faith include Luther, Calvin, Wesley, Kierkegaard and Tillich.

Fall: The doctrine that at some primeval stage in history humanity did something terrible that damned the race for all eternity. This is the event described in the third chapter of Genesis, where Adam and Eve are persuaded by the serpent to eat the fruit of the tree of knowledge and are subsequently cast out of the Garden of Eden. It was this event that Christ came to reverse. The doctrine is associated with the doctrine of original sin and has proved especially influential in Western Christianity, less so in the East. Today it is especially questioned because it seems to rely on the claim that Adam and Eve were real people and that human beings started off good but went bad—claims that modern science appears to contradict strongly. Important theologians to deal with the fall include Irenaeus, Augustine and Calvin.

free will: The doctrine that human beings are free to choose good and evil, that God does not force them one way or the other. The doctrine was important to Christians in early centuries, who inherited it from Platonism, but was later downgraded in favor of a more predestination-oriented outlook. Important theologians to defend the doctrine include Irenaeus, Origen, Gregory of Nyssa and Augustine.

God: One of the central elements of Christianity and other Western religions. God is the Creator of the universe and the ultimate object of worship and praise. Christians regard God as not only Creator but also Savior, and this is traditionally achieved, first, by understanding God as a Trinity and second, by identifying one member of the Trinity with Jesus Christ. Different theologians have described God in quite different ways: some have regarded him as material, others as immaterial; some have described him in positive terms, others in negative terms. Important theologians to focus especially on the nature of God (apart from the Trinity) include Irenaeus, Tertullian, Origen, Gregory of Nyssa, Pseudo-Dionysius, Gregory Palamas, Aquinas, Scotus, Schleiermacher, Barth, Bultmann, Tillich and Moltmann.

grace: The action of God that saves us, even though we do not deserve it. Theologians who emphasize grace tend to downplay free will and favor predestination. In Catholicism, grace tends to be understood as existing primarily in the context of the church and is administered through the sacraments; in Protestantism, grace is more likely to be understood as a matter between God and the individual directly. The most important theologian to write on the subject is Augustine, but Calvin and Barth are also important.

heresy: Any doctrine that deviates from orthodoxy. The term comes from a Greek word meaning "choice." Often it is applied to a doctrine only retroactively; that is, there may be no definitive orthodox position on a particular topic until somebody starts an argument about it. Eventually one side wins and becomes orthodoxy, and the other loses and becomes heresy. Other times, however, there is a defined orthodoxy, and heresy appears when people consciously protest against it. Some of the most important heresies of the past include docetism, Gnosticism, Arianism, Pelagianism, Nestorianism, Monophysitism and Monotheletism. However, in modern times many theologians have sought to go beyond the orthodoxy-heresy disjunction and tried to understand the heretics of old more sympathetically.

humanism: An important movement of the Renaissance that stresses the value of human achievements quite apart from their religious dimension. By resuscitating the study of antiquity and the origins of Christianity, the movement prepared the ground for the Reformation.

incarnation: The doctrine that in Jesus Christ God became human. This is one of the most central doctrines of Christianity, and it represents a basic affirmation of the goodness of the material world. How God became man and what it means to say that have been much debated over the centuries. Important theologians to have focused on this topic include Irenaeus, Athanasius, Maximus the Confessor, Anselm, Schleiermacher, Ritschl and Pannenberg.

Jesus: The founder of Christianity, Jesus lived in Palestine, probably from about 4 B.C. to about A.D. 30. Although he was crucified by the Romans, his followers believed that he had been raised up again and would return soon, and it was this faith that became Christianity. A distinction is sometimes made between Jesus the historical individual and Christ the divine figure who is worshiped by Christians and who appears in theological writing. Are they the same person, or do they actually have very little to do with each other? The point is that christological doctrines often seem rather abstract and may have little basis in the Jesus of history, about whom not an enormous amount is known. This distinction between "the historical Jesus" and "the Christ of faith" has been used constructively by some theologians, such as Bultmann and Tillich, but others, such as Pannenberg, feel it to be artificial and seek to unite them by basing Christian faith on the real Jesus of history.

justification: The doctrine that God cancels out our sin and makes us fit to be saved. The idea is one way of approaching the doctrine of the atonement.

kingdom of God: According to the first three Gospels, Jesus spent most of his time preaching that the kingdom of God was coming. Since the kingdom of God is mentioned very rarely by other New Testament authors, theologians have often found it hard to give it as prominent a place in their thought as Jesus himself did. They also differ over its meaning. Some, notably Schweitzer and Moltmann, have interpreted it eschatologically to mean that God will shortly intervene in history. Others have interpreted it to refer to a human society on earth, such as the church. This idea has its roots in Augustine and is found most clearly in Ritschl.

liberalism: A very vague term, sometimes used as an insult, as one step (and that a small one) removed from heresy. Generally, a "liberal" outlook does not regard traditional orthodoxy as infallible and seeks to reinterpret or even discard old doctrines where they seem problematic. In particular, it is used to refer to the school of 19th-century German theology associated with Schleiermacher and Ritschl, but more generally it could be applied to any of the Protestant theologians described in this book who come after them (with the possible exception of Barth).

Logos: A Greek word meaning "word," "speech," "discourse," "principle" and so on. In the philosophy of late antiquity it was used to refer to a lesser God who mediates between the high God and the world and who keeps the world running properly. The opening verses of John's Gospel apply the idea to Christ, and early theologians did the same thing. Logos theology was the forerunner of the doctrine of the Trinity and was gradually replaced by it. The most important theologian in its development is Justin Martyr.

Monophysitism: The doctrine that Christ had only one nature, not two. The Monophysites rejected the Council of Chalcedon and split away to form one of the two Coptic churches. The Orthodox Church hoped for some centuries to win them back to the fold, and this influenced the development of Byzantine theology.

mysticism: A mystic is someone who goes beyond normal understanding and experience to penetrate into deeper realities. In a Christian context, this means someone who undergoes an intense experience of union or closeness with God, or Christ, or perhaps the Virgin Mary or other saints. Mysticism has been an important influence on theology, since many great theologians have also been great mystics and their theology has been an attempt to set out what they experienced. Among the most important mystical theologians are Origen, Gregory of Nyssa, Augustine, Pseudo-Dionysius, Maximus the Confessor, Symeon the New Theologian, Gregory Palamas and Bonaventure.

myth: A story with a deeper meaning that reflects some profound truth about the world and humanity's place within it. A myth may be something that actually happened, but its importance lies in its ability to help those who tell and hear it to make sense of the world. The great stories of Christianity—Adam and Eve, the exodus, the life, death and resurrection of Christ—are all myths in this sense. Modern theologians have shown a new interest in understanding the nature of myth and understanding Christianity in this sense; among them are Bultmann, Tillich and Pannenberg.

natural theology: The belief that God can be known about independent of revelation, through looking at the world or using human reason. Natural theology is associated especially with the medieval theologians, particularly Anselm and Aquinas, and was also common in the Enlightenment. The philosophy of Kant showed up serious holes in much traditional natural theology, however. The crusade against natural theology is especially associated with Barth.

neo-orthodoxy: A name given to Barth's theological approach, because it aimed to rehabilitate traditional doctrines such as the Trinity and the Chalcedonian understanding of Christ that had been abandoned by 19th-century liberalism.

Nestorianism: The heretical doctrine that Christ's two natures are so distinct as almost to be separate persons. The Nestorians refused to accept the Council of Ephesus and split off from Orthodoxy as one of the Coptic churches. They were subsequently very important in bringing Christianity to Asia and the Indian subcontinent.

New Testament: A collection of twenty-seven books written in the hundred years or so after Jesus' death. Together with the Hebrew Scriptures (the Old Testament) they form the Christian Bible. The most important elements of the New Testament are the four Gospels—books describing Jesus and what he did—and the letters of Paul, a missionary who set out the basic doctrines of Christianity.

Nonconformists: British members of churches other than the Church of England—most commonly, Methodists and Baptists.

ontological argument: A form of reasoning that aims to prove God's existence through an analysis of the word *God* (ontology means "being"). The argument was formulated by Anselm and was later adapted by the rationalist philosophers Descartes, Spinoza and Leibniz but was greatly criticized by Kant. Since then it has been very unfashionable, although attempts are sometimes made to revive it.

original sin: The doctrine that the fall of Adam and Eve contaminated them and their descendants to such a degree that human beings cannot help sinning. It is important to distinguish between two versions of the doctrine. On the one hand, there is original sin as a force, a kind of inherited genetic disorder that pollutes free will and causes the sufferer to sin. On the other, there is the idea that Adam and Eve's descendants inherit their actual guilt, quite apart from guilt amassed on their own account for their own sins. The doctrine has been extremely powerful in the West but much less so in the East; it is associated above all with Augustine and also with Calvin.

orthodoxy: Not to be confused with the Eastern Orthodox Church, the word *orthodoxy* means "right belief." It is the notion and standard of a set of correct and official doctrines. Different churches have their own understandings of what counts as orthodoxy, which is why one can talk of orthodox Catholicism, orthodox Calvinism and so on. Orthodoxy is usually set out in the form of a creed.

pope: The bishop of Rome and head of the Catholic Church. Since the early centuries of the church the pope has steadily increased in power, until the declaration in the 19th century that everything he says in his official capacity is infallibly true. The reluctance of the Eastern Orthodox Church to accept this tendency was one of the causes of the split between the two traditions, and it remains a bone of contention today. Protestants similarly reject the pope's claims to greater authority than any other bishop, and a traditional feature of Protestant anti-Catholic propaganda has been to depict the pope as the antichrist denounced in the book of Revelation. Catholics for their part appeal to Matthew 16, where Jesus tells Peter, traditionally believed to have been the first bishop of Rome, that he is to possess the keys of heaven and earth.

predestination: The belief that everything that happens has been set up by God. The doctrine is the religious version of determinism, the theory that the universe works rather like a giant clock, mechanically and entirely predictably. It is formally inconsistent with free will, which is problematic because many Christians have tried to affirm both of them. The doctrine of predestination is associated with Augustine, Luther and above all Calvin.

priest: Someone who mediates between the people and God. In Christianity, Christ himself is the greatest priest of all, an idea first articulated in the New Testament book of Hebrews. But in Roman Catholicism, Eastern Orthodoxy and Anglicanism, the minister of a congregation is also called a priest, since they administer the sacraments and preach to the people. Protestants have traditionally opposed this idea, arguing that it seeks to set up church officials in the place of Christ, and so they preach the "priesthood of all believers." This means that the clergy have no special powers or dignity other than that possessed by all Christians. Important theologians to have written on the priesthood include Augustine, Aquinas, Wyclif, Hus and Luther.

Protestantism: The churches that split off from the Roman Catholic Church in the early 16th century, and their successors, are known as the Protestant churches. They generally emphasize the role of Scripture in the formulation of doctrine and practice. They are divided among an enormous number of different denominations, ranging from evangelicals and charismatics to middle-of-the-road Anglicans, Methodists and Lutherans, and are theologically extremely varied. They have a much greater tendency to informal styles of worship than other traditions and make less emphasis on the sacraments and the role of the priesthood. Throughout most of the Western world, the Protestant churches are the most vocal and visible of the Christian traditions. The most important theologians of Protestantism are Luther and Calvin.

resurrection: One of the most distinctive doctrines of Christianity since its early days has been the physical resurrection of all humanity at the end of the world. The doctrine has its roots in the resurrection of Christ, which in I Corinthians 15 is interpreted as the "firstfruits" of the general resurrection of the dead. Many early Christians, such as Justin and Irenaeus, were concerned to defend the doctrine against its detractors. Other theologians have found the doctrine difficult, however, and have either rejected or modified it, the most famous example being Origen.

revelation: The idea that God has told us certain things about himself and spiritual realities. Traditionally, the prime example of revelation is the Bible. The relative importance of revelation and other sources of knowledge, such as natural theology, is an important issue that was dealt with in particular by Erigena and Aquinas. In modern times, the most important theologian to make it central to his thought is Barth.

Roman Catholicism: In the way it does theology, the Roman Catholic Church is distinctive mainly in the importance it gives to the authority of the church itself in establishing doctrine and practice. Scripture and tradition are both important too, of course, but Catholicism gives a role to church authority that is lacking in other Christian denominations. That authority is vested primarily in the pope, the head of the Catholic Church. Roman Catholicism is also distinctive in its emphasis on the priesthood and the sacraments and in its devotion to the Virgin Mary and other saints. The Roman Church split from the Eastern Orthodox Church gradually throughout the early Middle Ages, and until the Reformation it was the only church in Western Europe. The most important theologians of Roman Catholicism are Augustine and Aquinas, and its most important defining council is the Council of Trent.

sacraments: Rituals of the church by which, according to traditional understanding, God's grace is administered. The Catholic Church has seven sacraments: baptism, confirmation, marriage, confession, the Eucharist, ordination and extreme unction. The Reformers rejected all of these as unscriptural except for baptism and the Eucharist, which is why the Protestant churches have only two sacraments. Important theologians to write on the sacraments include Augustine, Aquinas, Wyclif, Hus and Luther.

Scholasticism: A general term for rigid orthodoxy, often used negatively to mean the stifling of creativity with set answers to every question. In particular, the term is used less pejoratively to refer to the medieval synthesis of Christian theology and Aristotelian philosophy epitomized by Aquinas, Bonaventure and Scotus.

Scripture: The sixty-six books of the Bible. Christians have always taken Scripture to be different from other books, peculiarly authoritative. But they have disagreed over its precise nature and over how its authority compares with those of reason and tradition. Theologians who have addressed the issue include Tertullian, Origen, Augustine, Wyclif, Hus, Luther, Barth and Bultmann.

sin: What is wrong with humanity. Sin can be thought of either in the singular, as a kind of force that oppresses us, or in the plural, as particular acts that we do. How one sees sin determines how one will understand the atonement. Theologians to have made important contributions to the understanding of sin include Irenaeus, Augustine, Anselm, Abelard, Luther, Calvin, Schleiermacher, Barth, Bultmann, Niebuhr and Tillich.

soteriology: The doctrine of salvation, or the atonement.

tradition: Doctrines and practices that are passed down from previous generations. Different Christian churches place different weight on the importance of tradition: the Orthodox Church regards it as central, while the Protestant churches consider it a lot less important. In practice every church, just like every human society, relies on tradition to a greater extent than it might realize. For example, many Protestant evangelicals aspire to base their doctrine and practice solely on the Bible, but the way they understand the Bible is often determined to a large extent by their own traditions. Theologians who have looked at how tradition works include Tertullian and Newman.

Trinity: One of the most distinctive Christian doctrines. It states that although there is one God, he is known as three Persons—the Father, the Son and the Holy Spirit. How to balance the threeness and the oneness without slipping into tritheism or unitarianism is a traditional problem for theology. Theologians who have made major contributions to the doctrine include Justin Martyr, Tertullian, Origen, Athanasius, the Cappadocian fathers and Augustine. Landmark councils include the First Council of Nicaea and the First Council of Constantinople. The doctrine's modern restatement is especially associated with Barth.

universalism: The doctrine that all creatures will ultimately be saved and that damnation, if it exists, is not eternal. Some theologians have upheld this doctrine as an expression of God's desire to save his whole creation, but it can conflict with the doctrine of free will. Some theologians suggest that it is possible to be saved even while following another religion, while others reject this but argue that ultimately—after death or in a future life—everyone will come to the truth. Today some form of universalism is common among theologians, although not among most Christians. Prominent theologians with universalist tendencies include Origen, Gregory of Nyssa, Rahner and Moltmann.

virgin birth: The doctrine that although Christ's mother was a normal human being, she was a virgin when she conceived him. The doctrine is based mainly on Luke 2 and was developed in subsequent centuries. By the time of Origen, it had become the doctrine of Mary's *perpetual* virginity, which meant that she remained a virgin for the rest of her life (a problem with this is that the New Testament mentions Jesus' siblings). Shortly afterward appeared the doctrine of her virginity *in parturition*, which means that Jesus' actual birth occurred in some miraculous way that left Mary physically undamaged. The doctrine of the virgin birth has been important to Western theologians because it explains how Jesus could be born without the taint of original sin. This would suggest that original sin is inherited only from one's father, so by the Middle Ages it was supplemented by the doctrine of Mary's immaculate conception, according to which Mary was born in the normal way but miraculously preserved from the effects of original sin so that she would be fit to bear Jesus. Aquinas is especially associated with this doctrine. Today all of this, apart from the original doctrine, is rejected by most Protestants, and the notion of the virgin birth itself is a traditional stumbling block for liberal theologians, who often regard it not only as superstitious but as casting doubt on Jesus' true humanity.

works: The traditional counterpoint to faith—what we do as opposed to what we believe. A central plank of Protestantism has been that we are saved by faith alone and that any reliance on works is heresy and pride. Catholicism affirms that faith and works are both necessary to salvation and that the two are flip sides of the same coin. Theologians who take this approach are careful to distinguish their position from Pelagianism, the heretical notion that we save ourselves; and those who take the Protestant line must explain why anyone need bother doing good works at all. Important theologians in this debate include Augustine, Abelard and Luther.

Further Reading

This is not an exhaustive bibliography. I have included some of the most helpful introductions to the different periods and theologians, which represent the best next step for those curious to find out more. But there are many more out there—and all the books listed here will provide more reading suggestions.

In particular, there are several series to watch out for. Oxford University Press publishes the renowned Past Masters series, now reprinted as the Very Short Introduction series, each of which provides a short and readable introduction to a major thinker of the past. Several figures in this book are featured in the series, and it is equally useful for finding out about other thinkers who have influenced theology, from Plato to Heidegger.

There are also some similar series specifically dealing with theologians. Geoffrey Chapman publishes a series entitled Outstanding Christian Thinkers, now reprinted by Continuum, each volume of which presents the leading ideas of a major theologian. These are the ideal place to look for further information on the figure who interests you. Fount also publishes a series called Fount Christian Thinkers (published in the United States as the Great Christian Thinkers series by Triumph); these are shorter, extremely clear and helpful introductions, and it is a great shame that there are not more of them. At a more advanced level, Blackwell publishes several wide-ranging surveys of the different periods.

For primary texts, there are several series to look for. SCM Press and Westminster John Knox publish the Library of Christian Classics, edited by John Baillie, John McNeill and Henry van Dusen, which gives a good range of texts in clear translations, although they may be hard to find. Routledge publishes the Early Church Fathers series, devoted to the Fathers and Byzantine theologians, each of which gives a clear and detailed introduction to the theologian in question, together with a substantial selection of texts. Finally, Paulist Press publishes the outstanding and remarkably comprehensive Classics of Western Spirituality series. Each book in this series contains a substantial and helpful introduction to the featured mystic, followed by a very clear and readable translation of his or her principal spiritual works.

Probably the easiest way to find the writings of the most famous theologians is to look in the Penguin Classics range, as well as other popular "general" series such as Everyman. In addition to books like these, there is a wealth of further information—at every level—available on the Internet. This ranges from introductory material to advanced academic discussions. I have not listed any online resources here, because of their rapidly changing nature, but judicious use of any search engine will quickly take the inquirer to useful material. Be aware that some of it may be of variable quality: the

Internet is a haven for people with unusual or extreme points of view, and by their very nature the names of the great theologians of the past can often be found on sites of dubious value—both pro- and antireligion.

The Internet is an excellent resource for primary texts. The writings of the Fathers, the medieval theologians and the Reformers, as well as others, can be found here. It is often possible to find works online that are not available elsewhere.

General

First, several works that present the history of Christianity or serve as general introductions to theology.

Dowley, Tim, ed. *The History of Christianity.* Rev. ed. Oxford: Lion, 1990.
　　A very clear history with lots of pictures!

Ford, David. *Theology: A Very Short Introduction.* Oxford: Oxford University Press, 2000.
　　As it promises, a short and clear introduction to the way theology is done today.

McManners, John, ed. *The Oxford History of Christianity.* Oxford: Oxford University Press, 1990.
　　A readable and in-depth account of the story of Christianity.

Mursell, Gordon, ed. *The Story of Christian Spirituality.* Oxford: Lion, 2001.
　　This highly illustrated book tells the story of Christian mysticism and spirituality.

Ward, Keith. *Christianity: A Short Introduction.* Oxford: Oneworld, 2000.
　　This excellent book looks at each major Christian doctrine in turn and presents three possible approaches to them that different theologians have taken in the past. Very helpful for understanding the complexities of the issues.

Williams, Rowan. *The Wound of Knowledge.* 2nd ed. London: Darton, Longman & Todd, 1990.
　　This is a good and clear introduction to the history of Christian spirituality and mysticism, from the Fathers to the Reformation.

Here are some books introducing different Christian churches, their history, practice and theology.

Constantilos, Demetrios. *Understanding the Greek Orthodox Church.* 3rd ed. Brookline, Mass.: Hellenic College Press, 1998.
　　An excellent and more in-depth supplement to Ware's book, below.

Bokenkotter, Thomas. *A Concise History of the Catholic Church.* Rev. ed. New York: Doubleday, 1990.
　　Clear and interesting.

Giles, Richard. *We Do Not Presume.* London: Canterbury, 1998.
　　A very easy-to-read and entertaining introduction to Anglicanism.

McBrien, Richard P. *Catholicism.* 3rd ed. San Francisco: HarperSanFrancisco, 1994.
　　Totally all-encompassing.

Ware, Timothy. *The Orthodox Church.* New ed. London: Penguin, 1993.
　　The best introduction to Orthodox history, doctrine and practice—very well written and interesting.

The Origins of Christianity

Here are some suggestions for anyone who wants to find out about what happened before the narrative of this work.

Burkett, Delbert. *An Introduction to the New Testament and the Origins of Christianity.* Cambridge: Cambridge University Press, 2002.
An enormous book that will tell you everything you need to know on the subject!

Sanders, E. P. *The Historical Figure of Jesus.* London: Penguin, 1996.
A brilliant and very clear introduction to the very complicated business of unearthing the real Jesus.

———. *Paul.* Oxford: Oxford University Press, 1991.
Part of the Past Masters series, this is the best short introduction to the life and thought of the earliest and greatest Christian theologian of them all.

The Church Fathers

Barnes, Timothy. *Tertullian: A Historical and Literary Study.* Oxford: Clarendon, 1971.
This revisionist work sets out to demolish most of the "established" facts about Tertullian but is still a good introduction to Tertullian and his world.

Brown, Peter. *Augustine of Hippo.* 2nd ed. Berkeley: University of California Press, 2000.
The most famous, definitive biography of Augustine—very absorbing!

Butterworth, G. W. *Origen on First Principles.* London: SPCK, 1936.
The definitive edition of Origen's most daring and advanced book, painstakingly pieced together from all the surviving fragments, with useful introductions.

Donaldson, James, and Alexander Roberts, eds. The Ante-Nicene Christian Library. Edinburgh: T & T Clark, 1867-1872.
This series goes with Wace and Schaff's Nicene and Post-Nicene Series 1 and 2 (see below).

Grant, Robert. *Irenaeus of Lyons.* London: Routledge, 1997.
Part of the Early Church Fathers series.

Gregory of Nyssa. *The Life of Moses.* Translated by Abraham J. Malherbe and Everett Ferguson. New York: Paulist, 1978.
Part of the Classics of Western Spirituality series.

Meredith, Anthony. *The Cappadocians.* London: Geoffrey Chapman, 1995.
Part of the Outstanding Christian Thinkers series.

Meredith, Anthony. *Gregory of Nyssa.* London: Routledge, 1999.
Part of the Early Church Fathers series.

Oulton, J. E. L., and Henry Chadwick. *Alexandrian Christianity.* Library of Christian Classics 2. Philadelphia: Westminster, 1954.
Translations of three of Origen's treatises, together with some works of Clement of Alexandria.

Pettersen, Alvyn. *Athanasius.* London: Geoffrey Chapman, 1995.
Part of the Outstanding Christian Thinkers series.

Price, Richard. *Augustine.* London: Fount, 1997.
Part of the Fount Christian Thinkers series.

Trigg, Joseph. *Origen.* London: Routledge, 1998.
Part of the Early Church Fathers series.

———. *Origen: The Bible and Philosophy in the Third-Century Church.* Atlanta: John Knox, 1983.

Probably the best introduction to Origen, this biographical account introduces both his context and his leading ideas clearly.

Wace, Henry, and Phillip Schaff, eds. A Select Library of Nicene and Post-Nicene Fathers of the Christian Church. Series 1. Oxford and New York: Christian Literature, 1886-1900.

————. A Select Library of Nicene and Post-Nicene Fathers of the Christian Church. Series 2. Oxford and New York: Christian Literature, 1890-1900.

The standard sources for almost all the church fathers. These series have been reprinted by various publishers and are also available in their entirety at more than one location on the Internet. The volumes represent a fascinating insight into the 19th-century Church of England after the Oxford Movement: the Fathers are presented essentially as staunch Anglicans who happened to live a millennium or two too early, and for this reason the introductions are not reliable expositions of their thought—particularly the less orthodox ones such as Origen. The texts themselves tend to make the Fathers speak as if they were Victorian bishops, but they are still quite clear and accurate.

The Byzantine Empire

Louth, Andrew. Denys the Areopagite. London: Continuum, 2001.
Part of the Outstanding Christian Thinkers series.

————. Maximus the Confessor. London: Routledge, 1996.
Part of the Early Church Fathers series.

Maximus the Confessor. Selected Writings. Edited by George Berthold. Mahwah, N.J.: Paulist, 1985.
Part of the Classics of Western Spirituality series.

Meyendorff, John. Byzantine Theology: Historical Trends and Doctrinal Themes. 2nd ed. New York: Fordham University Press, 1979.
An excellent introduction to the theology of the whole period.

————. St. Gregory Palamas and Orthodox Spirituality. Crestwood, N.Y.: St Vladimir's Seminary Press, 1974.
A good account of Palamas and his place in the Orthodox tradition.

Palamas, Gregory. The Triads. Edited by John Meyendorff and Nicholas Gendle. New York: Paulist, 1983.
Part of the Classics of Western Spirituality series.

Pseudo-Dionysius the Areopagite. Complete Works. Edited by Colm Luibheid and Paul Rorem. New York: Paulist, 1987.
Part of the Classics of Western Spirituality series.

Rorem, Paul. Pseudo-Dionysius: An Introduction to the Texts and a Commentary on Their Influence. Oxford: Oxford University Press, 1993.
A detailed exposition of Pseudo-Dionysius.

Symeon the New Theologian. The Discourses. Edited by C. J. de Catanzaro and George Maloney. New York: Paulist, 1980.
Part of the Classics of Western Spirituality series.

The Middle Ages

Abelard, Peter, and Heloise. *The Letters of Abelard and Heloise.* Edited by Betty Radice. London: Penguin, 1974.
This also features the *History of My Misfortunes* and is very entertaining!

Anselm. *Anselm of Canterbury: The Major Works.* Edited by Brian Davies and G. R. Evans. Oxford: Oxford University Press, 1988.
Provides exactly what it says on the label.

Aquinas, Thomas. *Summa Theologiae: A Concise Translation.* Edited by Timothy McDermott. Westminster, Md.: Christian Classics, 1989.
A very readable version of Aquinas, miraculously contained in one volume.

Cross, Richard. *Duns Scotus.* Oxford: Oxford University Press, 1999.
A comprehensive introduction, although possibly rather hard going for the beginner.

Davies, Brian. *Aquinas.* London: Continuum, 2002.
Part of the Outstanding Christian Thinkers series.

Evans, G. R., ed. *The Medieval Theologians.* Oxford: Blackwell, 2001.
One of Blackwell's wide-ranging, scholarly introductions to the period.

O'Meara, John. *Eriugena.* Oxford: Clarendon, 1988.
This features a useful and readable paraphrase of *On Nature.*

Rout, Paul. *Francis and Bonaventure.* London: Fount, 1996.
Part of the Fount Christian Thinkers series.

The Reformation

Calvin, John. *Institutes of the Christian Religion.* Translated by Henry Beveridge. Grand Rapids, Mich.: Eerdmans, 1989.
Much more readable than you might expect—Calvin was an extremely clear and elegant writer.

Grosshans, Hans-Peter. *Luther.* London: Fount, 1997.
Part of the Fount Christian Thinkers series.

Lindberg, Carter, ed. *The Reformation Theologians.* Oxford: Blackwell, 2002.
One of Blackwell's wide-ranging, scholarly introductions to the period.

McGrath, Alister. *A Life of John Calvin.* Oxford: Blackwell, 1990.
A good introduction to his life and thought.

Marins, Richard. *Martin Luther: The Christian Between God and Death.* Cambridge, Mass.: Harvard University Press, 1999.
An excellent biography.

Tomlin, Graham. *Luther and His World.* Oxford: Lion, 2002.
An extremely good introduction to Luther's life and thought and the background to the Reformation.

Turner, John Munsey. *John Wesley: The Evangelical Revival and the Rise of Methodism in England.* Peterborough, U.K.: Epworth, 2002.
This gives a comprehensive and interesting account of Wesley and his times.

The Modern Period

Chadwick, Owen. *Newman.* Oxford: Oxford University Press, 1983.
    Part of the Past Masters series.

Clements, Keith. *Friedrich Schleiermacher: Pioneer of Modern Theology.* London: Collins, 1987.
    Good introduction and selected texts.

Gardiner, Patrick. *Kierkegaard.* Oxford: Oxford University Press, 1988.
    Part of the Past Masters series.

Gerrish, B. A. *A Prince of the Church: Schleiermacher and the Beginnings of Modern Theology.* Philadelphia:
    Fortress, 1984.
    A very good, easy-to-read introduction.

Heron, Alasdair. *A Century of Protestant Theology.* Cambridge: Lutterworth, 1980.
    This is a brilliantly useful book. Despite the title, it deals with all Protestant theology from
    Schleiermacher onward and is extremely clear and accessible.

Ker, Ian. *Newman the Theologian: A Reader.* Notre Dame, Ind.: University of Notre Dame Press,
    1990.
    A good introduction and selection of texts.

Newman, John Henry. *Apologia pro vita sua.* London: Penguin, 1994.
    His autobiography and probably his best-known work. It features the exchange of letters and
    pamphlets with Charles Kingsley that prompted it: watch in amazement as the greatest
    minds of 19th-century English religious life attack each other like small children!

————. *An Essay on the Development of Christian Doctrine.* Notre Dame, Ind.: University of Notre
    Dame Press, 1989.
    His most important theological work, and still easy to read.

Schleiermacher, Friedrich. *The Christian Faith.* Edinburgh: T & T Clark, 1928.
    Fairly dense but well worth the effort. It is amazing just how much subsequent Christian
    thought is anticipated in this volume: it is hardly outdated even now.

————. *On Religion: Speeches to Its Cultured Despisers.* 2nd ed. Cambridge: Cambridge University
    Press, 1996.
    The rhetorical style will leave some cold, but there's no mistaking the passion here.

Vardy, Peter. *Kierkegaard.* London: Fount, 1996.
    Part of the Fount Christian Thinkers series.

The 20th Century

Barth, Karl. *Church Dogmatics.* Edited by G. W. Bromiley and T. F. Torrance. 2nd ed. Edinburgh:
    T & T Clark, 1975.
    Not for the faint-hearted, although not really as intimidating as it might at first appear.

————. *Dogmatics in Outline.* Translated by G. T. Thompson. London: SCM Press, 1949.
    A short work based on an exposition of the Apostles' Creed. Barth's basic viewpoint in con-
    densed form.

Bethge, Eberhard. *Bonhoeffer: A Life in Pictures.* Philadelphia: Fortress, 1986.
    Short, readable biography by one of Bonhoeffer's closest friends and fellow convict.

Bonhoeffer, Dietrich. *The Cost of Discipleship.* London: SCM Press, 2001.
One of Bonhoeffer's most powerful books.

―――――. *Letters and Papers from Prison.* Enlarged ed. Edited by Eberhard Bethge. London: SCM Press, 1971.
Bonhoeffer's best-known work—easy to read, absorbing, with daring ideas.

Bowden, John. *Karl Barth.* London: SCM Press, 1971.
An old book but still the best short work on Barth. A brilliantly clear, easy-to-read introduction that still grapples with the basic issues and problems.

Brown, Robert McAfree, ed. *The Essential Reinhold Niebuhr.* New Haven, Conn.: Yale University Press, 1986.
Good Niebuhr reader.

Bultmann, Rudolf. *Existence and Faith.* Edited by Schubert Ogden. London: Hodder & Stoughton, 1961.
A good introductory selection of easily digestible pieces.

―――――. *Faith and Understanding.* Edited by Robert Funk. London: SCM Press, 1969.
Another selection of short essays.

Busch, Eberhard. *Karl Barth: His Life from Letters and Autobiographical Texts.* Translated by John Bowden. London: SCM Press, 1976.
Gives a vivid—and very full—picture of Barth the human being, complete with all his wit, eccentricities and aggressiveness.

Durkin, Kenneth. *Reinhold Niebuhr.* London: Geoffrey Chapman, 1989.
Part of the Outstanding Christian Thinkers series.

Dych, William. *Rahner.* London: Continuum, 1992.
Part of the Outstanding Christian Thinkers series.

Fergusson, David. *Bultmann.* London: Continuum, 1992.
Part of the Outstanding Christian Thinkers series.

Ford, David, ed. *The Modern Theologians.* 2nd ed. Oxford: Blackwell, 1997.
One of Blackwell's wide-ranging, scholarly introductions to the period.

Gutiérrez, Gustavo. *A Theology of Liberation.* Maryknoll, N.Y.: Orbis, 1973.
The quintessential book of liberation theology.

Kilby, Karen. *Rahner.* London: Fount, 1997.
Part of the Fount Christian Thinkers series.

Moltmann, Jürgen. *The Crucified God.* New York: Harper & Row, 1974.
Moltmann's first and most powerful work.

―――――. *Theology of Hope.* New York: Harper & Row, 1967.
His other major book.

Niebuhr, Reinhold. *Moral Man and Immoral Society.* New York: Charles Scribner's Sons, 1932.
Niebuhr's major work, in which he applies Christian ethics to society.

―――――. *The Nature and Destiny of Man.* New York: Charles Scribner's Sons, 1941, 1943.
His other major work, containing his anthropology and treatment of religious myth.

Pannenberg, Wolfhart. *Systematic Theology.* Translated by G. W. Bromiley. Grand Rapids, Mich.:

Eerdmans, 1991-1998.

Pannenberg's magnum opus is likely to set the standard for Christian dogmatics for many years to come.

Rahner, Karl. *Foundations of Christian Faith*. New York: Crossroad, 1978.

The closest Rahner came to a systematic theology.

————. *Theological Investigations*. 23 vols. New York: Crossroad, 1974-1992.

Those who like their theology short and dippable need look no further.

Rasmussen, Larry, ed. *Reinhold Niebuhr: Theologian of Public Life*. Minneapolis: Fortress, 1991.

Good introduction and selection of writings.

Ruether, Rosemary Radford. *Sexism and God-Talk*. Boston: Beacon Press, 1983.

The most important work on feminist theology; sets out the agenda.

Tillich, Paul. *The Shaking of the Foundations*. New York: Charles Scribner's Sons, 1948.

A book of sermons—a relatively easy way into Tillich's often complex theology.

Webster, John. *Karl Barth*. London: Continuum, 2000.

Part of the Outstanding Christian Thinkers series.

Weger, Karl-Heinz. *Karl Rahner: An Introduction to His Theology*. New York: Seabury, 1980.

Another book that does just what its title suggests.

Where Next?

Here are a few suggestions for those who want to explore possible future avenues for Christian thought. These books set out different agendas that readers may or may not agree with.

Cupitt, Don. *The Sea of Faith*. 2nd ed. London: SCM Press, 1994.

Cupitt represents a radical modern liberalism. He argues passionately for a religion that is based on values rather than on factual claims, one that rejects the notion of God as "out there" and instead acts on what the notion of God means to us. His book is extremely well written and easy to read and gave its name to the Sea of Faith Movement, a small but dedicated party within the Church of England whose members occasionally hit the headlines for their "atheism."

Küng, Hans. *Christianity*. New York: Continuum, 1995.

Küng is one of the best-known Catholic theologians writing today, but his relative liberalism has led his church to disavow his work. In books like this one he puts his enormous erudition to work in setting out a forward-looking Catholicism that remains well aware of the problems and opportunities set by the past.

Ward, Keith. *God: A Guide for the Perplexed*. Oxford: Oneworld, 2002.

A witty and engaging look at how the idea of God has developed over history and where it might go in the future. Ward represents a moderate liberal English version of Christianity, keen to use the insights of science and philosophy to take theology forward with an eye to the past.

Wright, Alex. *Why Bother with Theology?* London: Dartman, Longman & Todd, 2002.

A popular work that looks at possible future directions for theology.